ENEMIES OF THE ENLI

ENEMIES

of the

Enlightenment

The French Counter-Enlightenment
and the Making of Modernity

Darrin M. McMahon

OXFORD
UNIVERSITY PRESS

OXFORD
UNIVERSITY PRESS

Oxford   New York
Auckland   Bangkok   Buenos Aires   Cape Town   Chennai
Dar es Salaam   Delhi   Hong Kong   Istanbul   Karachi   Kolkata
Kuala Lumpur   Madrid   Melbourne   Mexico City   Mumbai   Nairobi
São Paulo   Shanghai   Singapore   Taipei   Tokyo   Toronto

and an associated company in Berlin

Published by Oxford University Press, Inc.
198 Madison Avenue, New York, New York 10016

www.oup.com

First issued as an Oxford University Press paperback, 2002

Oxford is a registered trademark of Oxford University Press.

Library of Congress Cataloging-in-Publication Data
McMahon, Darrin M.
Enemies of the enlightenment : the French counter-Enlightenment
and the making of modernity / Darrin M. McMahon.
     p.   cm.
Includes bibliographical references and index.
ISBN 0-19-513685-3; 0-19-515893-8 (pbk.)
1. Enlightenment.   2. Philosophy, French—18th century.   I. Title.
B1925.E5 M39   2000
944.04—dc21   00-045297

9 8 7 6 5 4 3 2

Printed in the United States of America
on acid-free paper

TO MY MOTHER,

who taught me commitment
and compassion, two values
so necessary to the scholar.

AND TO MY FATHER,

who through childhood
bedtime stories, and many
since, showed me the worth
of history as both soporific
and the stuff of dreams.

PREFACE

*T*he amused librarian in Paris who fielded my first, fumbling inquiries in 1994 about the material that would become this book greeted me, in turn, with a question of her own. *Vous êtes royaliste, monsieur?* Delivered in a tone that only one who has spent time in French libraries will fully appreciate (a distinct blend of candor, civility, and condescension), the question took me somewhat by surprise. Admittedly, I was seeking information on royalists, and what is more, on royalists of a particular kind. Catholics, conservatives, counterrevolutionaries, the first ideologues of the Right, all promised to figure prominently in my proposed study of cultural opposition to the Enlightenment in the eighteenth and nineteenth centuries. But that this might imply some immediate identification with the subject matter at hand struck me as odd. An undistinguished heir to the Irish peasantry and a native son of California, I had never even known a royalist. Did such a thing actually still exist?

No doubt I took the question a little too seriously. I was, after all, guilty by association, or at least so it seemed. As the historically minded French never failed to observe, my last name bears a damning resemblance to that of the infamous Maréchal MacMahon, a French general implicated in efforts to restore the monarchy during the Third Republic. There is, to my knowledge, no connection, but inquiries of a skeptical, even suspicious nature continued to follow me through France nonetheless—both in and out of the archives. Time and again I was asked to account for my subject, to explain *why* I had chosen to study what I had. Was I Catholic, a Counter-Revolutionary, an enemy of the Enlightenment, a man of the Right? Just what was I up to? For all the good-natured teasing in this interrogation, there was genuine suspicion as well. This fact is a subtle reminder of what the heated debates surrounding the revolutionary bicentennial of 1989 and the electoral successes of the extreme Right in the 1990s also emphasized: that neither the Enlightenment nor the Revolution is completely over in France. Both of these eighteenth-century upheavals continue to serve as benchmarks by which men and women gauge their allegiances and identity in the present. They still generate passion.

On European soil, then, my choice of topic retained the power to raise quizzical eyebrows. But across the Atlantic, a study of cultural opposition to the Enlightenment seemed, at least to me, perfectly innocuous. Moreover, it seemed timely, for Americans had just witnessed firsthand during the 1980s and early 1990s the disheartening spectacle of cultural divide. In what was perhaps the final flare-up of the implosion following the supernova of the 1960s, the American University became, once again, an important site in public consciousness, a key battlefield of what were termed the "culture wars." Endlessly explicated in both the academic and the popular press, these wars, at their best, raised fundamental questions about the nature of American identity at the end of the twentieth century. At their worst, however, and all too often, they degenerated into mutual shouting matches in which pundits and polemicists threw mud at caricatures of their opponents, providing a perfect example of the way in which intellectual adversaries are wont to create their own enemies from straw. While cultural conservatives attacked the allegedly monolithic power of 1960s radicals, well ensconced and burrowing away in the nation's media and universities, the Left countered with the fanatical specter of the Christian fundamentalist, puritanical, out of touch with modern America, but dangerously close to ruling it nonetheless. If there was truth in either claim, there was far more falsehood. But this didn't prevent the two sides from hurling insults past one another with ever-increasing ferocity. For all its remove from reality, this invective had very real consequences in the political landscape.

The Enlightenment was not always a divisive issue in these debates. In a strange twist, as I have occasion to discuss later, it even united the more extreme voices on the Right and Left in shared contempt. Yet the debates themselves, with their sharp, often artificial dichotomies between "politically correct progressives" and "reactionary fundamentalists," did appear to offer insight into the dynamics of cultural cleavage and intellectual divide. Mindful of the dangers inherent in allowing the present to shape one's understanding of the past, I came to see genuine merit in conceiving of the eighteenth century—with the French Enlightenment as its centerpiece—as a culture war of its own. As I hope this book demonstrates, the parallels are revealing.

While American critics bashed each other in a native war over culture, developments on the world stage also suggested that a study of religious opposition to the Enlightenment might illuminate broader issues and concerns. As an employee at the Office of Programs in Comparative Religion at the Graduate Theological Union while I was an undergraduate at Berkeley and then as an analyst of religious nationalist movements at the United States Institute of Peace in 1990–1991, I watched as not only the United States but also Israel, India and Sri Lanka, much of the Middle East, the former Soviet Union, eastern Europe, Africa, and Latin America experienced what appeared to be a worldwide revival of religion or, at the very least, its strong resurgence in public life. Ironically, at the very time that Western philosophers were proclaiming the demise of grand narratives, religious or otherwise, as the "end of ideology" or the onset of the "postmodern condition," religious activists around the world were making headlines and, at the same time, a mockery of the Enlightenment assumption that the "darkness of fanaticism" would naturally give way to the "light of reason." Defying what sociologists and political theorists had long held to be the relentless logic of modernity—increasing secularization and an ever-widening gap between the sacred and the profane—the world at the end of the twentieth century suggested that the connection might be more complicated. There would be no better time than now, it seemed, to explore the origins of that very divide—the moment at which Western culture squared off into the hostile, suspicious camps of the secular and the sacred. This book seeks to tell an important chapter in that story.

Enemies of Enlightenment, then, like all books, is in part the product of its time. It is also the product of the generous assistance, understanding, and advice of a great many friends and colleagues. At Yale, David Bell, whose stimulating seminars led me across the Pyrenees from an original (and ongoing) interest in Spain, has served all along as the model advisor, at once searching critic, patient reader, psychologist, strategist, and friend. I am deeply grateful to have been his first student. John Merriman, too, has given generously of his time, friendship, and vast knowledge of French history. I thank him and his family for sharing some of this with me. Frank Turner urged me on several important occasions in directions I didn't think I could go, directions that subsequently proved fruitful. He has been a perceptive critic and advisor. Since my time at Berkeley, Mark Juergensmeyer has served as *Doktorvater* and much more. I am still not convinced that he read every page of the manuscript, but those he did, he read with care. His influence is evident throughout. My first boss, Dr. David Little, then of the United States Institute of Peace and now of Harvard University, provided inspiration at a pivotal moment in my life, demonstrating to me and to many others that the notion of the gentleman-scholar is not an antiquated ideal.

At Columbia University, where from 1997–1999 I was Mellon Fellow in History at the Society of Fellows in the Humanities, colleagues Graham Burnett and April Shelford contributed greatly to a stimulating and congenial atmosphere. In the Department of History, Isser Woloch and Simon Schama were at once gracious and inspiring. David Armitage gave me the privilege of his sterling intellect and wit and also his friendship, and Eileen Gilooly, David Johnston, and my wonderful, wonderful students helped to make teaching in Columbia's contemporary civilization program the richest of pleasures.

A great joy of this profession has been the openness, receptivity, and goodwill of colleagues. As every young scholar knows, encouragement is gold, and though some of the men and women listed below may well have forgotten ever speaking to me, I have not. Their answers to my queries, suggestions, and assistance of various kinds have been more sustaining than they can know. In particular, I wish to thank Greg Brown, Jack Censer, Robert Darnton, Pascal Dupuy, William Everdell, Joël Félix, Dena Goodman, Jean Marie Goulemot, Lisa Graham, David Higgs, Margaret Jacob, Colin Jones, Tony Judt, Tom Kaiser, Emmet Kennedy, Thomas Keselman, Dale Van Kley, Sheryl Kroen, Richard Lebrun, Mark Lilla, Martyn Lyons, Maria Riasanovsky, Noë Richter, Jochen Schlobach, Alyssa Sepinwall, and Timothy Tackett.

A number of individuals—Greg Brown, Graeme Garrard, Tom Kaiser, Sheryl Kroen, John Merriman, Isser Woloch, and unflaggingly, David Bell (who from the beginning to the end has gone beyond the call of duty, and back again)—kindly read individual chapters and provided immeasurable insight. Roger Friedland, Mark Juergensmeyer, and the students in their graduate seminar on religious nationalism at the University of California, Santa Barbara, plowed through the entire manuscript, much to its improvement. The talented students in my own graduate seminar on the Old Regime, taught at Yale in the spring of 2000, provided careful feedback, great pleasure, and the reminder that teaching and learning are common endeavors. Finally, the task of revising and refining this manuscript has been immensely facilitated by two fine editors—Thomas LeBien, who took on the project and provided encouragement and insight from the start, and Susan Ferber, who saw it through to completion, providing careful readings and suggestions at every stage. I am deeply grateful to both of them and to the anonymous readers they solicited, who will see that I have incorporated many of their suggested changes.

Portions of this project were presented at the Washington, D.C., Old Regime Group, which kindly allowed me to run its gauntlet; the Society for French Historical Studies; the Western Society for French History; the Columbia University Seminar on Eighteenth-Century European Culture; the Society of Fellows in the Humanities; the Séminaire international des jeunes dix-huitièmistes in Saarbrücken, Germany; and the Université de Rouen, where Pascal Dupuy was, as ever, a gracious colleague and friend. The hosts of and participants in The Counter-Enlightenment and Its Legacy: A Symposium in Memory of Sir Isaiah Berlin, held at the University of Tel Aviv in January 2000, were nothing if not enlightened. My thanks, especially, to Shulamit Volkov and Joseph Mali; to Charles Rosen for a memorable evening in the spirit of Sir Isaiah; and to John Robertson and Robert Wokler for the sublime, if surreal, experience of touring Jerusalem with two committed sons of the century of lights.

Generous financial support was forthcoming from the Mellon Foundation, which quite simply made graduate school possible. The Smith Richardson Foundation financed a year's research in France, and Professor Paul Kennedy and the office of International Security Studies at Yale intervened to organize funding at a critical juncture, saving both me and my project. Florence Thomas and Valerie Van Etten at the Yale History Department and Judy Huyck, Jane White, and Marsha Manns at the Society of Fellows performed innumerable favors. My oldest friend, Fritz Kaplan, intervened on several occasions at short notice to prop up my sagging German, and Matthew Connelly never once objected when I told him tales of the naughty *philosophe*.

On a personal note, Douglas and Roseline Crowley took me into the heart of their extraordinary family during the course of this project, showering me with kindness, humanity, and grace, for which I am eternally grateful. In Paris, Ariane, Agnès, and the extended Pappas family did much the same, making me feel more at home there than in most places in the world. Andrew Davies and Ourdia Boucenna, Richard and Laura Watts, Emmanuelle Mosser and Sophie Verdejo, all favored me with their couches, their generosity, and their friendship, and Professors Tim Johnson and George Manners shared their passions for life and France, particularly the regions of Rhône, Bordeaux, Burgundy, and Loire. In New York, Michelle Ferrari, William Moses, Lyle Starr, and Elaine Sterling each helped, in their own ways, to push the boundaries of artistic and intellectual exploration far beyond the confines of the university. In Wales, Gordon Main, of England, did much the same. In Los Angeles and London, Eugene Shirley, Kate Clanchy, and James Younger provided desperately needed creative outlets and ever-heartening conversations, and in all these places, Michael Friedman demonstrated to me the meaning of true friendship, complaining only when I trod on his clean floors. My sister and my parents, to whom this book is dedicated, offered continual comfort and support, and finally, most recently, Courtney Burke has given patience, understanding, and affection. She is glad, I know, that this book is finished, as am I.

New York City   D. M. M.
January 2001

CONTENTS

ENEMIES OF THE ENLIGHTENMENT

INTRODUCTION

*I*t would be difficult to write a more dramatic denouement to the life of France's greatest man of letters.[1] The aging *philosophe*, famed throughout Europe, returns to Paris after years of exile to claim the rewards of eighty-four years of labor. His final play, *Irène*, will be performed at the Comédie française, but the "modern Sophocles" becomes ill while finishing the piece and is rumored to be on his deathbed. He manages, nonetheless, to complete the work, enabling thousands to attend the opening performance on March 16, 1778, in his absence, including the Queen, the King's brother, the Count of Artois, the Duke of Bourbon, and the cream of fashionable society. "Never was a gathering more brilliant," exults the *Correspondance littéraire*, a leading newsheet of the day.[2]

In the weeks following, the *philosophe* receives a constant stream of supplicants, well-wishers, and pilgrims. He has already administered a "blessing" to the grandson of Benjamin Franklin; given audience to the former first minister of state, M. Turgot; and encouraged his many subjects at the Académie française—d'Alembert, La Harpe, Condorcet, and Saint-Lambert. Now another wave of pilgrims descends, but he is forced to curtail these visits as his health is failing. The count of Argental and Jacques Necker, among others, are kindly told that the great philosopher is unwell, and are turned away at the door.

Such persistent demands, however, do not cease—the public's clamor is too great—and so, reinvigorated by his glory, the philosopher musters the strength to personally attend a performance of his play. On March 30, he departs from his accommodations in Paris, the lavish Hôtel de Villete, stopping first at the Académie française, where he oversees a special assembly convened in his honor. Ceremoniously ensconced in the president's chair, a king at court, he hears himself compared to the greatest figures of French literature. Outside, a massive throng of adoring subjects awaits expectantly. The philosopher emerges. The crowd chants his name in unison, accompanying his carriage to the Comédie. And there, the final triumph. Entering the theater, the *philosophe* is met by cries of joy, wild applause, and shouting. Tears flow from the old man's eyes. He is crowned with a garland of laurels. The curtain opens and his bust, the work of Lemoyne, is exposed on stage—a tribute to the glory of genius: "Long live our Homer!" (see Figure 1).

At the conclusion of the spectacle, thousands more await the *grand homme* outside the theater. A genuine social mix with a strong popular character, the crowd, as witnesses will later recall, is moved by "explosions of joy, frenzy, enthusiasm, collective delirium." Individuals mount the philosopher's carriage to get a better look at the man, and supplicants strive to touch him, "as if he were a saint."[3] "Long live the defender of Calas!" The coach fades into the night, gilded by the reflections of torchlight, leaving behind a penumbra of immortality. In a

Figure 1. The coronation of Voltaire at the Comédie française, March 3, 1778. Engraving by Charles-Étienne Gaucher, after the original by Jean-Michel Moreau. Photo courtesy of the Bibliothèque Nationale, Paris.

stroke worthy of no other, François Marie Arouet, Voltaire, has attended his own apotheosis.

The pomp and circumstance of the celebratory events of the spring of 1778, given perfect closure by Voltaire's timely death in May of that same year, have long attracted the attention of scholars. Rich in inherent drama, the apotheosis, too, is wonderfully symbolic, capturing perfectly the apparent triumph of the Enlightenment in France. The archenemy of the Catholic Church, a man who had been twice imprisoned in the Bastille, unceremoniously beaten by the lackeys of the Chevalier of Rohan, chased from the borders of his homeland, and forced to abide the public burning of scores of his publications, Voltaire, king of the *philosophes*, was now crowned in the country that had disowned him. By 1778, it seemed clear, the *philosophes* had arrived.

Yet not all viewed this arrival with the same enthusiasm as the revelers of March 30. However irresistable, however justified, historians' fascination with the glittering lights of 1778 has tended to blind them from the considerable number of men and women who read Voltaire's triumph in an altogether different way. Standing in the shadows and watching from the wings, a small group of clerics and writers, for example, gathered to protest the opening performance of *Irène* as if it were some hideous, eighteenth-century *Rite of Spring*. In their opinion, the return and reception of a man who had devoted his life to attacking religion was hardly indicative of the triumph of light. It reflected instead the onset of darkness. "All is lost!" cried out one of their number at a later performance, in the presence of Voltaire himself.[4] For Abbé Jean-Nicolas Beauregard, canon of Notre Dame Cathedral and a highly respected orator, Voltaire's apotheosis was also deeply disturbing— symbolic of the utter depravity of the century. As he sought unsuccessfully to impress on the king in a personal interview, the *philosophe*'s presence in France was an outrage, one that no Christian monarch could condone.[5] And for the prolific journalist François-Xavier Feller, Voltaire's "fame" was in fact infamy, a shameless notoriety based upon his many "crimes" against throne and altar, goodness, and truth. The warm welcome afforded this enemy of God could only herald the demise of France.[6] More a nadir than a highpoint, Voltaire's triumph ominously portended to these and other witnesses the crepuscular end of an era, not a bright beginning, a descent into darkness and folly, rather than the ascension of reason and light. Ironically, though, in articulating this sense of impending doom and cultural anomie, these same men and women were giving birth to something novel of their own, shaping the outlines of a powerful new way of looking at the world.

Who were these men and women, the anonymous figures clad in

priestly robes who sought to disrupt *Irène*, the pamphleteers and pulpit orators who attacked the *philosophes* and bemoaned their triumphs? These and many others I call "anti-*philosophes*"—not an arbitrary term, for they used it themselves, as did their enemies, who added it to a host of far less flattering epithets.[7] Militant clergy, members of the *parti dévot*, unenlightened aristocrats, traditionalist *bourgeois*, Sorbonne censors, conservative *parlementaires*, recalcitrant journalists, and many others, these were the so-called fanatics of the Enlightenment catechism. Since mid-century they had fought to check the onslaught of *philosophie*, and since mid-century they had watched in horror as their enemies achieved ever greater conquests. Before the rays of the *philosophes*' waxing sun, these figures burned with envy, anger, and incomprehension.

Observers in our own century may perhaps find such resentment unsympathetic. Yet it becomes more comprehensible when we consider the spectacular rise of the Enlightenment man of letters. Aided by a general increase in literacy, the expansion of print culture, and the *philosophes*' own determined efforts to gain access to polite society, secular men of letters carried out a dramatic transformation in both their status and their calling over the course of the eighteenth century. Penetrating circles from which they had been hitherto barred, they cast off negative stereotypes, earning the acceptance and respect of influential social actors.[8] "Banished from [good] society until the time of Balzac and Voiture," Voltaire himself observed, men of letters had since become one of its "necessary parts," as comfortable "in *le monde* as in the study."[9] His comrade Diderot largely agreed. "There is not a country in Europe," he noted in the late 1760s, "where the letters are more honored, more remunerated than in France."[10] As if to confirm the fact, the queen herself upbraided a courtier in 1786 for failing to address a poet with proper respect. "When the king and I speak to a man of letters," she reprimanded, "we always call him, *Monsieur*."[11]

It is important, of course, to draw distinctions. Although the general spread of the Enlightenment created unprecedented opportunities for writers and scholars of many kinds, not all were accorded equal status and compensation. Writing in 1788 in his *Tableau de Paris*, the journalist Louis Sébastien Mercier drew attention to this fact, entitling a chapter the "Misery of Authors." "The most deplorable of conditions," he reflected soberly, "is to cultivate the letters without fortune—the fate of the vast number of *littérateurs*."[12] This important qualification— explored, to great effect, in the work of Robert Darnton—nonetheless throws into spectacular relief the contrasting fortunes of those at the highest echelons of the literary world, the *grands philosophes* of the "High Enlightenment."[13] For these select few, the doors of the *ancien régime* were opened widely. Breaching exalted circles, they entered the salons, lodges, and literary societies of the fashionably rich and powerful, winning important contacts and protectors, whom they in turn used to further their own interests. One by one they gained access to the most eminent scientific and literary academies of the Old Regime, achieving the summit, the Académie française, in successive waves: Voltaire in 1746, Duclos in 1747, d'Alembert in 1754, Marmontel in 1763, Thomas in 1767, Condillac in 1768, Suard in 1774, Malesherbes in 1775, Chastellux in 1775, La Harpe in 1776, Chamfort in 1781, and Condorcet in 1782.[14] Monopolizing patronage networks; seizing the editorships of important journals; and taking the lion's share of sinecures, honoraria, and government posts, the *philosophes* of the High Enlightenment—to the great frustration of their enemies—could boast by the last decades of the *ancien régime* of having penetrated its loftiest reaches.[15]

Nor were they content merely to pontificate in elegant drawing rooms. Emboldened by their success, the *philosophes* claimed for themselves a new calling—the power to form and reflect public opinion. As Antoine-Léonard Thomas declared in an acceptance speech delivered at the Académie française in 1767, "[T]he man of genius has become the arbiter of the thoughts, of the opinions, and of the prejudices of the public."[16] Sébastien-Roch-Nicholas Chamfort concurred, arguing in a prize-winning essay of the same year that the genius of a few great "masters of humanity" shaped the character of any given historical epoch, "imposing its sovereignty on the mass of men" who flocked under the banners, and rushed to adopt the ideas of "great writers and bold *philosophes*."[17]

Undoubtedly this was hubris, a swelling confidence that piqued their opponents as the ultimate sin of pride. Yet the *philosophes*, in part, may be excused, for there were certainly ample signs that their own self-valorization was requited publicly in a cult of genius of which Voltaire's apotheosis was the supreme example. Sought out in their homes as modern oracles, called on by kings as correspondents and councilors, their images reproduced in popular engravings and paraphernalia, and the details of their private lives devoured in biographies and personality sketches, the *grands philosophes* enjoyed by century's end nothing less than the status of celebrities.[18] And with the masters, so with their art. In the final years of the Old Regime, *philosophie* flooded French society as a sort of fashionable kitsch, making it possible to smoke a pipe carved in Voltaire's likeness or to play with cards that were stamped with the images of the *nouveaux philosophes*.[19] There were those who retained the high seriousness of the calling, but for many *philosophie* became radical chic, a melange of set phrases, pseudolearning, and even quackery.[20] International heroes of the mind, the *philosophes* had not only penetrated the highest reaches of eighteenth-century society but, arguably, conquered them as well.

The impact of this process has long been a subject of debate. But although many have asked, from shortly after Voltaire's apotheosis to the present day, what the *philosophes'* triumph entailed (the first tick of the revolutionary countdown? the establishment of the Enlightenment? the enlightenment of the Establishment), few have examined the effect that this process had on the *philosophes'* opponents. Though endlessly invoked by the *philosophes* themselves as a dark specter impeding the course of light, the *philosophes'* enemies have received relatively little attention. As Robert Palmer pointed out in his classic 1939 study, *Catholics and Unbelievers in Eighteenth-Century France*, "It must be confessed that the thought of the Age of Enlightenment, more than that of any equally important period in modern history, has been studied from writings which express only one side of the question."[21] Over fifty years later, his assertion still holds true.

Palmer's work was, and remains, a notable exception to a general rule. But as an account of opposition to the Enlightenment, it is selective and incomplete. Setting aside what he called "the more absurd productions of the orthodox," Palmer concentrated solely on "men of ability," excluding "writings that were only cries of horror, wild assertions, and promiscuous calling of names." His aim was to show that able and reasonable believers opposed the *philosophes*, and in this he succeeded admirably. But he did so at the expense of occluding the radical rage and vehemence that moved a great many of the Enlightenment's opponents, whether in possession of "ability" or not. As Palmer himself acknowledged, his process of selection was prone to "give a false view of the real ideas of the time."[22]

Such exclusivity also characterizes the other great exception to the general neglect of the Enlightenment's contemporary opposition: the work of Sir Isaiah Berlin. It was Berlin, in fact, who first gave the term "Counter-Enlightenment" common currency, treating the subject in a famous essay of that name and elsewhere.[23] Sweeping back to the relativist and skeptical traditions of the ancient world, and forward to the vitalism and irrationalism of the twentieth century, Berlin's Counter-Enlightenment was not precisely demarcated in time. It was, however, for the most part, carefully bounded in space. Whereas the Enlightenment for Berlin was an overwhelmingly French affair, the Counter-Enlightenment was overwhelmingly German, assuming perfect expression in the writings of J. G. A. Hamann, Friedrich Jacobi, J. G. Herder, and Justus Möser. Relativist, historicist, vitalist, organic, and irrational, it was the antithesis to the alleged rationalism, universalism, and ahistorical mechanism of eighteenth-century French thought. Indeed, the only French-speaking writers to figure at all in Berlin's discussion of the Counter-Enlightenment were two postrevolutionary figures, Louis de Bonald and Joseph de Maistre. The former he dismissed as "deservedly forgotten," and the latter he made into a man whose true soul hovered somewhere east of the Rhine. In Berlin's reading, Maistre was "at one with German irrationalism and fideism" and even held the dubious honor of being an intellectual forefather of fascism.[24]

Like all his work, Berlin's writing on the Counter-Enlightenment has been extremely suggestive. But his exclusive focus, like Palmer's, on "men of ability" considerably limited the range of his inquiry.[25] To elucidate broader trends, we need to move beyond the confines of great thinkers and timeless thought, applying to the study of the Counter-Enlightenment the same tools that have been developed by students of the Enlightenment itself in the last thirty years. This is an approach that must also be brought to the thought of the Counter-Revolution, which, likewise, has remained narrowly restricted to a handful of figures, the familiar platoon of Bonald, Burke, Maistre, and their immediate cohorts.[26] Drawing on the insights and methods of recent cultural and intellectual history, this book seeks to do precisely this, branching out into the sometimes unpleasant worlds of the Counter-Enlightenment and the Counter-Revolution.[27] By and large its focus is on names that have been forgotten. And though the so-called men of ability who dominate the pages of earlier studies are not entirely absent here, this work attempts to situate their thought and their language in relation to a much broader current—one, significantly, that includes women as well.

What does one find in venturing out and down into this Counter-Enlightenment world? At the most basic level, it is clear, opposition to the Enlightenment was neither exclusively German nor predominantly philosophical. First and foremost French and first and foremost religious, it extended outward from there into other countries and realms of inquiry. Though new, this claim should not really surprise us. Scholars have long agreed that the Enlightenment coalesced earliest in France and developed there its sharpest vituperative edge.[28] It stands to reason that the reaction to the Enlightenment should also have occurred first in the place of its birth and been spearheaded by the very institution—the Catholic Church—charged with maintaining the faith and morals of the realm.

Admittedly, this was not a reaction marked by the sophistication of thought evident in Berlin's *Gegen-Aufklärung*. But sophistication, as the example of the lonely Vico movingly attests, is not a proper index of influence and is often a distorting lens.[29] In the case of opposition to the Enlightenment, it has blinded us from the literally thousands of religious apologies, books, pamphlets, sermons, plays, poems, and other works produced throughout Europe in the eighteenth century that decried the *siècle des lumières* with very little nuance but with a great deal of genuine revulsion. It has also limited and misshapen our conceptual understanding of the Counter-Enlightenment. For upon closer examination, it becomes perfectly clear that Berlin's own use of the concept was based on his idealist (and highly debatable) point of departure. Beginning with what he took to be the principal doctrines of Enlightenment thought, he then went in search of countervailing propositions, finding them in the authors mentioned above. The problem is that if one alters the departing definition of Enlightenment (as it is easy and, in fact, necessary to do), *Counter*-Enlightenment becomes another phenomenon entirely.[30]

The approach adopted here is very different. Rather than begin on high, with an abstract definition of what the Enlightenment entailed, I begin on the ground, examining what hostile contemporaries themselves said about the *siècle des lumières* and its actuating principle, *philosophie*. As we shall see, it was over and against their own construction of their enemies' doctrines—a construction, that is, of the Enlightenment—that the men and women in this study positioned themselves in direct Counter-Enlightenment opposition.

Being French, these figures were almost all Catholic and, indeed, tended to see the Enlightenment, as Hegel would later do, as a fundamentally Protestant emanation. But this is not to suggest that opposition to the Enlightenment was exclusively or uniformly a Catholic development. Just as there were many within the wide umbrella of the church who enthusiastically embraced the century of lights, there were many outside the Catholic fold who despised the Enlightenment for their own particular reasons. In the end, it is almost certainly the case that the Catholic Counter-Enlightenment discussed in these pages is only one of a range of oppositional responses to Enlightenment movements, spanning a broad, geographical spectrum of regional and confessional difference.[31] These other Counter-Enlightenments await their historian.

This said, there are important reasons for paying particular attention to France. Not only was France the birthplace of the Enlightenment on the European continent, and so the first country to generate a self-conscious Counter-Enlightenment response, but it also enjoyed unsurpassed intellectual prestige within the wider Catholic world. Religious apologists, theologians, and devout readers throughout Europe and the New World looked to French religious writers for guidance and leadership in the same way that intellectuals abroad looked to the *philosophes* in Paris, the capital of the *siècle des lumières*. In hindsight, we are not apt to think of the eighteenth century—and particularly the French eighteenth-century—as a time or place noteworthy for its religious prowess. But although the century produced no Bossuet or Bonaventure—a fact of which contemporaries themselves were acutely conscious—it did produce a startling volume of work across a wide range of genres and styles, whose poverty has been overstated.[32] Given the international currency of the French language, the venerable authority of French religious writing, and the international channels of exchange provided by the Holy Roman Church, France's reaction to the Enlightenment spread well beyond its borders.

Again, it should seem only natural that this was the case—that defenders of the faith abroad should have turned to those soldiers on the front lines in the fight against incredulity for aid in their own indigenous struggles. In addition to the reasons just given, it is also true that in many instances Catholic partisans abroad were waging war against the same authors—the same *French* authors—who drew the wrath of their comrades in France. In this respect, at least, Isaiah Berlin may have been right. To judge from the reactions of many Catholic opponents throughout the world, the Enlightenment did seem a thoroughly French affair. And so, using French fire to fight French fire, Catholic enemies of the Enlightenment in Europe and the New World borrowed from French authors, translated French books, and repeated French arguments that circulated freely through the worldwide network of the church. In short, it is possible to speak of a Catholic Counter-Enlightenment international, in which the French, as with the Enlightenment itself, enjoyed pride of place.[33]

To understand the French Counter-Enlightenment, then, is to begin to understand a movement with tremendous international impact, as well as to help understand the Enlightenment itself.[34] For surely any evaluation of the Enlightenment's character—indeed, its very definition—cannot be complete without an appraisal of those who opposed it in a contemporary context. As we shall see, opponents of the Enlightenment provided its first coherent portrait—a deeply unsympathetic one, certainly, but a portrait all the same—a fact that belies the claim made recently that the Enlightenment was only constructed retrospectively by the Revolution's proponents.[35] On the contrary, well before 1789 opponents of the *philosophes* had collapsed these various figures together into a consistent whole, warning repeatedly that the triumph of *philosophie* augured regicide, anarchy, and the annihilation of religion. Reiterating these admonitions through the 1780s, they greeted 1789 as the fulfillment of their worst fears.

That such predictions were in place long before the Revolution is important for it allowed enemies of the Enlightenment to argue later that they had foreseen the Revolution as the inevitable consequence of the triumph of *philosophie*. In the wake of the Terror, as Europe smoldered in the ash and blood of the revolutionary wars, arguments of this type seemed compelling. No longer could they simply be dismissed as the paranoid ranting of fanatics. Seizing this initiative, anti-*philosophe* polemicists grafted the concrete events of the Revolution to their earlier preconceptions to elaborate a historical reading destined to exert a powerful influence on subsequent interpretations of the Enlightenment. As we will see, enemies of the Enlightenment diffused this construction in tremendous volume in the aftermath of the Terror and well into the nineteenth century.

To repeat, this reading of the Enlightenment was a construction, and though extremely influential, was neither balanced nor kind. For this reason, scholars have largely ignored it. But to turn, in this way, a deaf ear to the "cries of horror" uttered throughout the eighteenth and early nineteenth centuries is to fail to understand the central context in which Enlightenment movements throughout Europe developed: that of militant struggle. The light of the *siècle des lumières* did not somehow miraculously shine forth from a historical black hole. It was refracted, turned, deflected at every juncture. The great pioneer of the cultural history of the eighteenth century, Daniel Mornet, understood this fact, acknowledging with a different metaphor that *philosophie* never flowed like an "unhindered river" but was forced to carve its way through "immobile masses" and "hostile terrain" that forever impeded its course.[36] Similar to the manner in which historians have taken to depicting the revolutionary process in terms of a continuum of force and counter-force, of Revolution and Counter-Revolution, the Enlightenment—Enlightenments—must be viewed in this way.[37] In none of its national manifestations was it uncontested, and rarely was it benign.

This is a lesson that many in our own day could stand to consider, for it must be admitted that critics in the postwar West have been particularly unkind to the Age of Enlightenment. The movement retains its spirited defenders,[38] but on the whole, Enlightenment bashing has developed into something of an intellectual blood-sport, uniting elements of both the Left and the Right in a common cause. From the one side, no shortage of conservative critics—many of them writing in the long shadow of the cold war—have insisted on presenting the Enlightenment as the *ur*-source of modern totalitarianism, the godless font of the Terror, the Gulag, and other atrocities committed in the name of reason.[39] From the Left, and particularly the postmodern Left, we hear the charge that the so-called Enlightenment project is alone responsible for much that is amiss in modernity, the germinating source of totalizing discourse, hegemonic reason, racism, misogyny, and holocaust.[40] United in their antipathy, these camps, too, have been united by their willingness to overlook the Enlightenment's *contemporary* opponents, a predisposition characteristic of a general indifference to historical context that has resulted in tremendous oversimplification and serious distortion. As we shall see, a good number of the more violent claims against the Enlightenment have been with us since the movement itself.

An examination of the *philosophes'* opponents, then, promises to help flesh out the contours of the Enlightenment. It also promises to lend insight into another subject that has received relatively little attention—the ideological origins of the Counter-Revolution in France and, more generally, those of the Right. Although to suggest a connection between opposition to the Enlightenment and later right-wing thought is not entirely without precedent, few studies have examined this relationship in detail.[41] The vast majority of scholars who deal with the Right, in fact, trace its origins to the Revolution itself. After all, they point out, this was the period in which the terms "Right" and "Left" first came into use, employed to signify seating arrangements in the Constituent Assembly.[42]

But the concept of Right entailed far more than geographical location—nor is it sufficient to explain its genesis simply in terms of reaction to the revolutionary process. The men who grouped together at one extreme of the hall of *menus plaisirs*, and those who from outside encouraged their action in deed and word, did so for a reason. They shared a language, a set of common beliefs, and a vision. And when one comes to consider this vision—the ideological convictions of the more dogged opponents of the Revolution—it is apparent that its main outlines had been elaborated well before the National Assembly held its first session.

This was not a wholly unified political plank, a specific platform or slate, but a nascent view of the world that involved a loose, though identifiable, set of mutual assumptions, a group of postulates, and a rhetorical style—what I term an "anti-*philosophe* discourse." Cultivated during nearly forty years of combat with the *philosophes*, this discourse was firmly in place before the Estates General had even met—an important contention, for it calls into question the view of those who allege that the Revolution's opponents in the early years were essentially a figment of a frenzied Jacobin imagination, a discursive invention of the Left.[43] As we shall see, the Revolution did not need to invent its enemies. They were there from the outset, and their presence exerted a powerful influence on the dynamics of the revolutionary process. Those who try to explain the terrible violence of the Revolution in the absence of this militant opposition do so in a vaccum and, as a result, unconvincingly. The Terror was the product of the clash of revolutionary and counterrevolutionary extremes, not of either force in isolation.

What were the elements of this emergent right-wing vision? The fundamental importance of religion in maintaining political order, a preoccupation with the perils of intellectual and social license, the valorization of the family and history, the critique of abstract rights, the dangers of dividing sovereignty, and the need for a strategic alliance between throne and altar—these all featured centrally in this new ideology. Even more fundamental was a Manichean readiness to divide the world in two: between good and evil, right and wrong, Right and Left. Marked by an unwillingness to compromise and the belief that to do so would imperil the social order in its entirety, this vision was a direct outgrowth of the apocalyptic rhetoric aimed at the *philosophes* during the final years of the *ancien régime*.

Two important points follow directly from this close link between opposition to the Enlightenment and the genesis of the Right, in France as elsewhere. The first is that given that right-wing ideology developed in response to a quintessentially modern phenomenon—the Enlightenment—it follows that it, too, was modern. This is something that Isaiah Berlin clearly recognized.[44] And although the perception caused him to subsume his Counter-Enlightenment thinkers into larger teleologies that sped headlong toward the twentieth century, the underlying observation was acute. Not "conservative" in any strict sense, not archaically traditional, not romantically medieval, the early Right was in fact radical, striving far more to create a world that had never been than to recapture a world that was lost. Granted, its vision was deeply and profoundly religious. No other force, this book will argue, played as central and important a role in the genesis of the early European Right as the Roman Catholic faith. But if in this respect, as in others, the Right necessarily drew on the legacy of the past, it used this legacy to continually look forward, summoning the horrible specter of a time, one day soon, when religion might not exist at all. In its very fundamentalism—itself a modern phenomenon—the religious Right raised concerns that continue to be our own, dramatizing from the start the cultural costs of disenchantment and laying bare the state of a world in which no appeal could be made to higher sources (religious, political, or moral).

Dwelling on the dark underside of modern rationalism, individualism, and materialism, the early Right created a distinctly new ideological culture. Its defense of tradition was not traditional, its reverence for history was a historical departure, and its arguments for the family and patriarchal power were a response to novel threats both real and perceived. Developing these and other innovative arguments in the face of innovative attacks, polemicists of the Right did so by direct participation in the new public sphere, also a uniquely modern product.[45] The incipient Right detested that sphere and was convinced that the free exchange of ideas produced devastating social consequences. But in the absence of other, viable means to curtail the Enlightenment's expansion, it was forced to adopt modern methods and modern technology, employing pamphlets, print culture, and the periodical press to compete openly in the new republic of letters.

I will have occasion to discuss the theme of the Right's modernity in greater detail later. Here let me make a second point: that just as France served as the spiritual homeland for an international, Catholic Counter-Enlightenment, so did it serve as an ideological source of subsequent right-wing doctrine abroad. I should perhaps qualify this statement, because the use of the term "Right" is a convention. There was never a single Right, any more than there was a single Left. Developing in individual and national contexts and across a spectrum of varying opinions, European right-wing movements nonetheless drew on a common stock of ideas and developed in the common contexts of resistance to the Enlightenment and, later, resistance to the French Revolution. The role of France in this process was crucial. For too long, if inevitably, given the experience of the twentieth century, scholars have allowed the case of Germany to eclipse other inquiries into the origins of the European Right. Yet arguably, France was as fertile a source, if not more so, feeding currents of Catholic authoritarianism that would flow with force into our own century in eastern Europe, Italy, Latin America, and Spain. It was, in fact, a Spanish observer, Javier Herrero, writing at the end of the Franco regime, who first appreciated this phenomenon. In a study of the eighteenth-century origins of Spanish reactionary thought, he observed in passing that there was "nothing traditional, or Spanish, about the great masters of the Spanish [reactionary] tradition."[46] His point was hyperbolic but nonetheless profound. The origins of Spain's right-wing tradition, he argued, could be traced to a more general "Counter-Enlightenment movement" (*movimiento antiilustrado*), which though intensely Catholic (which is to say, intensely international), stemmed ultimately from France. It was an insight that Herrero was quick to extend to other countries as well:

> The conflict between the Enlightenment and reaction in Spain is but an episode of a movement that embraces the near totality of the [European] continent and that extends to include the Americas. The fundamental sources of this movement are, of course, European as well, and as we are

dealing with the eighteenth century, the most important reactionaries, those which exercised the major influence on conservative Europe, were French. Its historical influence was immense.[47]

This book chronicles this immensely influential French Counter-Enlightenment movement, writing a chapter in what is, at once, the history of France, the history of Europe, the history of the New World, and in certain respects the history of modernity itself.

CHAPTER *1*

Listen to the modern *philosophes*,

lend an ear to their lessons,

receive and practice their doctrines and

all will be overturned. . . .

—Charles Louis Richard,

Exposition de la doctrine des

philosophes modernes (1785)

A CENTURY BLINDED BY LIGHT

*O*n the night of the opening of Voltaire's *Irène*, a small "cabal . . . excited principally by men dressed in the costumes of abbés" mingled with the enthusiastic onlookers who had come to pay tribute to the great *philosophe*. Little is known of these men, except that they were at odds with the majority of spectators. As a firsthand witness, Voltaire's personal secretary, Wagnière, reports, they attempted to disrupt the performance in "violent" protest before its onset. Their voices, however, "were snuffed out by the general applause," serving only to "enliven the room" before the raising of the curtain. Two weeks later, at the performance attended by Voltaire himself, the anti-*philosophe* contingent was even smaller. A single voice, that of the poet Nicolas-Joseph-Laurent Gilbert, cried out, "There is no more religion in France. All is lost!" He was forcibly subdued by the crowd[1] (see Figure 2).

The number of those opposed to Voltaire's Parisian presence—and to what it seemed to stand for, the triumph of *philosophie*—was greater than this meager collection of abbés and the lone Gilbert would suggest. Nor was religion lost in France. The pro-*philosophe* newsheet, the *Mémoires secrets,* was even ready to tip the balance in favor of Voltaire's adversaries. "Despite the great number of partisans and admirers of M. de Voltaire," it observed amid the pandemonium of the apotheosis, "he has even more enemies. He has against him all the party of the *dévots* and the clergy."[2] Yet to view the eighteenth century from the perspective of devoutly religious men and women is to understand their exaggeration. In their view, the so-called century of lights represented the single most concerted attack on the Christian religion in the history of humanity, and figures like Voltaire—self-styled *philosophes*—were directly responsible for waging this war. That France could now lionize a man long deemed by religious observers to be in close consort with the devil seemed to confirm that the most advanced country on the European continent had undergone a startling transformation (see Figure 3). As the esteemed orator the abbé de Cambacérès had already warned in a celebrated sermon preached at the court of Louis XV, modern disbelief was producing a "revolution" in "the morals and characters of the nation." In the face of this revolution, religion was "threatened, tottering on a precipice."[3]

What might a world in which religion had plunged to its demise, a world ruled by modern philosophy, entail? As we shall see in this chap-

Figure 2. Nicolas-Joseph-Laurent Gilbert (1750–1780).
Photo courtesy of the Bibliothèque Nationale, Paris.

ter, enemies of the Enlightenment left little to the imagination, painting
a portrait of the triumph of *philosophie* in vividly apocalyptic terms. In
doing so, they necessarily constructed an image of *philosophie* itself and
of the age in which it was formed—an image, that is, of the Enlightenment. However disfigured, this construction proved powerful and lasting. However far from the original, it served admirably as both a specter
and a foil: a specter of a modern world to come and a foil against which
to rally opposition. Conceiving of their century as a fallen age, enemies
of the Enlightenment refused to fall before it. Rather, they rose to the
challenge, bidding hitherto disparate groups and individuals to come together in a militant, Counter-Enlightenment response. In the process,
they forged not only new alliances but also a view of the world that was
every bit as modern as that of their adversaries.

Anti-*Philosophes* at the End of the Old Regime

Opposition to the *philosophes* did not begin in 1778.[4] In fact, Voltaire's
enemies were quick to view his apotheosis as symbolic of French de-

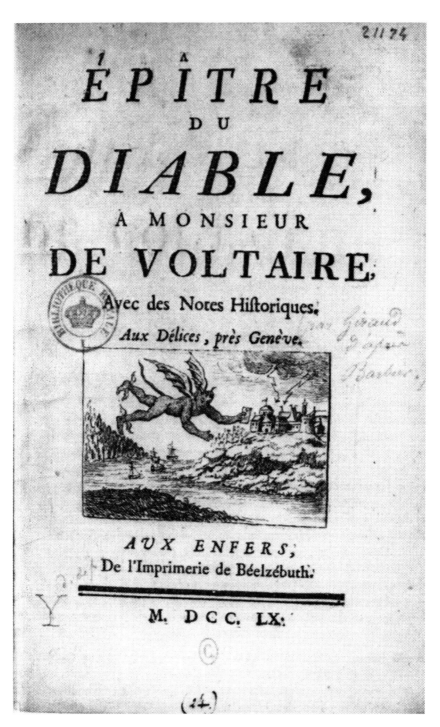

Figure 3. Frontispiece to the physician Claude-Marie Giraud's *Epistle from the Devil to M. Voltaire.* This brief work, chronicling Voltaire's traffic with Satan, was republished over thirty times between 1760 and the outbreak of the Revolution. Photo courtesy of the Bibliothèque Nationale, Paris.

cline, in large part because it reminded them—painfully—of their own, prior failings. From bases in important cultural institutions and circles of power, anti-*philosophes* had waged war from the middle of the century on what they saw as the corrosive effects of modern philosophy, seeking especially to eradicate the flow of illicit books. Thus, since 1755, each of the church's national general assemblies, held at least once every five years to coordinate policy and review fiscal matters, had taken up the problem of the "contagion" being spread "throughout the realm" by the poisonous writings of "so-called *philosophes*."[5] The learned doctors at the Sorbonne, too, had issued a steady stream of refutations of these works, denouncing the concerted effort to destroy the "religion of our fathers" and to undermine the "authority and power of kings."[6] Always these warnings were insistent and often graphic, confronting the crown directly with the prospect of "bloodied thrones" and the "horrors of anarchy" if it failed to act with haste.[7] Unable and at times unwilling to significantly curb the well-documented flow of subversive books in this period, the respective reigns of Louis XV and Louis XVI witnessed, instead, a dramatic increase in their circulation. In the years following Voltaire's apotheosis, this showed no signs of slowing. As Jean-Marie Dulau, bishop of Arles, complained in 1782, "enemies of revelation" now freely scattered "heaps" of "licentious productions" throughout his diocese, even daring to throw these works into the gardens and enclosures of convents.[8] No place, it seemed, was sacred. By the last years of the Old Regime, the General Assembly of the Clergy was forced to admit its defensive stance, alleging in 1785 that the "lessons of the *nouvelle philosophie*" now resounded "even in the workshops of the artisan and under the humble roofs of peasants."[9]

Likewise, in the provincial and Paris *parlements*, where influential men such as Jean-Omer Joly de Fleury and Antoine-Louis Seguier had fought consistently to defend the Catholic faith against the ravages of *philosophie*, anti-*philosophes* looked on in baffled horror at what they saw as the steady advances of their enemies.[10] As early as 1759, Fleury had complained that the *philosophes* "conspired" to "sap the foundations" of the state, urging authorities to take "sword in hand to smash . . . these sacrilegious and seditious authors."[11] Despite Fleury's efforts, however, these authors continued to produce their "poisonous" works. By 1781, speaking before the Grand'Chambre, Seguier presented their threat as more imminent still. "In vain," he intoned, has the "administration established the wisest precautions, in vain has it multiplied obstacles to the publication of writings that spread audacity and irreligion throughout society. The wisdom of government is annihilated, the vigilance of the magistracy destroyed. More and more the *esprit philosophique* becomes the spirit of the day."[12]

From the perspective of opponents of the *philosophes* in the church and *parlements*, then, the outlook was dire. So, too, did other intransigent defenders of the faith regard the *philosophes'* advances with consternation. At court, the militantly Catholic *dévot* faction had seen its partisans consistently pushed aside during the dissolute reign of Louis XV. Helpless to unseat an open protector of the *philosophes*, Malesherbes, as director of the book trade from 1750–1763, it suffered further ignominy when a coalition of Jansenist *parlementaires* and philosophic allies managed to orchestrate the expulsion of the Jesuits from France in the mid-1760s. As if to add insult to injury, 1765 witnessed the premature death of the *dévots'* leader and erstwhile heir to the throne, Louis Ferdinand, the pious son of Louis XV (see Figure 4). And although the heir apparent, Louis XVI, was noted for the conviction of his faith, his youth, vacillation, and susceptibility to persuasion did not favor the prospect of a sustained anti-*philosophe* crusade.[13] Such doubts proved well founded. Despite the presence in Louis XVI's early reign of leading *dévot* ministers, including Maurepas; du Muy; and most notably, the Count of Vergennes—all men convinced that the *philosophes* constituted a pressing threat to the realm—their influence was offset by less religiously inspired courtiers.[14] When Voltaire marched triumphantly into Paris in 1778, his presence unimpeded and his play conspicuously attended by an adoring Marie Antoinette, hopes that the young king would make fighting the *philosophes* a priority of his reign were even more difficult to sustain.

Beyond the reception halls and drawing rooms of court officials, royal magistrates, Sorbonne doctors, and practicing clergy, one other active group looked on with alarm at the advance of the century's new learning: anti-*philosophe* men of letters.[15] Though the *philosophes* might claim a preeminent place in the cultural landscape of France, they had not won this position without an, at times, dirty fight. Climbing to the top, they

Figure 4. (facing page) The 1757 frontispiece to the first volume of Jean Soret and Jean-Nicolas-Hubert Hayer's anti-*philosophe* journal, *La Religion vengée, ou Réfutation des auteurs impies*. True philosophy, in possession of the keys to the church, presents a copy of the work to the dauphin, Louis Ferdinand, who looks on approvingly as religion and wisdom trample false philosophy under foot. The latter bears a sign which reads in Latin, "He said that there is no God." Hopes that the heir to the throne would completely extinguish the torch of false philosophy, however, were themselves snuffed out with the dauphin's premature death in 1765. Photo courtesy of the Bibliothèque Nationale, Paris.

La Philosophie, sous les auspices de la Religion, presente l'Ouvrage à Monseigneur le Dauphin.

trod on rivals in the process, often intentionally and frequently with skill. Their vaunted social graces did nothing to impede their ability to slander. In a single work, Voltaire could dub one anti-*philosophe* adversary, the journalist Elie Cathérine Fréron, "a scribbler," "scoundrel," "toad," "lizard," "snake," "viper's tongue," "crooked mind," "heart of filth," "doer of evil," "rascal," "impudent person," "cowardly knave," "spy," and "hound."[16] As much as genuine difference of opinion, deliberate offensiveness of this kind—a desire not only to smash the infamous thing but also to rub one's face in the shattered remains—earned the *philosophes* vehement enemies. Thus, during the 1750s and 1760s, the abbé Gabriel Gauchat devoted his monthly journal, the *Lettres critiques, ou Analyse et réfutation de divers écrits modernes contre la religion*, to refuting the works of men who "combined against truth . . . the salt of irony . . . and the blackness of calumny."[17] Still others adopted the tactics of the *philosophes* themselves. Fréron consistently employed ridicule, defamation, and sarcasm to pillory his enemies in his influential *Année littéraire*, and many others mocked the *philosophes* in a host of satirical plays, libels, and novels published in the late 1750s, 1760s, and early 1770s. Despite this prodigious output, these writers could not deny the *philosophes'* gains. The poet Jean-Jacques Le Franc de Pompignan, who in 1760 had used the occasion of his election to the Académie française to condemn a century "drunk with the philosophic spirit . . . the scorn of religion, and the hatred of all authority," was regarding such drunkenness by the 1780s as total intoxication.[18]

These were the *philosophes'* principal enemies. At odds with their century, they conceived of themselves as a marginal, and marginalized, group, living in a world apart. As the anti-*philosophe* journalist J. M. B. Clément complained, those who resisted the "rally cry of *philosophie*" were "scattered, without leaders, without credit, and without honors."[19] Largely as a consequence, we know far too little about them. We have, for example, no study of the *parti dévot*, no treatment of the booksellers and distributors who traded in anti-*philosophe* writings, no consideration of their readership, no analysis of the anti-*philosophe* press. Only recently have scholars begun to acknowledge that conservative salons existed in the eighteenth century in which the *philosophes'* ideas were regarded with horror; and only recently have they have begun to consider the patronage networks and social geography that shaped anti-*philosophe* production.[20] Still, it is clear from even this attenuated cross section that the anti-*philosophes* drew from a varied lot, comprising lofty courtiers, influential ecclesiastics, and powerful *parlementaires*, as well as lowly administrative officials, minor abbés, and Grub Street hacks. Such diversity should warn us not to take the anti-*philosophes'* protestations of marginality too closely to heart. Clearly, some in their ranks enjoyed positions of power, although it was ultimately religious and cultural conviction, not social standing, that shaped their beliefs. And it was almost certainly the case that more men and women shared their disdain for the Enlightenment than the anti-*philosophes* themselves were ready to acknowledge. Jean-Jacques Rousseau was not the only cultural critic in the eighteenth century to adopt the stance of embattled minority.

Whatever their final numbers, the anti-*philosophes'* inability to halt the advance of *philosophie* was real and their frustration well founded. The very diversity of their ranks was undoubtedly a contributing factor. Although select royal officials and Catholic *parlementaires* might well share bitter resentment of philosophic triumph, they were just as apt to quarrel over the nature of the *parlements'* role in the legislative process or the limitations and checks on the power of the king. Ecclesiastics also engaged in endless disputes with both the crown and the courts on a number of issues, ranging from the boundaries of legal jurisdiction to the failings of the police in controlling the book trade to the amount of the church's contributions to royal coffers. Even the anti-*philosophes'* greatest institutional stronghold, the church, was by no means a house united. Rent by protracted battles between Jansenists and *dévots*, Gallicans and Ultramontanes, and the impoverished lower clergy and the wealthy hierarchy, it also harbored numerous members who were little inclined to view the *philosophes'* ascendance with displeasure. Part of what has been described as a European-wide "Catholic Aufklärung," these figures drank deeply of the new learning.[21] And although they at times paid lip-service to the fight against "infidelity," they took, on the whole, a benign view of the *siècle des lumières* and were even inclined to see the *philosophes* as a source of potential renewal and rejuvenation. The archbishop of Toulouse, Loménie de Brienne, is a perfect illustration of this type. When this close friend of d'Alembert was recommended as a candidate to assume the archbishopric of Paris, Louis XVI quipped that "at the very least" such a high-ranking official of the church "must believe in God." This didn't, however, stop the king from appointing Brienne controller-general of France in 1788.[22] With colleagues like these, opponents of the *philosophes* scarcely needed enemies.

Divided allegiances and crisscrossing interests of this kind effectively stymied any concerted campaign against the social influence and publishing prowess of the *philosophes*.[23] Scattered and set against themselves, men and women who shared a deep antipathy to the century's leading lights thus felt impotent before them. When an exultant supporter of the *philosophes* mocked his adversaries in 1776 as "powerless enemies of *philosophie*," his jibe carried more than an element of truth.[24]

But to cite these admissions, as many commentators have done, simply as testimony to the anti-*philosophes*' defeat would be to miss the genuine strain of revulsion in their rhetoric, the seething bitterness, and the apocalyptic note of terror.[25] Seemingly at odds with their century, these men and women looked at the society around them as one gone mad. "I no longer recognize my nation," grumbled an anonymous commentator in the *Journal ecclésiastique*, the leading professional publication of the clergy. "The *philosophes* are the men of the day."[26] "*Philosophie, philosophie*—voilà the tone of the times," complained another enraged opponent, the Franciscan Élie Harel. "One speaks now only of philosophic spirit, philosophic varnish, philosophic gloss."[27] Anti-*philosophes* lamented, even overstated, this plight, but they did not simply wither and blow away in the last decade of the Old Regime. On the contrary, the very triumph of the *philosophes* further embittered their adversaries, enjoining them to come together in the face of a common enemy. Hardened by their setbacks and frustrated by their failures, they fought on with continued vehemence, viewing their battle in cosmic terms as an eschatological struggle between good and evil. Far from succumbing to the triumph of *philosophie*, anti-*philosophes* waged an even more desperate struggle. Indeed, it is possible to speak of a reaction.

From Dark Despair to Dark Reaction

Certain contemporary critics were quick to note this shift.[28] Writing in April, 1776, the astute social observers of Grimm's *Correspondance littéraire* commented with perplexed fascination on the tremendous outpouring of religiosity associated with the jubilee celebrations in Paris of that year. Speculating that these "outbursts of zeal" were based as much on the "mood . . . against the party of the *philosophes*" as on genuine piety, the journal ventured that "it would be somewhat amusing if *philosophie* [through its very successes] unwittingly contributed to rekindling the faith of the century."[29] Two years later, at the time of Voltaire's apotheosis, an anonymous pro-*philosophe* pamphleteer was complaining that it had become "fashionable . . . to persecute the *philosophes*,"[30] a development that the *Correspondance littéraire* now seemed less inclined to view as "amusing": "Pamphlets of all kinds against *philosophie* and the *philosophes* multiply every day, and the goal of these writings is to accuse the sect of Encyclopedists for all our disorders, for all our woes: general depravation, the excesses of *libertinage*, the decline of taste, the progress of luxury, the weakening of all the orders of the State, bad harvests, and the increase in the price of bread."[31]

Sweeping condemnations of this sort were common in the last decade of the *ancien régime*.[32] Called forth by the general triumph of the *philosophes* symbolized by Voltaire's apotheosis and also by such specific episodes as the well-publicized effort to distribute Voltaire's collected works in the early 1780s, this anti-*philosophe* reaction took the form of hundreds of books, pamphlets, sermons, essays, and poems.[33] In part these condemnations were actively subsidized by the Assembly General of the Clergy's Committee on Religion and Jurisdiction, which spent close to 200,000 *livres* in the 1780s to fund antiphilosophic propaganda, including an unprecedented 46,600 *livres* in 1782 and 97,000 *livres* in 1785 alone.[34] They were also actively solicited by groups such as the Société des amis de la Religion et des Lettres, founded in 1778 to encourage anti-*philosophe* production by sponsoring essay contests and awarding prizes for the works that best defended religion.[35] Finally, these writings found outlets—for review, excerpt, subsidy, and advertisement—in a buoyant, anti-*philosophe* press. Established journals such as the *Année littéraire*, the *Journal historique et littéraire*, and the *Journal ecclésiastique* continued to make combating the *philosophes* their raison d'être. And more recent publications, such as the *Journal de Monsieur*; the *Journal de littérature, des sciences et des arts*; and the *Affiches, annonces et avis divers*, brought fresh vigor to the fight. Edited and staffed by the likes of Thomas-Marie Royou (1741–1792), Julien Louis Geoffroy (1743–1814), Jean-Baptiste Grosier (1743–1823), Louis-Abel Fontenai (1736–1806), Augustin Barruel (1741–1820), and François-Xavier Feller (1735–1802), these journals shared a common purpose. Their editors were intimates and associates and, significantly, all displaced Jesuits who would become prominent counterrevolutionary journalists.[36]

By combing through sources such as these, one obtains a sense of the contours and content of the anti-*philosophe* reaction of the final years of the Old Regime. Spanning a range of genre and form, the writing of this period tended to be simplistic and reductive, consciously avoiding the detailed theological arguments of formal Christian apologies and directing itself, on the whole, to a lay audience.[37] But it is this very simplicity that renders the anti-*philosophe* invective of the last years of the *ancien régime* of greatest interest. Abjuring tortuous explication and meticulous critique, this literature was content to make broad and brash assertions, drawing on a set of what by the 1770s were already well-established criticisms. Collapsing the diverse and variegated opinions of eighteenth-century philosophy into a reified whole, this literature repeated a number of consistent charges against the *philosophes* in a coherent, predictable, and fully articulated language. In broad terms, this language should be understood as a unified phenomenon, a linguistic strand—what I call an "anti-*philosophe* discourse."[38] Pulling together the more nuanced reflections of countless earlier apologists, this discourse radically simplified complex phenomena, providing a master narrative through which orthodox Catholics could understand the bewildering changes that seemed to be overtaking their society. In a manner similar to the way in which, as Robert Darnton has argued, an underground literature of political slander and libel closed off debate from the Left in the final years of the Old Regime, the anti-*philosophe* literature examined here closed off debate from the Right.[39] It, too, operated on the principle of "radical simplification," polarizing views and forcing the public to take sides in either-or, black-white terms. And it, too, reduced the history of the eighteenth century to "a central theme with a single moral." Whereas the libelists of the literary underground, however, saw only the degeneration of monarchy under despotism, anti-*philosophes* saw the degeneration of France under *philosophie*.

Constructing *Philosophie*, Constructing the Enlightenment

Before moving on to a more general discussion of this anti-*philosophe* discourse, it is useful to consider in detail a characteristic example: Charles-Louis Richard's *Exposition de la doctrine des philosophes modernes*, a sixty-nine-page pamphlet published in 1785. Born in 1711 to a noble family from Lorraine, Richard received a doctorate in theology from the Sorbonne and spent his life as a priest in the Dominican order. A prolific religious apologist who would later be put to death by the Jacobins for his outspoken counterrevolutionary views, Richard was no stranger to doing battle with enemies of the faith. He had even known some success.[40] Yet by his own admission, the majority of the writings of the century's Christian defenders had touched only "a certain number of people for whom they [were] the least necessary"—other theologians. They were, consequently, "useless to the multitude who, without arms and without defenses, succumbs rapidly to *Philosophie*. . . ." Richard conceived his work "with the design of putting in the hands of all those who know how to read a victorious weapon against the assaults of this turbulent *Philosophie*."[41] It is doubtful that the work fulfilled this ambitious goal, but the attempt is instructive.

Departing from the premise that there was such a thing as a "philosophic doctrine," a coherent body of ideas working toward mutual, pernicious ends, Richard grouped these ideas into three principal categories—physics, metaphysics, and ethics—to show that *la doctrine philosophique* collectively entailed a thoroughgoing materialism, a complete rejection of man's duties to God, and a morality based solely on self-interest and pleasure. In its conception of the physical world, the philosophic doctrine, Richard maintained, posited a universe moved solely by self-propelling particles of matter. Man and the world were only random assemblages of matter without purpose or design, a physical supposition with direct metaphysical and ethical consequences. Stripped of higher calling, the *philosophes* responded only to pleasure and interest, refusing to recognize God. The only being recognized by the *philosophes* at all, it seemed, was the self. "Read, if you can, the innumerable writings to which modern philosophy has given birth. You will see that the great motor of human action is love of the self, of this *me* that constitutes the center and final end of everything. All is related to the self and to one's well being, one's interests, one's pleasures. . . ."[42] Following from this radical individualism—the core of *philosophie's* ethics—was a complete denial of social responsibility. Just as the *philosophes* sacrificed society as a whole to the individual, so did they assert that "Kings, Czars, Sultans, and Emperors owe[d] their institutions, their ranks, and their authority to the people." The *doctrine philosophique* was thoroughly "republican." Not only did the *philosophes* allege that subjects could "freely establish and dissolve" their governments at will, but their "discourses and seditious writings . . . had no other goal than to arm citizens against their kings."[43]

None of Richard's principal allegations were new in and of themselves. Charges of materialism, atheism, ethical self-interest, republicanism, and sedition abound in earlier Catholic critiques. And indeed, when applied to particular works, they were not wholly without foundation. La Mettrie's *L'Homme machine*, for example, presented a radically materialist view of the universe, which denied the distinction between mind and matter, body and soul. The Baron d'Holbach wrote consistently in a similar vein, drawing clearly atheistic conclusions in such anonymous publications as *Du Bon sens* and *Système de la nature*. Helvétius's *De l'Esprit* did base its ethical propositions on the calculation of personal interest and a sensationalist epistemology of pleasure and pain, and the *Encyclopedia's* article on authority or Mirabeau's *Essai sur le despotisme* possess more than a whiff of republicanism. But though Richard cited all these authors, he lumped them together indiscriminately with a host of others—Voltaire, Raynal, Robinet, Diderot, and d'Alembert—quoting selectively and eclectically to construct a reified *philosophie*, a composite caricature of the complex and conflicting ideas of eighteenth-century philosophy, reduced to the sum of its worst parts. And regarding the general effects of the doctrine, he left little to the imagination:

The simple exposé that we have just made of the doctrine of the modern *philosophes* proves evidently that it can have no other result, as it has no other goal, than to corrupt the faith and its morals, to raise from the earth every manner of religion and religious worship, every idea of duty, of obligation, of law, of conscience, of justice and injustice, of vice and virtue, of God . . . and consequently, to lose without recourse—for this world and for the next—the entire human race. What a picture! What goals! What effects! . . . Voilà, the natural outcome of the philosophic doctrine.[44]

This was a voice of stupefaction at the blindness of an age, a voice of incomprehension, of outrage and hate. But although it must be admitted that Richard was among the more inflammatory of late anti-*philosophe* writers, his general tendency to reify *philosophie* in precisely these terms, dwelling on its terrible, adverse consequences, was entirely characteristic. The preliminary discourse to the Grub Street anti-*philosophe* Sabatier de Castre's *Trois siècles de la littérature française*, for example, drew together Holbach's *Système de la nature*, La Beaumelle's *L'Asiatique tolérant*, Voltaire's *Micromégas*, Raynal's *Histoire philosophique & politique des deux Indes*, Naigeon's *Militaire philosophe*, Rousseau's *Émile*, Helvetius's *De l'Homme*, and the *Encyclopédie*, among other works, to prove that the maxims of *la philosophie moderne* "breathed only trouble, sedition, and upheaval."[45] Madame de Genlis's 1787 primer for children, *La Religion considérée comme l'unique base du bonheur*, similarly quoted extensively from the works of Helvétius, Voltaire, Diderot, Mably, Holbach, Condorcet, Raynal, and others to emphasize modern philosophy's collective quest to "destroy religion," its ceaseless declamations against authority, and its violent enjoinders to "overturn thrones" in language all could understand[46] (see Figure 5). These were standard denunciations, intended, like Richard's work, to move beyond intricate theological debate and sustained refutation, reaching out in the process to the widest possible audience. As one exultant publicist for Sabatier affirmed, his works drew readers of all types—"men of the Church, men of letters, men of the world, women, and even the most frivolous spirits."[47] Given that the *Trois Siècles* went through at least seven editions prior to the Revolution, this may have been more than exaggeration.

Admittedly, we know very little about who, in fact, constituted the readership of these works, although there are strong indications that more were reading them than previously acknowledged. To take only one example, the abbé Barruel's epistolary novel, *Les Helviennes*, went through at least five augmented editions between 1781 and 1788. Barruel was every bit as violent in his treatment of *philosophie* as Richard. But

Figure 5. Stéphanie-Félicité Ducrest de Saint-Aubin, "Madame de Genlis" (1746–1830). Photo courtesy of the Bibliothèque Nationale, Paris.

arguably for that very reason the book was glowingly reviewed, often in multiple installments, in the *Année littéraire*; *Journal de littérature, des sciences et des arts*; *Journal de Monsieur*; *Journal historique et littériare*; *Affiches, annonces et avis divers*; and *Journal ecclésiastique*.[48] Clearly, some found this literature compelling.

Detailed understanding of the readership, publication networks, and communication channels of this work awaits further study, as does so much else in this forgotten, Counter-Enlightenment world. What can be said with certainty here is that the literature itself drew on arguments rehearsed over the course of decades to present the *philosophes* and *philosophie* in consistent, hypostatized terms. In the mind of anti-*philosophes*, *philosophie* was a "thing," a coherent entity, a unified whole, and the *philosophes* themselves were working toward mutual ends. As the abbé Grosier observed typically in the preliminary essay to his *Journal de littérature, des sciences et des arts* in 1779, "Let us stop for a moment to consider *Philosophie* from the simple perspective of league and confederation. One cannot deny that the *Philosophes* fulfill amongst themselves the mutual duties imposed by a strict confraternity. . . . Between them, what union, what accord, what reciprocity of zeal . . . !"[49]

In envisioning *philosophie* in this way, Grosier pointed most accusingly at what he termed the "Encyclopedic school."[50] Neither he nor his anti-*philosophe* comrades, in fact, had any doubt that the men who made up what is now referred to as the High Enlightenment were the principal architects and original agents of the philosophic doctrine. As such, they were portrayed as men of vast and diabolic strength—"new titans"—whose influence extended outward on a terrific scale. Revered by kings, they were also the "masters and doctors of the multitude."[51] But Grosier and others also referred to the many "apprentices" who studied the writings of the great *philosophes*, presenting these "Encyclopedic lackeys," too, as active disseminators of the *doctrine philosophique*. "Vermin," as Élie Harel observed, made fine carriers for their more celebrated hosts. The disease—*la nouvelle philosophie*—was common to both.[52] Such conflation was typical, and underscores just how few distinctions anti-*philosophes* were inclined to draw between "Enlightenments" low and high, early and late. From their perspective, *philosophie* was a continuum, flowing outward and downward from the pens of a few controlling evil geniuses to encompass all those dissidents who claimed to bear the torches of the *siècle des lumières*. Acknowledging few differences, anti-*philosophes* inveighed collectively against this hydra of many heads, employing a host of neologisms—*philosophailles, philosophistes, philosophesque, philosopherie, philosophisme*—that displayed their semantic, as well as ideological, disregard for fine distinctions.[53]

Language of this sort forces us to contemplate a strange irony: as a conceptual entity, an idea, the Enlightenment was "invented" as much by its enemies as by its friends. Long before Immanuel Kant had even posed his celebrated question—*Was ist Aufklärung?*—critics in France had answered him. The Enlightenment, or in their terms, the *siècle des lumières*, was an abomination; *philosophie* was a unified force, one that produced radical, even revolutionary consequences. Well before 1789 anti-*philosophes* were making this claim, reconciling and uniting their enemies well beyond their extreme differences, attributing to them common aims and common ends. Tautology aside, there is much truth to the claim that the Counter-Enlightenment invented the Enlightenment.[54]

Anti-*Philosophe* Discourse

At the most fundamental level, *philosophie* was accused of subverting the foundations of the Catholic religion, leading necessarily to the wholesale destruction of the faith. To the majority of anti-*philosophes* of the waning years of the Old Regime, this was the explicit aim of the *philosophes*, who had "conceived the design of arming all the forces of their reason towards the ruin of religion."[55] As the Sorbonne censors of Raynal's *Histoire philosophique* commented in 1781, "It is no longer the single individual who dares to raise his voice against the Lord and his temple, but a formal conspiracy, a numerous league . . . [that] seeks to destroy religion, wiping its every trace from the face of the earth."[56]

These observers spoke in the charged language of conspiracy, accusing the *philosophes* of overtly plotting the demise of Christianity.[57] Such language was common. But even those who did not dwell on the conscious agency of the *philosophes* still depicted the result of their doctrines as the weakening and annihilation of the faith. In their countless anticlerical tirades, their questioning of the authenticity of Scripture, and their arrogant confidence in the power of the unaided human mind, the *philosophes*, their enemies charged, "made pretensions to doubt all," bidding men and women to set foot on the slippery slope that led to disbelief.[58] Undermining the twin pillars of Catholic certainty (revelation and the tradition and authority of the church), they tempted their converts with the oldest of sins (vanity and pride), urging them to trust blindly in individual reason. "Unbelief," the Bishop and Duke of Langres proclaimed in a typical refrain, was "always born of pride."[59] Only in the law of the Gospel, in revelation, and in the church could man's reason be harnessed and employed effectively. Without this mitigating restraint, the individual necessarily fell prey to the vagaries of vain speculation.

As proof of this assertion, opponents of the *philosophes* frequently cited the wide range of the *philosophes'* religious speculations, presenting this very diversity as evidence of their inability to arrive at a constant truth. "I defy you," challenged a journalist in the *Année littéraire*, "to cite me an error, however absurd . . . that the *philosophes* have not adopted," guided solely "by the torch of reason, of *philosophie*."[60] For whatever the variety of its manifold conclusions on religious matters, *philosophie* stemmed from a single source, the arrogance of the human intellect, and tended in the same direction, the destruction of all belief. The fatal seeds of doubt might bear many vines, but they were all working to choke off belief in its entirety. As the abbé Liger summarized pithily, "[T]he boisterous philosophy of this century is, properly speaking, the art of disbelief."[61]

Again, the individual themes of this rhetoric were not particular to the final years of the Old Regime. The critique of pride, for example, as old as Ecclesiastes, was sharpened in the wake of the Reformation when the attack on the Catholic rule of faith and the revival of Greek Pyrrhonian skepticism provoked a flood of writing on the inevitable shortcomings of human reason.[62] Defenders of the church had also long held that atheism was the inevitable outgrowth of dissidence, leveling the charge consistently (and with great liberality) at a host of religious dissenters since the mid-seventeenth century.[63] But though their intellectual weaponry was battle-hardened, Catholic opponents of the *philosophes* who were fighting at the end of the century wielded it with their own innovative parries and thrusts, commanding their forces in new ways. Of particular importance was their willingness to use both Pascal and Rousseau to buttress their claim, as the abbé Gérard explained in his best-selling anti-*philosophe* novel, *Le Comte de Valmont, ou les Égarements de la raison*, that the "obscuring of reason . . . its aberrations, contradictions, and limits, proves to us the extreme need of more abundant aid, of a guide more sure"[64] (see Figure 6). Pascal, of course, had used this same argument in the *Pensées* to poignant effect, dramatizing the insufficiency of human reason and highlighting the consequent need of a "guide more sure" in a manner that disturbed even Voltaire. Yet his powerful fideistic argument for faith had largely been off-limits to orthodox Catholics, who were wary of Pascal's Jansenist

Figure 6. Philippe-Louis Gérard (1737–1813). Photo courtesy of the Bibliothèque Nationale, Paris.

convictions and his celebrated attacks on the Jesuits. Jansenism remained an orthodox bugbear at the end of the century. But when faced with the dire threat of corrosive, philosophic reason, many were increasingly prepared to borrow their weapons where they could, overlooking Pascal's shortcomings and drawing freely on his strengths.[65]

So, too, did orthodox religious defenders adopt this approach to the thought of Jean-Jacques Rousseau, whose influence on Catholic apologetic writing in the last decades of the Old Regime was immense.[66] Rousseau, of course, was by no means irreproachable either. But by quoting selectively and discounting his more "enlightened" propensities, anti-*philosophes* tended to set him apart. As even the unimpeachable F.-X. Feller was prepared to concede, Rousseau was "less guilty than the more decided *philosophes*, and one of their most ardent adversaries."[67] As a consequence, anti-*philosophes* borrowed from him extensively, citing Rousseau's passages against their common enemies; sharing his dissatisfaction with the corruption of the age; and echoing his belief that sentiment, emotion, and feeling were wellsprings of faith. Like Pascal, Rousseau argued convincingly that the heart had reasons that reason knows not, that when left to themselves our rational faculties left us lifeless and cold, uncertain and unsure. This was a powerful weapon in an "age of reason," and opponents of the *philosophes* drew on it repeatedly to attack the pretensions of those who would live by thought alone. Offering the bread of faith to the disillusioned, they sought to respond to the hunger and anxiety of a modern age.

In these ways, as in others, enemies of the *philosophes* looked more to the future than to the past, marshaling arguments in defense of religion that would soon be employed, with greater flair, by no less a modern than Chateaubriand. But it is perhaps less the argumentative nuance of this literature than the novelty of its drumming consistency and the coherence of its rage that should arrest our attention, for the vastness of the *philosophes'* assault on religion struck their opponents as unprecedented. Moreover, the apparent convergence of the *philosophes'* aims seemed without parallel. As the assembled clergy noted in a pastoral letter circulated in every parish in the country in 1775, "In previous centuries there were impious persons here and there, but without party and results. There were books that taught impiety, but [they were] obscure and little read. Today the unbelievers form a sect, divided as it should be, over the objects of its belief; united in the revolt against the authority of divine revelation."[68] This was clearly sacrilege on a scale that the world had never known, an "open war," as the *Affiches annonces et avis divers* emphasized, "on eighteen centuries of belief" that far surpassed any previous heresy or schism.[69] Left unopposed, the philosophic army would overrun France and then the world, leaving only charred remains in its wake. As the Marquis de Pompignan observed in a statement that captures perfectly the anti-*philosophes'* sense of the irreconcilable opposition between Catholicism and *philosophie*, "In order to light the torch of *philosophie*, the torch of religion is extinguished."[70] In the cosmic struggle between light and dark and good and evil, there was no room for shady middle ground.

If the destruction of religion was thus seen as an explicit goal and an inherent result of the teachings of the *philosophes*, one that threatened society on a vast scale, their opponents viewed this horrific outcome as both cause and effect of another of *philosophie's* pernicious consequences: the corruption of social morals. At the most basic level, anti-*philosophes* argued that by eliminating the fear of God and an afterlife, breaching the ramparts of Christian morality, and destroying respect for religious authority, the *philosophes* removed all impediments to humanity's basest tendencies. Stripped of the restraining bournes of religion and the self-controlling impulses of conscience, men and women would carry out every manner of depravity. "What have we seen as a result of this so-called century of lights but a frightening inundation of every sort of crime—impiety, injustice, cruelty, *libertinage*, deception, fraud, and suicide?" asked the Dominican Barthélémi Baudrand in what would prove to be an extremely popular work of anti-*philosophe* piety.[71] In his similarly successful anti-*philosophe* novel, *Les Helviennes*, the abbé Barruel charged that the "natural effect" of the *philosophes'* writings was to create "monsters," who could be seen at every level of society, from the *grands* down to the "brigand who lays his traps for travelers in the isolation of the forest, or the valet who assassinates his master in the shadow of night."[72] Having imbibed the teachings of the *philosophes*, these men were restrained by no moral restrictions, only by fear of punishment. Well before Dostoevsky, if with little of his subtlety, anti-*philosophes* were contemplating the plight of Raskolnikov.[73]

An increase in criminal offenses, however, was merely one of the ravages wrought by *philosophie*. Not content to remove the mitigating restraints of religion, the *philosophes* actively encouraged the most sordid human impulses as well. "Under the pretext that there are natural and necessary human penchants," observed the abbé Gérard, "a false and dangerous *philosophie* eulogizes the most unbridled passions."[74] It flagrantly celebrated self-love, avarice, ambition, and lust as "natural" instincts, the motive forces of human *grandeur* and greatness. And it urged its adherents to seek happiness in their satisfaction alone.[75] Unbeholden to an afterlife or the duties imposed by a higher power, *philosophie* based individual action simply on calculations of pleasure and pain, equating the good with what was pleasurable in the here and now and the bad with what denied it. The result was an ethics of utility that sanctioned the most frightful egotism, making personal interest the sole criterion of morality. As Liger commented in a typical refrain, "All the duties of men are reduced to personal interest and pleasure."[76] *Philosophie* was a prescription for the "most vile, the most absolute, the most fatal egoism," a recipe for personal indulgence of every kind.[77]

If the *philosophes* advocated the shameless pursuit of the things of this world at the expense of those of the next, the hedonistic gratification of the senses in place of Christian self-sacrifice and denial, it was no surprise, their opponents agreed, that lucre and sex were at the top of their list. Regarding the former, anti-*philosophes* read their enemies' praise for industry and economic development as blind slavishness to the profane. *Philosophie*, as one critic charged, pressed men to "search only for temporal happiness during their sojourn on earth, to amass riches that all-too-soon will be taken away."[78] Seeking satisfaction in the greatest extravagance, the *philosophes* were frank "apologists and defenders of *luxe*," the consummate "eulogists" of material splendor that further enervated the soul, the body, and the mind.[79] At the same time they sought to restimulate their blunted senses through sexual debauchery, for the two—"licentious passions and impious *luxe*"—went hand in hand.[80] Symptoms of a sensual society, they further promoted its decadence. The evidence shouted from the walls. "One hears nothing from all quarters but the cries of [sexual] passion," Élie Harel affirmed in alleging an intimate connection between *philosophie* and *libertinage*.[81] Barruel was more explicit. The *philosophes'* obscene morality sanctioned "hideous vices"—adultery, incest, and even the "love most contrary to nature" (homosexuality).[82] As Madame de Genlis affirmed, the *philosophes* scorned "all who recommended moderation of desire."[83]

It need hardly be stressed that these charges, like the great majority of anti-*philosophe* accusations, were vastly overstated and grossly unfair. Yet it is important to appreciate that they were not arbitrary either. There was a basis to the anti-*philosophes'* criticism, an element of truth, however exaggerated, that gave order and internal logic to their attacks. Anti-*philosophes* could point, for example, to a strong utilitarian current that ran through much of Enlightenment thought—a frank acknowledgment, from Locke to Condillac, Helvétius, and beyond, that the pursuit of pleasure and the avoidance of pain was a prime mover of human actions, one that should be factored into moral and political judgments.[84] Stemming from a sensationalist epistemology that discounted or rejected altogether the importance of innate ideas, this moral calculus rooted human thoughts in physical sensations. And although few *philosophes* went so far as to identify the good purely with physical enjoyment, most did seek to reclaim the moderate pleasures of the senses from the strictures of Christian asceticism. Moreover, by praising the fruits of modern civilization—the benefits of work, industry, and commerce—they readily granted an important place to material reward in the garden of earthly delights. Wealth, in the *philosophes'* view, was a respectable component of human happiness, not something to be shamefacedly excused.[85] In the same way, they were quick to "celebrate" the passions, almost uniformly rejecting the view that human nature had been vitiated by the Fall.[86] Rather than see such "natural" penchants as egotism, ambition, vanity, and covetousness as divine punishment for original sin, the *philosophes* pointed out instead the positive role these passions played in the development of civilization. Vanity, egotism, and sexual desire, Helvétius maintained in *De l'Esprit*, stood behind all the great events and discoveries of history. Taking the part for the whole, as they did so often, anti-*philosophes* could point to such apologies as proof of their accusations, condemning *philosophie* en masse.

In at least one other area—the bedroom—the *philosophes* provided their opponents with explosive ammunition. Not only did many preach a healthy appreciation of the pleasures of the body against what they regarded as the confining prudery of Catholicism, but they spiced their works with ample lubricious material as well. The dreamer of Diderot's *Rêve de d'Alembert*, for example, interrupts a disquisition on materialism to masturbate in the presence of his hostess (a general practice that is later prescribed liberally by the story's Dr. Bordeu), and *Les Bijoux indiscrètes* blurs the lines between pornography and *philosophie* even further, centering the story's action around two talking vaginas. Other great *philosophes* engaged in enlightened eroticism of this sort, using sexual awakening as a metaphor for intellectual expansion and growth. Moving down a notch to the depths of the literary underground, *philosophie* and smut were virtually synonymous. Lovers of knowledge here were also lovers of men, women, animals, and all combined, liberating themselves from the strictures of Catholicism, as well as the grasps of debauched clergy, to find freedom in the coupling of sexual pleasure and *philosophie*.[87] To the anti-*philosophes*, in little need of convincing, these books and scores of others provided conclusive proof that sexual depravity lay at the heart of the *doctrine philosophique* (see Figure 7).

Promoting carnal materialism, vicious egoism, and the unadulterated pursuit of worldly pleasure, *philosophie* reduced men and women to the level of beasts, creating "tigers," "lions," and "brutes."[88] A "poison," it tore away at the social fabric, dissolving the ties that bound individuals to friends, to family, and to country.[89] It flowed into the hearts and

Figure 7. Voltaire in flagrant delight with Madame du Châtelet, one of a number of "gallant scenes" that depict Voltaire, Rousseau, Diderot, and other freethinkers practicing the craft of free love. Though probably produced by the *philosophes'* admirers, such engravings only reaffirmed the anti-*philosophes'* contention that depravity of the mind led to depravity of the body. Photo courtesy of the Bibliothèque Nationale, Paris.

minds of youths, corrupting their sensibilities; it seduced women, bidding them to despise chastity and to throw off their marital vows; and it encouraged children to brazenly disregard the authority of their parents.[90] Having seeped into the most basic constituent element of society, the family, *philosophie* was rotting France from within, a theme the anti-*philosophes* returned to with great regularity. "Oh discord of families!"—the "horrible monster" created by the *philosophes*—lamented one typical observer, bemoaning the ease with which husbands and wives alike cast aside their oaths of fidelity to pursue their own selfish pleasure, the facility with which children disavowed their parents' strictures. Once an asylum from the evils of the world, the family was now a germinating source of its corruption. As "society as a whole" was nothing but an "imitation" of the order of families, the horrors within spread abundantly without. "It is the domestic virtues," the author continued, "that prepare the social virtues. And he who does not know how to be a husband, a father, a son, a friend, or a neighbor, will not know how to be a citizen."[91] The abbé Liger concurred wholeheartedly: families, being monarchies in which "fathers were rulers," and "empires," being "large families in which princes were fathers," to undermine the one was to subvert the other. The strength of the *patrie* depended on the strength of the patriarch and vice versa.[92]

The anti-*philosophes'* "family values" rhetoric, in this regard, drew on traditional monarchical conceptions that based social order and divine kingship on the paternal authority set forth in the Bible.[93] Insofar as these conceptions regarded domestic government as the model of public government, with patriarchal power seen as God-given, absolute, and indissoluble, the anti-*philosophes* were not entirely without cause in fearing the larger ramifications of the *philosophes'* assaults on the family. Not only did many *philosophes* advocate divorce—a practice that reduced marriage to a negotiable contract, with obvious parallels to the political process—but they also disputed the unlimited power of the father, the so-called *puissance paternelle* enshrined in *ancien régime* law.[94] Also an explicit metaphor for absolute sovereignty, *puissance paternelle* entrusted fathers with nearly limitless power over the persons and property of their children and wives. To contest this, anti-*philosophes* argued, to emphasize children's rights at the expense of their duties and to stress their reasonableness and independence from parental "tyranny," was to sever the first link in the chain of hierarchical authority that connected subjects to rulers and to God.

Relaxing the most elemental of all human bonds, *philosophie* was thus insinuating corruption into every level of society, at a rate that their opponents observed with horror. Since the birth of Christianity, intoned the archbishop of Lyon in a pastoral letter circulated in 1785, "public morals have never been as corrupt as they are today."[95] Other critics moved the comparison further back, arguing that contemporary France surpassed even the horrors of antiquity. "What Rome was during the decline of the Republic," warned the abbé Yvon, canon of Coutances, "Paris is today. Yes Paris, the center of all corruption and of all vices. It is there that a *nouvelle philosophie* has established its seat."[96] The *Année littéraire* compared the *philosophes*, rather, to the "Germanic hordes," the Goths, Visigoths, Lombards, Vandals, and Huns, who had brought about Rome's downfall: "Reason, religion, morality, dogma—they have attacked all, destroyed all, overturned all . . . ."[97] But by whatever measure, all agreed that the *philosophes* had carried out a frightening revolution in moral sentiment, transforming a world and citizenry once sober and devout. As the provincial academician and anti-*philosophe* author Rigoley de Juvigny summarized definitively in 1787,

> The destructive spirit that dominates today no longer has anything to stop it. *Philosophisme* has penetrated everywhere, has corrupted everything. . . . The outcome of this distressing revolution has been the general depravation of morals. And indeed how could morals remain pure when an all-consuming *luxe* corrupts them? when everything gives off a spirit of independence and liberty that leads us to sever the ties that attach us to State and Society, making of us egotists who are as indifferent to evil as to good, to virtue as to vice? when an ungrateful and false *philosophie* seeks to snuff out filial piety in our hearts, the love that we possess, from birth, for our kings, the attachment we owe to our country . . . ? when, in a word, we have lost all idea of duty, of principle, every rule of conduct, and every sentiment of religion?

These were, Rigoley hastened to add, neither "false nor exaggerated assertions" but a faithful picture of the "present state of society."[98]

Ruthlessly uprooting the seeds of the faith while sowing fetid immorality in putrid ground, the *doctrine philosophique* could hardly fail to have adverse political consequences. This, in any event, was the firm conviction of the anti-*philosophes*, who accused their adversaries of subverting the political institutions of the Old Regime with as much consistency and as little refinement as they attacked the *philosophes'* corruption of religion and morals. In their view, the *philosophes* were "enemies of the state," "evil citizens," "declared adversaries of throne and altar," and unpatriotic subjects guilty of human and divine treason. "Disturbers of public tranquility," "brigands," and "*frondeurs,*" the *philosophes* were engaged in destroying completely the existing political order.[99]

The great variety of the *philosophes'* political beliefs, ranging from mild republicanism to enlightened absolutism, presented their opponents with little conceptual difficulty in this regard. Just as in their treatment of the *philosophes'* religious and ethical views, the anti-*philosophes* were ever inclined to assume the worst, quick to see the most radical positions of their opponents as indicative of a general philosophic tendency. Thus, the anti-*philosophes* frequently accused their opponents of spreading "republican" and "democratic" ideas. The *philosophes*, they claimed, preached the sovereignty of the people, advocated "perfect equality," and spoke endlessly of "social contracts."[100] They lauded the political institutions of the United Kingdom, spreading a contagious "Anglomania" that held up Parliament and the limitations placed on the powers of the English crown as models to be emulated in France.[101] And they talked ad nauseum of "liberty and equality," natural rights, and the "rights of the people" without ever mentioning duties or obligations.[102]

Yet far more dangerous was the general spirit of independence that lay at the heart of the *doctrine philosophique*. The same unmitigated confidence in the power of the individual mind, the same boundless arrogance that led the *philosophes* to throw off all religious restraint, prompted them to attack all political authority. "Whoever does not fear God, will not respect his king," affirmed the abbé Proyart in his widely selling biography of the late anti-*philosophe* hero, the dauphin.[103] The abbé Pey confirmed the sentiment, observing that "impiety and heresy have in all times been as much enemies of kings as of the Church."[104] The subject who would not genuflect before God, in short, would not bend a knee before the sovereign. "The school of Raynal, of Voltaire, of Jean-Jacques, of Helvétius, of Diderot," Barruel clarified, "is one of rebellion, of insubordination, of anarchy."[105]

Once again, it is scarcely necessary to point out that few of the *philosophes* of the High Enlightenment, or even most of the underground hacks of Grub Street for that matter, preached anarchy or the wanton destruction of the monarchy. Yet it is important nonetheless to appreciate that from the refracted perspective of the anti-*philosophes*, these conclusions were perfectly logical, following naturally from their portrayal of the *philosophes'* assault on religion and morality. To the anti-*philosophes*, religion, public morality, and political order were inseparable, a tightly knit triumvirate enshrined in the canonical, if sadly ignored, phrase of the royal censors, "*la religion, la monarchie, les moeurs.*" As devout publicists had argued since mid-century, the altar was the necessary complement to the throne. To attack one was to attack the other. Likened to "two great trees whose intertwined branches offer to society delicious shade and sure asylum," religion and monarchy, in the anti-*philosophes'* view, were inseparably bound. They had little doubt that the *philosophes* were engaged in an effort to "hack down both these trees at the root."[106]

Envisioning the Future

The violence of this metaphor, replete with its image of an organic, naturally ordered world of God and king hacked to pieces by unnatural, unrooted *philosophes*, is instructive. Although the anti-*philosophes* were sometimes vague about the processes by which the *philosophes'* ideas would destroy the political order, they were explicit in detailing the end results. For example, in a discourse delivered at the church of the

Mazarin college, celebrating the birth of the new dauphin in 1781, the orator warned the heir apparent of the dangers posed by *la fausse philosophie*. After spelling out its "central principle"—namely, the denial of religion and the rejection of the belief in an active God—the speaker continued: "From this anarchy of the physical and moral universe results, necessarily, the overthrow of thrones, the extinction of sovereigns, and the dissolution of all societies. Oh Kings! Oh Sovereigns! Will you be strong enough to stay on your thrones if this principle ever prevails?"[107] Clearly, the speaker implied, they would not. Far more graphically, Charles-Louis Richard undertook to explain the fate that a society in the grip of *philosophie* could inevitably expect:

> Everywhere *philosophie* lights the torch of discord and of war, prepares poisons, sharpens swords, lays fires, orders murder, massacre, and carnage, sacrifices fathers by the hands of sons, and sons by the hands of fathers. It directs lances and swords at the heads and the breasts of sovereigns, placing them on scaffolds, which it yearns to see flowing with sovereign's blood—blood that it will drink in deep draughts as it feasts its eyes on the horrible specter of their torn, mutilated, and bloody members.[108]

One could multiply such extraordinary citations at much greater length, for they were common.[109] It is perhaps more instructive here, however, to ask whence this anti-*philosophe* obsession with violence, this unsettling fascination with blood?

Without doubt, the Bible itself was one important source, providing a constant reminder of the fury of divine wrath. In the books of the Old Testament, Catholics could find ample precedents for envisioning the violent fate of a faithless people. And though generally immune to the sort of eschatological reflection on the New Testament so characteristic of Protestant millenarianism, Catholics were not entirely averse to borrowing from the Book of Revelation when it suited their purposes. Marc Antoine de Noé, bishop of Lescar, for example, in a sermon printed as the keynote address for the 1785 General Assembly of the Clergy, painted a vision of the church in ruins straight out of John's apocalypse. "Six trumpets have already sounded; the seventh and the last is giving the signal," he warned, predicting a "sea of blood" and "a flood of fire" in France's future. The great beast of the end of the world was *philosophie*.[110]

As we shall see in greater detail in chapter 2, biblical associations of this kind certainly helped to shape anti-*philosophes'* expectations of the future. A more immediate influence behind their fears of violent social upheaval, however, were the lessons they drew from the past. Above all,

the cultural memory of the Reformation and the religious wars continued to haunt European Catholics well into the eighteenth century, serving as what Amos Hofman has called a "paradigm of civil disorder," a
terrible test case of the consequences wrought by a systematic attack on
the church.[111] Here was a graphic illustration of how religious heresy
led to political upheaval, of how dissent from the one truth faith could
unravel into the tangled web of internecine conflict and bloody civil
war. By unleashing the tight reign of Catholic tradition, dogma, and ecclesiastical authority, the Reformation had turned men and women toward the frenzy of the unbridled human intellect, seducing them to believe that they could arrive at truth independently through the private
study of Scripture and the private sounding of one's heart and mind.
This was pride of the ultimate sort, and the results were all too predictable: limitless, subjective speculation; continual conflict over Scripture; the dissolution of the original *protestants* into an endless babble of
conflicting sects and heretical factions; and ultimately the long series of
religiously inspired wars that had bathed Europe in blood.

These memories provided orthodox Catholics with a specter of the
perils of religious dissent, genuine historical precedent that seemed to
give substance to their fears of the violent consequences of *philosophie*.
They also helped to shape their response to *philosophie* itself. From the
vantage point of many anti-*philosophes*, there was something dangerously Protestant about the Enlightenment as a whole. Did not the
philosophes adopt as their spiritual heirs a range of Protestant thinkers,
from Tindal and Collins to Bayle, Locke, and Newton? Was not the
Protestant demand of "tolerance" the central battle-cry of the *philosophes*, for whom the heretic Calas was a Voltairean martyr and saint? And
like their Protestant forefathers, did not the *philosophes* continually attack the authority of the church, placing their trust in the subjective
prompting of individual reason alone? From this perspective, it was
fairly easy to view *philosophie* as yet another of the deviations wrought
by the Reformation. Catholic apologists of the eighteenth century reaffirmed the connection by employing many of the same terms to combat *philosophes* as their Counter-Reformation predecessors had used
against Lutherans and Calvinists.[112] The term *prétendu philosophe*, for
example, mirrored that of the *prétendu réformé* favored by French
Counter-Reformation writers, as did the continual references to the
philosophes as a "sect" or "cabal."

Similarly, anti-*philosophes*' constant attacks on their enemies as "fanatics" resonated with the violent overtones of the sixteenth century.
"Fanaticism," of course, was a charge consistently leveled by the
philosophes themselves to condemn the religious zealotry they deemed

responsible for the excesses of the religious wars. Anti-*philosophes* merely reversed the charge, denying their own fanaticism and imputing it to their rivals. As Madame de Genlis observed, characteristically,

> There was no longer any fanaticism in France before the sect of modern *Philosophes* was formed. But voilà the *Philosophes*—and indeed those most renowned, who exhort the people of every nation to destroy temples and places of worship, to massacre Kings and Sovereigns, to suffer no authority—except that of the *Philosophes*! I ask of every impartial person: Is this horrible fanaticism not a thousand times more dangerous than that inspired by religion?[113]

Following naturally from rhetorical questions of this type was the corollary assertion that the *philosophes'* demands for "tolerance" were insidious and insincere. On the one hand, anti-*philosophes* charged that the plea for tolerance merely confirmed their enemies' indifference to religious truth, laying bare a deeper, more sinister design. By treating all faiths equally, the *philosophes* sought to water down the one true faith in a deluge of relativism, drowning Catholicism in an endless sea of competing beliefs. On the other hand, the plea for tolerance itself was grossly hypocritical. Pointing to the *philosophes'* jealous monopoly of the literary world and to the scorn and ridicule they heaped on their religious opponents, anti-*philosophes* alleged the "extreme intolerance of those who preach tolerance the most."[114] As Feller observed with representative bitterness, "Sweet tolerance consists in giving free circulation to every error, and to opposing all that combats them with the arrogance of tyrants."[115]

An intolerant sect, a fanatic cabal, bloodthirsty tyrants incensed with pride—the range of the anti-*philosophes'* characterizations clearly drew on stock phrases and concepts from the Counter-Reformation's fight against heresy. It is hardly surprising, then, that when Louis XVI relented to long-standing pressure to grant limited civil status to French Huguenots in the 1787 Edict of Toleration, many orthodox Catholics viewed this as the direct result of the machinations of a joint Protestant-*philosophe* plot and warned of imminent bloodshed. In their view, Protestantism and *philosophie* were closely allied, their doctrines intermingled and intertwined.[116]

Enemies of the Enlightenment thus drew from the language and legacy of the Counter-Reformation, but they did so in a modern way. Their violent premonitions of the future were something more than mere regurgitation of the apocalyptic invective of old; their obsession with violence itself was novel in its own right. It is worth remembering in this connection that what Isaiah Berlin famously took to be the hallmark of Joseph de Maistre's modernity was his "preoccupation with blood and death."[117] In making this claim, Berlin overstated his case, ignoring completely the long tradition of Catholic writing out of which Maistre's own thought emerged, thereby attributing novelty to what was in fact a recurrent preoccupation. But Berlin's general point was still perceptive. There *was* something modern about the anti-*philosophes'* obsession with blood, for the same reasons that there was something modern about their radical fight against the Enlightenment itself. Whereas the anti-*philosophes'* Counter-Reformation forebears had struggled to preserve a world in which the Catholic faith would retain its predominance, the anti-*philosophes* struggled, in their view, for simple survival. They were acutely conscious of the difference.[118] This was, they believed, an unprecedented war of world-historical importance, a metaphysical fight to the death, an opinion that gave particular urgency to their appeals and that lent particular violence to their morbid imagination. The anti-*philosophes'* frequent references to blood and destruction provide illuminating insight into the sort of anarchic world they believed their enemies were bringing about. *Philosophie* was a specter of the future, not of the past. The terrible world created in its likeness could only scarcely be conceived. "Imagine," ventured the abbé Lamourette, "an exact picture of all the various crimes and random horrors in the history of the world. Add to this all the atrocities that up to this point have only been conceived. . . ." This was the terrible image created in the "books that one calls *Philosophiques*."[119] As the abbé Liger asked, with an equally morbid proleptic imagination, "My God, what theater of horror and confusion would society become if this murderous *philosophie* ever prevailed?"[120]

This was, to reiterate, conjecture, much of it purposely exaggerated to rally the faithful to the cause. Yet if not all anti-*philosophes* believed that Armageddon was inevitable or immediately at hand, the logic of their categories stressed that unless something was done to impede the spread of *philosophie*, France would soon be engulfed in horrors. Some were coming to see this as a distinct probability. In the late 1780s, the editors of the *Journal historique et littéraire* repeatedly drew attention to the *philosophes'* triumphs throughout Europe, with premonitions of coming disaster. "Within ten years," an article entitled "Philosophic Fanaticism" argued in 1786, "the ministers of God will not dare show themselves in public" but will be forced, as in days of old, "to celebrate the divine mysteries underground, in unknown catacombs."[121] Later in the same year, the journal reiterated this point at greater length, noting that "without wanting to predict or foresee the future . . . it must be said that the revolution that makes those who are still Christians shudder is in certain respects natural and inevitable." The corruption of the age portended far more than an overturning of "this or that Christian dogma by a particular heresy," but rather the "triumph of general impiety," of "skepticism and atheism." Quoting Fénelon, the reviewer emphasized, "The day of ruin is close at hand, time hastens to bring it about."[122]

One is always tempted to read in quotations of this nature "predictions" of the Revolution. Counterrevolutionary historians, as will be seen in subsequent chapters, did precisely this, seeking to establish thereby the clairvoyance of those who fought the *philosophes* before 1789. This, of course, is to succumb to the teleological fallacy: the imposition of an end result onto the thoughts and actions of individuals who were not conscious of this outcome at the time. Those who fought the *philosophes* in the waning years of the *ancien régime* did not—nor could they have done so—foresee the complicated events that would subsume France in the aftermath of 1789. But having made this important qualification, it is essential to stress that given their analysis of the state of France, social upheaval of a revolutionary character was more than conceivable to enemies of the Enlightenment. The *philosophes* had already carried out a "revolution" in moral and religious sentiment. It was a term that anti-*philosophes* used frequently.[123] And although they did so with pre-1789 resonance, it was clear to them that such "revolutions" led in turn to social and political upheavals more in keeping with our modern use of the word.[124] This, they argued, was the natural outcome of *la doctrine philosophique*. Left unchecked, it would destroy the church and bring down the crown, engendering anarchy, carnage, and dissolution on a scale hitherto unknown.

A Nascent Ideology of the Right

Ascribing to *philosophie* radical consequences and sinister intent, the anti-*philosophe* discourse of the end of the Old Regime presented France as a country imminently threatened by religious, moral, and political upheaval. A poison, a sickness, a disease, *philosophie* was corrupting the body of France, and unless arrested it would continue to do so until the body lay lifeless and cold.

That this characterization—of both the *philosophes* and *philosophie*—was a construction, a linguistic creation to a far greater degree than any reflection of social reality, has been observed. It should also be apparent that in this respect the anti-*philosophe* discourse served an ideological function. Raising the specter of a common enemy, it exhorted fellow partisans to overcome their differences to join together in mutual combat. "If we love religion and the fatherland," Harel affirmed, "let us work together to destroy this [philosophic] vermin." What interests did the anti-*philosophes* share? Under what banner did they group? "Let us speak openly," Harel answered. "It is for God, king, and country that we fight."[125] To wage war against "the dogmas of the Encyclopedic school," concurred the abbé Grosier, was to adhere "to a party"—a party of "honesty, morals, the religion of [our] fathers, and the laws of [our] country."[126] These, it is true, were somewhat vague propositions, a rather loose set of principles on which to found a party. As has been pointed out all along, however, the anti-*philosophes* themselves were a diverse lot, one that cut across any clearly demarcated social, or sociological, lines. Sharing a common conception of *philosophie*, anti-*philosophes* did not see eye to eye on every issue.

Yet to say that the anti-*philosophe* discourse fulfilled an ideological function is not to assert that it offered a fully developed political platform. Rather it provided a "symbolic template" through which to construe a perplexing and rapidly changing world, a number of "authoritative concepts" and the "suasive images" by which they could be grasped.[127] It was through this common template, and before their common construction of the Enlightenment, that men and women in France began to come together in the face of a mutually acknowledged enemy. In the process, they articulated common interests and common concerns that increasingly gave their "party" greater ideological coherence. And in doing so, they generated a set of themes that would assume a prominent place in subsequent right-wing thought.

Most essentially, the anti-*philosophe* discourse underscored the fundamental importance of the Catholic religion in maintaining the social order.[128] Anti-*philosophes* did not overlook the deeply *personal* role that Catholicism played in the lives of its adherents. Increasingly, in fact, they emphasized this aspect of the faith, arguing in a proto-Romantic vein that the *philosophes'* pretensions to define human happiness solely in secular terms was deeply misguided. Only by satisfying the longings of the soul, anti-*philosophes* argued, by fulfilling the demands of feeling, could human happiness be achieved.[129] But although the index of human suffering could thus be measured in individual terms, the anti-*philosophes* were more inclined to dwell on the social ramifications of *philosophie*. As we have seen, one of their principal complaints was that the *philosophes* exacerbated individual preoccupation at the expense of the social whole. To preserve that whole, anti-*philosophes* agreed, the Catholic religion was absolutely essential. It was religion that provided the motive for self-sacrifice and duty; religion that held together families; religion that prevented men and women from committing hideous crimes and horrible indulgences; religion that inculcated a sense of obligation and responsibility that extended beyond the self; religion, and above all the Catholic religion, that bred respect for hierarchy and power. Remove it, and the world would unravel, as indeed it already showed signs of doing.

Playing an indispensable role in preserving the moral unity and character of society, religion also served as the natural ally and buttress of monarchy. To attack the church was to attack the crown, and thus to counter this double philosophic threat, anti-*philosophes* urged the two targets to unite. The logic of their discourse underscored the importance of the strategic alliance between throne and altar. This, at any rate, was the theory. In practice, this alliance was always more complicated than it seemed, and as a consequence one can detect from early on a certain ambivalence in anti-*philosophe* attitudes toward the state. Under the notoriously dissolute reign of Louis XV, for example, pious observers frequently grumbled about the absence of religion in the person of the king. And though Louis XVI's personal life was unimpeachable, enemies of the Enlightenment bemoaned his concessions to the Protestants and deplored his less than resolute stance against the *philosophes*. The note of strained exasperation in the National Assembly of the Clergy's 1780 *mémoire*, requesting action against the circulation of philosophic books (*mauvais livres*), is revealing: "It is time, Sire, permit us to say it with the apostolic candor of our ministry, it is time to put an end to this frightening and deplorable lethargy."[130] In the minds of many enemies of the *philosophes*, the throne was not holding up its end of the alliance.

Frustration of this sort, however, reflected more than simple dissatisfaction with the personal shortcomings of the monarch. On a deeper level, it belied the tensions inherent in a gradual but monumental transformation that was taking place in the overall character of the state. In a process that historians have come to call "desacralization," European governments were slowly shedding their religious and confessional skins, and in the quest for greater administrative efficiency and utility, political power was becoming increasingly secular.[131] What is more, it was becoming stronger, often at the direct expense of religious institutions.

Perhaps the clearest case of this secular extension of the arm of the law was the European-wide expulsion of the Jesuits in the 1760s, an act that in itself engendered a great deal of lasting bitterness on behalf of men who were generally regarded as the *philosophes'* most able adversaries. If, as anti-*philosophes* widely believed, Jansenists and the *philosophes* ultimately lay behind the expulsions, European monarchs had nonetheless condoned them.[132] As Catholic opponents of the Enlightenment throughout Europe learned to their chagrin, the state could be their worst enemy. In the Spain of Charles III, the Tuscany of Peter Leopold, the Portugal of Pombal, and above all the Austro-Hungarian Empire of Joseph II, "enlightened" leaders pursued policies directly inimical to the interests of the church, extending secular power over Catholic jurisdictional autonomy and education, curtailing links to Rome, abolishing religious orders in the name of utility, scaling back the assiduously constructed edifice of Counter-Reformation piety, and in general taking an indulgent attitude toward the century's new learning. Orthodox Catholics in many parts of Europe regarded such developments as depressing betrayal, a sign that *philosophie* had worked its way into the highest echelons of power. In certain instances, they were right, and in any case, their suspicion that the priorities of government were slowly departing from their own was well founded. Slowly but certainly the sacred and the profane were going their separate ways, pitting those who would have governments rule in the interests of God against those who would have them rule more in keeping with the interests of the public.

This was, to repeat, a gradual process, one that assumed the level of open conflict in France during the Restoration and that would continue to plague European states down through the nineteenth century. During the Old Regime, the conflict was less clearly defined, for *officially* the French monarch was the "most Christian king," who ruled in the service and at the behest of God. But beneath the ideology of sacral absolutism, tensions simmered, creating for the anti-*philosophes* an awkward dilemma. Claiming to be the consummate defenders of throne and altar, they were, in truth, often less than pleased with the terms of the alliance and could even channel their dissatisfaction into a muted criticism of the throne from the Right.[133]

Ambivalence of this nature can also be seen in a third constituent element of this nascent ideology: the self-conscious defense of tradition, convention, and historical prejudice. As the anti-*philosophes* repeated time and again, their enemies "denied all, doubted all."[134] "Avid for innovation" and "ardent to destroy what so many centuries ha[d] established . . . in the way of genius, taste, reason, knowledge, and experience," the *philosophes* were quick to dispense with the heritage of the Christian past.[135] They severed the great chain of being that connected all men and women to the first men and women, all humans to God. Their abstract individual was thus cut off from the past, their abstract society cut off from all that came before it.[136] "We live in an irreverent century," observed the *Année littéraire*. According to the views of a few "modest *philosophes* . . . it seems that in order to think, the world had to await the arrival of these new prophets . . . They deplore the imbecility of our ancestors . . . disdain ancient establishments and usages, erode the foundations of society, destroy all, and put nothing in its place."[137] Well before Burke, observers in France were developing arguments for the inherent logic of prejudices and the need to respect "the collected reason of the ages."[138]

But here again, one must be careful not to identify this nascent ideology too closely with conservatism, with a desire, that is, simply to preserve the status quo. Although the anti-*philosophes* defended ancient laws, customs, and institutions, they held that all these things—that France itself—had been deeply corrupted. They were, consequently, profoundly dissatisfied with many aspects of their culture and, as we have seen, spread a rhetoric of decline that emphasized the thoroughly degenerate state of the national character. It is a curious irony, in fact, that the anti-*philosophes*' stress on the need to uphold virtue and the *patrie*; their tirades against *luxe*, sensuality, and egotism; and their constant lament for the decline of the family echoed motifs recurrent in classical republican thought. Yes, there were sound bases in Catholic theology for pursuing every one of these themes. Yet the overall emphasis on societal decline almost certainly owed something to other currents as well. In this respect, it is noteworthy that many anti-*philosophes* were frequently prepared to cite Rousseau in their behalf. Not only could they point to Rousseau's insistence on the shortcomings of reason, but they could also cite a steady theme in his writings, from the *Discours sur les arts et les sciences* (1750) onward, that equated the advent of *lumières* with a decline in virtue and social corruption. His constant criticism of pride and egotism (*amour propre*), his denunciations of *luxe* and depravity, and his critique of materialism and atheism could be, and were, cited by Christian apologists and defenders of the throne to support their own agendas.

Such indulgence reminds us of the protean and contradictory nature of Rousseau, of the way in which he could appeal to the most reactionary, as well as to the most progressive, minds. It also points to an inherent tension in the notions of anti-*philosophes* themselves. Although they claimed to defend a social order in imminent danger of collapse, they undoubtedly, if unwittingly, contributed to its decline. By forever insisting on the moral decadence of France, the anti-*philosophe* discourse underscored the profound shortcomings of contemporary society. Just like Rousseau and even a number of the proto-Jacobin hacks of Grub Street, who also inveighed with great enmity against the *philosophes* on high, the anti-*philosophes* traded in the alleged social rot of their century. Insistence of this kind did little to generate confidence in a sagging political regime and probably helped to undermine it.

Yet if the anti-*philosophes* shared themes with a broadly republican current in eighteenth-century thought, one should not exaggerate these similarities. Anti-*philosophes* might rail against the enervating effects of egotism and *luxe* and bemoan libertinism and the decline of the family, but they never spoke of the sovereignty of the people, nor did they conceive of virtue outside the guiding authority of the church. Moreover, unlike many of the "gutter Rousseaus" (the *Rousseau du ruisseau*) of the literary underground, the anti-*philosophes* refused to see the *philosophes* as the symptom of a wider social malaise, that is, as the *product* of a profligate aristocracy, a decadent monarchy, or a moribund church. Rather, they depicted the *philosophes* as the primary *cause* of these afflictions. To emphasize the point, they frequently alluded to a romanticized past before the onset of *philosophie* in which French men and women were pious, faithful, upright, and loyal to their king. For Rigoley de Juvigny, and as we shall see in subsequent chapters, for considerable numbers of anti-*philosophes*, this golden age was that of Louis XIV. "What a most memorable century!" Rigoley pined—a halcyon epoch in which a devout king "loved, protected, sustained, and conserved religion, banishing error from his states."[139] During that great time, Gérard added, the "love of kings was spread amongst all hearts and minds." Men were devout, moved by "valor, honor, patriotism," and a spirit of self-sacrifice that consolidated France in "precious unity." Today, however, "all these grand sentiments" are gone.[140]

By invoking this mythic golden past—one far removed in time and character from the classical city-states so revered by republicans—anti-*philosophes* revealed signs of a romantic, quasi-utopian yearning for wholeness and social unity that would characterize a strain in far Right thinking for years to come. And although the example of an allegedly harmonious epoch—one in which a strong and pious king commanded the obedience and fidelity of reverent subjects—did reflect badly on the present regime, it nonetheless highlighted the anti-*philosophes'* predilection for that regime's institutions. The throne and altar might not be what they were; the people of France might be corrupted. But remove the canker, and France would flourish anew.

In their militant opposition to the status quo and their implacable hatred of the existing state of society, the anti-*philosophes* were genuinely radical. But their profound dissatisfaction with the present notwithstanding, it should also be apparent that enemies of the Enlightenment were violently opposed to any change that could be construed as a further concession to the corrosive spirit of the century. Although the positive propositions of their ideology were still amorphous and inchoate, anti-*philosophes* agreed on what they despised. In *philosophie* they found the perfect foil to channel their mutual hatred, one that drew them together in the face of a common enemy. If the *philosophes* assailed religion, then anti-*philosophes* must protect it. If the *philosophes* attacked the king, then his authority must be upheld. If the *philosophes* vaunted the individual, then the social whole must be defended. If the *philosophes* corrupted the family, then its importance must be reaffirmed. And if the *philosophes* advocated change, then anti-*philosophes* must prevent it—if not in defense of the world that was, then at least in the name of a world that could be.

Reactive, reductive, Manichean, this thinking was less noteworthy, perhaps, for its particulars than for its general form. It was precisely this tendency to view society as a battleground between opposing camps that stands as a hallmark of the bipolar, Right-Left model of politics so fundamental to subsequent European history.[141] To anti-*philosophes*, as for the more mature French Right, cultural and political concerns were part of a zero-sum contest in which the entire social order was held in the balance. Dividing the world between good and evil, between the pious and the profane, anti-*philosophes* saw their struggle as a cosmic war in which the winners would take all. In the battle against *philosophie* there could be no compromise.

Such was the lens with which enemies of the Enlightenment viewed the France of the final years of the Old Regime and through which they observed and interpreted the initial events of 1789. Though they did not predict it, anti-*philosophes* greeted the Revolution as the perfectly natural outcome of over thirty years of philosophic success. And in keeping with the logic of their categories, they were inclined from the outset to assume the worst, seeing in even the mildest efforts at reform premonitions of horrors to come.

CHAPTER 2

[The National Assembly] would

more reasonably be called a *Sect of*

Philosophes, because it is a seditious

and murderous *philosophie* that is

the cause of our misfortunes.

—*De la décadence de l'empire françois,*

fruit de la philosophie moderne

adoptée par nos législateurs (1790)

THE REVOLUTION AS THE REALIZATION

OF PHILOSOPHY

*I*n January 1789, as French men and women argued vociferously over the composition of the upcoming Estates General, the archbishop of Lyon, Yves-Alexandre de Marbeuf, issued a pastoral statement (*mandement*) interpreting the events that seemed to be overtaking his country. France, he noted, was experiencing a "universal restlessness" and a "formidable crisis." "A spirit of vertigo had taken hold of men's minds"; "new ideas were brusquely substituted for ancient maxims," "sowing discord and defiance among our fellow citizens." At a time when the country was undergoing the "worst winter on record," a "general subversion threaten[ed] all political, civil, and religious institutions."[1]

In the archbishop's opinion, none of these calamities, whether climatic or social, was fortuitous. Rather, they provided clear evidence of the hand of an active providence, a vengeful God at work in the world. Quoting extensively from Isaiah, Marbeuf raised the apocalyptic specter of divine retribution meted out to a faithless people.[2] The same God whom Isaiah had prophesied would destroy Jerusalem and Judah for transgression of the law was now again poised to vent his terrible wrath. The "thunder sounds from afar," the archbishop warned, and "the lightning will soon strike."[3]

It should come as little surprise that Marbeuf traced the cause of this divine anger to the "long chain of unpunished crimes against civil and sacred authority" carried out by men adopting the "pompous title" of *philosophe*. It was they who had sapped the "foundations of throne and altar" and they who had "reduced the realm to the disastrous state" in which it found itself today. God, of course, willed France's punishment as ultimate orchestrator of the universe, but it was the *philosophes* who had summoned his wrath.[4]

Marbeuf's interpretative reflex was virtually instinctive to men and women who shared the assumptions of the anti-*philosophe* discourse. From the outset of the revolutionary process, they extended its categories to explain the causes of the present upheaval. And from the outset they found in contemporary events confirmation of their belief that *philosophie* was the Revolution's animating creed. Erstwhile anti-

philosophes quickly became counterrevolutionaries and in so doing exercised a profound influence on the dynamics and trajectory of the Revolution itself. Lending credence to the belief of revolutionary militants that hostile forces conspired against them, anti-*philosophes* in turn saw in the actions of the Revolution's proponents confirmation of their own theories of conspiracy. The fears and suspicions of the one fed the fears and suspicions of the other, fueling a process of spiraling radicalization that consumed both sides of the political divide, polarizing opinions, and sundering France with terrible results.

Providence, Conspiracy, and *Philosophie*

Marbeuf was not alone in invoking the specter of divine punishment for philosophic and revolutionary transgressions. F. Amable Coquet de la Minaudière, for example, canon of the Abbey of Notre-Dame de Val-Joyeux, published a *mandement* in the beginning of February that presented the approaching Estates General as an assembly that would "consecrate a unanimous, impious, and sacrilegious revolt" against God by destroying the Gospel of Christ.[5] Whereas heaven in the past had graced France with "frequent miracles," the "incredulity" of this "philosophic century" had put an end to such merciful intervention. "Celestial vengeance" was now poised to strike down "Sodom," eradicating "*philosophes*, politicians, and so-called patriots" alike.[6] Similary, the *Journal ecclésiastique* drew an extensive parallel in March between Paris and Babylon, warning that the French city faced an impending and similar fate.[7] And in a coup de grâce, Jean-Nicolas Beauregard, the same clergyman who had upbraided Louis XVI for permitting Voltaire's 1778 return, preached a sermon at Notre-Dame Cathedral in the spring of 1789 in which he invoked an ominous future: "Yes, your temples, Lord, will be stripped and destroyed, your feasts abolished, your name blasphemed, your worship forbidden."[8]

The thesis of providential action on which all these admonitions drew was common among French and European Catholics in 1789. Forming part of a broader Christian prophetic tradition that extended well beyond the confines of the church, the thesis quite simply held that God's will was at work in the world, rewarding, chastising, and shaping the events of human history. For supporters of the Revolution, in France and abroad, theories of this sort were employed early on to present the rupture of 1789 as heralding a millennial transformation, a great rejuvenation of the French people, blessed and sanctified by God.[9] But although historians have paid some attention to this Christian consecration of the Revolution, few have recognized the darker strain of the providential view. Those who discuss providence at all generally point to figures who were writing after the Terror (above all, Joseph de Maistre) as originators of the interpretation of the Revolution as divine punishment. They have seldom appreciated that this view was prevalent from the Revolution's onset.[10] The distinction is critical, for whereas in the later 1790s the providential interpretation served a retrospective function, explaining events that had already taken place, in 1789 it acted proleptically, warning of imminent danger to come. That is, rather than simply shaping the view of the past, providential interpretations shaped views of the present and future, configuring expectations in a manner that bore directly on contemporary events.

This dark, providential view, furthermore, was almost invariably a direct extension of the anti-*philosophe* discourse, a continuation of the jeremiad strain so prominent in the literature of the 1780s. Although it was perfectly possible to view providence as working independently of human conduct (and beyond human comprehension), observers were far more inclined to elucidate a direct source of God's anger. "The cause of these present disgraces," Marbeuf affirmed, was clear. *Philosophie* lay at their heart.[11] Also writing in January 1789, the abbé Barruel developed this point with even greater explanatory boldness in a long article published in the *Journal ecclésiastique*"[12] (see Figure 8). France, he exhorted, was finally sliding toward the "ruin" long foreseen by prescient enemies of the *philosophes* who had continually "predicted and proclaimed our present afflictions."[13]

> For half a century, a legion of ungodly men has risen up. We have received their adepts, and crowned the masters; we have devoured their works, smiled at their blasphemies, adopted their principles. Their school became for us that of wisdom. It was, nevertheless, a school of every vice. . . . Their lessons broke the bonds between parent and child, between husband and wife, between king and subject. In order to render us vicious, they made us impious. They raised our hearts against heaven.[14]

With France awash in *philosophisme*, it was no wonder that the social, political, and religious foundations of the country were crumbling—no wonder, either, that divine providence was beginning to rain punishment on an ungodly people (see figure 9).

But Barruel saw more than just the hand of God behind the tremors of early 1789, and he was inclined to read them as more than simply the general effects of *philosophie*. His language here hinted at a thesis that would later propel him to international notoriety with the publication,

Figure 8. Augustin Barruel (1741–1820). Photo courtesy of the Bibliothèque Nationale, Paris.

in 1797, of the *Mémoires pour servir à l'histoire du jacobinisme*: the theory of the *philosophe* conspiracy. He spoke, for example, of the "sect" that for nearly fifty years had worked to undermine throne and altar; he employed the terms "masters" and "adepts" to distinguish between an inner circle of plotting masterminds and an outer group of unwitting agents who carried the ideas of the *philosophes* without full knowledge of their aims. And he alluded to the secrecy that veiled the vast majority of the public from the *philosophes'* true goals. The early events of the Revolution, Barruel suggested, revealed evidence not only of the work of a wrathful God but also of a formal conspiracy, a secret plot long meditated in the minds of France's enemies.

The theory of the *philosophe* conspiracy, like that of the thesis of providential action, was already well in place by 1789.[15] Barruel himself had developed the theory alongside other anti-*philosophe* journalists in the pages of the *Année littéraire* in the 1770s, including in *Les Helviennes* a detailed account of a plot hatched by *philosophes* to topple throne and altar.[16] The abbé Gérard's widely selling *Comte de Valmont* was no less explicit in chronicling a continent-wide conspiracy to "breathe the spirit of republicanism into monarchies," to "arm subjects against their princes, and to make war on the kings of the earth and the gods of the

LA JUSTICE DIVINE

Figure 9. Divine Justice smites the famous statue of Voltaire by Jean-Baptiste Pigalle. Though produced, circa 1773, in response to efforts by the *philosophes* to raise money for the statue, this anonymous engraving captures perfectly the hopes and fears of enemies of the Enlightenment at the outset of the Revolution. Photo courtesy of the Bibliothèque Nationale, Paris.

sky."[17] And the abbé Crillon's *Mémoires philosophiques du Baron**** contained an elaborate description of the clandestine agents and subalterns, the secret meetings and suppers, and the charters and initiation rites overseen by conspiring philosophic masterminds.[18] Indeed, the language of plot (*complot*) and conspiracy (*conjuration*) is scattered throughout many of the works discussed in chapter 1. For the idea that the *philosophes* were secretly plotting to achieve the downfall of France was merely an extension—an extreme version—of the general anti-*philosophe* discourse. It gave, to be sure, a more formal coherence to the *philosophes'* designs, placing their malicious intentions in the worst possible light. It stressed their collective agency and their willful desire to destroy. It also emphasized the hidden character of the *philosophes'* true aims, alleging that the majority of their followers were unwitting dupes of the controlling directors, thus explaining how a conspiracy so vast could remain undetected by so few. In none of these ways, however, did the theory fundamentally depart from the received anti-*philosophe* view that their enemies were shredding the social fabric, tearing apart church and state. In all of its permutations, the anti-*philosophe* discourse highlighted the destructive character of *philosophie*. Therefore, whether invoking plots, providence, the manifest poison of philosophy, or some combination of all three, the *philosophes'* most vehement adversaries shared the assumption that horrors were on the horizon. They brought that assumption to bear on their analysis of contemporary events from the earliest stages.

The abbé Bertrand Capmartin de Chaupy provides a useful example. A battle-hardened *dévot* publicist who had defended the crown against Jansenist *parlementaires* in the 1750s, Capmartin perceived a new threat to the monarchy in the effervescence of the pre-Revolution. He sought to warn France of the impending danger in a long, rambling work begun in 1788 and first published late in 1789, intended to give its readers the means to "comprehend present affairs."[19] If the details of his account were somewhat convoluted, the main message was perfectly clear. What Capmartin termed *misophie* or *in-philosophie*, the hatred of genuine wisdom, was now determining the course of contemporary events. A blend of libertinism and impiety reduced to a system by Voltaire, *misophie* represented all that was opposed to the one true philosophy and the love of wisdom, that is, Catholicism. Whereas the latter was "capable of changing the earth into heaven," *misophie* would turn it "into hell," a prospect that was by no means hypothetical, for the Revolution was putting this hideous system into practice. Fulfilling the original intentions of the conspiratorial architects, Voltaire and his chief lieutenant, d'Alembert, faithful revolutionary agents were now busily carrying out their goals: the destruction of religion, the "overthrow of monarchy," and the institution of total "anarchy in the name of liberty."[20] If not successfully repulsed, these men would push until they had annihilated "all ancient institutions."[21]

An enjoinder to "fight the impure spirit vomited . . . from the mouth of *in-philosophie*," Capmartin's text was also a vivid description of the consequences of failure.[22] One-half of France "would be drowned in a torrent of blood," he warned, while the other would fall prey to aggressive foreign enemies invading the country during its hour of weakness. The result would be "the total dissolution of France, the end of even the name itself."[23] By dispelling the illusions that hid the true intentions of revolutionary agents, Capmartin aimed to confront his readers with a faithful picture of the *philosophe* conspiracy unveiled.

It is no easy task to think oneself into this mindset, to understand how otherwise rational individuals could reduce an event as complicated as the French Revolution to the scheming of a handful of men. Yet the continued prevalence of conspiracy theories in our own time should caution us from adopting a condescending stance toward these troubled observers at the dawn of the modern age. Historians, moreover, have devoted a good deal of energy in recent years to showing how conspiracy theories themselves are a distinctly modern phenomenon, employed widely by men and women of the eighteenth century as a conceptual tool for understanding the social and political developments of their time. On a popular level, belief in conspiracy under the Old Regime was common. Large numbers of Parisian citizens succumbed in the 1750s to the rumor that the crown was abducting orphaned children to prepare baths of blood for the king, and throughout the century many workers and peasants were moved by the so-called famine-plot persuasion, the belief that devious royal officials and financiers periodically hoarded grain to drive up its price and benefit financially from the people's misery.[24] From a more bookish persuasion, the Jesuit Duport du Tertre's ten-volume *Histoire des conjurations, conspirations et révolutions célèbres* sought to provide a rational understanding of much of Western history through means of the conspiracy. "There are few republics or monarchies that have not witnessed the formation of conspiracies," Tertre observed. His work undertook to chronicle them all, from the beginning of time to the late seventeenth century.[25]

Nor was conspiracy thinking confined only to religious and popular milieux. The *philosophes* themselves frequently invoked conspiracy as an explanatory and rhetorical tool, decrying the artful scheming of Jesuits and depicting Christianity's historical ascendance as the consummation of a priestly plot to keep the people in darkness.[26] The renegade Jean-Jacques Rousseau was likewise quick to see conspiratorial forces at work in the world. In his final book, published posthumously as the *Dialogues* or *Rousseau Juge de Jean-Jacques*, he vented his long-standing resentment against the *philosophes* in terms surprisingly similar to those employed by Catholic hard-liners. Drawing an extended parallel with the Jesuits, Rousseau noted that the *philosophes* were their "great imitators," who now governed minds with the same dexterity with which the defunct order had once governed consciences, persecuting their opponents with the "most lively intolerance."[27] Plotting explicitly to achieve European supremacy, they had united themselves into a "sect," "a corps grouped under chiefs" with the aim of becoming the "arbiters of public opinion." They sought out the rich and powerful—above all, those who like them were "disposed to secret intrigues and subterranean machinations"—to further their aims. And they propagated their ideas through "young students whom they initiated into the secrets of the sect" and who then acted as "emissaries" and "operatives." Their network of accomplices was now so large that the *philosophes'* hideous aims were safe from exposure: those in league kept watch over one another, ensuring that all "remain[ed] faithful to the plot." In this way had the century become one of "hatred and secret conspiracies."[28]

Rousseau's language is startling in its similarity to that of even the most militant Catholic anti-*philosophes*. Coming as it did from one who knew the *philosophes* personally, his theory of conspiracy was so convincing to some that even a Vatican censor could cite it years later as conclusive proof of the plot to destroy the *ancien régime*.[29] Again, it helps to remind us of the tremendous breadth and ambiguous legacy of Rousseau—of the fact that although a hero to Robespierre and the Jacobins, he was also, at least in the initial stages of the Revolution, a champion to many on the Right.[30] But Rousseau's charged invective also highlights another significant point: that the theory of *philosophe* conspiracy cannot be dismissed as the crazed ranting of archaic fanaticism or relegated to a negligible handful of "medieval" zealots. Itself a modern, if misguided, symptom of the need to account for all human phenomena through causal explanation, conspiracy thinking was integral to Western thought across the social and political spectrum at the dawn of the modern age.[31]

To those interested in the dynamics of the French Revolution, this point is extremely important. Although historians have looked closely at the role of conspiracy in revolutionary politics, they have concentrated their efforts almost exclusively on the political Left. For François Furet, arguably the most influential interpreter of the French Revolution of the postwar period, conspiracy was the central organizing principle of that monumental event, part of a discourse on power that allowed supporters of the Revolution to pit an "ideology of pure democracy" against its putative negation, the "anti-principle" of the aristocratic plot. A necessary and ubiquitous element of revolutionary rhetoric, conspiracy enabled the Revolution's most radical proponents to effect an "imaginary communication" with the people by identifying common enemies—duplicitous priests and aristocrats—who plotted to deprive the people of their true rights.[32]

There can be little doubt that conspiracy was a fundamental trope of revolutionary language. But this very fact highlights the inattention of Furet and others to the use of rhetoric of conspiracy by the Right.[33] In fact, it is a curious feature of his analysis, and that of much modern revolutionary historiography in general, that early opponents of the Revolution are conspicuous only by their absence. Whereas defenders of the Old Regime simply disappear, we are told, with the power vacuum created by the rupture of 1789, genuine opponents of the Revolution itself apparently did not materialize at all until much later.[34] Thus, we are urged to believe that the revolutionary's own obsession with conspiracy was simply mass hysteria. Led solely by an "imaginary discourse on power," the Revolution "invented formidable enemies for itself." They were, it seems, a "figment" of a frenzied Jacobin imagination.[35]

This analysis is no more convincing logically than it is empirically. The Revolution did not need to invent "fanatical" enemies. They were there from the start. And though there was undoubtedly something hysterical about the Jacobin's obsession with plots, the same can be said about the conspiratorial obsessions of the Right. Their theories were not imitations of revolutionary versions of conspiracy. Nor, it is clear, did they develop gradually out of the revolutionary turmoil: they were in place before it began. Recent research, in fact, would suggest that in the Revolution's early stages, conspiracy theories were more prevalent on the Right than on the Left.[36] Independently and from the outset, they provided a narrative framework, like the anti-*philosophe* discourse as a whole, that emphasized the inherently destructive course of the Revolution while dramatizing the terrible costs of the failure to stop it. At the very moment that the radical Left was coming to see the Revolution as imperiled by the constant danger of being thwarted, the radical Right was pressing the need to do precisely this. Such contentions fed one another, seeming to give substance to the fears of radical revolutionaries, just as their own rhetoric seemed to give substance to the fears of the Revolution's most militant opponents. It is in these mutually reaffirming apprehensions—the dialectical logic of competing conspiratorial claims—that one should look for insight into the Revolutionary dynamic and ultimately the terrible violence that was its product.

Confirming Worst Suspicions

Almost all of the warnings examined so far were uttered at an extremely early stage of the revolutionary process—even before the meeting of the Estates General. A direct outgrowth of the anti-*philosophe* discourse of the 1780s, they reflected a predisposition to view the Revolution as inherently noxious, tending necessarily to the extreme. With the actual opening of the Estates General, the creation of the National Assembly, the storming of the Bastille, the wave of provincial urban uprisings and unrest in the countryside in July, and finally the tumultuous night of August 4, 1789, those inclined to see the forces of *philosophie* at work in the Revolution had further material for their morbid conjecture. Writing shortly after the declaration of the Tennis Court Oath, the abbé Jacques Linsolas exposed the Third Estate's defiance of the crown and the heated disputes between the three orders of clergy, aristocrats, and commoners as evidence of *philosophe* subversion:

> One has witnessed the so-called *philosophes* strive—directly themselves as well as through their adepts—to carry out a religious and civil revolution planned for close to a century. One has seen men, already revolutionaries at heart, throw an apple of discord amid the clergy, lead ministers of the Second Estate to subordination against the first, heap disdain upon the nobility . . . while inciting men against the first two estates of the realm. One has heard impiety insult Christ and his teachings, and the Church and its ministers, more brazenly than ever before, repeating the blasphemy of the patriarch of Ferney: *écrasez l'infâme.*[37]

In the cries of contemporary assailants of the church one could hear the overtones of Voltaire, and in the efforts to wrest sovereignty of the nation from its rightful trustees, the astute would discern the fulfillment of goals in place for over a century.

Antoine Sabatier also quickly brought his nearly two decades of anti-*philosophe* acumen to bear on revolutionary events, commenting in July in one of the first organs of the counterrevolutionary press that the violent talk circulating at the Palais-Royal and in other radical circles augured a "philosophic Saint Bartholomew's Day." In this case, however, Catholics and nobles would be the victims, and *philosophes* the oppressors.[38] Neither could another veteran opponent of the *philosophes*, F.-X. Feller, resist interpreting the Revolution through the categories he had developed consistently in the 1770s and 1780s. "It is the *philosophie* of the day," he proclaimed, "the principles of *libertinage* and irreligion, that have prepared men's minds for the total, destructive anarchy that is laying waste to this beautiful realm."[39]

Both Sabatier and Feller, of course, enjoyed long-standing reputations as inveterate opponents of the *philosophes* and faithful defenders of throne and altar. It was only natural that they should confront the first upheavals of the Revolution with familiar reflexes. There is indication, however, that others were being won over to the anti-*philosophe* cause by the pace of events. In the view of the contemporary Parisian chronicler Siméon-Prosper Hardy, the archbishop of Paris, Antoine-Elénore-Léon Le Clerc de Juigné, was one such convert, popularly believed to have convinced Louis XVI to hold his royal session in the National Assembly on June 23 by raising the specter of a Protestant and *philosophe* challenge to throne and altar.[40] The Parisian *parlementaire* Augustin Jean François Chaillon de Joinville, who in 1784 had published a ringing encomium of Voltaire, Helvétius, and other principal *philosophes*, quickly recanted his previous errors in the early stages of the Revolution.[41] Embracing Catholicism with all the ardor of the newly born, he decried the "*fausse philosophie* of the so-called *philosophes*" now espoused by members of the National Assembly. Were these men "to continue . . . to put in practice their ridiculous and subversive ideas of liberty," Joinville warned, soon "nothing sacred would remain" in the crown or the church.[42] Similarly, an anonymous delegate to the Estates General came away from his early confrontations with fellow representatives convinced that "the project of *philosophie*," by which he meant the total destruction of the church and the abolition of the crown, was "today close to consummation."[43]

Given the fact that professional *hommes de lettres (philosophes)* accounted for only a tiny fraction of the deputies to the Estates General, these associations are somewhat ironic.[44] Yet they were not altogether lacking in internal logic. Aggressive anticlericalism was a common attitude of many of the deputies, particularly those of the Third Estate.[45] Outside the Assembly hall, too, enthusiastic proponents of the Revolution took full advantage of relaxed censorship laws to publish militant tirades against "fanaticism."[46] Those who had long associated *philosophie* with impiety and anticlericalism and who were little inclined to draw distinctions between the two could thus point to such fulminations as an indication of the "philosophic" character of the Revolution.

Equally damning, they could point to the words of the revolutionaries themselves, for it was not simply opponents of the Revolution who alleged the intimate connection between *philosophie* and contemporary events. Right from the onset, revolutionary enthusiasts, too, hailed the *philosophes* as their spiritual forefathers. By claiming the *grands philosophes* of the Enlightenment as their intellectual ancestors, the revolutionaries grounded their actions in a historical narrative, providing parentage and legitimacy to their break with the past.[47] They also opened themselves to the further accusations of their opponents. When Jean-François La Harpe proudly proclaimed in December 1789 that the *philosophes'* attack on "despotism" lay behind all the changes that had thus far transformed France, the *Année littéraire* could not have agreed more completely: "According to M. de la Harpe, it is *philosophie* that has all the honor of destroying the nobility and the clergy; it is *philosophie* that has made the revolution. Nor is he entirely wrong. *Philosophie* is effectively the principal cause of the disasters we have witnessed."[48]

Later in the next year, when La Harpe led a delegation of playwrights before the National Assembly to protect the rights of dramatic authors, the *philosophe* reiterated his claim, noting that "men of letters had been the first engines of this grand and happy revolution." "They and they alone," La Harpe waxed grandiloquently, "liberated the human spirit," breaking the chains of ignorance placed on man by religious, political, and moral oppressors.[49] Once again, opponents of the *philosophes* could only agree. As Montjoye's *L'Ami du Roi*, one of two successors to the defunct *Année littéraire*, commented sharply,

> If by *gens de lettres*, M. de la Harpe means the Diderots, the la Mettries, the Helvétiuses, and their servile imitators and fanatical disciples—well then yes we agree with him wholeheartedly that these sorts of writers caused the revolution in the fullest sense—the upending of all principles of shame, of honesty, of morality, of politics, of religion. Yes, we agree that they were, to borrow his own words, the sole and principal engines of this revolution. They broke the first link of the moral, civil, and religious chain.[50]

In words such as these, anti-*philosophes* cum counterrevolutionaries found convincing proof of the Revolution's origins.

But it was not, of course, in revolutionary words alone that opponents of the *philosophes* found confirmation of their indictment of *philosophie*. In revolutionary *actions*, they detected from very early on evidence that their worst fears were being realized. The general upheaval of the spring and summer of 1789, culminating in the Third Estate's defiance of the king, the sporadic outbreaks of violence in July, and the extraordinary night of August 4, could be read as evidence that *philosophie* was finally bearing its bitter fruit—long predicted to engender social breakdown, anarchy, and the disintegration of established laws and institutions. Anti-*philosophes* drew their most damning proof of the philosophic character of the Revolution, however, from two principal undertakings of the National Assembly: the passage of the Declaration of the Rights of Man and the Citizen in late August 1789 and the prolonged assault on the church that gathered force in the fall of the same year.

In the first of these enterprises, critics saw enshrined not only the dreaded tenets of the *doctrine philosophique*—religious tolerance, popular sovereignty, and freedom of the press—but also a general willingness to make the abstractions of *philosophie* the underlying basis of the entire social order. The declaration's talk of metaphysical rights and theoretical principles was, in this respect, profoundly disconcerting. As the *Journal politique-national* noted concisely in August,

> The *philosophes* of today draw up their republic, like Plato, on the basis of a rigorous theory; they have an ideal world in their heads, which they want always to put in place of the world that exists. They prove very well that priests and kings are the greatest plagues of the earth, and when they become masters their first step is to incite the people against the Church and against authority. This is the path they have followed in France.[51]

Present himself in the National Assembly debates, the First Estate deputy Louis-Jean-Baptiste Le Clerc de Lassigny complained in a letter to his wife that "good Catholics" in the chamber were being outmaneuvered by "philosophical reasoning."[52] Though outflanked, resistance to what opponents deemed the "metaphysical abstractions" of the declaration was nonetheless significant, cutting across class lines to unite representatives to the Assembly of all three orders.[53]

Judgments of this type followed naturally from long-standing Catholic concerns about the dangers of overreliance on reason. As anti-*philosophes* had charged repeatedly, the inevitable result of haughty confidence in the powers of the human intellect was error, aberration, and distortion. The criticism of abstraction, though, was also the classic theme of Edmund Burke, who in his *Reflections on the Revolution in France* (1790) consistently denounced what he termed the revolutionaries' "philosophic system," their "metaphysic sophistry."[54] Certainly, Burke's *Reflections* was read widely in France, selling ten thousand copies by the end of 1791.[55] But although the work undoubtedly popularized the critique of abstraction, there is indication that Burke actually borrowed it from French sources with whom he was in contact, a debt he partly acknowledged.[56] A close reading of the *Reflections* does suggest that Burke shared many of the assumptions of enemies of the *philosophes* across the channel, providing evidence that he already sub-scribed to what he later would acknowledge explicitly to the abbé Bar-ruel: a full-fledged conspiracy theory of the Revolution.[57] The work abounds in references to the "intolerance," "intrigue," and "fanatical" proselytism of the philosophic "sect," observing that this "literary cabal had some years ago formed something like a regular plan for the de-struction of the Christian religion."[58] It was not entirely without reason that militant anti-*philosophes* quickly sought to claim Burke as one of their own.

Regardless of where they drew their beliefs, however, all of these observers viewed the central document of the Revolution as over-whelming proof of its *philosophic* imprint, what another critic, the sea-soned anti-*philosophe* the abbé Royou, later described in the introduc-tory prospectus to his counterrevolutionary newspaper as "a false and dangerous metaphysics . . . unworthy of those who would weigh the destinies of a great empire.[59] In these men's opinions, the revolutionar-ies were creating—with smoke, incense, and fire—a world of dreams. But their greatest chimera of all, the Declaration of Rights, would have very real consequences. By declaring that sovereignty resided in the na-tion and that law was the expression of the general will, this founding revolutionary document dealt a direct blow to traditional conceptions of monarchy, placing power in the hands of the people while inciting the imaginations of the dispossessed. This, in turn, was to disrupt the *natu-ral* world, the world of experience, tradition, and history. Over and against the *philosophes'* alleged realm of dreams, the anti-*philosophes* placed their own, "real-world" propositions.

In this world—no more "real" of course than the *philosophes'* own, but one that theorists of the Right have nonetheless invoked consis-tently to the present day—men and women were deeply corrupt. Ac-cording to some, this was the result of inherent depravity, of the total, vitiating effects of the Fall in the Garden. Increasingly, in fact, the events of the Revolution would appear to underscore the wisdom of this venerable Christian doctrine, enhancing its appeal in Catholic cir-cles. But even those less inclined to emphasize the innate evil of the human soul could point to the historical circumstances of France, argu-ing in a vein stressed as much by Rousseau and Montesquieu as by deeply committed Catholics that a people of lapsed morals could not rule itself effectively. The corruption of France was not in question; this had been a central tenet of the anti-*philosophe* discourse. The French were corrupt and the *philosophes* had corrupted them, a fact that not only explained the origin of the Revolution but also helped dictate the course of action one should pursue at the present juncture. As Feller observed, politics was a function of morality: "Amongst the different peoples of the world, all is controlled by the national spirit, and the national spirit is the result of morals. Morals are thus the key to history; it is through morals that everything is explained. The science of morals is the basis of all [true] philosophy and politics."[60] Given that the *philosophes* had introduced *luxe* and impiety in France, casting off the "yoke" of the church, perverting minds, and prompting men and women to debauchery, egoism, and vice, it was preposterous to speak of perfecting France by decree.[61] The influential rightist deputy Vicomte "Mirabeau-Tonneau" concurred, prescribing the only proper cure for the French people: "Give them morals; convince them that it is only by the exercise of domestic virtues that they can prepare themselves for the practice of public virtues; convince them that he who does not know how to be a husband, a father, a neighbor, or a friend, will not know how to be a citizen. . . ."[62] If one were to begin the process of regeneration anywhere, it should be within the family, but meanwhile the wise legislator should concentrate on harnessing France's depraved citizens, not on further "liberating" them.[63]

Yet the men of the National Assembly seemed intent on doing precisely the opposite. The Declaration of Right's sanction of free speech gave license to the most perverted souls to preach with impunity, allowing "atheists and deists to blasphemy God" and wicked firebrands to urge the "bloodying and overturning of thrones."[64] Its rhetoric of liberty and equality further excited unrealistic expectations that clashed in the face of lived experience, for in the natural world hierarchy and inequality were endemic to human existence. Social creatures by definition, men and women did not exist as isolated individuals. "We are born in the greatest dependence, the most shameful subjection," emphasized Étienne Bremont, canon of Notre Dame Cathedral, in a long, biting attack on the *philosophes* in 1789, beholden to our parents, to our king, and ultimately to God.[65] "Whatever the *nouveaux philosophes* of the National Assembly say," Chaillon de Joinville echoed, "men are not born free or equal."[66] "Inequality," another stressed, was built into "the nature of things."[67] By attacking hierarchy and touting equality, the declaration dangerously subverted the natural order of France. It severed essential ties that bound men and women together, removed necessary social restraints, and turned subjects toward the whims and passions of individual desire—all in the name of a groundless set of abstract principles.

If the declaration, then, gave convincing indication of the Revolution's philosophic origins and future course, the revolutionaries' protracted intervention in church affairs seemed an even more perilous assault on the social fabric. As anti-*philosophes* had always argued, to attack religion was to fundamentally undermine society, inducing anarchy and lawlessness by removing the gentle yoke of faith. "It is in this way," confirmed the anonymous author of *Reflexions intéressantes sur les principes de la nouvelle constitution de la France* in 1790, "that the foundations of society are loosened. Impiety has always armed citizen against citizen. It has always been the enemy of peace, of subordination, and authority."[68] The revolutionaries' religious legislation provided the ultimate confirmation that the Revolution itself was the incarnation of *philosophie*, that it would not cease until the church and faith had been completely destroyed. Thus, the further extension of religious tolerance granted in the Declaration of the Rights of Man and the Citizen, despite its partial nod to Catholicism, seemed a continuation of the "relativist" strategy so decried at the time of the passage of Louis XVI's 1787 Edict of Toleration. As the author of *Du Tolérantisme, et des peines auxquelles il peut donner lieu* argued in perfect echo of those who had opposed the 1787 edict, by allowing freedom of conscience the revolutionaries were directly fulfilling the *philosophe* plan to destroy the one true faith by tolerating all. The "sect" that had been at work for over "half a century" was now "taking off its mask amongst us," the author warned, employing the specious dogma of "universal tolerance" to fulfill its nefarious goals.[69]

Nor did the National Assembly tarry in providing further evidence of its creeping strategy to eradicate the faith. Shortly thereafter, in November 1789, it placed all church property at the disposal of the nation, prompting Feller to comment matter-of-factly that "the possessions of the clergy have always been the great object of the covetousness of the *philosophes* who now form the greater part of the Assembly."[70] In February 1790, the National Assembly dissolved France's monasteries and convents as useless institutions, and finally, in June 1790, it passed the monumental Civil Constitution of the Clergy, which destroyed the old dioceses; drastically reduced the number of parishes; and made all clerics electable state officials to be voted on by the laity, including nonbelievers. When, in the same month, the *Ami du Roi* noted in its preliminary discourse that "our opinions, our presumptions, our morals, our laws, even the form of our government, everything is changed," it did not exaggerate unduly.[71]

These acts are familiar to students of the French Revolution. It is worth pausing here, however, to reflect on the rapidity with which they were carried out. Within scarcely a year after the opening of the Estates General, one of the most powerful institutions in France had been radically transformed and its independence severely curtailed—measures unthinkable even twelve months previously. To the men and women who are the subjects of this study, the scale of the devastation was mind-boggling. "All that was, is no longer," the *Journal ecclésiastique* already bemoaned in January: "All is overthrown. . . . Venerable antiquity crumbles before us. . . . All that was sacred . . . is no longer."[72] In the journal's view, the cause of the ruin was clear: "*Philosophie*, enemy of God, has triumphed."[73] It warned, however, that some day the French would wake up "to discern the role that this restless, impious *philosophie* was playing in the Revolution."[74]

Indeed, it was precisely in this period—the first six months of 1790—that ever greater numbers of French men and women were awakening to the dangers inherent in the National Assembly's headlong assault on the church. Jean-Jacques Duval d'Eprémesnil, for one, an Old Regime *parlementaire* who had flirted with the radical Committee of Thirty in 1788 before taking fright and organizing a conservative group of aristocrats in response, warned of the sacrilegious efforts to "found a system of laws based on atheism." He urged Frenchmen to "finally understand" that the National Assembly's patent move in this direction "was nothing other than an attempt by modern *philosophie* on the throne and altar."[75] Others in Eprémesnil's extreme Right coalition of nobles and clergy in the National Assembly seem to have agreed. The moderate *patriote* Jean-Bernard Grellet de Beauregard remarked in reference to the growing ideological gulf that divided his colleagues that, "much of what is happening today has been influenced by the old quarrels between the sect of philosophers and the clergy."[76] By the conclusion of the debates on the Civil Constitution, a large number of the far Right "Capuchin" coalition in the National Assembly was convinced that its opponents were "godless philosophers" intent on eradicating Catholicism.[77]

Outside the National Assembly, Léon de Castellane-Mazaugues, bishop of Toulon, certainly had no doubts. As he emphasized in a pastoral letter written just after the vote on the Civil Constitution,

> Look around you, my dear brothers, and consider dispassionately, if that is possible, the evils that have afflicted you, and that threaten you still. . . . You will easily recognize in the fatal present the work of our modern *philosophes* who have preached an impious doctrine, enemy of God and men. Not content to destroy all religious principles, they have undertaken to completely annihilate the social order. . . . [78]

In the bishop's opinion, the Revolution was the perfect realization of *philosophie*, whose advocates had worked for thirty years toward the destruction of the church. It was *philosophie* that had "dictated the laws destructive of religion"; *philosophie* that had "destroyed the monasteries"; *philosophie* that had "carried off the Church holdings." "Modern *philosophie*" had "caused all these evils," the bishop insisted, and it "promised evils even greater still."[79] The author of the *De la décadence de l'empire françois, fruit de la philosophie moderne* agreed. "It is a seditious and murderous *philosophie* that is the cause of our present misfortunes," he warned.[80] Like a "corrosive powder that after having consumed the dead flesh of a wound then ate away the living," *philosophie* would not stop until it had decayed the bones and would continue until the marrow.[81]

This is by now a familiar refrain. For the anti-*philosophe* discourse had always emphasized the unrelentingly destructive character of *philosophie*. If, in the opinion of the author of *De la décadence*, "rivers of blood" were already beginning to flow, far worse could be expected in the future. "Pillage," "conflagration," "massacres in the country," fanaticism, and tyranny of all sorts lay on the revolutionary horizon. The final incarnation of an insidious force that had rotted France for decades, the Revolution seemed to confirm this belief at each successive step, revealing yet another dimension of its profoundly philosophic character. With such an enemy, there could be no compromise. "Honest souls [can] not unite too quickly to deal death blows to the Sect of Demagogues," the author stressed.[82] To read the Revolution as the realization of *philosophie* was to oppose it.

From Anti-*Philosophe* to Counterrevolutionary

To assert this connection between the anti-*philosophe* discourse of the Old Regime and opposition to the Revolution is not to imply that all who fought the *philosophes* prior to 1789 necessarily became counterrevolutionaries. To take one concrete example, the abbé Antoine Adrien Lamourette, whose *Pensées sur la philosophie de l'incrédulité* figured largely in chapter 1, was clearly able to overcome his once venomous hatred of the *philosophes,* or at least he failed to draw the connection between their thought and the Revolution. A constitutional bishopric was too tempting an offer to put aside. By 1792, as a deputy to the Legislative Assembly from the Rhône-et-Loire, he was urging opponents to come together in fraternal embrace in the famous kiss of Lamourette.[83] Others, if not always in so loving a fashion, made similar conversions.

Nor can one say even of those anti-*philosophes* who opposed the Revolution that they all did so in precisely the same way. To study the French Right during this period is to know that the word itself, though essential, is misleading. There was not a Right, there were *Rights*—a spectrum of opinions ranging from moderate constitutionalists to those who would restore the Old Regime in full, with considerable range and fluidity in between.[84] Although they all resisted the Revolution, they did so for different reasons, at different stages, and mindful of different concerns. As the comparatively moderate count of Montlosier lamented, "[A]mongst the dissatisfied, there exist numerous views as to the means of re-establishing order in France." He proceeded to list eight different political remedies touted by opponents of the Revolution, commenting that although they were "in agreement on a number of points," notably the "necessity of giving the king great authority," the ultimate unifying factor was their hatred of the "common enemy."[85] This, clearly, was not enough to overcome their differences either in France or abroad, where the petty squabbling of émigré factions is notorious. A problem that had plagued the anti-*philosophes* themselves continued to haunt opponents of the Revolution.

But even with these important qualifications, it is nonetheless true that the anti-*philosophe* discourse developed during the Old Regime provided a lens and a language that predisposed its proponents not only to opposition to the Revolution but to opposition of the most unyielding sort. Almost invariably, the people under consideration here tended to the extreme, advocating a version of what is generally referred to as integral absolutism, or the politics of throne and altar. A theocratic vision of the state, it stressed the essential unity between God and king, linking human sovereignty to the divine. From this perspective, a return to the political institutions of the Old Regime was a point of departure. *All* the changes carried out since the convening of the Estates General were tainted with the philosophic blemish and thus would have to be undone.

This does not mean, however, that such a vision was purely and simply reactionary. As the unabashed anti-*philosophe* editor of Montjoye's *L'Ami du Roi* noted in the review's opening prospectus in June 1790, "One would strangely mistake our intentions if they expected to find in this new journal . . . *simply* a censure of the vast changes brought forth by imperious circumstances. The *ancien régime* had its abuses— intolerable abuses." Having admitted as much, the author proceeded directly to advocate a "general restoration," arguing that to remedy the shortcomings of the Old Regime, it must first be restored.[86] This point of view was perfectly in keeping with the views of the anti-*philosophes* developed in chapter 1, who as we have seen were deeply dissatisfied with many aspects of their corrupt world. To heal it, that world, including the sacred realm of the church itself, would have to be purged, purified, and cleansed of its offending elements, which now included not only the terrible accretions of *philosophie* but also its revolutionary precipitate.[87]

Militant and aggressive, this vision was in its own way profoundly radical—a point that is missed by those who conceive of the Right as wanting only to recover privileges lost or to restore a world that had been. Rather, the Right sought to remake society in keeping with an ideal image, one that frequently conflicted with concrete political realities, both present and past. For this reason, the far Right was paradoxically often at odds with the very institution it claimed to defend—the crown. Just as enemies of the *philosophes* had been suspicious of the king during the *ancien régime* for not doing more to fight *philosophie*, voices on the far Right berated Louis XVI until his death in 1793 for his foolish compromises with the Revolution.[88] Later, during the Restoration, the Ultras, too, would part company with the king, adopting an attitude that was, in effect, more monarchist than the monarch.

How many shared the views of this radical extreme in the early stages of the Revolution, and what power did they really have? To be sure, such figures were a relative minority, a militant fringe defining one end of the revolutionary spectrum. Nor did they pose a direct military threat to the Revolution and in fact, given their Catholic convictions, were never unanimous in sanctioning armed resistance.[89] They were no less important for that. Vehement and vocal, they declaimed with strident defiance, even before the meeting of the Estates General, employing a violence of language that was in itself deeply menacing. During the first year of the Revolution, moreover, they were able to count on support from within the National Assembly itself. As the historian Timothy Tackett has shown, factional groupings took shape there early on, drawing partisans and opponents alike to revolutionary and counterrevolutionary extremes. Around one pole formed a body of patriots and radicals who by November 1789 had organized into a coherent Jacobin block; around the other coalesced men of the Capuchin and Augustinian clubs, whose adherents shared the deeply religious convictions of enemies of the *philosophes*. As these factions gesticulated across the aisle, their supporters outside the Assembly gestured through discursive space, clenching words into fists and pummeling their opponents with incredible ferocity.

Herein lies the true power of the militant extreme on either side of the political divide. Just as radical journalists were already articulating the main themes of Jacobin discourse by the summer of 1789, anti-*philosophe* polemicists, too, were voicing the essential elements of an ideology of the Right.[90] Each gave substance to the fears of the other, summoning their enemies into being. Whereas members of the radical

Left were inclined to see demonic "aristocrats" and seductive "fanatics" conspiring to check the Revolution at every step, polemicists on the far Right pointed their fingers at *philosophes*. In both cases, the terms were only of limited sociological content. For the Jacobins, the label "aristocrat" quickly came to encompass far more than just the aristocracy, serving as a metonym for privilege, hierarchy, royal authority, social inertia, and all that threatened to impede the revolutionary goal of equality.[91] "Priests," in turn, were frequently portrayed as occult seducers, men trading in the illusory powers of superstition, and "fanatics" were all those who blindly gave them support. For the far Right, *philosophes* extended far beyond the circle of Old Regime men of letters and their revolutionary admirers, including all who were opposed to the former society—who pressed unceasingly for change; attacked religion; and fought order, hierarchy, and tradition in the name of liberty, equality, and progress. They, too, possessed diabolic powers, "conjuring" illusions that seduced the gullible and mislead the innocent.[92] And like the demonic fanatics and aristocrats who were driving the political imagination of the Left, *philosophes* were ubiquitous. The National Assembly was a "sect of *philosophes*"; the Jacobins, *philosophistes*. Employing the term with indiscriminate breadth during the Old Regime, anti-*philosophes*, now counterrevolutionaries, leveled the charge even more broadly. In this political hall of mirrors, conspiratorial enemies were everywhere.

One might almost say that the most radical proponents of the Revolution and its most vehement enemies needed each other, for they constituted themselves—and were so constituted—in the eyes of their hostile beholders. Inverted images, or mirror opposites, they nonetheless could appear strangely similar. As is so often the case with those who hate each other intensely, Jacobins and their devout enemies bore a greater resemblance than either was prepared to admit. Each charged the other with fanaticism, intolerance, and corruption of the social whole. Each traded in the moral rot of the century, bemoaning (with Rousseau) the decline in virtue; the demise of the family; and the horrible effects of individualism, self-interest, and *luxe*. Each underlined the central importance of protecting the unity of the sovereign, be it the king or the people. And each agreed that France must be remade, refusing to countenance the legitimacy of opposition to that final goal. Perhaps, in the end, it is not so surprising that a few former anti-*philosophes* like Stanislas Fréron, son of Élie Cathérine Fréron and one-time editor of the *Année littéraire*, threw in their lot with the radical Revolution.[93] As the ever stalwart F.-X. Feller could admit, the Jacobins were at least "frank and sincere, embracing and professing all the consequences of impiety" while showing none of the "hypocritical moderation" that characterized the *monarchiens* and other temperate supporters of the Revolution. "Tigers and lions," he emphasized, were to be preferred to snakes "that slithered on the ground." There was grudging respect in his words.[94] In the other direction, too, as we shall see in the next chapter, there were men and women ready to reciprocate the compliment, abandoning their former allegiance to the radical Revolution to embrace its most vehement opponents.

In pointing out these similarities between militants on either end of the political spectrum, I don't mean to deny their essential differences but rather to emphasize how the very resemblance of their rhetoric reinforced opposing views. Each gave credence to the other's claims, confirmed each other's suppositions, and substantiated each other's fears. Polarizing opinions and reinforcing inverted views, they justified the other's existence, permitting the far Left and the far Right alike to divide the world into two while claiming to protect it from the other. In the process, they radicalized the Revolution, radicalized the Counter-Revolution, and radicalized themselves.

Varieties of the Plot

It is in this connection that the Right's preoccupation with conspiracy is most instructive. If from the Jacobin perspective an obsession with the unity of the collective will (the sovereignty of the people) led quickly to the identification of faction with "aristocratic" conspiracy, then from the perspective of the far Right a similar apprehension about the dangers of divided sovereignty (in this case, of the king) led also to conspiratorial accusations. The theory of *philosophe* conspiracy, in fact, was almost always a defense of absolutism, a dramatization of the pernicious effects of allowing the indivisible sovereignty of the king to be challenged by appeals to public opinion.[95] By admitting the principle of public politics, conspiracy theorists warned, the door was opened for plotters to deceive the people, "conjuring" illusions that would lead them horribly astray. And this, of course, was precisely what conspiracy theorists claimed the *philosophes* had done.

Thus, whereas the "aristocratic plot" became the lever of an egalitarian ideology, the *philosophe* plot and its various permutations served as levers of absolutist doctrine. For it was not simply *philosophes* who were seen to be working behind the veil of perceived reality, but also their manifold accomplices and agents—Protestants, Jansenists, Masons, Illuminati, Rosicrucians, and others. The anonymous author of the brief pamphlet *Causes et agens des révolutions de France*, for example, argued that the Protestants were in fact the original instigators of the conspiracy to overthrow the French church and crown. Angered by the revocation of the Edict of Nantes and "emboldened by the anti-Monarchical principles of their doctrine," they had formed a "league" that for over a century had plotted to institute a republic. The *philosophes* who joined them at mid-century had only come to the conspiracy after the fact. Nonetheless, they formed consummate allies. In Diderot's dictum that "the people would only be happy when the last king had been hung by the entrails of the last priest," the Protestants heard the perfect echo of their own doctrine. The Jacobins, the latest initiates in the plot, were currently working toward fulfilling just these ends.[96]

As we have seen, the anti-*philosophes'* vocabulary had always resonated with language that stemmed from the Counter-Reformation's fight against heretical "sects." At the time of Louis XVI's Edict of Toleration, many drew explicit connections between Protestants and *philosophes*, arguing that to grant religious tolerance was to pave the way to civil turmoil, republicanism, and ultimately the destruction of the faith. Such claims took on ever greater force as the Revolution unfolded. At the same time that the Declaration of Rights of Man and the Citizen proclaimed further religious tolerance, the Revolution began its systematic assault on the church, seemingly confirming the anti-*philosophes'* assertion that the rally cry of tolerance was really a cover for the destruction of religion. The presence of Protestant radicals in the National Assembly and the leading roles played by such avowed admirers of the *philosophes* as Jean Paul Rabaut Saint-Étienne and Antoine-Pierre Barnave in the reorganization of the church only further confirmed anti-*philosophe* suspicions.[97] By the time of the outbreak of sectarian violence between Catholics and Protestants in the Midi in the summer of 1790, anti-*philosophes* were charging that the "massacre" of Catholics was the result of joint Protestant and *philosophe* machinations, a grim reminder of the atrocities of the religious wars and a horrible premonition of the tumult to come.[98]

Assertions of a collective Protestant-*philosophe* conspiracy thus flowed naturally from far Right pens. They frequently implicated Jansenists as well (see Figure 10). As Feller commented in October 1790, Jansenism had formed a "strict union" with *philosophisme*, a union that had been in place for some time.[99] Jansenists had, of course, long endured accusations of "crypto-Protestantism." They were also recurrently associated with the *philosophes*.[100] Charged with subverting dogma, challeng-

Figure 10. The *philosophe*-Protestant-Jansenist conspiracy to destroy the church, as described by the counterrevolutionary journalist Jacques-Marie Boyer Brun in his *Histoire des caricatures de la révolte des français*, 2 vols. (Paris, 1792). *Philosophisme*, represented by the degenerate Bishop Talleyrand, and Protestantism, personified by the dark-robed Rabaut de Saint-Étienne, have seized control of the church, depicted here as a woman in white. Rabaut plunges a sword into her breast as Talleyrand prepares to hand her over to the Jansenist Camus in return for a worthless pile of *assignats*. The desecrated cathedral in the background symbolizes the end result of this conspiratorial exchange. Photo courtesy of the British Library.

ing church hierarchy, and evincing dangerous republican tendencies, Jansenists were easily incorporated into the anti-*philosophes*' counterrevolutionary triumvirate of principal enemies. Given their important role in the development of an anti-absolutist, parliamentary constitutionalism during the Old Regime and the prominence of Jansenists like Armand-Gaston Camus in spearheading the National Assembly's attack on the church, the anti-*philosophes*' hostility is not difficult to understand. Jansenism was only another of the many apostasies unleashed by the Reformation. It found receptive allies in its brethren heretics—the Protestants and the *philosophes*.[101]

One other group was at times implicated in the *philosophe* plot—Freemasons. Some, it is true, saw in the secret fraternal order the sole cause of the Revolution. They could point in proof of their assertion to the vast European network of Masonic lodges, to the presence of leading Masons such as the Duke of Orléans at the radical end of the revolutionary spectrum, and to genuine historical precedent.[102] For in the 1780s an *actual* conspiracy had been uncovered in Bavaria, led by a young professor at the University of Ingolstadt, Adam Weishaupt. Having formed his own secret society, the Illuminati, Weishaupt and his collaborators sought to infiltrate established Masonic lodges throughout Europe, using these bases to further their own republican, egalitarian, and anticlerical beliefs. Uncovered before it could have any real impact, the conspiracy nonetheless produced an ensuing scandal and panic. Not just in Germany, but throughout Europe, a denunciatory literature revealed the Illuminati's intentions, drumming up fear and feeding an already ingrained suspicion of Masonic orders in general.[103] With the coming of the Revolution, many naturally pointed their fingers at one or another of the many brotherhoods—the Masons, Templars, Rosicrucians, and the Illuminati themselves.

In the hidden chambers of the Masonic orders, then, some found a complete explanation of the revolutionary conspiracy. Most, however, preferred to see the Masons as part of a larger whole, comprising Protestants, Jansenists, and *philosophes*.[104] Whereas the organizational structure of the lodges, with their cells and secret rites, levels and grades, and interior and exterior degrees, provided a general image and vocabulary for the theory of conspiracy, it was the ideas of these other groups (or rather, those attributed to them) that were seen as the driving force behind Freemasonry. In the eyes of their detractors, the lodges were breeding grounds for the subversive theories of deviants, seedbeds of Protestant heresy, republicanism, atheism, and sexual perversion. Needless to say, these negative stereotypes were greatly exaggerated, although some of them contained at least a kernel of truth. The lodges, Margaret Jacob has shown, were places where the Enlightenment was "lived," where rationalism, constitutionalism, and the criticism of superstition were carried out concretely and in practice.[105] Given this intimate connection, it is not surprising that hostile critics portrayed Masons and *philosophes* as working in close concert. As the abbé Baissie charged in his 1790 pamphlet, *L'Esprit de la franc-maçonnerie dévoilé*, they were like "two orders, two classes of perverted citizens who have the same goal, but who seek it in different ways."[106]

Conspiracy theories of all these varieties were, in the earliest stages of the Revolution, above all the property of the militant extreme. But as the Revolution progressed, taking on an increasingly rapid and violent character, the contention that insidious plotters had consciously master-minded this destruction, and were continuing to do so, seemed to many an eminently logical explanation of France's predicament. Writing home to his erstwhile constituents in the summer of 1791, the Count of Pannetier, a noble deputy to the Estates General from Couserans, ex-plained that the Revolution had been masterminded by the Protestant Necker and his *philosophe* associates. These diabolical conspirators, he charged, had set in motion a plan to "destroy the monarchy, to engulf the realm in anarchy . . . to overturn altars, and to establish a repub-lican government."[107] Another immediate observer, the abbé Jean-Siffrein Maury, arguably the most influential orator of the far Right dur-ing the first year of the Revolution, came away from his experience in the National Assembly speaking the language of conspiracy.[108] And the Count of Antraigues, an important prerevolutionary *patriote* and ardent admirer of Rousseau, quickly went over to the Counter-Revolution, or-ganizing an extensive émigré spy network and publishing several vi-cious books in which he described in copious detail the plot hatched by Voltaire, Diderot, d'Alembert, Helvétius, and their *philosophe* and Jansenist adepts to destroy the throne and altar.[109] By 1791, allusions to *philosophe*, Protestant, and other conspiracies were appearing frequently in the right-wing press, filling the pages of such journals as the *Gazette de Paris; Annales monarchiques; Journal général de France; Journal du peuple, Rocambole;* Montjoye's *Ami du Roi;* and Royou's journal of the same name, reiterating accusations that had been standard fare for the *Année littéraire, Journal ecclésiastique,* and *Journal historique et littéraire* since the first days of the Revolution.[110] Writing to France in the spring of 1791, Pope Pius VI, himself, invoked the *philosophe* plot, denouncing the *philosophes novateurs* who now formed a majority in the National As-sembly and who had "conspired" to abolish Catholicism. "Protect your-selves from lending an ear to the seductive voice of the *philosophie* of the century," he implored, "[for] it leads to death."[111]

Opponents of the Revolution proved receptive to theories of con-spiracy not only because they presented otherwise bafflingly complex events in simple, cogent terms but also because they were useful. First, they excused those who, like the count of Antraigues, had advocated in the initial, heady stages of the Revolution enlightened reforms of one sort or another. Such talk could now be explained away as admittedly naive but nonetheless not ill-intentioned. Little did some men know that they were fulfilling the insidious designs of those manipulating the

Revolution. Yes, good men and women had been "duped," but this merely pointed out in more emphatic terms the danger of the conspiracy and the pressing necessity of total retraction and resistance to compromise. Second, plot theories exonerated Old Regime society as a whole. France had been infected on a vast scale, but this did not imply that the body itself was unsound. Once the criminals were removed and the sickness rooted out at its source, Catholic and monarchist France would again stand firm. Finally, right-wing plot theories in general reaffirmed the either/or persuasion from which they derived, undergirding the logic of total inflexibility. The enemies of France—enemies of God—might be many and varied, but they all stemmed from a single impulse: the desire to break with the absolute sovereignty of the king and the religious hegemony of the Catholic Church. Protestants, Jansenists, *philosophes*, and Masons alike shared this desire. To allow cracks in the foundations of throne and altar was to allow hell itself to spit up a host of enemies. Those cracks would have to be filled.

In their distinctions between the real and the apparent, the actual and the potential, the seen and the unseen, right-wing conspiracy theories also reaffirmed a judgment manifest in both the providential and the general anti-*philosophe* viewpoints: the Revolution, at any given moment, was always worse than it seemed. Moved by forces discernible only to the clear-eyed observer, the Revolution would continue to enslave, ravaging and destroying until France acknowledged the magnitude of its error. As the author of an extended anti-*philosophe* allegory of the Revolution, *L'Isle des philosophes*, warned in 1790, "Believe me . . . French nation, lend an ear to the seductive oracles of a *fausse philosophie* . . . and soon, in the name of liberty, it will carry trouble, anarchy, and desolation in your breast."[112]

Once more, it is important to emphasize that if admonitions like these could be dismissed in the early stages of the Revolution as alarmist and extreme, they were more difficult to discount as the Revolution progressed. By the middle of 1791, anti-*philosophes* could argue with a considerable degree of plausibility that they had been right all along. The nobility and France's former legal system were totally abolished, and each member of the church had been forced to take an oath declaring adherence to the new Civil Constitution of the Clergy. Nearly half refused, their decision validated by Pius VI's formal condemnation in the spring of 1791.[113] Refractory priests—those who refused to sign the oath of adhesion—were banished and in many instances publicly persecuted. In June of that year, the king himself declared unequivocally his view of the Revolution by fleeing to the border. His failure to escape only highlighted the moribund state of monarchist France.

As the enemies of the *philosophes* had long warned, the Revolution *had* fundamentally altered the existing institutions of society. It *had* unleashed "anarchic" forces, fomenting the people, the peasantry, and the political clubs. It *had* attacked the church openly and unabashedly. And it *did* flaunt its philosophic badge, frankly proclaiming the *philosophes* as its progenitors and forebears. Was it not perfectly logical to assume that this creeping transformation would continue until the world of old was no longer recognizable, until, as Capmartin had warned, France was drowned in "a torrent of blood"? If violent upheaval had always been regarded as the natural telos of *philosophie*, that judgment was seemingly confirmed by the course of revolutionary events.

By the summer of 1791, in fact, men and women of the Right had grown to think of what we now refer to as the Terror as not only conceivable but also to be expected. Ironically, though, in voicing these fears, the Revolution's most adamant opponents were undoubtedly helping to give them substance, perpetuating a climate of reaffirming hostility and conspiratorial suspicion that in that same summer was taking hold of ever wider segments of the Left as well.[114] On both sides of the political divide, conspiracy was the order of the day—an order that when carried out would produce terrible results.

The Revolution Crowns Its King

Enemies of the Enlightenment could thus point to the political developments of the first two years of the Revolution as proof of their prescience, testimony to the logic of their claims. But if any remained unconvinced of the Revolution's philosophic character, the revolutionaries themselves provided the ultimate proof in the spring and summer of 1791, voting to move the remains of Voltaire from his former estate at Ferney to the Church of Sainte-Geneviève, recently transformed into the resting place of the *grands hommes* of the Revolution—the Pantheon. In the lavish celebration of his internment held on July 11, the revolutionaries shed the last of their veils in open acknowledgment of the origins and ends of their undertaking.

Voltaire, of course, was already something of a deity.[115] He had been treated as such at his "first" apotheosis, the Parisian reception of 1778, and the events of the Revolution only heightened his stature. Proclaimed as the patriarch of the Revolution, he was a natural choice for men who, as Mona Ozouf observes, were obsessed by the need to give "sacral" status to their new regime.[116] What better way to do this than by coopting a preeminent symbol of the old? The Church of

Sainte-Geneviève, erected by Louis XV to his patron saint at vast expense after his "miraculous" recovery from a life-threatening illness, exemplified both the capriciousness of regal "despotism" and the "fanaticism" of the Catholic faith. By converting it into a profane basilica, the revolutionaries replaced the world of the Old Regime with the values of the new, values given concrete form in the statues that adorned the Pantheon's revamped peristyle: *philosophie*, law, force, the *patrie*, liberty, and equality.

All this made perfect sense to the enthusiastic deputies who proposed the Pantheon and then put forth Voltaire as a prime candidate for admission. But for the same reasons, the project struck the Revolution's opponents as the quintessence of blasphemy. Entailing a grand cortege from Ferney to the Pantheon itself, with calculated stops at the Bastille, the Opéra, the Comédie française, and other strategic "stations" along the way, the "translation" of Voltaire's remains mocked traditional Catholic processions, constituting a direct affront to the faithful[117] (see Figures 11 and 12). That the king of the *philosophes* was now canonized as a saint—his remains placed in a secular sepulcher in what had once been a vast monument to the glory of God—was defilement and provocation difficult for even some defenders of the Revolution to comprehend. In a petition to the National Assembly several hundred "friends of the constitution" questioned the wisdom of erecting a temple in which "all would be gods except God Himself."[118] At a time when the National Assembly was already facing enormous expenditures, the pomp of the procession seemed unnecessary. More gravely still, it would further exacerbate the divide created by the recent controversy over the oath to the Civil Constitution of the Clergy, "offering to non-juring priests a veritable triumph." "Adversaries," the petition predicted, would claim that "the friends of the Constitution [were] not those of religion."[119]

The drafters of this petition were only too right. Adversaries of the Revolution saw in Voltaire's pantheonization the final proof of its fundamentally "philosophic" nature, using the event to assail the character of the new regime. To Feller, long accustomed to seeing in the Revolution the workings of *philosophie*, the National Assembly's celebration, though deeply horrific, was no real surprise. It seemed natural that the Revolution should honor the man who was "one of the principal causes of the evils that afflict France." After all, Feller alleged, the majority of the members of the National Assembly owed their places to him.[120] Other commentators expressed greater shock. The *Journal de la cour et de la ville* (better known as the *Petit Gautier*), the best-selling journal of the Right, with a daily circulation of some ten-thousand copies, found it incredible that the "most relentless enemy that Hell had ever vomited up

Figure 11. Voltaire's remains led through Paris on July 11, 1791. Photo courtesy of the Bibliothèque Nationale, Paris.

Figure 12. The order of the cortege of Voltaire's second apotheosis. Note the bearers of a replica of the Bastille in the center right. The pantheon can be seen in the upper-left corner. Photo courtesy of the Bibliothèque Nationale, Paris.

against the Christian religion" was now being honored in a church of Christ.[121] The *Journal de la noblesse* was equally damning. In a parody of a hymn composed by André Chénier for the internment, it noted that one should not shed a tear for "the most guilty of all Frenchmen" but rather rejoice at seeing him in ashes.[122] Montjoye's *Ami du Roi*, which enjoyed a daily press run of close to three thousand, noted that by choosing to honor a man who had spent "three quarters of his life unraveling the laws that should govern empires, insulting our religion and priests, and writing obscene novels," the National Assembly revealed all too well the sad criterion it used for discerning "great men." With constitutional bishops now at the head of the church, Montjoye mused, the people might one day worship directly before the remains of Voltaire, Rousseau, and other *philosophes*.[123]

Such comments, drawn from among the most important journals of the right-wing press, illustrate how ubiquitous the identification of the Revolution and *philosophie* was by this stage.[124] If the National Assembly could lavishly honor a man described by Fontenai's influential *Journal général* as the "most obstinate and dangerous enemy of Religion," one who, in the opinion of another leading publication of similar persuasion, was the "Apostle and Patriarch of impiety and corruption of every kind," then clearly *philosophie* had worked its way into even the remotest corner of that sullied chamber.[125] As this satanic rite confirmed, *philosophie* was the Revolution's creed, its diabolic faith.

Over a century later, Émile Durkheim would argue in his groundbreaking *The Elementary Forms of Religious Life* (1915) for the essential unity of religious and social experience, citing the French Revolution as a particularly striking example of "society's ability to make itself a god or to create gods."[126] With this proposition, at least, the men and women studied here would have agreed. To them, Voltaire's pantheonization reflected perfectly the values, the religion, that upheld the society of the new order. A demonic religion, a religion of *philosophie*, this modern faith had taken hold of its disciples with relentless fanaticism. The principal *philosophes* of the Old Regime had been seductive "evangelists," and the National Assembly, in adopting their creed, had tempted the French people as Satan had tempted Jesus in the wilderness.[127] Unlike Christ, however, France had not withstood the devil's offer, and now his voice echoed through the din. As Chaillon de Joinville intoned in a two-volume work published in late 1791, "And still the serpent hisses, and he is wrong, but we do not destroy him, and we are wrong, and the *philosophes* print their systematic madness, and they are wrong, and we read their works, and we are wrong."[128]

The title of this text, *La Révolution de France prophétisée*, as well as its lapidary style imitating the prophetic authority of the Old Testament, is revealing. Whereas in 1789 Joinville had been primarily concerned to warn of coming danger, by the end of 1791 he was looking back into the past, seeking revelation there to explain the present state of France. He did not neglect the future entirely, asserting that "the time will come" when the French people will join "the party that fights against the dominant authority," operating a "counter-revolution in the ignorant, feeble minds of the seduced."[129] But although he placed that date, improbably, in 1792, the burden of his text emphasized the weight of the past—the sinister logic of the *philosophe* conspiracy that was born in the early reign of Louis XVI and its preordained, satanic goals of regicide, tyranny, and atheism.

With the ever greater consolidation of the Revolution and the concomitant marginalization of its most virulent opponents in late 1791 and early 1792, anti-*philosophes* displayed an increasing tendency to share Joinville's morbid preoccupation with the past. To be sure, they continued to warn of dangers on the horizon, emphasizing the expansive principle of *philosophie*. As Sabatier stressed in 1791, "One can not hide the fact. The writings of the *philosophes* . . . have excited a fermentation in the spirit of all peoples—the result of which will be to bring about a new order of things in the various European states. . . . Can one really believe that the *esprit philosophique* will limit itself to France?"[130] Evidently not, for philosophic "fanaticism" was determined to propel itself outward. When news trickled into France of the bloody slave revolt touched off in Santo Domingo in August 1791, anti-*philosophes* read this as an inevitable consequence of philosophic proselytism. "Modern *philosophie*," the count of Antraigues stressed, "which has the universe for its goal," could claim "one more trophy" in the death and destruction in the West Indies.[131] As France inched to the precipice of war in late 1791 and early 1792, Sabatier's rhetorical question appeared entirely apt. If "in former days religious fanaticism led millions of men to their graves in Palestine," stated the rabidly royalist *Journal pie* in early 1792, "now it is philosophic fanaticism that has designs on every king."[132]

Enemies of the *philosophes*, enemies of the Revolution, then, did not cease to invoke the specter of the future, warning of impending "philosophic crusades."[133] Yet these same exhortations contained a tacit admission of what had been harder and harder to deny since Voltaire's apotheosis: in France, at least, *philosophie* had triumphed, giving it the power to consolidate its forces within and to project them without. As an ephemeral publication of the far Right commented in April 1792 with dramatic finality, "The fall of kings has been decided."[134] Whether that aim would be fulfilled depended now on the strength of foreign armies.

In the meantime, anti-*philosophes* increasingly turned their attention toward the direction signaled by Joinville. In looking back in anger over the recent history of France, it appeared uncanny to many that not more had perceived the telltale signs. "It is another unique characteristic of this revolution," commented Fontenai's *Journal général* in a long article of early 1792 devoted to chronicling the history of the *philosophe* conspiracy, "that long before its explosion, it was unveiled. For at least thirty years, our magistrates in their indictments, our Christian orators in their pulpits, and our Doctors in their public theses—all these men announced that the throne was in danger, as well as the altar."[135] Sadly, few had heeded their warnings. Now their sagacity was more clear. "It would be easy," the author continued, "to cite fragments [of these writings] from twenty to thirty years prior to the great shock—fragments that make up, to some degree, the history of the revolution."[136] By putting these fragments back together, one could write the history of the Revolution. The way in which like-minded authors did precisely this, constructing a history of the Enlightenment and an attendant history of the Revolution, forms the subject of the next chapter.

CHAPTER 3

What do counter-revolutionary

writers do? They attack *philosophie*

with such a fury that they lack only the

power of Philip II to send the *Philosophes*

to the pyre, just as that king disposed

of the Protestants. . . . Yes, there is

a very discernible coalition

preaching against *philosophie*.

—Honoré Riouffe,

Discours lu au Cercle Constitutionnel,

Le neuf messidor, an V (1797)

THE TERROR AND THE INTERNATIONAL
CONSTRUCTION OF THE ENLIGHTENMENT

*W*ith the storming of the Tuileries palace on August 10, 1792, what remained of the tattered French monarchy was destroyed. Shortly thereafter, in early September, as Prussian and Austrian troops marching in step with French émigrés bore down on the nation's capital, Parisian *sans-culottes* invaded the city's prisons, massacring upward of eleven hundred suspected opponents of the Revolution, including over two hundred priests. Pleased with this purging—for which they were publicly congratulated by the directing municipal authority, the Paris commune—many of these same men then rushed to the aid of the struggling French army, which made its famous stand at Valmy on September 20, halting the counterrevolutionary armies to the cry of *Vive la Nation*.

Consecrated in blood, the newly elected National Convention voted on the very next day to establish a republic, the first in a series of genuinely revolutionary decrees that broke definitively with France's past. In November, it vowed fraternal assistance to all peoples seeking to recover their liberty, and in the following months it gave alarming credence to these words by declaring war on Great Britain, the Dutch Republic, and Spain. Fighting for "freedom" without, the National Convention battled "tyranny" within, decreeing the guilt of Louis XVI in early January and sending him to the guillotine shortly thereafter. His blood mingled with that of countless other men and women who, like him, fell to French, not foreign, hands as the country descended into civil war in the spring and summer of 1793. In parts of Normandy and Brittany, in the area around Bordeaux, and in a broad swath in the east stretching from Franche-Comté to the Dauphiné, "Federalists" rose in defiance of increased tax and troop requisitions, levied to sustain the Revolution's escalating military campaigns. They blended—at times indistinctly—with more ideologically committed opponents of the Revolution, who also brought the sword to their compatriots. Revolutionary justice, in all cases, was swift and severe. Sixteen thousand alleged enemies of the Revolution were executed by the blade of the guillotine alone during the Reign of Terror of 1793–1794, a great number of them innocent peasants and workers.[1] Thousands more were killed summarily or en masse without so much as a pretense of a mock trial. In frightening premonition of later political atrocities, revolutionary columns in the Vendée and Lyon shot prisoners into open graves by cannon fire or exploded them with dynamite in subterranean caverns.

In and of themselves, these developments more than fulfilled the worst fears of numerous aghast onlookers. Their horror was accentuated by the equally terrifying spectacle of the ideological crusade carried out against the remnants of the previous order. Not content to abolish the forms of the Old Regime, the revolutionaries sought to cleanse the country of all atavistic traces of royalist, Christian France. In 1790 they had redrawn the country's map, obliterating the lines of the traditional provinces with the more rational demarcations of the *départements*. During the National Convention, revolutionaries carried this process of spatial reconfiguration further, changing the names of streets and public squares (fourteen hundred in Paris alone) to expunge all references to kings, queens, and saints. They even renamed themselves. Men christened with the unfortunate Louis became Brutus or Spartacus, and families *Léveque* ("Bishop") or *Le Roi* ("king") were dubbed *La Loi* or *Liberté*.[2] So, too, did the revolutionaries assail the former temporal order, abolishing the Gregorian calendar to mark time not from the birth of Christ but from the founding of the Republic itself. And finally, in the general movement known as dechristianization, revolutionaries attacked wholesale the outward manifestations of "fanaticism," destroying churches and desecrating sanctuaries, plundering altars, and forcing priests and nuns to marry. By the end of 1793, the public worship of Christianity had ceased in all but the most remote regions, replaced by profane festivals that blended pagan forms and revolutionary rhetoric in a "transfer of sacrality" from the values of the Old Regime to those of the new.[3] In the most famous of these, held on November 10, 1793, at the newly christened Temple of Reason (formerly Notre Dame Cathedral), revolutionaries worshipped directly before an altar of *philosophie* (see Figure 13).

To many hostile observers, such open obeisance was no longer revealing; it was gratuitous. The Revolution, plainly, was *philosophie*, a charge to which revolutionary actions testified more vividly than revolutionary rituals or revolutionary words. In the great din of destruction in the 1790s, enemies of the *philosophes* heard their most convincing vindication, the most telling proof to date of the perspicacity of those who had warned of the dangers of *philosophie*. And in the Terror itself, they saw the ultimate revelation of the Enlightenment's true character, its damning confession and its terrible avowal. Armed with this evidence of both sight and sound, enemies of the Enlightenment now turned to the

Figure 13. Young women worship before a "temple of philosophy" constructed during the Festival of Reason, November 1793. Photo courtesy of the Bibliothèque Nationale, Paris.

task of condemning the guilty. With growing cultural authority, they pleaded their case, linking the *philosophes* to the worst excesses of the Revolution while spreading their renewed construction of the Enlightenment throughout Europe and throughout the world.

The Power of Prophecy

Those who carried out this great historical inquest did so under trying circumstances, prosecuting their enemies from afar, in hiding or in absentia. Catholic opponents of *philosophie*, like Catholic opponents of the Revolution, were hardly welcome in France after the fall of the monarchy. They fled in massive numbers. No fewer than six thousand to seven thousand refractory priests were resident in the British Isles by the end of 1792, and another six thousand escaped to Spain. Many others, clergy and lay alike, took up residence in Holland, Italy, Germany, eastern Europe, Russia, and the Americas. Soon, Hamburg was host to an émigré community of close to forty thousand, as was London. Small pockets of exiles formed anywhere they could, as far afield as Charleston, South Carolina in the West and Saint Petersburg in the East.[4]

By no means all, or even most, of these figures were *pures et dures* ideological opponents of the Revolution, still less of the Enlightenment. A great many ordinary people fled only to spare themselves the up-heavals of civil war. But that very upheaval, coupled with the disruptive experience of exile, created a climate in which scapegoats flourished and recriminations festered. Those trading on both found a receptive audi-ence among the émigrés, where the critique of the *philosophes* elabo-rated prior to the Revolution was picked up and spread as a "sort of propaganda." Tales of plots and conspiracies enjoyed a remarkable cur-rency.[5] Natives of these foreign havens, too, as we shall see shortly, proved extremely receptive to the anti-*philosophe* criticism, using it to drive indigenous reactions against the Enlightenment and as a weapon in their own respective wars against revolutionary expansion. Finally, even in revolutionary France itself, growing numbers came to embrace the strident rhetoric of anti-*philosophes*. The fall of Robespierre in July 1794 and the subsequent reaction against his excesses created a climate much more conducive to violent opposition to *philosophie*. Gradually, if fitfully, enemies of the Enlightenment reemerged to air their views.

By 1796, in fact, a surviving *philosophe* himself, André Morellet, could complain that the "accusation carried out against *philosophie* of having precipitated the evils of the Revolution is so widespread . . . and has taken on such credit, even among reasonable minds, that one would be astonished to not see this false and absurd opinion combated if one did not think that the friends of *philosophie* simply refuse to conde-scend to enter into this battle."[6] In the following year, a moderate re-publican and former Girondin, Honoré Riouffe, urged such condescen-sion, delivering an address at the prominent Parisian political club, the Cercle constitutionnel, in which he warned of a "league of writers paid . . . to wipe out *philosophie*" now acting on a scale that only the "stu-pid" could deny.[7] In the present circumstances, Riouffe stressed, "an anti-*philosophe* was an anti-republican." To refuse to enter into this bat-tle was to imperil the Revolution.

In lashing out at this "discernible coalition preaching against *philoso-phie*," Riouffe drew attention to the changed political circumstances of France in 1797, in which a discredited republican government, the Directory, struggled to retain power in the face of a resurgent royalist threat. Yet he also was acknowledging, despite himself, the discernible if distressing realization that anti-*philosophes* could claim renewed convic-tion and renewed credence, in no small part because of their own deeply held belief that recent French history corroborated their claims.

No sooner had the Revolution begun, in fact, than opponents of the *philosophes* were claiming for themselves the prescience of prophets.

Even beforehand, in January 1789, the abbé Barruel had hailed those "true sages" who had "foreseen" and "announced" the present crisis.[8] Shortly thereafter, in 1790, the successors of the *Année littéraire* drew attention in the opening prospectus of the *Ami du Roi* to the men and women who had predicted the "dreadful conspiracy" that was consuming France, lavishing praise on the prophetic powers of Fréron, who had "foretold the revolution that this proud sect would some day carry out."[9] Such claims were legion. But as Barruel lamented, those who had sounded these alarms were received as "false prophets," their "warnings" scorned as frivolous and superstitious fears.[10]

With the radical turn of the Revolution, however, warnings of this sort could no longer be dismissed out of hand. Yesterday's false prophets, seen through time and harrowing circumstances, now seemed to many to be remarkably prescient visionaries. As such they were hailed, and as such they hailed themselves, pressing repeatedly the prerevolutionary predictions, both real and attributed, of far-sighted anti-*philosophes*. Thus, the author of the *Instructions aux Catholiques, sur les causes de la Révolution*, a pamphlet originally delivered as an address in Burgos, Spain, in the spring of 1792, praised the foresight of those men, like himself, who had "seen the clouds gathering around the Church" and warned of the *philosophes'* diabolical design.[11] The abbé Duvoisin, former canon and vicar-general of Laon, observed from exile in 1795 that the "fanatical zeal with which the *philosophes* propagated their doctrine and their bold maneuvers to seize hold of public opinion announced to all clairvoyant men" the design to destroy the Christian religion and its political safeguard, the Bourbon monarchy. He applauded the few who had the foresight to signal the imminent danger, despite the blindness of so many.[12] Barruel, too, repeated his earlier praise—and with much greater precision—devoting several pages of the *Mémoires pour servir à l'histoire du jacobinisme* to extolling the men and women who had joined in the fight against the *philosophes* "that began with the conspiracy itself."[13] Others added to this pantheon of prophets, including in their lists Barruel himself, whose writings were cited alongside many others as unambiguous predictions, perfect prophecies of the horrors to come.[14]

Needless to say, such claims were greatly exaggerated and in some cases openly apocryphal.[15] By attributing anticipatory meaning to the words of Old Regime writers, these critics paid little attention to context and circumstance, in the process doing a grave injustice to the past. No one, however close the seeming correspondence between his or her prerevolutionary warnings and the actual events of the Revolution, could legitimately claim to have foreseen it in any of its contingent complexity. The product of numerous and complicated circumstances, the Revolution was neither foreordained nor reducible to any single cause, a fact as evident to many contemporaries as to subsequent observers.

But this straightforward rejoinder notwithstanding, there was a remarkable concurrence, however superficial, between anti-*philosophe* expectations and revolutionary events. At the most basic level, had not the anti-*philosophes* stressed time and again that the *philosophes'* assault on the foundations of the *ancien régime* would bring about calamities of an Old Testament nature? They warned of anarchy and blood, of regicide and the destruction of religion, of license and depravity, fanaticism, intolerance, and the wrath of God. Had French men and women not witnessed these very same developments, carried out by the revolutionaries' own admission in the name of *philosophie*? Seen in this light, the most extreme of the Old Regime anti-*philosophes*—the Barruels, the Fellers, the Richards, the Harels—with their consistent evocation of blood and violence, seemed in retrospect to be the most astute. The specter painted by Capmartin de Chaupy in 1789–1790 of a France "turned into Hell," rent by civil war and "drowned in a torrent of blood," was no longer an admonition but a vivid description of recent French history.

Reductive, simplistic, and superficial, these parallels were for the same reason powerful and convincing. Their apparent foresight gave to enemies of the *philosophes* a credibility far greater than they had previously enjoyed, and the excesses of the Revolution itself imbued the anti-*philosophe* discourse with renewed explanatory power. Providing a ready means to comprehend the otherwise incomprehensible, the anti-*philosophe* discourse was now directed at the past, indicting the *siècle des lumières* and its leading lights in sweeping, historical judgment.

Reconstructing *Philosophie*,
Reconstructing the Enlightenment

Those who sought in the aftermath of the Terror to pass judgment on *philosophie* did not fundamentally depart from earlier conceptions. They restated them in graphic, tireless refrain. At first sporadically, in sundry pamphlets and ephemeral publications written in exile or in hiding after the fall of the monarchy, and then gradually, in the wake of Thermidor, with ever greater boldness in France itself, counterrevolutionary writers emphasized the continuity between past and present, between philosophic cause and revolutionary effect. And although their arguments were largely derivative—in many cases boringly repetitive—they possessed a sharpness, a coherence, and a consistency that focused the earlier construction of *philosophie*, tying it explicitly to the horrors of the Revolution.

The first and most important element of this renewed assault was the unbreakable link between *philosophie* and the Terror. Just as the anti-*philosophe* writers of the Old Regime depicted *philosophie* as the sum of its worst parts, their successors viewed the Revolution as the product of its extremes. The Revolution *was* the Terror. The two were inseparable, underwritten and explained by the murderous doctrine of the *philosophes*.

This, of course, was and remains a highly contentious charge. Indeed it was precisely at this moment, in the wake of Thermidor, that repentant republicans and constitutional monarchists began to elaborate a view of the Revolution that would characterize the liberal position until well into the twentieth century. In this view, the Terror, admittedly, was an abomination. But it was also a perversion, an aberration, in no way related to the glorious achievements of the first, moderate revolution of 1789–1792. If the monster Robespierre and a few bloodthirsty cohorts had succeeded in subverting the laudable principles of 1789, this did not cast aspersion on the revolutionary project itself but rather underlined the pressing need to strengthen these same principles. The search for viable means to ensure them—through the balance of power, constitutional guarantees, and the rule of law—constituted one of the central problems of French politics in the aftermath of the Terror, exercising the faculties of liberal theorists from Madame de Staël and Benjamin Constant to those of important critics in our own day. To these observers, the principles of the Enlightenment—human rights, religious tolerance, freedom of speech, and civil equality—produced the most noble aspects of the Revolution. Under no circumstances could they be held accountable for its excesses.[16]

To the writers under consideration here, however, the attempt to separate 1789 or 1791 from what came after was a false and deeply insidious dichotomy. The revolutionary project was a unified undertaking, the Terror inscribed in the dynamics of *philosophie*. Jean-Thomas Richer-Sérizy, for example, returned to this theme repeatedly in the pages of his appropriately entitled *L'Accusateur public*, published clandestinely in France between 1795 and 1797. A former associate of the radical Cordelier Camille Desmoulins, Richer-Sérizy had since transformed himself into a counterrevolutionary journalist and conspirator. The conversion sapped none of his former vehemence.

> You who have prepared our glorious Revolution, who exalt the progress of reason and light—mob of ridiculous Encyclopedists and

Economists—come out from your graves and stand before the ruins and cadavers. Explain to us how in this so-vaunted century, thirty tyrants who legislated murder were able to find 300,000 executioners to carry out their orders. Interrogate [the bloodiest revolutionaries]—your writings are in their pockets, your maxims on their lips, your pages shine in their government reports. It is in the name of virtue that the most terrifying atrocities have been committed; in the name of humanity that two million men have died; in the name of liberty that 100,000 Bastilles have been erected. There is not a single one of your works that is not present in the offices of our 40,000 revolutionary committees.[17]

The Revolutionaries, in short, were the *philosophes'* willing executioners.

Richer-Sérizy's rhetoric was remarkable for its inflation and intensity. His general charge was not. The conviction that the *philosophes* had opened the door to the worst excesses of the Revolution was central to the rhetorical position of the Right, providing a litmus test that marked off this end of the political spectrum from other colors and shades. As the venerable anti-*philosophe* J. M. B. Clément pointed out in his newly founded *Journal littéraire* in 1797, many were the opportunists who rushed to condemn the Terror in its aftermath. But to do so without attacking its philosophic source was to hide behind a "mask of hypocrisy," condemning the effect but not the cause.[18] Antoine Rivarol perfectly agreed (see Figure 14). A celebrated *homme de lettre* during the Old Regime, a skeptic, and always an independent thinker, Rivarol had nonetheless opposed the Revolution unhesitatingly from the outset, collaborating with Antoine Sabatier on one of France's first counterrevolutionary newspapers, the *Journal politique national.* "If you pretend to deny responsibility for the enormous crimes of your allies [the Jacobins]," he challenged the *philosophes* directly in what would prove to be his anti-*philosophe* magnum opus, *De la Philosophie moderne* (1797), "posterity will pass judgment. It will decide between the architects of the crime and those who carried it out, and it will see whether or not principles are always guiltier than their consequences." Rivarol himself had no doubt about which way the verdict of history would fall. Many others, he predicted, would "paint the tableau of this *reign of terror,* to the eternal shame of ambitious fools." And they would see "how the most obscure disciple of *philosophie moderne* [Robespierre] raised himself to his throne by walking the path that the *philosophes* had cleared for him with their hands, and paved for him with their minds."[19]

Given the deluge of writings that would pour from anti-*philosophe* pens in the coming years, Rivarol's prediction was well founded. He need hardly have deferred to the future for judgment, however. His immediate contemporaries were already pronouncing strongly against the *philoso-*

Figure 14. Count Antoine de Rivarol (1753–1801).
Photo courtesy of the Bibliothèque Nationale, Paris.

phes in precisely these terms and had been doing so for some time. "Whatever accusation that one chooses to level at the usurpers of France," wrote an anonymous counterrevolutionary pamphleteer from exile in London in 1793, "whatever horrible action or crime, one can respond that they have all been preached or extolled in works . . . infected by the maxims of the *Philosophes.*" In this author's view, the word "Jacobin" was only a "nickname" for the sect of *philosophes.*[20] Worthy linguistic successors to their Old Regime and early revolutionary predecessors, anti-*philosophe* polemicists writing in the wake of the Terror employed the latter term with indiscriminate breadth, ranting against the "*philosophe* Robespierre," the "*philosophes* Marat and Hébert," "*philosophes* Tyrants," "*philosophes* Montagnards," and "*philosophes révolutionnaires.*"[21] What one journalist termed the *rage philosophico-révolutionnaire* swept up all factions in its midst, linking them to a central source and cause—*philosophie.*[22] With some justice, the Thermidorian statesman and subsequent Napoleonic minister Jean-Étienne-Marie Portalis complained in 1798 that "never has a word been more susceptible to different meanings . . . never has a thing been more decried than *philosophie* itself."[23]

It should not be supposed, however, that the *philosophes'* enemies merely transferred the term to those who carried out the Revolution, forgetting in the process the men who had made the title one of opprobrium in the first place. Those who had done the most to pave the path to the Terror, all agreed, were none other than the members of the High Enlightenment pantheon of old. Their names were forever present in the anti-*philosophes'* diatribes, juxtaposed immediately with lesser figures of the *siècle des lumières* and with the most violent perpetrators of the Revolution itself. "The Voltaires and Rousseaus, the Helvétiuses, the Diderots and d'Alemberts," Rivarol affirmed, "need not blush at the homages paid them by the Convention."[24] They fully deserved their praise and posterity's vilification. As Joseph de Maistre observed symptomatically in 1797, "This Voltaire whom blind enthusiasts transported to the Pantheon is perhaps, in the judgment of God, guiltier than Marat. For it is likely that Voltaire made Marat, and it is certain that he did more evil than him."[25]

There is some irony in these associations between the *philosophes* and the Jacobins, given Robespierre's own well-documented dislike for the men who had vilified his beloved Jean-Jacques. In a celebrated incident, Robespierre had even publicly smashed a bust of Helvétius, observing that *philosophes* like him would "never have embraced the cause of liberty."[26] By this stage, however, enemies of the Enlightenment were little inclined to credit such distinctions. On the contrary, they widened their list of the accused to make room for the one man they had often treated as an exception, Jean-Jacques Rousseau. There were those who continued to excuse him as the "most tolerant of *philosophes* and constantly their victim," arguing that he had been unjustly coopted by the Jacobins.[27] But Rousseau's placement in the Pantheon in 1794 and the prominence of the principles of the *Social Contract* made it increasingly difficult to set him apart (see Figure 15). He, too, was called before the tribunal, judged guilty, and condemned. Henceforth, Rousseau would figure centrally in the anti-*philosophes'* canon of criminals against humanity.

The *philosophes* bore a heavy onus, the weight of guilt that their detractors loaded steadily onto their tombs in the wake of Thermidor. The fulfillment of prophecy, the Terror was at once the confirmation of anti-*philosophe* prediction and the matrix through which these writers looked back into the past. Although they sought to bury forever these "enemies of humanity," anti-*philosophes* could not resist defiling their graves. Time and again they returned to their tombs to taunt and disfigure, reiterating the charges of the Old Regime in light of revolutionary atrocities, bringing the two together in symbiotic union.

Figure 15. The Internment of Rousseau in the Pantheon, 1794. Photo courtesy of the Bibliothèque Nationale, Paris.

Thus, the most ubiquitous prerevolutionary accusation—that of the *philosophes'* atheism and unremitting hatred of religion—was leveled continually to illuminate both eighteenth-century cause and revolutionary effect. "Is it certain that modern *Philosophie* formed the project of destroying religion?" asked François-Marie Bigex, former bishop of Chambéry, in his *Le Missionaire Catholique, ou Instructions familières sur la religion*. Already in its third edition in 1797, the work answered with a resounding yes, spelling out in simple language the *philosophes'* elaborate conspiracy, as well as the evident role of providence in bringing it about. Similarly, the abbé Barruel dedicated the entire first volume of his multi-thousand-page elaboration of the *philosophe*, Mason, and Jacobin conspiracy to chronicling the anti-Christian machinations of the original directors of the plot: Voltaire, d'Alembert, and their Encyclopedic brethren. These men, he contended, had conspired to wipe religion from the face of the globe, taking as their "greatest object" the "destruction" of the Christian faith.[28] Seeking to prove this charge incontrovertibly, Barruel combed the writings of the eighteenth-century *philosophes* with systematic thoroughness, accumulating mountains of "evidence" to support his claims. This was not, certainly, rigorous scholarship. But by isolating incendiary passages, quoting out of context, and drawing extensively from the private correspondence of the principal *philosophes*, Barruel made up for quality with quantity, presenting what to many contemporaries seemed a deeply convincing case. The *philosophes'* successful effort to poison public opinion, their pleading for tolerance and religious pluralism, the expulsion of the Jesuits, the inundation of France with anticlerical and atheistic tracts, and the corruption of the clergy itself—all this was put forth as so many exhibits in a protracted, inquisitorial trial. Guilty as charged, the *philosophes* had masterminded a conspiracy whose success French men and women could see for themselves.

The details of this plot—recounted by other scholars and, in any case, merely an elaborate embellishment of conspiracy theories already in place—need not concern us.[29] What is important to emphasize here is that even those writers who did not dwell on the explicit conspiratorial intentions imputed by Barruel shared many of his general characterizations, as well as his methods. They, too, returned to the principal texts of the Enlightenment, finding in the *philosophes'* countless anticlerical outbursts, in their undermining of revelation and church doctrine, and in their consistent branding of Christianity as fanaticism ample reasons to draw close links between *philosophie* and the anti-Christian campaigns of the Revolution. The religious apologist Louis-Jacques Briel observed in a multivolume anti-*philosophe* tract of 1797 that "a simple reading of the correspondence of Voltaire, d'Alembert, and their company" was enough to convince anyone of the *philosophes'* profound hatred of religion and authority. Philosophy, quite simply, was the "enemy of all religion."[30] Antoine Joseph Barruel-Beauvert, count and editor of the counterrevolutionary journal the *Actes des Apôtres*, concurred, observing that the *philosophes* had substituted "throughout France their cult of reason for the faith of our fathers."[31] To view the *siècle des lumières* through the smoldering haze of the Revolution was to see the darkness of a gathering storm.

Denunciations of this sort, emphasizing the essential antagonism of religion and *philosophie*, were widespread. Consolidating the main themes of the anti-*philosophe* discourse of the Old Regime, they continued the process of reifying and distorting the Enlightenment, reducing it to the sum of its most radical parts while effacing the manifold religious distinctions drawn throughout the century by *philosophes* low and high. What Joseph de Maistre described in 1797 as the contemporary "war to the death of Christianity and *philosophisme*" was thus carried back into the past, shown to be the defining characteristic of the *siècle des lumières*.[32] The Enlightenment was only a dress rehearsal for the open battle of the Revolution, "a never forgettable struggle" pitting "*philosophie* against Christianity."[33]

With regard to religion, then, polemicists writing after the Terror picked up, sharpened, and restated long-standing anti-*philosophe* charges, altering them only to accentuate *philosophie*'s inherent trajectory toward the revolutionary telos. They treated other aspects of the anti-*philosophe* discourse of old with similar respect. Thus, the allegation of the *philosophes*' valorization of the passions was recalled frequently to explain the violence and anarchy of the revolutionary experience. By "ripping every sentiment of piety from the heart of man," Briel observed, by "flattering the passions and license of the multitude, false philosophy found itself naturally at war with all those who sought to contain them." It "finished by overturning the social edifice onto all the orders of the state."[34] Shamefully materialist, the *philosophes* had vaunted the things of this world at the expense of the duties and strictures demanded by the next. Shamefully ambitious, they had attacked hierarchy and the mitigating influence of institutionalized inequality. And shamefully dissolute, they had corrupted the family, championing divorce and the heedless pursuit of bodily pleasure. Claiming to liberate, the *philosophes*, in truth, had turned men and women over to themselves, casting off the very restraints that made us decent while justifying the lust for power, lucre, and flesh that Christian moralists had long sought to curb in fallen humanity. "Modern *philosophie*," Rivarol summarized, "was nothing other than passions armed with principles."[35] As prerevolutionary anti-*philosophes* had constantly warned, to empower the passions in keeping with the *philosophes*' injunctions was to create monsters, brigands, and thieves. Once again the Revolution provided proof. Unbound, Prometheus was a ravaging beast.

By reinvigorating Old Regime discussions of the passions with chronicles of Jacobin horror, anti-*philosophes* at once explained the excesses of the Revolution while pressing the need to harness citizens through the constraining yokes of religion, the family, hierarchy, and duty. At a time when the destructive effects of license and the potential for human evil were plain for all to see, such arguments carried force. In the same way, other elements of the anti-*philosophe* discourse took on renewed persuasive power in the aftermath of the Terror. The long-standing charge of the *philosophes*' intolerance, for example, could not fail to resonate with men and women who had witnessed firsthand the persecution of priests and ideological dissenters. Fréron's grim warning of 1772 in the *Année littéraire* appeared, nearly a quarter-century later, remarkably apt: "If the wise *philosophes* of the century, who demand tolerance with so much ardor and interest . . . were ever themselves at the head of government, armed with the sword of sovereignty or of law, they would perhaps be the first to deal severely with those who had the audacity to contradict their opinions."[36]

Seemingly borne out by the facts of history, this prediction, and countless others were cited with self-righteous relish, their arguments repeated with reborn conviction. As Duvoisin commented, "It was easy to predict, and Rousseau, who knew them so well, foretold that if the *Philosophes* ever became masters, they would be the most intolerant of men. The Revolution made them all-powerful and Rousseau's prediction was confirmed."[37] He proceeded to develop at length how "in proclaiming the indefinite tolerance of all cults, the Constituent Assembly meditated and prepared the proscription of the Catholic religion."[38] The *philosophes'* cry of tolerance, as their enemies had incessantly warned, was a sham, a devious strategy intended to annihilate the faith and reign in tyranny over its crumbled remains. "Oh how the tolerance of the *philosophes* is intolerant," lamented the editor of the *Invariable* in a typical refrain. "They have taken away from the clergy its property, its repose, its political existence, its name. They have massacred, drowned, burned, and starved priests by the thousands."[39] Benign in theory alone, in practice the *philosophes* were despots, their conquest of the Old Regime republic of letters a bitter foretaste of the tyrannical political power they wielded during the revolutionary republic.

Such experience seemed to some to shed light farther back than the eighteenth century. Had not philosophers in all ages acted with this same, inherent intolerance? demanded a letter to the editor in the Royalist *Déjeuner* in 1797: "Admire this lovely phrase of Plato: 'republics will be happy, if philosophers govern, or if those who govern philosophize.' What a false idea. Consult history and it will teach you that the greatest unhappiness that can come to an empire is to let it fall into the hands of one of these pedants, of a man entirely buried in books."[40] J. M. B. Clément was equally sweeping. After also quoting Plato's famous passage from the *Republic*, he beseeched, "Someone please explain to me by what strange fatality the disciples of philosophers have almost always been tyrants?"[41]

Clément's question was rhetorical, for both he and his fellow partisans had a ready response: the gap between the abstract notions of the mind and the concrete realities of social and political experience was vast. By abjuring, in their mania to change all, the accumulated wisdom of the ages, the *philosophes* had stripped society of the institutions and customs that rendered power gentle, that made human beings generous and kind. In doing so, they had shown tremendous aptitude, not only poisoning the hearts and minds of France's citizens but also corrupting the French language itself. Through the subtleties of words, they equated religion indiscriminately with fanaticism, monarchy with despotism, hierarchy with slavery, and ingrained belief with prejudice and superstition. And in place of these concrete institutions and noble attributes, they preached vague and beguiling notions—humanity, charity, philanthropy, reason, wisdom, liberty, equality, fraternity. As the revolutionary experience showed all too clearly, however, such "pretty-sounding names" were merely abstractions, hollow phrases that covered over the hypocrisy of *philosophie*.[42] "Oh anathema to the *philosophes*," bemoaned a typical article in the royalist *Thé*, "who abandoned the field of experience for the nothingness of systems" and the emptiness of words.[43]

Having attacked and "denatured all," undermined a centuries-old monarchy, subverted religion, removed conscience and the fear of God, touted equality and the injustice of social hierarchy, and inflamed the very passions these natural institutions had benignly restrained, the *philosophes* had opened a gaping void—one that could be filled only by naked, unmitigated power.[44] Here was the response to Clément's question, the answer to the alleged perennial link between philosophy and tyranny. Swept up by the monstrous abstractions of their systems, the *philosophes* and their followers had proselytized with all the fury of crusading zealots. They were, despite their insidious misappropriation of the term, history's true "fanatics," their doctrine pure "fanaticism." Indeed, more than one hostile observer was wont to point out the religious character of what the *Politique chrétienne* termed the *irreligion philosophique*.[45] Like the one true faith, the *"religion philosophique* had [developed] for many years its dogmas, its priests, its missionaries, its flock."[46] And in the Revolution itself, its frenzied enthusiasts had prostrated themselves before the temple of reason, rising in zealous waves, "the *droits de l'homme* in hand," to convert the infidel through force of arms.[47] Their millenarian hopes notwithstanding, the *philosophes'* perverted religion of abstract reason had born only blood and devastation. As Richer-Sérizy summarized in his inimitable way,

> I suppose, *philosophes*, to adopt your own pompous, charlatan term, that your project was to found universal reason, to give to humanity its rights, to overthrow tyrants, and to liberate the world. . . . So sure were you that general happiness would follow directly from [the institution of your divine government], that once put into effect, your plan, erected on indestructible foundations, would overcome any uncertainty,

any obstacle. But *philosophes*, to risk overturning your *patrie* on a doubtful theory, was, and this is to put it mildly, imprudent. For what horror has not been seized upon in the wake of this experiment? Blood has flowed, and continues to flow, in torrents. . . .[48]

An abstract system, intolerant, fanatical, atheistic, and radical—responsible at once for the moral corruption of the Old Regime and the bloody excesses of the Revolution—these were the charges for which *philosophie* stood condemned and convicted. Whereas anti-*philosophes* during the Old Regime and the early Revolution had looked for signs of the apocalypse on the horizon of the future, their counterparts in the 1790s believed they had witnessed it firsthand. Now it was the past that illuminated the present and the present that illuminated the past. Binding the two inseparably, anti-*philosophe* polemicists joined the Enlightenment to the Revolution in completion of a process of construction they had begun during the Old Regime. It was a portrait of the *siècle des lumières*, as we shall see in greater detail in subsequent chapters, destined to exert a powerful influence on historical perspectives of the Enlightenment well into the twentieth century, shaping the way both proponents and opponents of *philosophie* viewed the thought of the eighteenth century.

It should be stressed that this construction of the Enlightenment was an extreme discourse, one of a number of competing perspectives on the eighteenth century and the causes of the Revolution forged in the aftermath of the Terror. At the other end of the political spectrum, unrepentant Jacobins continued through the 1790s to pursue their radical revolutionary project, decrying the reversal of Thermidor and at times citing *philosophie* in their behalf. When the protocommunist François Noël Babeuf, for example, was placed on trial for attempting to overthrow the Directory in the famous "conspiracy of equals" of 1797, he cited the *philosophes* in support of his actions, claiming to have found in Jean-Jacques, Diderot, and Helvétius an "invitation to universal happiness and sublime equality" on which he based his principles. As the none-too-sympathetic journal *Politique chrétienne* observed, "Babeuf [speaks] with precision . . . when he calls to his aid these deist *philosophes*, these materialists and atheists."[49] However unjustly, Babeuf's candid confession and others like it reaffirmed the beliefs of men and women on the Right, strengthening their view that *philosophie* remained an active and radical presence, both within the republican Directory and without.

Babeuf and his kind represented the other extreme—the refusal to apologize for either *philosophie* or the radical Revolution. Many more sought a middle course, attempting to rescue the *siècle des lumières* from unfair imputation or association while at the same time striving to defend what were construed as *philosophie*'s elevated goals. In a speech before the National Convention, defending the proposed Constitution of the Year III in 1795, for example, one of its principal drafters, François Antoine Boissy d'Anglas, upheld the spirit of 1789, noting defiantly that the early Revolution was the "result of *lumières* and civilization . . . the fruit of centuries of *philosophie*" that had "dissipated the darkness . . . of error, despotism, superstition, and ignorance." To claim, he charged, that such a vast upheaval as the Revolution was the work of "a few individuals" or, more gravely still, that these same philosophic luminaries were in any way responsible for the Terror was absurd, a belief that could only be held by "delirious, ignorant men who sought to destroy the Revolution." No, the Terror did not represent the culmination of *philosophie* but rather its complete rejection. In seeking to restore the basic rights that the Jacobins had destroyed, the new constitution was simply reaffirming the moderate, tolerant goals for which the *philosophes*, in Boissy's view, had always stood.[50]

Claims of this kind—efforts to disengage the *philosophes* and *philosophie* from Jacobin outrage while retaining their loftiest principles—were common. In France they were probably predominant throughout the 1790s.[51] Yet Boissy and others clearly recognized as early as 1795 that the criticism of *philosophie* that emanated from the Right was a force to be reckoned with. Though not new, the anti-*philosophe* discourse was improved, if only by dint of circumstance; and though within France these circumstances were still not entirely amenable to the full flowering of a Counter-Enlightenment reaction, they were growing ever more so abroad.

The Counter-Enlightenment International

The massive exodus of refractory French priests and counterrevolutionary polemicists, all of whom bore grudges and, many, seeds of the anti-*philosophe* discourse, ensured that criticism of the Enlightenment spread far beyond the borders of France. Dramatically intensified by the emigration, this phenomenon of Catholic intellectual exchange and Counter-Enlightenment proselytization nonetheless long preceded it. Both in person and in print, French enemies of the Enlightenment were forging contacts with foreign associates well before the Revolution. And abroad, those fighting the importation of French *philosophie* and its various indigenous manifestations looked to France for guidance and support.

Consider, for example, the case of François-Xavier Feller, whose *Journal historique et littéraire* has already figured prominently[52] (see Figure 16). Born in Brussels in 1735, the son of a wealthy civil servant ennobled by Maria-Theresa, Feller studied at the Jesuit college in Luxembourg and then at Reims, where he pursued a doctorate in theology in the 1750s. Initiated into the order in 1754, he remained in France until its dissolution in 1763, traveling widely thereafter in eastern Europe and teaching at Luxembourg, Liège, and Tournau before devoting himself entirely to journalism. In 1769, Feller began contributing articles to the *Clef du cabinet des princes de l'Europe*, transforming the review under his editorship in 1773 into the bimonthly *Journal historique et littéraire*. A refuge and intellectual clearinghouse for Jesuit exiles, the journal united numerous contributors, including H. I. Brosius, J. L. Burton, J. H. Duvivier, J. N. Paquot, the *père* Dedoyar, and others in a continent-wide war against incredulity, fusing literary criticism with cultural commen-

Figure 16. François-Xavier de Feller (1735–1802). Photo courtesy of the Bibliothèque Nationale, Paris.

tary and militant, *dévot* piety. Published from Luxembourg until 1788 (afterward at Liège until 1791 and then at Maestricht until 1794), the journal followed French and pan-European affairs intently, making the fight against the *philosophes* its raison d'être, a truly international concern.

Feller's anti-*philosophe* polemic, as we have seen, was voiced in precisely the same terms as that of his French colleagues. To reaffirm the point, he regularly reviewed with enthusiasm the writings of France's most militant polemicists, lavishing praise on the likes of Barruel, Liger, Genlis, Pey, and others.[53] He also wrote in the international language of French, directing his most pointed criticism at French *philosophes* themselves, warning of their pernicious effects throughout Europe. All of this helps to underscore the fact that Catholic enemies of the Enlightenment conceived of themselves as a genuinely "catholic" community in the eighteenth century, an international alliance engaged in an international struggle—one whose front lines lay in France but extended outward to span national frontiers.

This is not to deny the important regional and national particularities of Catholic discourse in the eighteenth century, any more than it is to maintain that the Enlightenment itself was an uncomplicated whole. Nevertheless, within Catholicism's complex web of tense and even discordant traditions, one can identify closely gathered strands of the same intellectual fiber, spun and bound within the framework of the "universal" church. Militant adversaries of the *philosophes* across Europe knew who their friends were, and they called on them to fight not only native and imported versions of *philosophie* but the older heresies of Protestantism and Jansenism as well. Particularly in those countries where Jansenism entered into tactical alliances with reforming monarchs, on the one hand, and blurred, on the other hand, almost imperceptibly into variants of the Enlightenment, it should not surprise us that "the pejorative 'filósofos'" was uttered almost synonymously with that of "Jansenist."[54] Feller and his French comrades had long decried the "strict union" of the two,[55] and by 1789 orthodox religious apologists such as the Italian Rocca Bónola and his Spanish translator and editor, the Marqués del Mérito, were publishing screeds that warned of the joint machinations of a Jansenist-*philosophe* alliance.[56] Just as the leading scholar of French Jansenism, Dale Van Kley, has begun to explore what he describes as a "Jansenist international," cutting across Catholic Europe, one can speak of an international axis of the orthodox marshaled to refute both the Enlightenment and its Jansenist fellow travelers.[57]

Where it was a genuine political and ecclesiastical force, then, in conjunction with Enlightenment currents (above all, the Austrian Nether-lands, Italy, and Spain), Jansenism helped to crystallize orthodox reactions that were simultaneously forming in response to indigenous and imported versions of Enlightenment thought. Again, one must be sensitive to distinctive national characteristics and styles. Yet to speak only of the image of the *siecle des lumières*, the similarities between the French construction of *philosophie* and these international Catholic reactions is striking. In many instances, they were identical. Given the prestige and volume of eighteenth-century French religious apologies and anti-*philosophe* polemic, Catholics abroad often simply translated French works verbatim. Richard Herr, for example, notes in his classic study of eighteenth-century Spain that native opponents of the Spanish *ilustración* were quick to "turn to French sources for their ammunition," translating, among many others, the likes of Omer Joly de Fleury, Claude Marie Guyon, Louis-Antoine Caraccioli, the abbé Nonnotte, and later the abbés Gérard and Barruel.[58] On the Italian peninsula, too, orthodox polemicists fearful of the innovating tendencies of *illuminismo* looked to French authors to buttress what was in its own right a significant anti-*philosophe* response.[59] The Jesuit theologian Gian Battisti Roberti, for example, who since the publication in 1754 of his *Della religione rivelata contra gli ateisti, deisti, materialisti, indifferentisti* had made waging war against the *spiriti forti* of the eighteenth century his central preoccupation, embellished his writings with frequent references to French comrades in arms. He was not alone.[60] As far away as French-speaking North America, the Belgian priest Bernard Well was filling the pages of the *Gazette littéraire de Montréal* in the 1770s with anti-*philosophe* invective culled directly from the pages of the French apologist Louis-Mayeul Chaudon.[61]

Even when anti-*philosophe* partisans writing outside of France did not draw directly on the *words* of their French colleagues, they frequently shaped their *arguments* in similar ways. Not only did the authority of French religious authors and the international currency of the French language ensure that Catholics abroad were familiar with their work, but the Enlightenment itself was perceived by many to be preeminently French. And so, as the writings of French *philosophes* made their way into the Low Countries, floated across the Rhine, descended the jagged peaks of the Pyrenees and Alps, and gradually pushed their way into eastern Europe, they not surprisingly provoked like-minded responses among their Catholic adversaries. Their enemies, after all, were the same. Voltaire, d'Alembert, Rousseau, Diderot, Helvétius, Raynal—these great men of the French pantheon appear as commonly in the works of Italian, Spanish, and German apologists as they do in those of their French counterparts.[62] In the Catholic lands of the Habsburg empire—Austria proper and Hungary—as well as in devout Poland, the French *philosophes* loomed large, generating hostile, religious reactions.[63]

As the names were the same, so, frequently, were the charges. Fanaticism, intolerance, libertinism, moral transgression, atheism, materialism, and the subversion of throne and altar—such indictments appear again and again in international Catholic writings, traced to the common sources of pride and the Ur-revolt of the Protestant Reformation and drawn out in tales of conspiracy that culminated in blood-chilling accounts of the horrors to come. In a work like that of the Spanish apologist Fernando de Zeballos, published in Madrid in 1775–1776, all this is evident in a translation of the title alone: *False Philosophy, or Atheism, Deism, Materialism, and the Other New Sects Convicted of Treason Against Sovereigns and their Privileges, Against Magistrates and Legitimate Powers, Wherein are Combated those Seditious Maxims Subversive of All Society and Humanity Itself.*[64] The title was longer than most, but the first phrase, "false philosophy" (*falsa filosofía*), said it all. To significant numbers of Catholic Europeans at the end of the eighteenth century, these words alone summoned terrible connotations.

With the advent and radical turn of the French Revolution, the persuasive power of this international Catholic discourse was heightened dramatically, just as it was in France. Polemicists abroad could appeal to the same prescience and predictive acumen to which their French counterparts constantly referred. And they could pound meaning into their grisly tales of revolutionary atrocities to the sound of the boot steps of advancing French armies. The specter, and reality, of a "philosophic" war of conquest waged in the name of reason and light did little to enhance the prestige of the Revolution's avowed forefathers. In such an environment, indictments of *philosophie*—French *philosophie*—flourished.

In the German-speaking lands, for example, the proliferation of indigenous secret societies, the discovery of the Bavarian Illuminati plot of the 1780s, and a native tradition of hostility to French philosophy combined to feed a strong anti-*philosophe* current that burst forth in the early years of the Revolution. By 1792, the enlightened Karl Friedrich Reinhard was complaining in the *Moniteur universel* that the term *Aufklärung* and its French equivalent, *Lumières*, had been completely transformed into "subject[s] of scandal," used now only as "word[s] of war."[65] Leopold Hoffman and Johann Starck conceived of them as such, consistently presenting the Revolution as the outcome of a formal *philosophe* conspiracy in the pages of their respective journals, the

Wiener Zeitschrift and *Eudämonia*.[66] Many joined in this onslaught of religious criticism of the Enlightenment.

In Spain, too, the land of refuge for thousands of refractory French priests, anti-*philosophe* polemicists found receptive audiences. From the pulpit, the Spanish clergy denounced *la filosofía criminal y falsa*, blaming it for the destruction of the French throne and altar and exhorting France's citizens to "root out its Rousseaus, Voltaires, Helvétiuses, Bayles, and Masons."[67] Spanish presses translated the works of French anti-*philosophe* writers to shed light on the conspiratorial origins of the Revolution and published countless native polemics that unveiled the *philosophe*, Protestant, Jansenist, and Masonic machinations behind the present turmoil in Europe.[68] Likewise in Italy there was no shortage of men and women ready to ascribe the fall of France to conspiratorial forces and to warn of the contemporary threat of *philosophie* in their own lands.[69] As far away as Russia, ex-Jesuits and the itinerant Joseph de Maistre spread tales of the *philosophe* conspiracy, where they were received with great favor.[70]

So powerful was this Counter-Enlightenment language that even countries that had experienced little of the Enlightenment itself in the eighteenth century now adopted it as a prophylactic discourse. Thus, in the western Iberian peninsula, as David Higgs observes, "the Portuguese anti-philosophical and counter-revolutionary discourses at the end of the eighteenth century . . . were of immense significance to government attitudes which marked Portugal and Brazil during the first half of the nineteenth century and later."[71] Despite the fact that Inquisition scribes in Lisbon had so little familiarity with the chief figures of the Enlightenment that they transcribed Voltaire's name phonetically as "Vulter" in the 1790s, they feared his influence all the same.[72]

In the Portuguese colonies, similarly, fears of the influence of French *philosophie* were rampant in the 1790s, fed not only by developments in France but also by the discovery of an *actual* conspiracy in Brazil in 1789, plotted by influential colonists with the aim of wresting independence from the Portuguese crown.[73] When a cache of Enlightenment texts, including the *Encyclopédie*, Raynal's *Histoire philosophique*, constitutional commentaries by Mably, and works by Voltaire and Condillac, was found to have circulated among the conspirators, authorities drew predictable conclusions: the influence of French *philosophie* was at work in the New World.[74] Notwithstanding the negligible penetration of the Enlightenment in the country at large, Brazilian authorities took no risks, overturning every stone in search of the pernicious writings of "Vulter" and company and investigating the disbanded members of an innocuous literary society that had formed in Rio in the 1790s with the aim of discussing "philosophy in all its aspects."[75] Well into the next century the association of French philosophy with dangerous innovation was immediate in the minds of many Brazilian Catholics.[76]

In Spanish Latin America, too, defenders of throne and altar in the church, the Inquisition, and the various vice-regal administrations pursued the infiltration of French Enlightenment doctrine with vehemence. As in Brazil, the eighteenth-century impact of the Enlightenment there was comparatively small.[77] Yet the expulsion of the Jesuits in 1767, the circulation of anti-*philosophe* and anti-Jansenist writings produced in the Spanish metropole, and ultimately the impact of the French Revolution gave orthodox Catholics in the New World cause for fear of *philosophie* on native soil. Thus, the Cathedral Chapter of Mexico City could draft a letter to the king in November 1799, complaining that decisions prejudicial to the church taken by civil magistrates could be traced to Freemasons and French *philosophes*, with whose "pernicious doctrines . . . a few unfortunate officials have been contaminated."[78] And when the New World exploded in a series of national wars of independence amid the uncertainty created by Napoleon's occupation of Spain, supporters of Catholic orthodoxy found little trouble in attributing this ferment to the accursed doctrines of *los filósofos*. During the temporary respite created by the restoration of the Bourbon monarchy in 1814, the Peruvian defender of empire Blas Ostolaza, ex-canon of Trujillo, accused twenty-four prominent figures of complicity in the struggle for Peruvian independence. In his view, the dangerous political views of all these men "were inspired by the doctrines of the encyclopediasts."[79] In New Spain, similarly, supporters of the Spanish crown condemned all those who had participated in the temporarily thwarted civil war for Mexican independence of 1810–1814 in terms reverberating with themes of the anti-*philosophe* discourse. As the grand inquisitor of Mexico, Manuel de Flores, observed in 1815, the men and women who had sustained the struggle for liberal constitutionalism were infected by the "nonsense of the modern libertines, Voltaire, Rousseau, and their disciples and partisans."[80] Such condemnations of *filosofismo* were widespread.[81]

In various parts of the New World, then, the anti-*philosophe* discourse born in France and spread throughout Europe enjoyed sustained vitality well into the nineteenth century. This discourse was, as I have stressed, profoundly Catholic, but it is worth noting briefly that its influence was not limited solely to the Catholic world. Anglican England, for example, showed itself receptive to condemnations of the *philosophes*. It was in London, after all, that the abbé Barruel first published the *Mémoires pour servir à l'histoire du jacobinisme*, a work cited, reprinted, and quoted extensively in contemporary British sermons, books, and periodicals.[82] Upon receiving a personal copy, no less a figure than Edmund Burke responded to his exiled acquaintance, then living in England, with fulsome praise. "I cannot easily express to you," Burke wrote to Barruel in 1797, "how much I am instructed and delighted by the first Volume of your History of Jacobinism. The whole of the wonderful narrative is supported by documents and proofs with the most juridical regularity and exactness."[83] Burke, whose own *Reflections* of 1790 and subsequent works were rich in references to the *philosophe* sect, to their fanaticism, atheism, and perversion of public morals, added, "I have known myself, personally, five of your principal conspirators; and I can undertake to say from my own certain knowledge, that so far back as the year 1773, they were busy in the plot you have so well described."[84] Barruel, for his part, was more than prepared to return the compliment, commenting that "the immortal Burke" had already seen in 1790 the true origins of the Revolution and that everything published subsequently had been merely a "commentary on his text."[85]

Not all viewed the *Mémoires* as uncritically as Burke,[86] yet the great British statesman's readiness to countenance the main lines of Barruel's thesis is revealing; the stunning success of Barruel's work, in itself, is convincing testimony to the changed fortunes of the anti-*philosophe* discourse in the aftermath of the Terror. Published in both London and Hamburg in 1797, the four-volume, multi-thousand-page work tore through four revised French editions by 1799 and was translated into English, German, Italian, Spanish, Swedish, and Russian, countless editions of which were issued separately in London, Hamburg, Augsburg, Strengnàs, Luxembourg, St. Petersburg, Dublin, Hartford, Lisbon, Palma de Mallorca, Vic, Naples, and Rome before the fall of Napoleon, making it, as one scholar has observed, "one of the most widely read books in its day."[87]

Still others independently took up Barruel's arguments. In the United Kingdom, the Scottish scientist John Robison, described by Sir James Mackintosh as "one of the greatest mathematical philosophers of his age" and praised by the inventor of the steam engine, James Watt, as "a man of the cleverest head and the most science of anybody I have known," published in 1797 his *Proofs of a Conspiracy against All the Religions and Governments of Europe, carried on in the Secret Meetings of the Free Masons, Illuminati, and Reading Societies.*[88] The work, published in four London editions by 1798, printed in New York (1798) and translated into French (London, 1798–1799), German (Königslutter and Hamburg, 1800), and Dutch (n.d.), chronicled a joint *philosophe*, Mason, and Illuminati conspiracy to "root out all the religious establishments, and overturn all the existing governments of Europe."[89] Less detailed but arguably more refined than Barruel's text, the *Proofs of a Conspiracy* nonetheless corroborated the main outlines of the *Mémoires pour servir à l'histoire du Jacobinisme*. As Barruel himself commented upon learning of the work after the third volume of his own *Mémoires* had gone to press, "Without knowing it, we have fought for the same cause with the same arms, and pursued the same course."[90] The two books spawned a flood of anti-*philosophe* sermons and numerous publications that reiterated their central theses.[91]

In the United States, too, a country in which conspiracy language had long formed a staple of political discourse, the criticisms of Barruel and Robison found receptive listeners.[92] The Reverend Timothy Dwight, president of Yale, who had already noted the alarming progress of "the infidelity of Voltaire and his coadjutors" among impressionable undergraduates, preached a sermon in New Haven on July 4, 1798, in which he denounced the orchestrated plot, hatched by Voltaire, Frederick II, the Encyclopedists, and the Society of the Illuminati to destroy the Christian religion and abolish the French monarchy, citing Barruel and Robison in support of his claims.[93] An infectious virus, "philosophism," Dwight warned, had spread throughout the continent and now gravely imperiled the United States.[94] Fears of this nature were extensive, spawning a national panic from 1798 to 1790 in which influential segments of the clergy, important journals like the *Porcupine* and the *Aurora General Advertiser*, and leading Federalist statesmen including Alexander Hamilton charged republicans in general, and Thomas Jefferson in particular, with involvement in a vast conspiracy linked to the Bavarian Illuminati to spread the principles of the *philosophes* and the Jacobins to the New World.[95] Such was the degree of tension that one historian, the distinguished scholar of the American Revolution, Gordon Wood, asserts that during the height of the Illuminati scare in 1798 the country was brought to the verge of civil war.[96]

The manner in which extraneous theories of *philosophe* subversion and conspiratorial plots were thus incorporated into the internal politics of countries outside of France is a subject beyond the purview of this study. It is worth noting briefly here, however, that as in France, the language of opposition to the Enlightenment lent itself ideally to the language of opposition to the Revolution, with which it was consistently fused. In those countries that faced the threat or the reality of French invasion, French *philosophie* could easily be targeted as the motive force that was propelling French armies and presented as a foreign incursion that would also have to be expelled. In this way the Enlightenment was implicated, however unfairly, in the great continental wars that endured through the reign of Napoleon, bound up in emerging romantic movements for national liberation and national definition. In many minds, the Enlightenment was a French disease, as alien to native soil as the soldiers who bore it.

Anti-*philosophe* constructions of the Enlightenment thus enjoyed a startlingly vast and rapid diffusion outside of France in the immediate aftermath of the Terror—the product, at once, of the efforts of dogged French polemicists in exile, the fear of the spread of the Revolution beyond the frontiers of Gaul, the general prevalence of conspiracy language in eighteenth-century political vocabulary, and indigenous reactions to the *siècle des lumières*. In the somewhat less fettered regions beyond the reach of revolutionary jurisdiction, Counter-Enlightenment polemicists could no doubt inveigh with the greatest liberty. Yet even within France, there were telling signs that erstwhile supporters of the *philosophes* were undergoing a change of heart.

Philosophie, the God That Failed

To live without divine guidance is a difficult task; some would say, an impossible one, terrifying, directionless, and confused. If this remains true today, it was far more so during the first age in the history of humanity in which considerable numbers of men and women contemplated life without God (or gods). The outright atheism of the Enlightenment has been exaggerated. But this does nothing to change the fact that more travelers in the eighteenth century than ever before ventured forth into the twilight of the idols, plotting their journeys in a world in which God, though not banished, was at least set aside. Many, understandably, charted this new voyage with instruments of old, investing such abstractions as society, humanity, or the nation with quasi-divine power.[97] Some stumbled; others lost their way. And in the aftermath of the Terror, growing numbers came to doubt the wisdom of the journey itself, stopping in their tracks, only to turn back toward familiar ground.

In fact, the end of the eighteenth century laid another milestone in the history of Western civilization—the advent of the phenomenon of the ideological deconversion of the secular intellectual. Like the Whittaker Chambers and Arthur Koestlers of more recent times, men and women in the 1790s came in from the cold, renouncing *philosophie* as a "god that failed."[98] There is no more perfect illustration of this development than the dramatic defection of the former *philosophe* Jean-François La Harpe and the publication in 1797 of his *Du Fanatisme dans la langue révolutionnaire*, printed in a remarkable nineteen editions shortly thereafter.[99]

Du Fanatisme was the clearest indication of La Harpe's disavowal of his philosophic past, but it was not the first. The ardor of the man described as "Voltaire's disciple" cooled progressively over the course of the 1790s, although only gradually.[100] As we have seen, La Harpe had no trouble appearing before the National Assembly in 1790 to claim responsibility for the *philosophes* in bringing about this "grand and happy revolution," and outwardly he supported both the National Assembly and the National Convention from his post at the republican Lycée well into the Terror.[101] But despite protestations of unflagging support for the regime of Robespierre, suspicion of La Harpe's connections to Old Regime society grew, and in March 1794 he was imprisoned by the Committee of Public Safety. The experience was a revelation. Encountering there a host of unrepentant Christians, including the bishop of Montauban, Le Tonnelier de Breteuil, and the pious widow of Stanislas de Clermont-Tonnere, La Harpe took to reading the Bible and Thomas à Kempis's *The Imitation of Christ*. Struck by the fortitude of the faithful, he began translating the psalms and discussing the principles of the faith with his fellow inmates, undergoing something on the order of a conversion experience.[102] When he was released from prison after the fall of Robespierre, La Harpe was a new man. And though he did not at first criticize the Directory, which hailed him initially as a republican martyr, La Harpe was soon upbraiding the *philosophes* and defending his newfound faith in his resumed lectures at the Lycée, laying the groundwork for what was to come.

Du Fanatisme, nonetheless, was by far the most dramatic statement to date of La Harpe's transformation, evincing strong support for the refractory clergy, defending the Vendée revolt, and chronicling in gory detail the atrocities of the Terror. But clearly the most striking feature of the 135-page pamphlet was its wholesale adoption of the militant anti-*philosophe* line. The Revolution, La Harpe contended, was the work of "God who [had] punished a nation in order to instruct and preserve the world"—divine retribution leveled in just response for the errors of a fallen people.[103] Who had led French men and women astray, drawing upon them the wrath of the Almighty? La Harpe left no doubt, picking up the refrain that we have heard so often: "It is you, *grands philosophes*, who have provoked Providence for fifty years. You will not dare deny that it is your *philosophie* that has made the Revolution."[104] Leaving the definition of both these words deliberately vague, noting only that "the *philosophie* that I treat here with all the scorn that it deserves, is none other than that of the writers who called themselves *philosophes*," La Harpe avoided, for the most part, citing individual names.[105] A feeble attempt to avoid drawing scrutiny of his own intimate association with the great *philosophes* of the eighteenth century, the strategy could not hide the fact that La Harpe was indicting *philosophie* in the broadest possible terms, lumping together *philosophes* of both the Low and High Enlightenment, as well as the sanguinary revolutionaries to whom they allegedly gave birth. These *philosophes*, La Harpe accused, had "preached atheism, irreligion, and impiety, the hatred of all legitimate authority, contempt for all moral truths, and the destruction of all social ties." It was thus no difficult matter to prove that their "doctrine," ostensibly conceived to "enlighten the people," had in fact plunged them into the greatest "ignorance and absurdity." In brief, the *philosophes* of the eighteenth century were the "worthy precursors of the *hommes révolutionnaires*, the Chaumettes, Héberts, and Marats."[106]

To prove this assertion, La Harpe devoted the better part of his text to an examination of the deleterious consequences of the generalizations of philosophic language, focusing explicitly on the prerevolutionary use of the term "fanaticism." Properly speaking, La Harpe argued, "fanaticism . . . [was] blind, excessive, religious zeal," an abuse of religion, an aberration, and by no means inherent in the law of the Gospel.[107] Although La Harpe admitted that during the wars of religion, both Catholics and Protestants had been carried away by their human passions to excesses of fanaticism, he resolutely denied that this reflected on the faith itself. In any case, Christians had since succeeded in expunging fanaticism from their midst, a fact that the *philosophes* stubbornly refused to acknowledge. Consistently equating the abuse of religion with religion itself, they branded all faith blind fanaticism. Through their incessant denunciations, they had succeeded in creating a vast chimera, distorting reality to such a degree that their specter of religion no longer bore any relationship to Catholicism as a concrete faith. The only true fanaticism reigning in France in 1789 was of the philosophic variety, the "fanaticism of irreligion carried to an excess of intolerance and fury of which the writings of the *philosophes* furnish infinite examples."[108]

Developing this theme in great detail, La Harpe then proceeded to draw the connection with the militant anticlericalism of the Revolution itself. The "grand rallying cry" uttered endlessly by the Jacobins, the popular societies, and the National Convention was *guerre au fanatisme*.[109] "Am I wrong in saying," he asked, "that the word 'religion' was effaced from the French language . . . replaced generically by that of 'fanaticism'?"[110] And could the *philosophes* deny that it was from them that the revolutionaries "had taken their word of proscription"?[111] "It was you, *philosophes*, who taught the revolutionaries to denature ideas and words. Dare you say that you were not the first of the guilty?"[112] Dehumanizing their victims as fanatics, the revolutionaries had carried out the single greatest persecution of Christianity since the time of Caesar. Men and women had been "massacred like wild beasts, tortured in every conceivable manner, incinerated, drowned, decapitated, mutilated, and shredded for no other reason than their belief."[113] And though La Harpe acknowledged, much like Rivarol, that the *philosophes* of the *ancien régime* had not themselves perpetrated these crimes and likely would have been repulsed by them, he saw this as of little consequence: "You have not massacred or set fire, I admit, but you [*philosophes*] put the sword and the torch in the hand of those who were ready to make use of both these weapons."[114] "I swear," he continued, "I want to take away from our *philosophes* every excuse, every pretext, every subterfuge."[115]

In his refusal to draw distinctions between *philosophie* low and high and his dogged insistence that the *philosophes* of the *ancien régime* bore ultimate responsibility for the excesses of the Revolution, La Harpe was speaking from the heart of the militant anti-*philosophe* position. He voiced other classic anti-*philosophe* charges as well, stressing how the *philosophes*' intolerance undercut their own claims of toleration and structured the revolutionaries' refusal to endure dissent. He lambasted the deification of reason and emphasized how the *philosophes*' liberation of the passions exacerbated the violence of the Revolution.[116] Even his charge of the *philosophes*' indiscriminate conflation of fanaticism and religion was, of course, a standard anti-*philosophe* complaint. But La Harpe's emphatic focus on this theme and his innovative concentration on the power of language to transform and disfigure were in many ways original, bearing, as the leading revolutionary historian, Lynn Hunt, has recognized, more than cursory dismissal.[117] Undoubtedly, his argument as a whole suffered the exact same fault of which he accused the *philosophes*—the confusion of the abuse with the thing itself. Nor was this the least of his hypocrisies. With several minor exceptions, La Harpe avoided entirely the issue of his own intimate involvement with the *philosophes*. From a man who had endlessly decried "superstition" and "fanaticism," publicly supporting the Revolution well into 1793, this was hard for many to stomach. Defenders of the *philosophes* spared no opportunity to point out this glaring irony.[118]

Yet for all his rhetorical excess and self-serving avoidance of contrition, La Harpe found an audience eager to bring him into the fold. "Providence has delivered us a savior worthy of praise," rejoiced the *Annales religieuses* in the first of several glowing reviews of the work, "a man who, not a priest, cannot be accused of bias, a man whom the enemies of religion must fear all the more because he has observed them first hand."[119] The *Journal général de France* concurred, musing that "it perhaps took a man, like Saint Augustine, a renegade from the party of error, to truly know, to de-mask, to pursue and crush falsity with so much superiority and force."[120] "This is a work that ought to be translated into every language," raved the *Actes des Apôtres*, commending La Harpe's "noble style," and his "firm, tight, argumentative logic" in a number of admiring articles.[121] The *Déjeuner* resisted the temptation to cite long extracts from the text, emphasizing instead that *Du Fanatisme* "ought to be read in its entirety," for it was a work whose "every page" resounds with "virtuous indignation," "sweet religion," and the "imprint of genius."[122] La Harpe's "imperious logic, his inflexible reason, and his firm and moving eloquence," provided convincing evidence, remarked *Le Véridique*, that La Harpe was fighting "on the side of God Himself."[123] As *L'Historien* summarized, the philosophic apostasy of this "cherished disciple of Voltaire" presented a clear triumph for Christianity."[124]

However outlandish this praise, it left little doubt about the warm and widespread reception granted to La Harpe by the men and women who shared his hostility toward the *philosophes*. The tremendous success of *Du Fanatisme* is instructive, illustrating not only the growing willingness in France, as elsewhere, to countenance the most damning indictments of *philosophie* but also a general shift toward reexamining former beliefs in light of the revolutionary experience. La Harpe was perhaps the most dramatic example of one moved to disavow his former convictions, but he was not alone:

> M. de La Harpe is not the only one whom the Revolution has cured of being a sage. How many have deserted the banner of *philosophie* since this epoch began! How many blind and passionate admirers of Voltaire, of Raynal, of Jean-Jacques, and other poisoners of humanity have smashed their statues and burned their books! How many have been disabused of the grand words—tolerance and humanity, charity and liberty—that have seduced so many dupes![125]

As we shall see in the next chapter, there was truth to the claim. The cataclysms of the age were dissolving recently cherished convictions, undermining the certainties of the time. "The great phrase of the day," Maistre commented in a characteristic flash of acuity, was *Je n'y comprend rien*—"I don't understand anything."[126] In such an environment, the anti-*philosophe* discourse provided the means to comprehend. Persuasively simple and comfortingly familiar, the same charges that had fallen on deaf ears during the Old Regime now commanded attention.

La Harpe's conversion was thus indicative of a wider cultural transformation. Bearing testimony to the stirrings of a nascent religious revival, it underscored how effectively enemies of the Enlightenment were able to spread their view of the French past in the aftermath of the Terror, consolidating a causal explanation of the Revolution and a construction of the Enlightenment that would endure. At the same time, they were working to consolidate their political vision of the French present and future. As Barruel emphasized in 1797, contemporaries must "instruct themselves through the misfortunes of the past" and "draw the necessary lessons."[127] But to draw—let along to apply—these lessons remained a great challenge under the government of the Directory, and after the Fructidor coup of 1797 it was an impossibility. Putting a temporary end to a royalist resurgence, the coup reinstated men of a more committed revolutionary cast, resulting in the suppression of the right-wing press and increased vigilance over suspected Bourbon sympathizers. La Harpe, among others, fled Paris, accompanied, amusingly, by his new friend Richer-Sérizy.[128] Others followed or went into hiding. They would return, with far greater force, during the reign of Napoleon, using more propitious circumstances to refine the principles on which France and the world might build the future.

CHAPTER *4*

On what, then, is based this great

clamor that rises up today against

the *philosophes* and *philosophie*?

—*L'Antidote* (1800)

In those days, we could only

arrive at politics through

literature. Bonaparte's police

listened between the lines.

—Chateaubriand, Preface,

Mélanges littéraires

CONCRETE LITERARY POLITICS DURING
THE REIGN OF NAPOLEON

*L*ate in 1800, an ephemeral publication in Paris complained of a
sea change in French culture. A "great clamor rises up today
against the *philosophes* and *philosophie*," the journal lamented,
drawing attention to a bevy of familiar names—La Harpe, Clément,
Genlis, Grosier, and Geoffroy—as well as to the younger partisans,
Chateaubriand, Fiévée, Esmenard, and their many "collaborators . . .
not worthy of being named." Writing for such newly reestablished
newspapers and reviews as the *Année littéraire*, the *Journal des débats*,
and the *Mercure*, these men and women, together with their sacerdotal
allies, formed a "black militia" that aimed to "hunt down and extermi-
nate" *philosophes*. They were, the author alleged, "the principal directors of our present morale."[1]

Rhetorical, inflated, and deeply anticlerical, a journal that depicted
the sexual corruption of ten-year-old boys as being among the Catholic
priesthood's more noteworthy contributions to Western civilization
could hardly be counted on for dispassionate cultural commentary. Still,
the review's very title, *L'Antidote*, was indicative of a widespread feeling
among defenders of the *philosophes* that they were losing ground before
a powerful new onslaught. Just as anti-*philosophes* had long inveighed
against *philosophie* as a poison that was infecting the body of France, insinuating its way into even the remotest corners, pro-*philosophes* now
derided "anti-*philosophie*" as a ravaging virus of epidemic proportions.
"Fanaticism is spreading every day with fresh success," complained *La
Décade philosophique, littéraire et politique*—a journal founded by the
ideologues to maintain the ideals of the *philosophes*—"dominating the
beau monde, finding apologists amongst our men of letters, our *beaux
esprits*, and becoming the fashion even in our novels."[2] Marie-Joseph
Chénier, a former *conventionnel* and present member of the National Institute, agreed, satirizing the "new saints" of the anti-*philosophe* crusade
in a long, scurrilous poem, warning that they were "numerous, zealous," and preached their message everywhere—in "sermons, journals,
novels, and songs." "*Pour la philosophie, oh!*," Chénier mockingly complained, "*c'est le temps passé*."[3]

Philosophie had not completely run its course in France, a point that anti-*philosophes* themselves emphasized consistently. In journals such as *La Décade*, *Le Citoyen français*, *Le Journal de Paris*, and *Le Publiciste*; in the halls of the National Institute and the Athenée; in the circle of the ideologues; and in the persons of such important Napoleonic advisers as P.-L. Roederer and Joseph Fouché, the *philosophes* found devoted and able defenders. Yet if the days of *philosophie* had not entirely passed, if the complaints of its disciples were polemical and overstated, it was nonetheless true, as the *Antidote* emphasized, that the lines of debate in France were shifting significantly. Until only recently a persecuted minority, forced to conduct their campaigns in exile, in hiding, and in fear of revolutionary reprisals, anti-*philosophes* could now boast a burgeoning cultural authority. As a commentator in the *Journal des débats* gloated in early 1802, "Just a few years ago, those who called themselves *philosophes* . . . dominated despotically. . . . Today, this is no longer the case. . . . Religious men, friends of order, may now make themselves heard."[4]

Writing years later from the safety of the Restoration, Chateaubriand would look back on this period as a seminal moment in French history, crediting these same "friends of order" with guiding the country through a difficult moment of transition. "When France, tired of anarchy, settled into despotism," he observed, "[these men] formed a sort of league . . . to bring us back, through sane literary doctrines, to the conservative doctrines of society."[5] Chateaubriand's collaborator, Charles-Marie Dorimond de Feletz, was even more explicit, claiming that this league acted as a "sort of opposition to the tyranny of [Napoleon]." Speaking to a "new generation . . . tired of pernicious doctrines, and enlightened by their sad results," these critics put forth a "course of literary, philosophic, moral, and religious principles" tailored to a new age.[6]

However self-congratulatory, there was truth to these observations. Although historians have largely ignored the fact, the turn of the century was a critical moment in the coalescence of what Chateaubriand termed "conservative doctrines." In the first half of Napoleon's reign and under his aegis, anti-*philosophes* consolidated their political vision of the Right, refining a set of principles on which enemies of the Revolution would trade for years to come. In certain respects, as we shall see, these principles undercut the legitimacy of Napoleon's rule, lending credence to the claim that they fueled opposition to his reign. Yet in other ways, Napoleon was able to exploit them for his own benefit, using the anti-*philosophes* as he was able to use their enemies—the much celebrated, perhaps overdiscussed ideologues. In the end, his instrumental, symbiotic relationship with the antiphilosophic "league" was probably of greater consequence in defining the character of his reign than his fleeting dalliance with the *philosophes'* heirs.

Napoleon, the Revolution, and Anti-*Philosophie*

Shortly after Napoleon Bonaparte's infamous coup d'état of 18 Brumaire (November 9, 1799), the Corsican general abruptly declared that the Revolution was over, "established on the principles which began it."[7] At once ambiguous and sanguine, the statement papered over the contentious question of what in fact the principles of 1789 were, and denied the obvious: the Revolution, at this stage, still lived. In the summer preceding the events of Brumaire, neo-Jacobins had once again demonstrated that they remained a significant political force, mounting a sustained offensive in the press, reviving political activity in their Parisian and provincial clubs, and forcing a shakeup in the Directory in the month of Prairial—activity that served, however disingenuously, as the immediate pretext of Napoleon's coup. Popular royalism, too, re-emerged in 1799, with peasant rebels (*chouans*) and émigré conspirators taking to arms in the Vendée and the Midi. Finally, French forces, brandishing the *tricolore,* continued to engage allied armies throughout Europe. To say that the Revolution was over was an assertion based more on hope than on reality.

Napoleon was well aware of these ambiguities. In fact, he exploited them fully to forge a delicate path between revolutionary and counter-revolutionary extremes. Eschewing clear ideological commitment in favor of practical expediency, he vowed to rule above the factions in the spirit of reconciliation, combining calculated repression with strategic accommodation to both coerce and cajole. On the one hand, he effectively quelled Jacobinism as an active force, closing down its organs of publication, preventing meetings and assemblies, and in 1801 deporting or executing 130 prominent leaders for past political crimes. On the other hand, he stamped out the popular royalist rebellions in the west and south. But although he did not hesitate to use violence there when necessary (and would do so again later when it served his interests, most notoriously in the brutal kidnapping and assassination of the Bourbon prince, the duc d'Enghien, in 1804), he also displayed, to a much greater degree than in his dealings with the Left, a willingness to compromise.[8] Thus, he quickly moved to efface the most "hideous traces of revolutionary government," extending a conciliatory hand to moderate Catholic and royalist opponents of the Revolution. In a series of successive measures, he allowed Christians to resume worship on Sundays;

abolished the oath of hatred of royalty; ended the commemoration of the execution of Louis XVI; and ordered solemn obsequies for Pope Pius VI at the time of his death in 1799, quickly making known his willingness to work constructively with Pius's successor, Pius VII. Simultaneously, Napoleon drastically reduced the list of proscribed émigrés, ignoring or overturning revolutionary legislation that exacted punitive measures against exiles and their families.

The immediate result of these policies was to encourage a religious revival already gathering force in France (one that would be officially sanctioned with the signing of the Concordat in July 1801), as well as to hasten the return, in significant numbers, of lay royalists and refractory priests.[9] In most cases, their return was not a sign of active support for the new regime. Initially, many émigrés hoped that Bonaparte would use his privileged place to restore the monarchy, and even when it became apparent that these hopes were unfounded, there is little evidence to suggest that large numbers of returning royalists embraced Napoleon with any enthusiasm.[10] The majority viewed him only as a tolerable alternative to ten years of social upheaval. As a popular royalist *bon mot* of the period emphasized, "One does not love Bonaparte, one prefers him."[11] Considering Napoleon's suppression of the Jacobins, his successes on the battlefield, and after 1801 the blessing and sanction of the pope, it made sense to await the Bourbons in France. No less a defender of throne and altar than the abbé Barruel saw the logic of this position, returning to his homeland in 1802.[12] He was not alone.

Given that in the early stages of his rule Napoleon's regime was more gravely threatened by the Right than by the Left, this policy of tolerance and tactical compromise was certainly not without risk—a point pressed on him by numerous republican advisors. Yet in the short term at least, the gamble paid off. Isolating the Bourbon pretender and the dwindling group of unreconciled monarchists who remained beyond the frontiers, the policy effectively neutralized the armed Counter-Revolution, reducing it to a series of hapless conspiracies and assassination attempts. In the longer run, though, it introduced into France a significant number of men and women who shared a deep hostility to the Revolution and who were little inclined to view Napoleon as more than a temporary expedient. Not only did they hesitate to rally actively to the new regime, but also their more outspoken members—in particular a group of anti-*philosophe* journalists—clamored tirelessly against the Revolution, reviving its cultural battles and eventually proving to be a thorn in Napoleon's side.

The men and women who waged this fight, dubbed disparagingly by *La Décade* as "the apostles of prejudice," were a diverse lot.[13] They included refractory priests like the abbé Étienne-Antoine Boulogne; repentant *philosophe* fellow travelers and early supporters of the Revolution like La Harpe and Louis de Fontanes; radical revolutionaries reborn like Jean-Joseph Dussault; long-time anti-*philosophe* partisans including Geoffroy, Grosier, Clément, and Madame de Genlis; leading émigré ideologues and emissaries such as Louis de Bonald and Joseph Fiévée; and a legion of younger writers marked by the upheavals of the revolutionary experience, of whom the most famous was Chateaubriand. Having lived long in exile or been banished more recently, following the Directory's post-Fructidor purge in 1797, they slipped back into France in the wake of Napoleon's ascension, grouping together in Paris and forming, as more than one alarmed republican charged, a "party." This accusation they only half denied, claiming disingenuously that the "First Consul ha[d] declared that . . . there no longer existed parties in France." Yet they worked closely together, frankly acknowledging their formation of an "ever-growing cabal" to "dethrone the gods of *philosophie*," and they proudly assumed the mantle of "anti-*philosophe*."[14] As Geoffroy explained in the *Année littéraire*, refounded with the abbé Grosier in 1800, "If, in order to merit this epithet, it is enough to combat atheists, bad writers, fools, in a word the undergrowth of the human race, oh yes, we are anti-*philosophes*. If by that word one means friends of order, of law, of peace, of religion, the enemies of factions and disturbers of civil tranquillity, yes, we are anti-*philosophes*."[15]

Basing their attacks here, as well as in the abbé Boulogne's *Annales philosophiques, morales et littéraires*; Chateaubriand's weekly, the *Mercure de France littéraire et politique*; and the widest-selling daily newspaper of the Napoleonic period, the *Journal des débats*, these anti-*philosophe* polemicists wrote together and fought together, letting loose from 1800 "a furious and venomous campaign against the Enlightenment"[16] (see Figure 17).

To a great degree, this campaign reiterated the portrayal of the *philosophes* and *philosophie* elaborated during the 1790s. In book reviews, editorials, poems, and theater criticism; in long treatises and short essays; anti-*philosophes* continued to build on the construction of the Enlightenment worked out in the wake of the Terror, grafting *philosophie* ever closer to the Revolution and its excesses while continuing to present eighteenth-century *philosophie* in the sweeping, dismissive terms of their predecessors. When I say "philosophy of the eighteenth century," commented Joseph Fiévée concisely and characteristically, "I mean all that is false in morality, in legislation, and politics."[17] The *Mercure* spoke frequently with similar abandon, dismissing the *Ency-*

Figure 17. A satirical rendering from 1804 of the veteran anti-*philosophe* Julien-Louis Geoffroy. The collected writings of Geoffroy and his colleagues are weighed against a single volume of Voltaire, but despite their prolific output the anti-*philosophes* are evidently outmatched.

clopédie as an assemblage of "skepticism, materialism, and atheism," principles on which the philosophic "sect" had organized its "conspiracy" to overthrow the Old Regime.[18] And the *Journal des débats* consistently denounced the eighteenth century in the broadest possible manner. "What we understand by *philosophie*," it explained in 1803,

> is this impious language that teaches the people to disdain the faith of their fathers, this seditious language that teaches them to revolt against authority, this corrupting language that outrages morality, encourages vice, and removes all impediments to the passions . . . this *philosophie*, in short, that sullies nearly every one of the pages of the *philosophes* of the eighteenth century . . . a code of atheism . . . a code of immorality . . . a code of bloody revolt.[19]

One could multiply declamations of this nature *ad infinitum*, for anti-*philosophes* writing under the rule of Napoleon repeated them tirelessly, furthering the process of tying the Enlightenment to the concrete events of the Revolution.

But if in this respect early nineteenth-century anti-*philosophes* merely restated—and widely disseminated—a view of the Enlightenment in large measure already established, there was another aspect to their vitu-perative campaign: the attempt to provide France with the intellectual foundations for a counterrevolutionary rebirth. As the republican *Le Citoyen français* commented in early 1801 with reference to the *Année lit-téraire*, "One sees the faithful friends of throne and altar . . . work without end to ruin republican government and to infect society with the most corrupting principles."[20] To what degree these principles were "corrupting" was a contentious issue. But that the journal possessed "principles"—political principles shared in large part by its anti-*philosophe* allies—was beyond doubt, and that they used the relative tolerance and burgeoning cultural prominence of the first years of Napoleon's rule to spread them was also a certainty. As the French lit-erary historian Paul Bénichou observes aptly, it was in France itself, in the critical first years of the nineteenth century, that "the intellectual capital on which the French Counter-Revolution would trade for the next twenty-five years was gathered and made precise."[21] Just as un-reconciled émigrés continued to develop the ideological foundations for a Bourbon restoration beyond the frontiers, anti-*philosophe* militants within France prepared similar ground. In the process, they consoli-dated their ideological vision of French politics and society, developing a fully articulated language of the Right.

Religion

Central to this language was the valorization of religion. This had al-ways been a key element of the anti-*philosophe* critique, the raison d'être—the *raison d'agir*—of anti-*philosophe* partisans who fought both prior to and during the Revolution. With the renaissance and reflower-ing of the faith at the turn of the century, however, such argumentation assumed even greater force. The Revolution as the realization of *philosophie* proffered striking evidence of religion's truth and necessity and of the corresponding poverty of secular philosophy. As the *Annales de la Religion* observed, "[The truth of Christianity] becomes more sen-sible through the disastrous reign of this immoral *philosophie* that was put in its place. Thus does the darkness of a tempestuous night render all the more precious the rays of the star that enlightens us during the day."[22] The *Annales philosophiques, morales et littéraires* made much the same point, extolling the revelatory role of Providence and going so far as to "thank" this "truly regenerative Revolution" for opening France's eyes to the poverty of *philosophie*.[23]

Not all, perhaps, were as grateful for the events that ensued in the wake of 1789. But insofar as they provided convincing rhetorical "proofs" against their philosophic enemies, the great majority of anti-*philosophes* were deeply beholden to them. The Revolution as the fulfillment of *philosophie* reaffirmed what anti-*philosophes* had always argued, demonstrating more clearly than any mere treatise or polemic the potential depravity of humanity and the absolute necessity of binding religion steadfastly to the social order. To divorce ethics from superordinate sanction, to sever law from religion, was inherently perilous. "Civil law," the *Journal des débats* emphasized, was not enough to "restrain the human passions." It was only a "barrier" that opposed a "torrent." "Divine law," by contrast, presented "an insurmountable dike that continually resists the tide of passions that strike against it."[24] As Chateaubriand argued in his tremendously influential *Génie du christianisme*, "In the present state of society, can you repress an enormous mass of peasants—free and far away from the eye of the magistrate; can you, in the *faubourgs* of a great capital, prevent the crimes of an independent populace without a religion that preaches duties and virtue to all? Destroy religious worship, and you will need a police force, prisons, and an executioner in every village."[25] This, of course, was precisely what the anti-*philosophes* alleged had occurred during the Revolution, and as Chateaubriand observed elsewhere, even such ubiquitous repressive force was inadequate. "It is certain," he noted in the sixth book of the *Génie*, "that when men lose the idea of God, they plunge headlong into every manner of crime—*in spite* of laws and hangmen."[26]

Arguments of this nature were clearly and unabashedly utilitarian, intended to underline the indispensable necessity of religion as a means of social control. But whereas no anti-*philosophe* doubted religion's utility, it is important to stress that for the great majority, religion—and more specifically, the Catholic religion—was not merely useful, it was *true*. At a time when many chastened republicans, such notable fellow travelers of the *philosophes* as Madame de Staël and Benjamin Constant and, of course, Napoleon himself, were acknowledging the *instrumental* importance of religion with precious little faith and more than a touch of Voltairean cynicism, the distinction was critical. To argue that religion was useful but nothing more, necessary to the people but superfluous to the cultivated mind, was dangerous. By foisting religion on the masses while disavowing its veracity, hypocrites introduced corrosive doubt from above, seeking to found society on a lie. As the *Annales philosophiques, morales et littéraires* affirmed in an article devoted to the subject in 1801, "It would be the most revolting impiety against Providence, the most atrocious calumny against mankind, the most bloody outrage against reason, and the most complete reversal of certainty to claim to establish the welfare of society on the basis of a chimera, offering us deception as the basis of world happiness."[27] Religion was only "useful and necessary" insofar that it was "good and true," and thus it was incumbent upon all those who genuinely desired the welfare of society to embrace it with sincerity and conviction.[28] As the experience of the eighteenth century showed all too clearly, when the "directing classes" of a nation allowed their faith to lapse, when *philosophes* were permitted to spread their doctrines with impunity, the rest of society followed.[29] "Christianity," the *Annales de la Religion* confirmed, "desires every knee to bend before the same altar. It has but one law for all, without distinction of rank or knowledge."[30]

To so genuflect before this altar promised not only social stability but also personal happiness. As in so many other respects, the Revolution reaffirmed the emptiness and audacity of the *philosophes'* pretension to achieve human felicity of their own accord, to build a city of man on the foundations of the profane. Prior to the Revolution the *philosophes* had led many to believe, the refractory priest Blanchandin-le-Chêne observed, "that *philosophie* alone could effect the happiness of man. It required the most fatal experience to convince peoples of their incapacity to sustain these pretensions."[31] In truth, *philosophie* left its disciples cold and alone, disenchanted with the world and alienated from all that could give solace and succor.[32] As the *Journal des débats* argued in a remarkable passage,

> Nothing is more suited than this metaphysics [of *philosophie*] to dry up—to the bottom of the heart—every source of felicity. It substitutes abstractions in place of sentiments, desiccates and stains the soul, sucks the color from the canvas of the universe, snuffs out every flower of life on the vine, and destroys happiness by dint of analysis. In reasoning on every one of our duties, in submitting every one of our penchants to calculus, we finish by taking away from them this charm that is the natural recompense of good sentiments and healthy actions. All becomes reasoning, computation, combination.[33]

"True philosophy," that is, Christianity, was "the surest guarantor of happiness." Consisting of "fulfilling one's duties, submitting oneself to necessity," and "moderating one's desires" through the light and grace of God, Christianity reenchanted the world, restoring color to life's canvas. In poverty or in splendor, in times of joy or adversity, the Christian could "abandon himself with confidence to the hand of Providence—this guide that never errs—and enjoy, in advance, the prize that awaits him at the end of life."[34] In the "religious sentiments" of the "heart," the author stressed, in simple "good sense," one could find the repose that so eluded the *philosophe*.[35]

These stark oppositions between cancerous reason and the fecundity of religion, between the insatiable, corrosive doubt of eighteenth-century philosophy and the comforting, regenerative peace of faith, were employed frequently by anti-*philosophes* in the early years of the century. Marked by a neo-Pascalian emphasis on the truth of sentiment and the shortcomings of reason, they presented Christianity as a repository of certainty in a world of doubt.[36] As a later article in the *Journal des débats* confirmed, "Human reason is limited, and the desires of men are infinite. Excited, without end, by an insatiable curiosity to rush toward the first principles of our being, reason will necessarily fall into the most deplorable errors, unless it is restrained by an irresistible authority."[37] Catholicism was this authority—a consoling shepherd to which the flock could be led by the very yearnings for happiness that *philosophie* summoned but did not fulfill. It was by listening "to the objections" of one's own "heart," Chateaubriand and others emphasized with increasing resonance, by seeking to appease the "desire for happiness that torments us" continually but that "the entire universe does not satisfy," it was thus that one could find the nurturing "breast of God," there that one could quench the "thirst for felicity" and taste drops of the eternal happiness that awaited beyond the grave.[38]

Such warm, maternal images, however, such talk of social harmony and personal tranquillity, should not eclipse the harsher side of this language. If anti-*philosophes* offered the gentle "yoke" of religion as a means to individual happiness and social stability, many prescribed a much sterner harness for those who refused to submit willingly to religion's restraints. To tolerate error in the face of truth was to foolishly imperil both individual souls and society as a whole, a fatal mistake committed by the late rulers of the Old Regime and one that must not be repeated again. "We know," commented a contributor to the *Mercure* in 1802, "that the former government contributed to its ruin by according a foolish tolerance to the firebrands who melted its authority and who attacked religion. This is enough to decry all manner of political and religious tolerance."[39] In more cases than not, the journal seemed inclined to favor such blanket censure, repeatedly denouncing the *tolérantisme* of the *philosophes* while stressing the perils of religious and political indifference.[40]

The basis of this anti-*philosophe* argument against tolerance was twofold. On the one hand, anti-*philosophes* repeated the claim that the *philosophes'* doctrine of *tolérance*—what Louis de Bonald described as the "stronghold of the philosophy of the last century"—was really a hypocritical strategy of total "indifference" to all religious opinion.[41] To advocate the tolerance of conflicting moral and religious beliefs was to renounce the central question of religious truth, something the *philosophes* did quite happily throughout the eighteenth century. By affecting to tolerate any religious belief, they revealed their disdain for all, undercutting the foundations of moral certainty of religious experience in general and of Catholic Christianity in particular. On the other hand, pernicious in and of itself, this doctrine was doubly so because the *philosophes* themselves did not practice what they preached. "Hypocritical extollers of tolerance," they "persecuted all those who combated them," both prior to the Revolution and then during it, when, imbued with power, they revealed plainly the true meaning of their doctrine.[42] "As soon as it was seated on the throne," Bonald observed in a familiar refrain, this "doctrine [of tolerance] that had promised the happiness of kings and the liberty of peoples, massacred the ones and enchained the others."[43]

It followed from these assertions that men and women properly enlightened to the true principles of religion, morality, and government should necessarily be intolerant. As an author in the *Journal des débats* observed, "It has been said that the Christian religion is intolerant. If by this it is meant that it is the only divine religion . . . and that this separates it from all other religions, then yes, I admit frankly its intolerance."[44] To remain indifferent to error while in possession of truth was not only perilous but also absurd. As Bonald confirmed, "The most enlightened man would be he who is the least indifferent, the least tolerant regarding opinions." What was true for individuals was even more so for society as a whole. "The more enlightened a society," he continued, "the less one finds absolute tolerance, or indifference regarding opinions."[45]

Both Bonald and his cohorts hastened to add that this was not a prescription for the persecutory violence proscribed by the Gospel—what Madame de Genlis described as the "cruelties, and pyres of the inquisition."[46] Yet their reasoning fully supported a rigorous censorship of opinion. As Bonald stressed, the *philosophes*' cry of freedom of thought—*liberté de penser*—was, like tolerance itself, a sophism, analogous to demanding the freedom of the circulation of the blood. God himself did not seek to curtail this liberty; nor could the most capricious tyrant. But the demand for "freedom of thought" was in reality something else—the demand to "think out loud," the demand to spread one's opinions freely, the demand to "act." To allow this would be to willfully subvert "peace and good order," to "overthrow society from top to bottom"—political and religious folly of the highest degree.[47] The mistake had been made, and it should not be made again. As the indomitable Antoine Sabatier insisted, "One would have to be extremely blind to deny that the first and most important cause of the Revolution was the abuse of this magic and terrible art" of writing and publishing. To "regenerate the European mind," then, it was indispensable that religious and political authorities "took away from individuals the means to print." Sabatier urged "a league and union" against the "anarchic and philosophic spirit," advising rulers to "expropriate the exclusive use of printing presses, to suppress papers . . . to purge public and private libraries of all licentious works, and to destroy all literary societies."[48] The *Journal des débats* recommended action of an equally repressive sort. After castigating the works of Rousseau, d'Alembert, Voltaire, and Helvétius, the paper noted, "To justify these *philosophes*, it would be necessary to begin by burning their books, and it is precisely this that we desire."[49] Less attentive to sordid details, Madame de Genlis pressed a similar case: "Religious intolerance was so useful, so necessary to kings and to the tranquillity of peoples, that without it, no political system of government [could] be perfect."[50] In this way was the great battle cry of the Enlightenment transformed into a word of opprobrium. Tolerance was only weakness and indifference to truth.

The Patriarchal Family

Religion—stern, unyielding, intolerant religion—provided the sine qua non of harmonious social relations, personal happiness, and good government. It was, however, merely one of a constellation of sources on which anti-*philosophes* drew in forging their image of a well-ordered society. Of near equal importance was the family. The womb of morality, the cradle in which the young imbibed patterns of deference, respect, and duty that shaped their comportment in the world at large, the family bore heavily on the quality of government of any society. As the *Mercure* observed in 1801, "the experience of all centuries teaches us, in effect, that upon the good or bad constitution of the family depends . . . that of the state."[51]

Anti-*philosophes* prior to the Revolution had frequently invoked the essential unity of the family and the state, reiterating long-standing models of patriarchal authority that portrayed the family as a monarchy and the monarchy as a family. At the same time, they warned that the *philosophes'* advocacy of secular marriage, sexual license, divorce, and limitations on the power of fathers over children was tearing apart the social fabric—an admonition that was seemingly confirmed by the revolutionary experience. For in addition to their onslaught on the political institutions of the Old Regime, the revolutionaries undertook a vast overhaul of legislation regarding the family. Abolishing the sacramental basis of conjugal union, they rendered marriage a purely civil institution—a mere contract—that allowed partners to join in matrimony without regard for divine sanction. Legalizing divorce, they flouted the indissolubility of this sacred tie, enabling spouses to separate through mutual consent or through incompatibility of character, asserted by either sex. And curtailing the *puissance paternelle* of the Old Regime father, they abolished his right to incarcerate errant children through a *lettre de cachet* and scaled back his control over property, inheritance, and the careers and marriage choices of his offspring.[52] The result, anti-*philosophes* charged, was a domestic anarchy that mirrored perfectly the political anarchy of the Revolution. As the *Année littéraire* stressed in 1801, "The family is the image of the state. Domestic government is intimately tied to public government—the one cannot be altered without the other suffering."[53] The devastation wrought by the Revolution extended into hearth and home.

The charge of the Revolution's destruction of the patriarchal family would prove a staple of conservative thought well into the twentieth century.[54] It was rendered a commonplace by the anti-*philosophe* polemic of the Napoleonic period. The state of French domestic life, all agreed, was bleak.[55] Only through the regeneration of the family could France as a whole be restored. While Napoleonic administrators labored in the first four years of the nineteenth century to complete a Civil Code that would govern the legal aspects of all manner of French life, including matters domestic, anti-*philosophes* carried out a heated campaign to reestablish the family on sound foundations. In the process, they completed the construction of patriarchy they had begun under the Old Regime.

Of primary importance in this regard were two salient principles to which anti-*philosophe* partisans returned repeatedly: the restoration of the authority of fathers, allegedly destroyed during the Revolution, and the abolition of divorce. In reference to the former, the *Mercure* proclaimed in 1801, "Amongst the first questions of morality and legislation, there is not a single one that is more worthy of consideration, in all its aspects, than that of paternal power."[56] Rooted in nature, established in history, and confirmed by the revelation of scripture, patriarchy, anti-*philosophes* argued, constituted the basis on which all other social relations were built. As the *Journal des débats* observed,

> Paternal authority is the foundation of morality and of society. The enemies of all manner of authority, the fiery partisans of a chimerical equality, the most extravagant men . . . sought to overthrow the natural and legitimate authority that fathers exercise over their children in

the heart of their hereditary homes. Neither the testimony of history nor the example of the ancient legislation that they decided to destroy completely could restrain these madmen whose ignorance was matched only by their perversity.[57]

The revolutionaries' attack on paternal authority, their attempt to carry "liberty and equality" into the heart of the family, was seen as a necessary concomitant, at once cause and effect, of their wider assault on political authority.[58] Parricide, anti-*philosophes* believed, went hand in hand with regicide, for in the power of fathers over children and husbands over wives, they saw enshrined the elemental principles of hierarchy, deference, obligation, and responsibility that constituted the central foundation of the well-ordered society. The very term "power," Bonald observed, was "in every religious and political society called *paternity*," just as subjects were called "children."[59] To subvert it in either its domestic or public forms was to undo a central restraint that bound together all members of the social order. Just as religion harnessed the will of individuals by instilling in them a sense of duty to a higher source, so did the authority of fathers foster obeisance, respect, and interdependence—principles that when consecrated by religion formed the core of social virtues. "Morals," the *Journal des débats* continued, "are the laws of families. To strike a blow at paternal power is to attack them at their source. To surround the patriarchal throne with all the attributes that belong to it, to honor it with all the veneration that is due, is to confirm . . . the foundations of morality."[60]

Such assertions rested unabashedly on belief in the inherent inferiority of women, or at least on their starkly different prerogatives. Men, under God, provided the source of power in the family, as in society at large, and women assumed a subsidiary role. "Sensible wives, tender mothers, loving links of society, friends of order and moderation, of morality and religion—voilà all that woman should be, and all that nature has intended them to be," commented the *Journal des débats*.[61] "To live for our happiness," echoed the *Mercure*, "to be the end of our hopes—this is the lot of women in this world."[62] Sentiments of this sort were common and in themselves did not differ markedly from republican encomiums that praised women as good mothers and domestic keepers. Yet anti-*philosophes* of this period added another quality to their praise: extravagant regard for specifically feminine religiosity. "Women are born for religion, and they carry its sentiment to a degree of delicacy that men rarely attain," commented the *Année littéraire*.[63] "Of all the virtues that women possess," the *Mercure* seconded, "there are none that are more ardent than the tender and religious virtues."[64]

Possibly reflecting the salient role played by women in the religious revival that began in the late 1790s, lauding declarations of this type in any case bestowed on women a central mission.[65] Whereas the patriarchal father ruled, like God and the sovereign, with justice that was necessarily stern and strong, tender mothers elicited the sweeter side of the faith. Through their ministry, they rendered the home an organic whole in which authority was coupled with compassion.[66] As Chateaubriand rhapsodized,

> The wife of the Christian is not a simple mortal: she is an extraordinary, mysterious, angelic being. She is the flesh and blood of her husband, and man, in uniting with her, does nothing less than take back a part of his substance. His body, his soul are incomplete without her. He has force, she has beauty. He combats the enemy and works the field of the *patrie*, but he understands nothing of domestic detail. Women is necessary to him to prepare his bed and his meals. He has sorrows, and she accompanies him at night in order to pacify them. His days are difficult and troubled, but he finds her chaste arms in his bed, and he forgets all his woes. Without woman, he would be hard, coarse, and solitary. Woman suspends around him the flowers of life. . . . [67]

With such stark oppositions between male virility and female softness, between masculine engagement in the world and chaste, feminine withdrawal to the home, passages like these read as if they were culled directly from the pages of Rousseau's *Émile*. Given Chateaubriand's acknowledged debt to the Genevan philosopher, they may have been. Yet the comparison extends beyond simple literary and stylistic influence, highlighting, once again, the peculiar convergence between the political thought of the Right and the more radical republican tradition both shaped in the image of Rousseau. Shorn of its Christian trappings, this anti-*philosophe* language bears more than a passing resemblance to the profoundly masculinist rhetoric that a number of leading scholars have identified as central to classical republican thought in the eighteenth century and, as a consequence, to the political culture of Jacobinism.[68] In this influential view, a gendered ideology of two spheres, which banished women from public life and relegated them to the home, was born in the eighteenth century from republican discourse and so made central to modern constructions of male hegemony. Several scholars have taken this important argument even further, asserting that not only Jacobinsim and the Rousseauian republican tradition were marked by this gendered discourse (a claim that would seem irrefutable) but also that the Enlightenment, liberalism, and modern civil society as a whole were profoundly structured by inherently misogynist assumptions, marked, as it were, at their birth.[69]

These latter (far stronger) claims are controversial and, indeed, have drawn sharp criticism from scholars quick to point out the perils of reifying the Enlightenment and/or of conflating Jacobinism, classical liberalism, and modern civil society.[70] What few of these observers have recognized, however, is the degree to which enemies of the Enlightenment attacked the *philosophes* as patriarchy's greatest scourge, men responsible for weakening, not empowering, the authority of fathers and the prerogatives of men in public life. Though the anti-*philosophes'* assessements of their enemies' positions were seldom pristine, it does seem clear that the *philosophes* were hardly the eighteenth century's most prodigious patriarchs or the greatest advocates of the exclusion of women from the public sphere. That dubious honor belongs to their enemies, who were engaged in constructing an image of paternal and patriarchal authority from the Right at the very time that Rousseau and his Jacobin heirs were building a new republican image of masculine authority from the Left. Arguably, it was this strange convergence that caught up more radical defenders of women's rights in the middle, displacing them, with women themselves, from the public sphere. Those commentators intent on seeing male hegemony as central to modernity should at least accord its greatest defenders their due. It was precisely in defense of interests perceived as threatened—first by the Enlightenment and then by the Revolution—that Counter-Enlightenment forces shaped their own self-conscious justification of patriarchy that would play a central part in right-wing discourse into the twentieth century. In the strong, near-absolute power of the father; the subservient, ministerial role of the mother; and the passive obedience of the child, anti-*philosophes* and their successors discerned "the source," as the *Mercure* observed, "of the great majority of relationships and obligations of civil society."[71]

It followed naturally from this conviction that to allow the willful dissolution of the family—divorce—was unthinkable.[72] Not only did divorce induce deep personal suffering, explicitly contradict Catholic teaching, and reject the experience of centuries, but it also introduced a dangerous principle of individual license and revolt at the most basic, constituent level of society. It was on this social plane that anti-*philosophes* saw the question's greatest import. As Bonald observed in one of the many extracts of his monumental *Du Divorce*, carried in the *Mercure* and the *Journal des débats*, "The question of the indissolubility of the conjugal tie is the first of all social questions after the existence of God."[73]

In Bonald's judgment—shared widely by anti-*philosophe* partisans—divorce was the twin product of the Protestant Reformation and "modern philosophy." Bearing the seeds of the spirit of independence by which both these movements had flouted political and religious authority, the practice reduced the most sacred of human bonds to a contract that could be negotiated and dissolved through the caprice of individuals. It was no coincidence, Bonald argued, that the Revolution had admitted divorce, for by treating marriage as a purely voluntary association formed for the convenience and gratification of its members, the revolutionaries gave expression to their larger political philosophy—one that likewise saw human society as a contrivance erected for the fulfillment of individual pleasure, not as a necessary, natural, and divinely consecrated means of attaining order. By allowing individuals to freely break their marital ties, the revolutionaries reproduced in the family the same subjective impulse at work in the democratic state, establishing on every level the insidious principle that all human society was a contract, to be constituted or dissolved at will. This, Bonald maintained, was a principle as dangerous as it was false. The family, like the state, was a natural institution bestowed by God to provide human order. When consecrated with his blessing, it could not be freely disbanded. To do so was to sever the link that bound divine power to secular institutions, opening the way to the anarchy of which the Revolution provided the most graphic illustration.[74]

To restore French society to health, then, it was necessary to abolish this terrible practice. "Divorce . . . destroys the natural links of the family . . . introducing democracy there," the *Annales philosophiques, morales et littéraires* warned in a glowing review of *Du Divorce*. "It will produce the same effects in the State [unless abolished]."[75] Evidently, Napoleon did not agree. Although the completed Civil Code of 1804 took pains to reestablish the strong authority of the father in domestic relations, it nonetheless allowed for divorce in certain circumstances—largely upon Napoleon's personal insistence.[76] Given the proscription against commenting directly on imperial law, anti-*philosophes* remained silent. But in light of the heated polemic conducted against the practice in the first years of the century, their dissatisfaction was undoubtedly great.[77]

History

If in the microcosm of the family anti-*philosophes* found a rich source of principles from which to create their image of the well-constituted society, they turned with equal relish to history for instruction and guidance. "History," the *Journal des débats* proclaimed, "is politics in action and morality in practice."[78] The font of wisdom and the record of lived experience, the past defined the parameters of the present. It is in history, the *Mercure* reaffirmed, that "one must investigate what we were, in order to know what, and why, we are."[79] This elemental truth—proclaimed endlessly by anti-*philosophes*—was one, they charged, that the *philosophes* of the eighteenth century had entirely ignored. "It is above all in the practice of history," the *Mercure* asserted typically in a glowing review of the abbé Gérard's *Les Leçons de l'histoire*, "that the *philosophes* displayed their extreme ignorance and recklessness."[80] Treating the past as a long chronicle of errors, the *philosophes* exploited history not to extract meaning and knowledge but to condemn the putative "darkness" that had preceded their shining "light":

> That which especially characterizes the *philosophes* is their absolute contempt for experience. They regarded all the lessons of the past as so many errors; the maxims consecrated by the wisdom of the centuries were only, in their eyes, superannuated stupidities. Their presumption put the most respectable traditions amongst the number of most ridiculous tales. Thus it was in vain that humanity has aged. Thus it was in vain that thousands of years amassed our knowledge, enriching the treasure chest of history and furnishing modern generations with resources of instruction. . . .[81]

Four years later, the *Journal des débats* was still drumming this theme, lavishing scorn on the *philosophes'* "manner of treating history"—one that reduced the record of human achievements to a morality tale, a "fable," in which were recounted nothing but the "disorders, wars, public and private misfortunes, and other crimes carried out by Despotism and Superstition."[82]

Such arrogant refusal to look honestly at the record of human achievement, anti-*philosophes* agreed, had not only distorted the past—slandering, to take but one prominent example, the notable contributions of Christianity to Western civilization—but had also deeply perverted the *philosophes'* view of the present. Foregoing lived experience and concrete example, the *philosophes* based their theories on nebulous abstractions and false ideals, the most elemental being their appraisal of human nature. A former lawyer and member of the Council of Five Hundred, Joseph Bernardi, observed that "the fundamental error of the *philosophes*" was to treat men and women "not as they are, but as they had conceived them," imputing an inherent goodness to humanity that flew in the face of the historical record.[83] "When one leaves the cloudy regions of *Philosophie*," he continued, "putting aside all these dreams of the natural goodness of men to consider them in the light of the experience of all times, the scene becomes very different." The record of history provided vivid testimony of human capacity for evil, offering a vast "tableau of the excesses, the outrages, and the cruelties which men in all times had carried out against their fellows."[84] To close one's eyes to the darker side of human nature was to embark on all discussions of political matters from a false point of departure. "Every theory made by man," Bonald emphasized, "that begins by refusing to recognize his true nature . . . is an absurdity."[85]

History, then, provided empirical evidence of the truth that Christian moralists, in the tradition of Augustine, found embedded in Scripture: human nature was flawed, corrupted, marred by a tendency to evil, and impaired by the limitations of reason. Confirmed graphically by the recent experience of the Revolution, this truth reaffirmed the need for strong social institutions—religion, the family, and the state—to harness errant mortals. It also gave the lie to hopes for the moral perfectibility of humankind espoused, anti-*philosophes* charged, by the *philosophes*. As Geoffroy stressed in a hostile review of Madame de Staël's *De la Littérature considérée dans ses rapports avec les institutions sociales* (1800), a work that argued for the progressive moral perfection of humanity,

> Not only does human reason not perfect itself with time, but this perfection is impossible. It would be necessary to discover new relationships among men, new duties, new moral truths—something that cannot take place in the wake of the Gospel. . . . Nothing beyond Christian morality has been discovered. It is evident that it is the *non plus ultra* of true philosophy, that it is beyond the capacity of human faculties to go farther.[86]

Even for nonbelievers, Geoffroy continued, two thousand years of history testified to the "fact" that the *philosophes*' "system of perfectibility" was a hopeless illusion. Nowhere in the chaotic tumult of secular beliefs and social structures that littered the past could one locate an indefinite march of progress. An article in the *Journal des débats* entitled "Sur la perfectibilité" made this point emphatically, arguing that history provided evidence that nations, like individuals, waxed and waned in keeping with human limitations:

> Indefinite perfectibility is nothing but a brilliant chimera. All things human have their progress and their limits, their growth and their decline. History teaches us that a nation has its days of obscurity and its days of glory, its epochs of barbarism and its epochs of refinement: here the excess of ignorance, there an excess of reason. Between the two lies the road of wisdom and truth. The moment that we stray from this route, we degenerate.[87]

All of these writers admitted that in one area alone, the natural sciences, humanity had made sustained advances. In astronomy, chemistry, physics, and geometry, new discoveries based on long observation and painstaking research had led to novel inventions and to an increased understanding of the physical world. Yet to deduce from this "incontestable progress" the corollary progress of the capacity of human reason, of morality, and of the art of governance was unsustainable folly.[88] Advances in science "added nothing to the competence of the soul," impinged in no way on the eternal principles of morality, affected not in the slightest the laws devised to rule men. "Let us guard against calculating the progress of human reason and social institutions," the *Mercure* implored, "on that of mathematics and physics."[89] This was a fatal occlusion, a millenarian dream, and one that as the experience of the Revolution showed led to catastrophic results. For like all those who believed in the possibility of limitless human progress, the *philosophes* were not content to allow "the progressive march of knowledge to usher in a state of perfect independence and happiness" on its own. They "formed a league to destroy every obstacle that opposed the development of perfectibility," waging unrelenting battle on the manifold vestiges of the past, a "war to the death on prejudice."[90] Picked up, in turn, by the revolutionaries themselves, this utter disdain for history— this utopian belief that one could level all and begin anew—lay behind France's recent horrors. Indeed, the *Mercure* affirmed, in all places and times where "the dream of *philosophic perfection* takes hold of minds . . . empires are threatened by plagues."[91] The "fatal chimera of perfectibility," Geoffroy concurred, the belief that men and society could be remade, regenerated in keeping with an ideal image of perfection, had "covered the earth in blood and crimes."[92]

Prejudice, Custom, and Tradition

The myth of human perfection was born out of blindness to the inherent limitations of humanity, as well as disregard for the lessons of the past. Considering these two factors in their proper light made apparent that the very "obstacles" deemed by *philosophes* as impediments to human progress were rather restraints that were molded by time to prevent human misery. What the *philosophes* termed "prejudices"— inherited customs, traditions, and beliefs—were indispensable sources of social cohesion, wellsprings of sagacity and virtue. As the root of the term in both English and French indicated, prejudices (*préjugés*) were opinions held prior to judgment, prior to reflection. Forged through generations of adaptation to particular circumstances and challenges, they formed the stock of accumulated wisdom of peoples, a body of received beliefs on which individuals could rely in the absence or aid of reason. Without them one was lost. As Joseph Michaud explained in a long article on the subject in the *Mercure*,

> Imagine a man seeking to live without prejudices, and forced, as a result, to examine the motives behind the most diverse customs, the most familiar ideas, the simplest actions. He would be embarrassed at every step; all that experience and time have consecrated would be lost for him. He would be no more advanced than a savage who, for the first time, leaves the forest, without ever having heard of a regulated society [*société policée*].[93]

Surrounding one from birth, prejudices provided a constant source of "authority" and "example." The "product of centuries," they shaped the individual's environment, making of one's work, one's studies, one's pleasure, and "even the most indifferent actions" a sort of "imitation," an "unthinking repetition," a "commonplace." Although Michaud admitted that in certain instances prejudices could "expose [the individual] to . . . errors," in more cases than not they grounded one in "the experience of generations and of a great number of enlightened men." The wise would thus do well to admit that "there is perhaps more wisdom in the centuries than in the books of the *philosophes*."[94]

This was, of course, a classic theme of Edmund Burke. Michaud quoted the great British statesman amply to emphasize that "in place of exploding general prejudices," men and women should "employ their sagacity to discover the latent wisdom that prevails in them."[95] Michaud, however, hardly needed to call on the author of the *Reflections* to give authority to ideas that already formed a stock of received wisdom in their own right. In anti-*philosophe* circles, at least, the defense of prejudice had become a prejudice of its own, a truth "so clear that it need barely be stated."[96] As in so many other respects, the Revolution had laid bare the collected wisdom of the ages.

Lending order and cohesion to society, prejudices were particular to countries and peoples, forming, as one commentator observed, part of "the very air" citizens breathed.[97] It followed naturally that neither they nor the institutions they served to uphold could be readily transferred— a further error, anti-*philosophes* charged, committed by their eighteenth-century adversaries.[98] Not content to abolish French prejudices and institutions, the *philosophes* had sought to replace them with the practices of another country—England. "This love of the English constitution," the *Journal des débats* asserted, "was a type of religion for the *esprits forts*" of the eighteenth century.[99] And "why did the *philosophes* praise England without end?" asked Joseph Fiévée in a long work that condemned the twin errors of *philosophie* and *anglomanie*: "For hatred of France." *Philosophisme* and Anglomania were one.[100]

Accusations of this nature were leveled by anti-*philosophe* polemicists of the Old Regime, who saw in the *philosophes'* praise for England the chief cause of the century's "Anglomania," as well as yet another proof of the *philosophes'* treasonous disloyalty to France. Viewed through the lens of the Revolution and from the perspective of a new sense of the weight and importance of the past, these charges seemed doubly apt. "Every nation that loses the idea of its antiquity," Fiévée asserted, "is necessarily led, through hatred of itself, to undergo the systematic experiments of innovators."[101] It was folly to treat with scorn France's own long and fecund history, and even more so to see in England a country whose institutions and form of government were worthy of emulation. Despite the tireless commendations of the *philosophes*, England was not a model. Not only could the organic laws and traditions of one country not be transferred to another, but also English institutions, in themselves, were wanting. "Is this [English] government so worthy of admiration?" asked Madame de Genlis. In the last two centuries the English people had experienced more "bloody revolutions" than any other country, "forever imprisoning and dethroning its kings, abolishing the monarchical state, hunting down and proscribing the reigning family, and placing foreigners on the throne." In addition, "having changed its religion," "thousands of sects" had formed in England, adding further to the political precariousness of the country. The result, Genlis concluded, was far from inspiring: "Combats, quarrels, and sedition are daily occurrences amongst the English people."[102]

This emphasis on the inherent instability of English society was a common theme, one traceable, anti-*philosophes* argued, to the country's Protestant character and to its chastened monarchy.[103] Having broken definitively with the Catholic Church, England disbanded the essential chain of authority that fastened humans to God, exposing its citizens to the multiplication of heretical cults that ensued in the wake of the Reformation. Hazardous in and of itself, this religious pluralism was all the more so given the temper of independence and revolt that lay at the root of every Protestant heresy. As the *Journal des débats* explained in praising Mathieu-Mathurin Tabaraud's *Histoire du philosophisme anglais, depuis son origine jusqu'à son introduction en France* (Paris, 1806), "[W]hen the reformers of the sixteenth century established that every man was the judge of the doctrine he wanted to receive," they set a dan-

gerous precedent, "consecrating the principle of independence," the belief that the "individual conscience could trust to its own voice," and
throwing off the yoke of authority necessary to the regulation of matters of doctrine.[104]

Deeply ensconced within English society, this terrible principle of individual judgment had resulted not only in philosophic deviations and
the proliferation of religious sects but also in a system of government
that was fundamentally flawed.[105] A monarchy in name alone, England
had seen the power of the crown whittled away by revolution and successive popular encroachment to the point that it was now "almost a republic."[106] With sovereignty residing outside the unity of the throne,
authority was divided and the constitution mixed. As the Revolution
demonstrated, such division of power was perilous. The "most frightening slavery" was "always the certain result of every political combination to weaken authority," the *Mercure* observed in reference to
France's recent past: "Powers cannot be divided."[107] "Every kingdom
divided against itself," Bonald agreed, "will perish." He went on to
argue at length that this would be the fate of England's "mixed constitution," indeed, of "all governments where power is multiple and divided." The future of the West, including the United States, he predicted, with the breadth if not the foresight of Tocqueville, lay in a
return to the only form of natural government—absolute monarchy.
Sooner or later, England, as all other countries, would return to its natural place, "independent royalty, the alpha and omega of all societies."[108]
Not every anti-*philosophe* shared Bonald's robust optimism about the
future of absolute monarchy, but the great majority agreed with him in
staunchly opposing England as a model of government.

Many also shared Bonald's incipient distrust of English political
economy and the new market society that was apparently being fash-
ioned in its image.[109] "The system of Adam Smith reigns today among
us," complained the *Journal des débats* in rehearsal of what would become a more consistent criticism of economic (and political) liberalism
during the Restoration: "He has a mob of admirers."[110] In an article
comparing French and English society, the *Mercure* observed similarly
that during the eighteenth century the "great and generous institutions"
of France had fallen into the "commercial slavery" that had long held
sway in the United Kingdom.[111] The fact that Smith was now being
held up as the "chief" of a "sect of economists" (the ideologues) was a
disturbing sign, a throwback to the discredited eighteenth-century effort to import English models that were as unsuitable as they were unsound.[112] The attempt to regenerate France in the manner of England
had been exposed by the Revolution and clear-eyed observation as an

egregious error, a truth that applied to economic, as well as to political, considerations. As Fiévée affirmed, a "country with fourteen centuries of existence" would do better to look to its own past, "to rummage through [its own] ancient laws," to locate models of good government and socioeconomic organization.[113] In one epoch in particular, he and his anti-*philosophe* partisans agreed, France had achieved a degree of greatness that commended it above all others.

The Great Age of Louis XIV

The valorization of the *beau siècle de Louis-le-Grand* was an incessant, ubiquitous theme of anti-*philosophe* polemicists under Napoleon.[114] They repeatedly expressed their "admiration, so legitimate, so well-founded" for the age of the Sun King, contrasting it in the most unflattering terms with the century that followed.[115] "Today," declared the *Journal des débats*, "now that the prestige of vain theories has dissipated before the torch of experience . . . it is easy to appreciate the superiority of the seventeenth over the eighteenth century.[116] "The eighteenth century grows smaller each day in perspective," Chateaubriand affirmed in what was a pervasive theme of the *Génie du christianisme*, "while the seventeenth century ascends. The one sinks, while the other rises in the heavens."[117] Indeed, the pinnacle achieved under Louis XIV was a graphic illustration of the fallacy of the notion of perfectibility, for all that had ensued in its aftermath, anti-*philosophes* maintained, was decadence and decline. "Since the century of Louis XIV," the *Mercure* proclaimed, "we have been traveling incessantly backward."[118] Whereas in the century of Louis XIV "Christianity was generally recognized as the basis of morality," the eighteenth century had been one of skepticism and irreligion.[119] Whereas in the age of Louis XIV France was "the first nation of the universe" and "looked upon the English people rightly as the very opposite of the French," the eighteenth century had spurned its history and traditions, succumbing to an enervating "Anglomania."[120] Whereas the seventeenth century had been a time of "politeness," "urbanity," and "noble gallantry," the eighteenth century was marked by moral corruption, dissolution, and domestic breakdown.[121] And whereas the great age of Louis XIV had galvanized France in social unity, engendering duty, self-sacrifice, and a sense of honor, the eighteenth century had produced glaring egoism, individualism, and social fracture.[122] "It had taken only a century," Michaud lamented, "for the French to pass from respect to disobedience, from docility to revolt, from the laws of a temperate monarchy to the furors of demagoguery."[123] To speak of perfectibility given such striking contrasts was absurd.

Devout, noble, and self-contained, the age of Louis XIV had produced, as striking evidence of its superiority, a literary culture before which that of the eighteenth century paled by comparison. "What are the *philosophes*," asked the *Journal des débats*, "measured against the powerful geniuses of the century of Louis XIV?" Believing themselves *grands hommes*, they were in reality meager men, petty minds who had seduced in place of ennobling.[124] In the writings of such giants as Bossuet, Racine, Corneille, La Bruyère, La Fontaine, La Rochefoucauld, Pascal, and others, anti-*philosophes* found models of supreme elegance, superior taste, and elevated thought. They lauded the poetic achievements of the seventeenth century, alleging that they had been destroyed by the desiccating, overanalytical spirit of *philosophie*. They praised seventeenth-century dramatists for their harmony and balance and in general asserted the superiority of seventeenth-century style on every level. What the *Mercure* described as the "flower of polish and cultivated sprightliness of the fortunate geniuses of the century of Louis XIV" had been sadly "dried up in the hands of avid *philosophes*" who could only "fill hearts with desolate doctrines."[125]

Such emphasis on the putative literary superiority of the seventeenth century was not, in itself, new. Anti-*philosophes* of the Old Regime had pressed this theme before, as we have seen, and even the *philosophes'* defenders had been inclined on occasion to speak of the "literary decadence" of the eighteenth century.[126] But what characterized the anti-*philosophe* critique of the Napoleonic years was its strident insistence on the symbiotic relationship between literature and society. If the writers of the age of Louis XIV were great, this greatness stemmed from the religious and political values of the time. To praise the literary superiority of the age of Louis XIV was to underline its political superiority, an observation that lends insight into Bonald's pregnant phrase "literature is the expression of society."[127] As the viscount himself explained,

> Literature arrived at this point without effort, by the sole influence of a firm constitution that consecrated the power of the monarch, the dignity of the minister, the respect and love of the subject; a constitution that, engraving in morals what was not written in laws, put religion in the army, and public force in the courts; made of the civil magistracy a priesthood, and of the priesthood a political magistracy; and maintained, between all the different persons of society, those natural relationships that constitute social order. Order, this primary source of beauty, even literary beauty.[128]

Madame de Genlis similarly pined for the "brilliant and religious century of Louis XIV," an age when an "enlightened sovereign" understood that authority depended on justice, and subjects in turn "were persuaded that there was neither security, happiness, nor repose without submission to their laws and rulers."[129] It was an age of order, a Christian age, an age whose wholesome values were reflected and reaffirmed by its authors. Unlike the eighteenth-century *philosophes*, their predecessors, it seemed, did not contest the authority of their king, denigrate their country, or challenge religious truth. Rather, they sang their glory. They were "all religious, all Christians, all the honor of the Church and state."[130] As F.-G. de la Rochefoucauld maintained in a work that rings with praise for the authors of the seventeenth century (and hatred for those of the eighteenth), "It must be remarked that the great writers of this [seventeenth] century all had the same opinions regarding religion and order as their monarch. Not a single one of their works calls for revolt, or announces principles opposed to the institutions of the monarchy." "All were pious," Rochefoucauld continued, and "the king was at the center of their glory."[131]

This portrait of a mutually reaffirming monarchy and literary clerisy was, of course, highly romanticized. It did not dwell on Pascal's involvement in the Jansenist controversy or the anticlerical satire that drew on the author of *Tartuffe* the displeasure of the *parti dévot*. Neither was it quick to recall the bloodiness of Louis XIV's foreign wars, his wranglings with the pope, his aggressive taxation, his subjugation of the aristocracy, or his devastating financial policies. In fact, for all their valorization of history, the anti-*philosophes* were poor practitioners of the craft. Their past was every bit as much of a morality tale as that which they attributed to the *philosophes*. Whereas for the latter history was a long series of darkness illuminated at last by the shining light of the *siècle des lumières*, for anti-*philosophes* the light of the past had been snuffed out by the sophists of the eighteenth century. From the great age of Louis XIV—a monarch who had revoked the Edict of Nantes, worked hard to quell the Jansenist heresy, and ruled with absolute authority after a period of civil unrest—France had passed into utter depravity.

Criticism of Napoleon and Napoleon's Cooptation of Anti-*Philosophie*

The political implications of this romanticized portrait lay only just beneath the surface. For Napoleon's close advisor Pierre Roederer, they were straightforward enough. As he warned the First Consul in a long memorandum in 1803 that singled out the *Journal des débats* for particular attack,

> The journal calls attention without end to the *siècle de Louis XIV*. It is in this age alone that it finds great writers, great magistrates, great warriors, illustrious pontiffs, a great king. . . . The conclusion that discontents pull from the ensemble of its pages is that in order to restore public happiness, it is necessary to attach and to submit the future of France to the end of the reign of Louis XIV—that is, to the absolute power of the prince over his subjects, and of the clergy over the prince. It is necessary, in other words, to have recourse to the Bourbons to begin again the reign of a Bourbon.[132]

As Roederer charged, both here and elsewhere, the anti-*philosophe* critique as a whole undercut the foundations of Napoleon's reign. "The attacks unleashed on the eighteenth century," he stressed in a pointed article in the *Journal de Paris*, "and on *philosophie* fall on the Revolution, on its principles, on the men that it has put in place, and finally, on the government that is its great and important result. When one attacks the philosophy of the eighteenth century, it is the government of the nineteenth century that is attacked."[133]

A former *constituent* who had long defended the *philosophes*, Roederer was no unbiased observer. Yet it is difficult to deny a large degree of truth in his assertion that the anti-*philosophe* discourse represented an implicit criticism of Napoleon.[134] By putting forth the reign of Louis XIV as a golden age, insidiously corrupted by the principles of *philosophie*, the anti-*philosophes* presented both the eighteenth century and the Revolution in its entirety as an unnatural rupture, a break with a form of government consecrated by fourteen centuries of history. Insofar as Napoleon was a product of this Revolution, it followed that his government, too, however expedient for the time being, could not provide an adequate basis on which to found the future of France. To attack the Revolution in full was necessarily to cast aspersion on the phoenix who had risen from its flames.

Having said this, it must be emphasized that the anti-*philosophes'* primary enemies were, of course, the *philosophes* themselves—the demonic eighteenth-century sophists who had corrupted France and all those who claimed to share in their inheritance. Although their arguments ultimately bore on the foundations of the Napoleonic state, it was also true that in them Napoleon could find much of worth. "If the chatter of the journals has its inconveniences," he admitted in 1805 with specific reference to the *Journal des débats*, "it also has its advantages."[135]

For its Bourbon coloring aside, the anti-*philosophe* discourse of the Napoleonic period articulated a set of convictions that were broadly authoritarian in character. Napoleon might, for example, scoff at the ostentatious religiosity of the anti-*philosophes*, yet he certainly shared their belief in the fundamental importance of religion as a means of social control. Whereas Napoleon failed to see the indissolubility of marriage as one of the "first of all social questions," permitting divorce in the Civil Code of 1804 and exercising the prerogative himself in 1810, he certainly viewed the strong paternal family as an essential pillar of society. If Napoleon accepted the "dangerous" principle of religious tolerance, granting civil rights to Protestants and to Jews, he did not abide the indefinite *tolérantisme* of the *philosophes*, and he used the state to repress works deemed threatening to religion and the state. Though Napoleon refused to find in France's past a golden age of Edenic perfection, he recognized the importance of history and prejudice in moving men, the perils of ruling through abstraction, and the shortcomings of foreign—namely, English—political forms as models for French government. And though Napoleon of course did not see in the Bourbon monarchy an ideal of governmental practice, he nonetheless perceived the shortcomings of parliamentary rule and the need for unity of power, ruling with the authority, if not the consecration, of the absolute monarch. Finally, whereas Napoleon certainly did not regard the *philosophes* of the eighteenth century with the opprobrium of the anti-*philosophes*, he did share an almost obsessive distrust of their nineteenth-century counterparts, repeatedly disparaging "metaphysicians" and this "vermin, the ideologues," men he deemed worthy of "throwing in the fire."[136] In the so-called liberal intellectual opponents of his realm—the Staëls and Constants; the Cabanis, Chéniers, and Tracys—both Napoleon and the anti-*philosophes* found a common enemy.

There was, in sum, a good deal of convergence between the authoritarian doctrine espoused by the anti-*philosophes* and the authoritarian ideology of Napoleon.[137] As a consequence, Bonaparte was inclined for some time to overlook the royalist sympathies of the majority of anti-*philosophes* in order to profit from their services. A reliable source of counterrevolutionary invective, the anti-*philosophes* provided him with a valuable foil against those who wished to give a more revolutionary cast to his regime. He thus allowed them to pursue their war against *philosophie* with relative impunity. In return, the anti-*philosophes* gave Napoleon at least tacit support, and in some cases actively served him. Joseph Fiévée's intimate involvement in the 1790s with émigré monarchists and his subsequent role as an Ultra ideologue during the Restoration, for example, did not preclude his rendering assistance to Napoleon as an aide and prefect. Fontanes, likewise, gladly accepted numerous posts in the Napoleonic state, including the semiofficial position of lover to Napoleon's eldest sister, Elisa Bacciochi; leadership of the Corps Législatif; and the rectorship of the Imperial University, where he appointed such cronies as Bonald, Gueneau de Mussy, and Pierre Royer-Collard. Even Chateaubriand, a man who would later pride himself on his opposition to Napoleon, eagerly solicited the position of secretary to the French ambassador to the Vatican in 1803, and in 1811 he gladly accepted a seat in the Institut de France.

Despite these and other examples of collaboration, however, it remains true that the anti-*philosophe* discourse as a whole undermined the stability of Napoleon's reign. The points of convergence with Napoleon's own authoritarian beliefs notwithstanding, the differences were apparent. Indicting *philosophie* for all the troubles that had beset France, the anti-*philosophe* discourse served as a cipher to condemn the Revolution as a whole, a strategy that could only implicate the legitimacy of Napoleon's rule. By continually reviving the cultural battles of the Revolution, making war on those who hoped to give a more republican flavor to the new government, the anti-*philosophes* frustrated Napoleon's stated objective of reconciling the factions under a transcendent government of accommodation. Thus, in the end, he came to accept the logic of arguments of those like Roederer and his chief of police, Fouché, who warned that the Counter-Revolution was "overrunning the newspapers and literature" of France in an effort to "control public opinion."[138]

Responding in 1805 to a note by Joseph Fiévée that defended the *Journal des débats*, Napolean gave clear indication of his growing doubts. "In reading the journal with more attention than the others because it has ten times the number of subscribers," he observed, "we note there articles directed in a spirit highly favorable to the Bourbons, and constantly with indifference to the great affairs of state." Characterizing its owner, Bertin de Veaux, as a man "sold to the émigrés in London," Napoleon added that "one could cite a thousand . . . articles of the *Journal des débats* written with evil intent." He ordered that its name be changed to the *Journal de l'Empire* (the previous title "brought back memories of the Revolution") and charged Fiévée with guaranteeing its content, forbidding all favorable allusions to the Bourbons.[139] Two years later, having remarked with chagrin that the journal continued to "speak without end of the Bourbons," the emperor lashed out at its incessant war on the *philosophes* and *philosophie*. The *Journal de l'Empire*, he accused, "attributes all the misfortunes of the Revolution to *philosophie*. . . . The spirit of party being dead, I can only look upon this constant scandal mongering of a group of impudent journalists, without talent and without genius, as a calamity and indignity carried out against the most respectable men."[140] Removing Fiévée as censor, he installed the pliable Étienne in his place, a man kindly disposed to the *philosophes*, significantly altering the journal's character. At nearly the same time, Napoleon used the pretext of an unflattering comparison drawn between his reign and the despotism of Nero by Chateaubriand in the *Mercure* to confiscate that journal. By late 1807, Napoleon had effectively muzzled the anti-*philosophe* press. And although in the remaining years of his reign isolated attacks on the *philosophes* were not uncommon, never did they achieve the degree of virulent consistency that marked the preceding period.[141]

Despite these definitive setbacks, it was nonetheless true that for seven years anti-*philosophes* in France had waged a consistent struggle against *philosophie*, and with palpable results. "It takes a kind of courage," complained the organ of the ideologues, *La Décade*, in late 1803, "to publish today, under the title of Philosophie, an important treatise on metaphysics or grammar. By what trick of fate has the first of the human sciences fallen into discredit? By what trick of fate . . . is the very name *philosophe* now belittled?"[142] When in the following year the aging *philosophes* Suard and Morellet sought, from their citadel at the Institut de France, to promote apologies of *philosophie* by offering a prize for the best essay on the "Tableau littéraire de la France au XVIIIe siècle," they received blunt answers to these questions.[143] Time and again the submitting contestants complained of the powerful "sect" that "desecrated the ashes" of the great *philosophes* of the eighteenth century.[144] "If we still love the sciences and letters," one essay lamented, "we must almost be surprised. . . . For the coryphaeuses publish every day hefty volumes and petite pamphlets against *philosophie*. . . . They have journals at their disposal . . . and they are not without partisans and power."[145] "Like wolves howling in the forest," another complained, the anti-*philosophes* hurled endless insults against the eighteenth century. "Preaching incessantly against *philosophie* in novels, in brochures, in periodicals, in prose and in verse," these wolves sought to "bring back the centuries of futility." "Cease," the author implored, "cease to cover us seven days a week . . . with your bile."[146] If *philosophie* had fallen into disrepute, it seemed clear, the cause was not fate.

Nor, moreover, was the anti-*philosophes*' vendetta merely a war against the past. As we have seen, their constant denigration of *philosophie* entailed a political vision that struck not only at those who dared continue to defend the *philosophes* in the present but also at Napoleon himself. This was, certainly, a muted criticism, one forced by the exigence of circumstance to take cover behind the cloak of literature. If, as Tocqueville would later charge famously (though unfairly), the philosophy of the eighteenth century represented an "abstract, literary politics," then the anti-*philosophe* vision of the early nineteenth century was a *concrete* literary politics.[147] Stressing the force of history and tradition, human beings' inherent capacity for evil, and the dangers of intellectual license, it fused the anti-*philosophe* discourse of the Old Regime with the experience of the 1790s to put forth the truth and necessity of religion, the strong patriarchal family, and the divinely consecrated and inalienable sovereignty of political authority as the sole means to prevent the recurrence of horrors of which the Revolution stood as an ever present reminder. Seeing in the unity of throne and altar allegedly achieved during the reign of Louis XIV a model of harmonious government, it preached a return to a romanticized past to ensure the future. And though, like all opposition under Napoleon, this vision was eventually quelled, it nonetheless successfully forged in France the essential outlines of an antiliberal ideology that was, in itself, new. When joined to the thought of returning *émigrés* during the Restoration, this vision would form the intellectual underpinnings of the Ultra-Royalist Right.

CHAPTER 5

The Revolution owes its origin principally

to *philosophie.* The *philosophes* began it.

They were the perpetrators of all the crimes,

and of all the excesses that accompanied it.

This impious and anti-social sect is still alive today

in full vigor. . . . Let us not be mistaken. At all

times, we must judge the future by the past.

—J.A.P.,

De la Monarchie avec les philosophes,

les révolutionnaires et les Jacobins (1817)

THE FUTURE OF THE PAST:
THE RESTORATION STRUGGLE AGAINST
THE ENLIGHTENMENT

*A*t 11:00 P.M. on February 13, 1820, the Duke of Berry, only son of the Count of Artois, nephew of Louis XVIII, and second in line to the French throne, was struck down as he left his box at the Paris opera. The assassin, Louis-Pierre Louvel, a journeyman saddler and fanatical devotee of Napoleon, readily admitted that he had acted to extinguish the Bourbon line. In this aim, he would be foiled, for although Berry was at the time the sole member of the dynasty who was capable of producing an heir, his wife gave birth to a son seven months later—an event that devout royalists quickly attributed to the hand of God. Divine intervention, they asserted widely, had facilitated the "immaculate conception" of this "miracle child."

Pious royalists thus insisted on seeing the birth of the future Bourbon pretender, the Count of Chambord, in providential terms. They regarded the death of his father in a more profane light. "The monster [Louvel]," declared the Duke of Fitz-James in the Chamber of Peers on the day after the murder, "is only . . . an instrument, a dagger, similar to the one that pierced the heart of our unhappy prince. The hand that directed the blow must be sought elsewhere." In his opinion, Berry's death was not "the work of an isolated fanatic," but rather of a larger, more insidious force.[1] Across the way, in the Chamber of Deputies, the Count of Labourdonnaye traced Berry's assassination to a similar cause, seeing in Louvel's calculations the necessary result of "pernicious doctrines that sap all thrones and all authorities, attack civilization in its entirety, and menace the world with new upheavals."[2] "Oh crime!" bemoaned the Ultra-Royalist daily, the *Drapeau blanc*, "the horrible plots of revolutionaries, of regicides, are made manifest by assassinations."[3]

Just who, precisely, were the shadowy figures who stood behind these plots and conspiracies, directing the hand of Louvel? And what, in effect, were the perverse doctrines that moved them? The names, we shall see, were changing, for the demons of old were assuming new forms. "Liberalism," its enemies now charged, was the force that threatened Europe and was the immediate cause of the death of the Duke of Berry.

The ideas of this new creed, however, and its tactics were eerily familiar. Scratch the surface and one found in liberalism only another permutation of that inveterate foe, *philosophie*. Imputing to liberals the same ends and means that they ascribed to their philosophic forefathers, enemies of the Enlightenment understood the ultimate source of Berry's assassination to be the Enlightenment itself. In the years before his death, they warned ominously that a failure to eradicate a resurgence in the publication of philosophic books would result in horrors. And in the years after, they used Berry's death as confirmation of this fact to wage an aggressive war against all traces of the Enlightenment inheritance. Only against this background of dire expectations confirmed and even more terrible predictions of evil to come can one fully understand the Restoration's extraordinary campaign against the eighteenth-century Enlightenment and its nineteenth-century progeny. And only in light of the failure of this campaign can one understand why important segments of the European Right would remain obsessed with the Enlightenment and its liberal offspring ever after.

A Fleeting Ultra Dawn

Although the dominant tenor of Ultra-Royalist political rhetoric throughout the Restoration was one of dark warning and recrimination, it is important not to overlook the ephemeral dawn of 1815–1816. In that brief period separating the victory at Waterloo from the Ultra setback of September 1816, dreams flourished and then were dashed: of a French people absolved and made whole again through the unity of the holy Catholic Church; of an aristocracy restored in title and fortune to its rightful place at the head of a society of orders; of a divinely consecrated king, ruling with justice and with strength over a penitent people; of a France purged of every trace of its revolutionary inheritance. Cultivated in both intellectual and physical exile over the course of a quarter century, these dreams were just that, dreams, inflated expectations at odds with the social and political realities of postrevolutionary France. As returning émigrés and long-suffering counterrevolutionaries would soon learn, the Revolution would not simply go away. The past twenty-five years, no less than the past twenty-five centuries, possessed an inertia of their own, a fact that would force men and women who called themselves "conservatives" to chew on the irony of the term. What they sought to conserve no longer existed, if it ever had. The Revolution, now, was history.

This truth highlights a dynamic at play in the thought of the Right from the end of the eighteenth century onward: the refusal to accept the world as given and the visionary desire to reshape it in keeping with an ideal. That this ideal was deeply unsavory to many—both at the time and since—does not alter in the slightest the fact that the project of the Right during the Restoration was, in its own way, utopian and, as a consequence, revolutionary. What historian François Furet has aptly called the "revolution against the Revolution" carried out in the aftermath of Waterloo was nothing less than a radical attempt to remake the world.[4]

Anchored in the so-called *chambre introuvable*, the overwhelmingly Ultra-Royalist assembly returned after the upheaval of the Hundred Days, this conservative revolution set out to cleanse France of the men and spirit of 1789. Throughout the country, exceptional courts and special jurisdictions tried and punished revolutionary criminals. In the civil service and royal administration as many as fifty thousand to eighty thousand former officials were stripped of their positions, and in the church, the army, and the universities, similar purges were encouraged, although on a smaller scale. In the provinces, particularly in the Midi, marauding gangs took matters into their own hands, hunting down revolutionary collaborators and settling old scores in a great bloodletting known as the White Terror. And in countless parish churches, reconstituted seminaries, and cathedrals throughout France, the faithful set about preparing themselves for what would prove to be the most concerted effort of Catholic reconquest since the Counter-Reformation. After years of persecution and expiation, many now allowed themselves the fleeting pleasure of confidence in a new tomorrow. Preaching before a large audience at Saint Sulpice, in February 1816, Monseigneur Frayssinous, bishop of Hermopolis, indulged such hopes:

> For over twenty years, we have endured punishment for the failings of our forefathers. . . . But Providence has made all bow before it, and when the hour sounded . . . nothing could stop the hand of God from smiting impiety. . . . Yes, gentleman, we no longer have anything to fear from the enemies of God; celestial vengeance has crushed them. . . . No, this throne will never perish. . . . Heaven has been reconciled with the earth.[5]

Just as providence had long rained punishment on France for its sins, now it would bless a king and a people atoned, promising a resplendent future if only the country kept its faith.

This qualified optimism was accompanied by one other attendant condition: the total proscription of the writings held responsible for France's long suffering. Despite their guarded hopes, counterrevolutionaries had not forgotten the danger of *philosophie*. The health of

France demanded that it be remembered well. Thus the leading organ of the clergy during the Restoration, the *Ami de la religion et du roi,* could comment with satisfaction that "no one doubts any longer that the writers known as *philosophes* of the eighteenth century formed, for the destruction of the Christian religion, a real conspiracy . . . one that exploded before our eyes in the most horrible manner."[6] When coupled with the fact that the "irreligious writers of the last century" had seemingly fallen into total disrepute, it was possible to entertain confidence in France's prospects for renewal. "Today," the same journal maintained, "the likes of La Mettrie, Helvétius, Diderot, or Holbach are no longer read. Their memory fades . . . and the generation that follows avenges the doctrine that these men attacked without even seeking to do so—by no longer opening their books, by letting their names expire little by little in shameful oblivion."[7] Only on the basis of such cautionary remembrance and salubrious neglect could France guard against the errors of the past while opening itself to the restorative faith of tomorrow. It was a condition, enemies of the Enlightenment would soon learn, that France was unprepared to meet.

Confronting Enemies of Old

The painful revelation that the long-awaited Ultra dawn would not break smoothly came quickly, the product of both political and cultural forces at play toward the end of 1816 and the beginning of the following year. On September 6, 1816, Louis XVIII dissolved the newly constituted *chambre introuvable,* to the great horror of the Catholic Right. Goaded by his moderate minister and personal favorite, Élie Decazes, Louis distrusted the overwhelmingly Ultra cast of the National Assembly, fearing its intransigent refusal to compromise with any vestige of the Revolution, its exaggerated religiosity, and its resolute efforts to exact retribution from the "criminals" who had sullied France. Hoping to reconcile the nation through a more temperate course, Louis presided instead over further division. For in dissolving the *chambre introuvable* not only did he alienate a good number of the monarchy's most loyal supporters—creating the ironic situation of a royalist opposition avowedly more royalist than the king—but he also opened the chamber to forces that would eventually spell the regime's undoing. The elections held between 1816 and 1820 returned an ever-growing number of representatives who scarcely hid their admiration for the first, moderate phase of the Revolution. Known by the general label Liberal and grouped around such leaders as Jacques Manuel, Jean Casimir-Périer, the Marquis of Lafayette,

Jacques Lafitte, and Benjamin Constant, this Constitutional, or Independent, party defended popular sovereignty and individual rights, denigrated the role of the church (often in overtly anticlerical terms), and looked to England as a political model for France.[8] Constituting a minority within the chamber as a whole, the faction nonetheless controlled sufficient votes to force the government of Decazes, based on several non-Ultra, centrist groupings, to grant concessions. Outside the chamber, the Liberals boasted an active and flourishing press.[9]

In and of itself, this abrupt reversal of fortune was viewed by those called or calling themselves Ultra-Royalists as catastrophic, an unthinkable betrayal of the "true" royalist cause by the very man entrusted to lead it.[10] Ultra bitterness, as a consequence, flowed in abundance, given perfect expression in the new rally cry of the Right, *Vive le roi quand même* ("Long live the king despite him"). A product of the disillusion wrought by unrealistic expectations, this bitterness also stemmed from the genuine conviction that to compromise in any way with the forces of the Revolution was to jeopardize the very existence of the Restoration monarchy. If the recent past had taught anything, Ultras held, it was that conciliation—what many would come to term *modérantisme*—was the first step toward disaster. The Right would find ample opportunity to argue the truth of this maxim. It seized on its first occasion, the announcement in late 1816 and early 1817 of the forthcoming publication of collected editions of the works of Voltaire and Rousseau, with relish.

It is perhaps surprising that the ostensibly "reactionary" Restoration should permit the publication of writers widely held to have caused the Revolution. Whatever its shortcomings in other respects, the Restoration proved remarkably faithful to the principle of freedom of the press enshrined in Article Eight of the Charter. Several efforts to curtail this freedom notwithstanding, neither Louis XVIII nor his successor, Charles X, seriously undermined it. Ironically, the "conservative" Restoration was undoubtedly the most liberal period in French publishing history to date, providing a considerable degree of freedom to parties on both sides of the political divide. This situation allowed tremendous publishing opportunities for the writings of the *philosophes*. Between 1817 and 1824, Restoration publishers, often with active, Liberal assistance, produced more than two million copies of the works of Voltaire and Rousseau alone, as well as hundreds of thousands of books by other important Enlightenment figures.[11] Despite the fact that these works quickly became important symbols of anticlerical and anti-Bourbon dissent, their publication continued, the presses in the final years of the Restoration flooding the market with hundred of thousands of cheap, small-format editions, readily affordable to artisans and peasants.[12]

Fervent Catholics could only regard this development with horror. The government's unwillingness to curtail the writings of the undisputed forefathers of the Revolution seemed perilous folly. As a group of "Catholic faithful" stressed in a pamphlet released shortly after Parisian publishers made known their intentions to publish the collected works of Voltaire and Rousseau, these two men had been denounced so often as the progenitors of the Revolution that it was no longer possible for anyone to deny the fact. Left unchecked, "the same writings would bring down new calamities upon France, placing arms in the hands of thousands ready to overthrow . . . religion and the state." Surely, the faithful demanded, France's leaders would not remain unmoved in the face of these "same tactics and these same writings," being so blind as to treat the "experience of twenty-five years as a pure loss?"[13]

Written with the expressed purpose of urging the hierarchy to bring pressure on the crown to put a stop to the new publication efforts, the pamphlet achieved, at least in part, its primary objective. Within weeks, the Vicars General of Paris issued a stern *mandement*, sounding an "alarm" against the dangers of the collected works, which was followed in turn by a flurry of other anti-*philosophe* pronouncements and publications.[14] Prescient in this respect, the letter of the Catholic faithful was also emblematic, for in its principal arguments it pursued a strategy that would be repeated by fellow partisans throughout the Restoration: establish the absolute necessity of countering the *philosophe* threat; invoke in graphic detail the horrors of the past; and lay out with equal precision the great risks of inaction.

Ideologues of the Catholic Right invariably sought to emphasize, even at this early stage, the magnitude and gravity of the *philosophe* question.[15] As the authors of *Les Fidèles catholiques* argued, to extinguish the writings of the *philosophes* was the most "important task" facing France, an opinion shared wholeheartedly by the Parisian Vicars General.[16] There simply was no issue worthier of "being thoroughly investigated" than the matter of the new editions of the works of Voltaire and Rousseau reaffirmed the prolific Ultra ideologue Claude Hippolyte Clausel de Montals in a forty-eight-page pamphlet published in March 1817. The "future happiness" of France depended on it.[17] As the veteran anti-*philosophe* Élie Harel asserted in early 1817, the time to sound the alarm was "now or never"[18] (see Figure 18).

This was a contention that the Catholic Right based overwhelmingly on its reading of recent history. It returned to this history repeatedly, highlighting both the blindness and the prescience of their forefathers. In what was a standard trope of Restoration invective, Catholic polemicists cited prerevolutionary documents at length, including bish-

Mentita est iniquitas sibi. Psalm. 26.

LE DESESPOIR DES PHILOSOPHES

ops' *mandements*, Sorbonne censures, and other writings to show how perceptive observers had long foreseen the dangers posed by the *philosophes*. They also emphasized that if Louis XVI himself had been slow to acknowledge the enormity of the *philosophe* threat, he at least did so belatedly, commenting from his prison cell in the Temple that "these two men [Voltaire and Rousseau] have ruined France." The phrase was widely repeated during the Restoration.[19]

By pointing out the foresight and the retrospective contrition of historical actors, Catholic partisans drew attention to the weighty precedent that justifyied their own, contemporary warnings. The "kings and men of state" of the Old Regime might be forgiven their blindness, for regrettably "they [had] recognized too late" that the *philosophes'* writings had sewn principles that would lead to "universal upheaval" and "civil war."[20] When confronted with the patent consequences of this blindness, however, similar neglect was inexcusable. As Clausel de Montals asserted frankly, "inaction" on the part of the state in the face of the resurgent *philosophe* challenge "would reveal it to be the supporter and protector of irreligion and licence." To fail to combat religion's enemies would be to "seem to join in league with them, to encourage them through criminal connivance."[21]

This note of exasperated warning was the third constant feature of so many of these writings. As the authors of *Les Fidèles catholiques* cautioned, a negligent government "would soon meet its ruin."[22] The warning was repeated widely. When set against the actual horrors of the revolutionary past, this appeal to the future had the effect of taking one back to the point of revolutionary origin—to the time when "the Revolution was rendered inevitable by the failure to halt evil at its source."[23] To commit the same mistake again would be to launch France on a trajectory that could end only with regicide, anarchy, and terror. The image of tomorrow was that of yesterday. As the Ultra author known simply as J. A. P. commented in 1817, in the citation that serves as the epigraph to this chapter, "At all times, we must judge the future by the past."[24]

Figure 18. (facing page) The Despair of the *philosophes*. Frontispiece to the 1817 edition of the prolific anti-*philosophe* Élie Harel's *Voltaire: Particularités curieuses de sa vie et de sa mort*, new ed. (Paris, 1817). Christ reigns supreme over a fallen medusa, who vomits up the *Encyclopédie*, Rousseau's *Émile*, Voltaire's *Dictionnaire philosophique*, and other key Enlightenment texts.

The logic that underlay this conception—that the past would necessarily repeat itself unless action were taken to the contrary—demanded a constant, vigilant attention to France's history. To forget, or worse, to ignore, recent experience was to condemn oneself to suffer it anew. Hence, the religiously minded strove to keep this past forever before French eyes, a strategy that pitted the church against the crown for much of the Restoration. As historian Sheryl Kroen has demonstrated, the state's policy of *oubli*—the "compulsory forgetting" of the period 1789–1815 in an attempt to allow old wounds to heal and troubling questions about the legitimacy of the restored Bourbon monarchy to fall by the wayside—placed it at loggerheads with a church determined to seek atonement through expiation and a constant reliving of the past so it would never have to be repeated. Reviving church-state conflicts with deep roots in French history, these contrasting approaches to the politics of memory created tensions between the two institutions, a truth that belies overly facile assumptions of an untroubled, reactionary, throne and altar entente during this period. The two, in fact, were frequently at odds.[25]

What was true of the church as an institution was even more so for those Catholic counterrevolutionaries on the front lines of the war against the *philosophes*. Compulsory remembering rather than forgetting was the rule, and a strong note of concern at the government's apparent insensitivity to the *philosophe* challenge is evident from the start. With the subsequent announcements of plans to publish three more collected editions of the works of Voltaire and another of Rousseau, of Raynal, and of Diderot in the year 1817 alone, such concern turned quickly to disbelief. Not only did the government seem willing to tolerate these ventures, but also its permissive attitude toward the press sanctioned a campaign of philosophic apology and promotion carried out in such Liberal newspapers as the *Constitutionnel*, the *Mercure*, and the *Minerve Française*. Lauding the new publishing ventures and seeking to disassociate the *philosophes* from revolutionary atrocities, these papers missed no opportunity to lash out at the alleged "fanaticism" and "intolerance" of "defenders of the Christian religion."[26] Here, once again, were the philosophic battle-cries of old, the initial strains of what would develop during the Restoration into a sustained and aggressive anticlerical campaign. As the *Ami de la religion et du roi* observed in the early summer of 1817, the scale of the assault was frightening:

> Fifty years ago, a party incensed against Christianity rose up, circulating evil books at low prices in public and in secret amongst all classes. These books could be found in salons, in kitchens, anti-chambers, and the peasant's hut. They were thrown into boarding houses and religious estab-

lishments with the aim of corrupting innocence and tempting piety itself. . . . It seems that philosophic proselytism has lost nothing of its vivacity, and has even renewed its attempts to insinuate its productions into the asylums of faith. We learn that copies of the *Prospectus* of the new editions of Voltaire have been directed at Christian virgins.[27]

It was this act that had so incensed the Bishop of Arles at the 1782 General Assembly of the clergy. Whether real or apocryphal, the rumor that philosophic proselytes were once again forcing their writings on unsuspecting nuns could only have triggered unpleasant associations. In any event, the story was symbolic of the scale of the perceived advance. Just a little over a year since proclaiming France's healthy neglect of the writings of the *philosophes*, the editors of the *Ami de la religion et du roi* were in despair.[28] As Clausel de Montals summarized in a new work written in May 1818, "In effect, this saintly religion sees itself plunged once more into incertitude and alarm."[29]

Clausel's sentiments were by no means singular, nor was the explanation he provided to account for this troubling state of affairs. In his view, the precipitate change in the fortunes of the church, this "overflowing of impious books . . . and periodicals that each day are spread throughout the realm" could be understood in only one way: "Let us unveil a type of conspiracy that reveals more than simply a present aversion to the faith, but the design of stopping it up at its source and depriving it of all future."[30] Already, in 1817, Harel had considered the horrible possibility that "new conspirators" were forming "a new conspiracy against throne and altar."[31] By 1818, more and more observers shared the same fear. As the *Ami de la religion et du roi* commented in February of that year,

> Those who have refused to believe in the existence of a plot formed in the last century to debase and to destroy religion need only, today, open their eyes to be convinced that this plot was no chimera. Not only did it exist, but it exists still, manifesting itself in a thousand ways. It is revealed in the re-printing of old books, and in the publication of the new. Never, in effect, have presses been more active in reproducing the old systems of *philosophie*.[32]

If the tremendous activity of Restoration presses was thus an indicator of contemporary conspiracy, the question immediately arose: just who were the conspirators? The weapons might be old, the final objectives unchanged, but the conspirators themselves were necessarily new. To reveal the cunning masterminds who stood behind these plots reborn, to unmask the modern equivalent of the eighteenth-century *philosophe*, would prove to be an essential task.

Philosophes in New Clothing

From as early as 1815, at least one perceptive observer, Félicité de Lamennais, was struggling to fulfill this duty. Arguably the most important Catholic intellectual of the first half of the nineteenth century, Lamennais possessed a knack for anticipating, well in advance, issues that would later occupy his brethren. He is most famous in this regard for his later advocacy of the separation of church and state and the need for religion to play an active social role in the lives of ordinary people. He made his early career, however, as an ideologue of Ultra-Royalism. In this capacity as both priest and journalist, he was no less prescient, giving ample proof of the fact in an important essay first published in 1815.

The title of the piece, the "Influence of Philosophic Doctrines on Society," was indicative of its central concern.[33] In many ways a straightforward summary of well-established anti-*philosophe* themes, the essay took pains to present *philosophie*'s corrosive effect on the social whole, emphasizing its atheism and materialism, its denial of history, and its destruction of the family. By rendering the individual the "universal center of society," *philosophie* had cut away all social ties, substituting personal interest, equality, and anarchy for duty, hierarchy, and order. The litmus test of the philosophic experiment, the Revolution, had exposed *philosophie* as empty and depraved.

In these respects, Lamennais's arguments were well established, even tired. He offered, however, one critical innovation on the anti-*philosophe* discourse of old, cautioning that although *philosophie* had indeed been thoroughly discredited by the Revolution, in many people's minds this was more nominal than substantial. The ideas underlying the sullied term were still very much alive and were slowly taking shape under a new banner: "Read the numerous pamphlets that give birth each day to philosophic deliriums. Every anti-social reverie is renewed in them, exalted, consecrated under the name of *liberal ideas*, a sacramental expression, whose calculated obscurity hides from the eyes of the vulgar the redoubtable mysteries of the philosophic religion."[34] For Lamennais, *libéral* was just a cipher for *philosophe*, a screen to conceal the awful meaning behind the term. Let one not be deceived, Liberals were merely *philosophes* in new clothing, men who sought to reclaim and exercise the power they had wielded during the Revolution. Unless they were opposed with defiance, they would do precisely this. The struggle, Lamennais stressed, was "a fight between life and death."[35]

Lamennais's criticism of the Liberal as a latter-day *philosophe* and of liberalism as a reincarnation of the *philosophisme* of old was original and precocious. Insofar as it posited an essential link between liberalism and the Enlightenment, moreover, it was not entirely unfounded. In fact, Restoration Liberals sought continually to incorporate the *siècle des lumières* into their wider project of defending the first, moderate phase of the Revolution.[36] Just as they argued that the latter was necessary and advantageous, betrayed by the Terror but bearing no relationship to it, so did they defend the *philosophes* from charges of extremism, arguing that their humanitarian ideals had also been betrayed by subsequent misinterpretation. The *philosophes* did not cause the Revolution, which was the product of myriad other forces: fiscal crisis, administrative despotism, antiquated privilege, and the like. But that they had fought on the side of reason and justice—combating superstition and fanaticism in the name of tolerance and humanity—there could be no doubt. For these reasons, Liberals emphasized, Enlightenment authors were still worthy of the greatest respect and the widest readership. In the eyes of critics like Lamennais, this affinity was revealing. Liberals, they believed, understood full well the revolutionary consequences of philosophic writings, and they were consciously using the republication of such works to this end. The defense of the *philosophes* was merely a cover for their own conspiratorial designs.

Lamennais's warning was prescient in 1815, but within several years fellow partisans of the throne and altar had taken up its essential logic and were using it as a tool to understand the political developments of Restoration France. Here was a way to comprehend the seemingly incomprehensible: the resurgence in publication of philosophic books, the rise of an exculpatory campaign in the press devoted to the defense of eighteenth-century authors, and the corresponding Liberal electoral successes in the two chambers. This creeping Liberal presence, and Decazes's willingness to give Liberal concerns a hearing in his coalition government, struck many Ultras as nothing short of mad. Was it not logical to see these developments as the result of a conscious conspiracy? France, it seemed, was being swept up again in what the *Ami de la religion et du roi* termed the "the great trial between Religion and philosophy," the world-historical struggle that would determine its final fate.[37]

The tendency to see France (and Europe as a whole) as the battleground of contesting, Manichean forces—so pronounced in earlier anti-*philosophe* rhetoric—returned to the fore in the year prior to the Berry assassination. Not only did the publication of *philosophe* texts continue unabated in this period, but also, in 1819, the infamous Abbé Grégoire, a leading figure of the constitutional church and a noted regicide, was elected to the Chamber of Deputies alongside a number of other men with only slightly less incendiary revolutionary pasts.[38] Grégoire's seat was denied amid public uproar, but the very fact of his election reaffirmed Ultra suspicions that the slide to the Left would continue until forcibly arrested or the country was plunged anew into revolutionary chaos. Although the various Liberal factions that were vying for a place in the two chambers and in the country at large might call themselves by any number of names, the common source that united them was the same.[39] "There are only two parties in France," affirmed Antoine-Eugène Genoude in the *Conservateur*, a leading Ultra journal that enjoyed the collaboration of Bonald, Chateaubriand, Fiévée, Fitz-James, and Lamennais. "One defends the doctrines of the Revolution, the other opposes them."[40] To pretend otherwise was to fall prey to the great error of the past—the assumption that one could compromise with the *philosophes* and the Revolution they made—an error that was being repeated now in the form of governmental complicity with liberalism. Moderation toward individuals might be a virtue, Bonald stressed, but when applied to doctrines that struck at the heart of monarchy, this was foolish indifference and, in the context of contemporary France, political suicide. By making concessions to the "spirit of the century," the government risked "losing all."[41]

Given the background of these dire warnings, the Ultra response to the assassination of the Duke of Berry is more fully comprehensible. Although the accusation of larger complicity in his death—pointed, immediate, and overwhelmingly consistent in Ultra circles—rested on no actual evidence, it was perfectly in keeping with the logic of Ultra categories.[42] Jean-François-Amable-Claude Clausel de Coussergues, brother of Clausel de Montals, may have overstated matters when he rose in the Chamber of Deputies on the day after the murder to accuse Decazes himself of being "an accomplice in the assassination of M. the duke of Berry."[43] Yet it reflected the general sentiment of the Ultra-Royalist minority in the two chambers and, more broadly, right-wing political opinion as a whole. In the eyes of these men and women, Decazes was criminally negligent, responsible, if only through indifference, for the resurgence of Liberal political sentiments throughout the country. And this, Ultra-Royalists agreed, was Decazes's greatest crime. In the ensemble of opinions dubbed indiscriminately *libéral*, they found the ultimate source of the powers that moved Louvel's hand. "I have seen Louvel's dagger," commented Charles Nodier famously in the *Journal des débats*, "and it was a Liberal idea."[44] What had been latent for so long was now clear. In the eyes of Ultras, the assassination removed the final veil from Restoration *libéralisme*, revealing it as a force with maximalist, revolutionary intentions. Pointing up the failure of the policy of accommodation followed since Louis XVIII's dissolution of the *chambre introuvable* in September 1816, it seemed to justify the Catholic Right's many warnings about the dangerous consequences of philosophic license and ushered in an extended period of political reaction.

Perhaps as important for the long-term political history of France, the assassination solidified the Right's nascent critique of liberalism. If there were ever any doubts among supporters of the throne and altar about the substance of Lamennais's warnings, they were now put to rest. The truth of liberalism lay in its philosophic past—a contention that the assassination reaffirmed and that Catholic critics would flesh out in great detail over the coming years. Fusing the terms in symbiotic union, they spoke of the "liberalism" of eighteenth-century *philosophie* and the *philosophie* of liberalism. They decried modern *philosophes libéraux* for defending the works of their eighteenth-century forefathers, and they tore into these same luminaries for sowing *idées libérales* in the past.[45] The critic L.-F. de Robiano de Borsbeek, for example, spoke interchangeably of *philosophie*, *lumières du siècle*, and *idées libérales* in his 1820 examination of the epic struggle between *philosophisme* and Christianity.[46] And the *Drapeau blanc* repeatedly condemned both the "*philosophisme* of the eighteenth century" and the "*libéralisme* that issued from it."[47] The two terms were virtually synonymous.

There was more to this criticism, however, than a simple exchange of labels. In conflating eighteenth-century *philosophie* with nineteenth-century liberalism, critics transposed the principal categories of the anti-*philosophe* discourse onto the modern adversary. Thus, whereas anti-*philosophes* had repeatedly decried *philosophie* as a system—one made up of heterogeneous parts but tending, nonetheless, toward common ends—so did their modern counterparts condemn the *système libéral*.[48] The abbé Beauchamp, curate of Bucy-Le-Long in the diocese of Soissons, enjoined in his 1822 study, *Du Libéralisme*, "Let us read the writings that seep from the pen of *libéralisme*, listen to the speeches of its orators, and everywhere we will see that they profess the same principles."[49] In effect, these could be boiled down to two: a virulent hatred of the Catholic religion and the desire to usurp all royal authority. But under the rubric of these overarching goals, internal variations were extensive. "Liberalism will admit into its ranks and under its banner anyone who comes to it," Beauchamp alleged, provided that they "abjure Catholicism and avow an implacable hatred towards its ministers, with the goal of attacking its dogma and its maxims more openly, and swear an eternal war not only against royalty, but against all kings and those who . . . show themselves faithful subjects of their legitimate princes." "[Liberalism's] hatred for religion and royalty has carried it to admit all systems presented to it—even those diametrically opposed."[50] Just as anti-*philosophes* had long characterized *philosophie* as an amalgam of internally inconsistent principles subordinated to common goals, Beauchamp presented liberalism without fear of contradiction as perhaps only a Catholic could: the system was both many and one.

Anti-*philosophes* of the Old Regime frequently justified this apparent discrepancy by drawing links to *philosophie*'s alleged Protestant roots. The Reformation, in throwing off the sacred yoke of dogma, tradition, and ecclesiastical authority, had unleashed humankind's errant reason to indulge in a frenzy of subjective speculation. The resulting explosion of conflicting sects and doctrines, united only by their common will to protest, was seen as an inevitable consequence of the haughty reliance on the unchained human mind. Not surprisingly, Restoration counterparts drew similar connections, seeing in liberalism yet another long-term consequence of the Protestant rejection of Catholic authority. As the author of the "anti-philosophic song" *Le Libéralisme dévoilé* maintained in 1822, the spirit of liberalism could be traced to Luther.[51] The *Mémorial catholique*, a monthly journal, was equally direct, calling liberalism "political Protestantism" and seeing in its many variations a mirror of the schisms and conflicts of the Reformation.[52] As the same journal explained in greater detail, "Those who have knowledge of modern history know the lineage of this doctrine [liberalism], which carries death to the heart of society. The innovations of the sixteenth century introduced amongst us the license of opinions." Soon, this rejection of spiritual monarchy was followed by an attempt to throw off the political authority of princes, a rebellion that was speciously termed "the liberation of the human spirit." *Philosophisme* and now, finally, liberalism were simply the latest incarnations of this horrible, foundational revolt.[53]

In light of this common intellectual pedigree, Catholic critics saw no problem in flagellating the son with the same weapons they had used against the father. Recycling the anti-*philosophe* vocabulary almost in its entirety, they denounced Liberals as "fanatics" bent on destroying all vestiges of the *infâme*. They lashed out at the calls for "tolerance" as a hackneyed stratagem to spread religious indifference, the ultimate hypocrisy of intolerant men.[54] They vilified the Liberals' pride and self-love, decrying their arrogant pretensions to be "the only master whom we should slavishly obey, the only guide whom we should follow."[55] And they decried in liberalism the same impetus toward egoistic individualism that they had condemned in *philosophie*, seeing the Liberals' talk of rights in place of duties, their sanctification of the individual at the expense of the social whole, as clear throwbacks to the eighteenth century.

Accentuated by their apologies for material gain and personal interest, this rampant egoism seemed ever more destructive now at a time when the love of wealth threatened to pull apart a society in the grips of rapid economic expansion. The twin forces of *philosophisme* and "industry," the *Drapeau blanc* affirmed, were "operating the dissolution of modern Europe," "isolating individuals in their opinions and their interests." The ideas of Adam Smith and such French emulators as the ideologue J. B. Say drove the spirit of the century, fusing the *tendance philosophique* to the *tendance industrielle*.[56] Economic liberalism and political liberalism went hand in hand, a suspicion that was apparently confirmed by French Liberals' open admiration for the English, a sentiment consistent with the *philosophes'* inveterate Anglomania. Left to their own devices, Liberals would wrench France in the direction of Protestant Albion, denaturing its religion, deforming its absolute monarchy, and transforming its subjects into shopkeepers of the profane.[57]

The reality of liberalism, then, was always worse than its appearance. Like the *philosophes* before them, Liberals hid behind specious maxims, pulling a veil over their true intentions. However much they might protest to the contrary, they were intent on razing the Restoration monarchy to the ground and bringing the church with it. "It is a fact that today has acquired universal evidence," warned *La France Chrétienne* in 1821. "The Liberals are in permanent conspiracy against legitimate governments. They conspire in the assembly, in their pamphlets, in their clubs; they conspire by their principles, their maneuvers, and their emissaries; they conspire every single day, and in every place."[58] The *Ami de la religion et du roi* decried in the following year the Liberals' "double project" to overthrow throne and altar:

> Do not the Liberals seek without end to advocate or excuse our Revolution and those who took part in it? Do they not constantly praise the revolutions and revolutionaries of other countries? Do they not constantly rally together all seditious persons and all those who are enemies of established governments? And the same party, does it not continually laud Voltaire and Rousseau and the editors of the complete editions of all the *philosophes* . . . ?[59]

The answers to these questions were well known, but opponents of the Liberals continued to pose them nonetheless, reminding all who would listen of the dangers inherent in *libéralisme* and the *philosophisme* from which it derived. Like its philosophic predecessor, liberalism would rage outward unless checked, engulfing not only France but also the world. With the spate of Liberal-inspired revolutions on the continent in the 1820s, this prediction took on increasing weight. With revelations of *actual* Liberal participation in a number of conspiratorial organizations, chief of which was the Carbonari, fears of Liberal designs were further confirmed. To root out these conspiracies, to snuff out *libéralisme* at its philosophic source, would prove the overwhelming objective of partisans of the Catholic Right in the years to come. Although obliged to leave the breaking down of doors and the capture of criminals to other forces, they launched an offensive of their own. Continuing to decry the publication of *mauvais livres*, they fought fire with fire, printing hundreds of thousands of *bons livres* in an effort that one scholar has termed, appropriately, the "battle of the books."[60]

Fighting Bad Books with Good

The Berry assassination was undoubtedly a turning point in the history of the Restoration, signaling to Louis XVIII the shortcomings of his policy of conciliation and opening the way for the return of the Ultras. It also confirmed revulsion toward the *philosophes* at the highest levels of society. As a noted contemporary historian, the Liberal Augustin Thierry, observed shortly after the death of Berry, "A relentless hatred, an implacable hatred, a hatred that history will record amongst the most celebrated aversions is that of the nobles today against the *philosophie* of the last century."[61] Yet strangely this hatred did nothing to halt the publication of philosophic books. Despite an ongoing debate over the censorship of *contemporary* literature (particularly newspapers), government authorities showed themselves unable or unwilling to curtail the publication of books from the past. Many, certainly, decried this lapse, but their protests could not stop Restoration presses from continuing to pour forth editions, collected and otherwise, of eighteenth-century authors.

Just a month before the Berry assassination, the *Ami de la religion et du roi* was complaining that Voltaire's alleged "burning desire"—that of selling his writings at "such a low price" that they would be available to the common people—was finally being realized, with works against religion sullying "everything" and "everyone."[62] By October 1820, eight months after the duke's death, the situation had apparently worsened. "It is an amazing thing," the same journal lamented, "this intensification of interest in Voltaire and his writings that has seized our Liberals."[63] Since 1817 publishers had released no fewer than seven collected editions of the *philosophe*'s works. The article bemoaned the recent announcement of an eighth, to be sold as a set of fifteen for thirty francs, or forty sous a volume. Such a price, it seemed, would allow "cooks" and "cobblers" to "dip into this useful collection," fulfilling Voltaire's ultimate aim of spreading *philosophie* to its farthest reaches.[64]

Whether Voltaire himself would have applauded this proliferation is as debatable as whether many cobblers and cooks were buying his works. Still, to his enemies, who waged war in the aftermath of the Berry assassination, the continued publication of philosophic texts, above all those in cheap editions potentially within reach of the common people, was deeply troubling. The government's apparent readiness to tolerate this license seemed utter folly. Once again, key figures in the church felt obliged to denounce the negligence. "Of all the scandals . . . that have heretofore afflicted religion and virtue," the battle-hardened Étienne-Antoine de Boulogne, now bishop of Troyes, intoned in a widely publicized pastoral letter of August 1821, "there is not one more alarming in its consequences . . . than the printing of so many impious writings . . . in a thousand different formats"[65] (see Figure 19). Singling out for particular invective the works of Voltaire and

Figure 19. Étienne-Antoine de Boulogne (1747–1825).

Rousseau—books whose every page revealed "a plan of attack against throne and altar"—Boulogne asked how a regime that considered itself Christian could permit their circulation. Were the countless rituals that conferred divine sanction on royal power "merely vain formalities and ceremonies without consequence?"[66] If not, then surely the state had an obligation to halt the terrible loss of souls that was ravaging its citizenry. The evidence of a renewed conspiracy against throne and altar was overwhelming and the effects certain. And though vigorous ecclesiastics would do everything in their power to prevent it, "if these fatal editions continued to sully French presses . . . irritating heaven . . . and bringing upon us the weight of its wrath," the throne of Saint Louis would have only itself to blame.[67]

Boulogne's angry invocation of a coming "deluge of misfortune" highlighted the belief, increasingly common among men of his stripe, that the state could not be trusted to look after its own interests. Whereas, for some, this implied a spiritual withdrawal to Rome, a quiet journey "over the mountains" in flight from the turmoil of France, others, ultramontane or not, were less willing to concede defeat on native ground. As *La France Chrétienne* and the Ultra-Royalist daily *La Quotidienne* affirmed in praising the "fine" and "eloquent" *mandement* of the Bishop of Troyes, religion must now "redouble its vigilance and zeal" to "impede the propagation of evil."[68] For these authors, as for the new grand master of the Parisian University, Frayssinous, the continued publication of philosophic texts was nothing less than a summons to war. "Evil . . . threaten[ed] France with the greatest disasters." The enemy must be defeated, and soon.[69]

The problem was how? The question exercised Catholics throughout the Restoration, eliciting a lively examination of past efforts to control the flow of subversive literature, with particular emphasis on the failed eighteenth century.[70] Many continued to place hope in the efficacy of a vigilant censor backed by government determination. But even the partial realization of this dream—culminating, under the more proactive reign of Charles X, with the appointment of Bonald as royal censor in 1826—did little to halt the circulation of eighteenth-century texts. That very year Clausel de Coussergues rose in the Chamber of Deputies to denounce the utter failure of existing press laws, claiming that no fewer than 2,741,000 books by Voltaire, Rousseau, Diderot, and their eighteenth-century disciples had been published in France between February 1817 and December 1824. Taken from an 1825 report commissioned by the Ministry of Interior, the figure was, if anything, low.[71] But when illustrated graphically by a number of accompanying tables that charted the press runs, titles, and publication dates of individual authors, it was more than enough to give Clausel's speech a sense of urgency (see Figures 20 and 21). Only against this background of concern with the proliferation of philosophic books can one properly understand Clausel's and others' calls to crack down on the press with an iron fist. Whatever their shrillness to modern ears, they sprang from an internal logic with a long history and an overwhelming sense of despair.

This was also the case with an even more disturbing effort to end traffic in *mauvais livres*: incineration. Catholic missionaries succeeded on at least twelve occasions between 1817 and 1828 in prompting the faithful to relinquish caches of philosophic books in great public conflagrations.[72] In cities as far afield as Bourges, Nevers, Vannes, Clermont, Avignon, Orange, and Chinon, missionaries preached rousing sermons against the *philosophes*, heaping upon them responsibility for the horrors of the Revolution and warning of their continued power to defile. In response, the gathered faithful brought forth their texts, placing them on the pyre in ritual expiation. One missionary in Grenoble boasted of having single-handedly burned a private library of ten thousand books; others took it upon themselves to excommunicate those who owned— and presumably would not surrender—copies of Voltaire, Rousseau, Condorcet, and Helvétius. In Montpellier, a published "antirevolutionary" catechism advised on various techniques of incineration.[73]

Although these accounts today evoke the terrifying image of Berlin Nazis, burning books in the 1930s, we should be wary of letting this awful foreground distract our attention from the more important historical background to these early nineteenth-century incidents. Restoration Catholics were not Nazis, and their sporadic efforts to extinguish philosophy by fire was more a defensive reaction than a totalitarian *Kulturkampf*. Stemming from the deep-seated belief in a direct, causal relationship between philosophic books and violent revolution—a relationship affirmed and reaffirmed for decades—they gave vent to the frustration of enemies of the Enlightenment at their inability to confine the philosophic phoenix to the ashes of history. In this respect, it is no coincidence that the first recorded book burning of the Restoration took place in March 1817, just months after the vicars general of Paris and others had warned of the renewed *philosophe* offensive.[74] By 1829, after the publication of millions of *mauvais livres*, the Archbishop of Bourges could write in disgust, "Ahh! burn these loathsome books that have caused so many evils!"[75] The cry was as much one of desperation, an admission of defeat, as an injunction to act.

Understood on their own terms and in their proper context, the book burnings testify to the tremendous power that Restoration Catholics attributed to the written word: books had the power to make revolutions,

ÉDITIONS DES OUVRAGES DES PRINCIPAUX ÉCRIVAINS IRRELIGIEUX DU XVIIIe SIÈCLE,

PUBLIÉS A PARIS DEPUIS ET COMPRIS LE MOIS DE FÉVRIER 1817 JUSQU'AU 31 DÉCEMBRE 1824.

AUTEURS.	ÉDITEURS.	TITRE DES OUVRAGES.	DATE de la publication.	NOMBRE des exemplaires.	NOMBRE des volumes.
Helvétius.	Ve Lepetit.	Œuvres complètes, 5 vol. in-8°.	4 avril 1818.	2,000	6,000
Id.	Dupont.	De l'Esprit, 2 vol. in-18.	15 sept. 1822.	2,000	4,000
Diderot.	Belin.	Œuvres complètes, 12 vol. in-8°.	14 mars 1817 au 20 mars 1819.	1,200	14,400
Id.	Brière.	Id., 20 vol. in-8°.	31 oct. 1821 au 4 juin 1823.	1,500	30,000
Id.	C. Taillard.	La Religieuse, in-18.	7 juin 1822.	3,000	3,000
Id.	André de Coudome.	Id., in-12.	20 novembre.	1,000	1,000
Id.	C. Taillard.	Jacques le fataliste, in-18.	18 juin.	1,000	1,000
Raynal.	Didot jeune.	Histoire philosophique, 10 vol. in-8°.	1er décembre au 4 avril 1820.	1,500	15,000
Id.	Polanteu.	Des peuples et des gouvernements, in-18.	15 nov. 1822.	1,000	1,000
Saint-Lambert.	P. Jalal.	Œuvres complètes, 2 vol. in-18.	4 mai.	2,000	4,000
Id.	Mesnard et Desenne.	Id., 2 vol. in-18.	9 janvier 1824.	1,500	3,000
Condorcet.	Masson.	Des progrès de l'esprit humain, in-8°.	24 mai 1822.	1,500	1,500
Id.	Pain.	Id., in-18.	22 mai.	2,000	2,000
Id.	C. Chantpie.	Id., in-18.	1er février 1823.	2,000	2,000
Id.	Bossange.	Id., in-18 (en espagnol).	3 février.	2,000	2,000
D'Holbach.	Lemonnier.	Système de la nature, 2 vol. in-8°.	28 février 1820.	1,000	2,000
Id.	Ledoux.	Id., 2 vol. in-8°.	31 octobre 1821.	1,500	3,000
Id.	Dumesnil.	Id., 4 vol. in-18.	12 juillet 1822.	1,500	6,000
Id.	Bossange.	Id., 4 vol. in-18 (en espagnol).	8 août.	1,000	4,000
Id.	Niogret.	Système social, 2 vol. in-18.	30 septembre.	1,000	2,000
Id.	Masson.	La morale universelle, 3 vol. in-8°.	31 août 1820.	1,500	4,500
Id.	Niogret.	Essai sur les préjugés, in-18.	21 mai 1822.	2,000	2,000
Id.	Bossange.	La contagion sacrée, 2 v. in-18 (en espag.).	23 janvier.	1,000	2,000
Dupuis.	Auguis.	Origine des cultes, 7 vol. in-8°.	15 juillet 1822 au 28 décembre.	1,000	7,000
Id.	[illegible]	[illegible]	3 août 1820.	1,500	1,500
Id.	Chasseriau.	Id., in-18.	17 octobre.	2,000	2,000
Id.	Moreau.	Id., in-18.	26 nov. 1822.	2,000	2,000
Id.	Touin.	Id., in-18.	20 août.	2,000	4,000
Id.	Bossange.	Id. (en espagnol), 2 vol. in-18.	17 avril 1817.	1,000	1,000
Volney.	Ve Courcier.	Les Ruines, cinquième édition, in-8°.	29 avril.	1,000	1,000
Id.	Id.	Id. (en espagnol), in-12.	18 mars 1820.	2,000	2,000
Id.	Baudouin.	Id., 7e édit., in-18.	22 juillet.	1,500	1,500
Id.	Gellot.	Id. (en anglais), in-18.	7 décembre.	3,000	3,000
Id.	Id.	Id., in-18, 9e édit.	14 sept. 1821.	3,000	3,000
Id.	Id.	Id., in-18, 10e édit.	21 novembre.	1,000	1,000
Id.	F. Didot.	Id., in-18, 11e édit.	9 février.	1,000	1,000
Id.	Id.	Id., in-18, 12e édit.	28 novembre.	6,000	6,000
Id.	Cellot.	Id., in-12, 13e édit.	16 mai 1823.	3,000	3,000
Id.	Migneret.	Id., in-18, 14e édit.	1er janvier 1821 au 21 juillet.	1,000	7,000
Id.	Bossange.	Œuvres complètes, 7 vol. in-8°.			
Destutt-Tracy.	Courcier.	Éléments d'idéologie, in-8°.	29 mai 1817.	1,500	1,500
Id.	Id.	Id., in-4°.	10 juillet.	1,000	1,000
Id.	Desoër.	Commentaire sur l'esprit des lois, in-18.	27 mai 1822.	1,500	1,500
Id.	Bellegarigue de Toul.	Id., in-12 (en espagnol).	7 décembre.	1,000	1,000
Id.	Ve Dabo.	Id., in-18.	24 mai.	3,000	3,000
Id.	Tastu.	Éléments d'idéologie, in-18.	27 déc. 1823.	2,000	2,000
Montesquieu.	Didot.	Lettres persanes, 3 vol. in-8°.	[illegible] juin 1820.	1,500	4,500
Id.	Mesnard et Desenne.	Id., 2 vol. in-18.	[illegible] août.	1,500	3,000
Id.	Id.	Id., in-12.	28 février 1823.	1,000	1,000
Id.	Debure.	Id., 2 vol. in-32.	11 août 1824.	2,000	4,000
Marmontel.	Mesnard et Desenne.	Bélisaire, in-12.	13 juillet 1818.	2,000	2,000
Id.	Lebègue.	Id., in-12.	28 avril 1820.	2,000	2,000
Id.	Sanjin.	Id. en portugais.	24 mai.	1,000	1,000
Id.	Bossange.	Id., in-32.	1er mai 1822.	4,000	4,000
Id.	Tremblay, à Senlis.	Id., in-18.	19 mai 1824.	1,500	1,500
Fréret.	Masson.	Apologistes de la religion chrétienne, 18.	12 nov. 1822.	2,000	2,000
Id.	Lavel, à Bordeaux.	Id. (en espagnol), in-12.	19 novembre.	2,000	2,000
Id.	Id.	Id., in-12 (en espagnol).	20 novembre.	1,000	1,000
Id.	Béraud.	Id., in-18.	22 novembre.	2,000	2,000
[illegible]	Guiraudet.	Qu'est-ce que le tiers état, in-8°.	27 novembre.	1,000	1,000
Payne.	Poulet.	Le sens commun, in-8°.	31 août.	3,000	3,000
				108,700	207,900

(180)

(181)

Figure 20. Editions of eighteenth-century irreligious writers published between 1817 and 1824. Tables of this nature were used by Clausel de Montals to illustrate the dangerous proliferation of philosophic books before the Chamber of Deputies in 1826.

EDITIONS DE VOLTAIRE ET DE ROUSSEAU,

PUBLIÉES À PARIS, DEPUIS ET COMPRIS LE MOIS DE FÉVRIER 1817 JUSQU'AU 31 DÉCEMBRE 1824.

NOMS des ÉDITEURS.	DATES de la première livraison	de la seconde livraison	NOMBRE des ...	NOMBRE des volumes ...	NOMBRE total des volumes à l'édition.
VOLTAIRE.					
Desoër	8 févr. 18 ?	1ᵉʳ oct. 1818	3,000	36 vol. in-8°	78,000
Plancher	21 mars	17 avril 1820	2,000	44 vol. in-12	88,000
Vᵉ Pérronean	18 avril	9 nov. 1822	3,000	56 vol. in-12	168,000
Lefèvre et Deterville	1ᵉʳ juillet	14 nov. 1818	2,000	41 vol. in-8°	82,000
Lequien	15 juin 1820	non termin.	2,500	70 vol. in-8°	175,000
Thomine et Fortic	21 juin	30 oct. 1822	3,000	60 vol. in-18	180,000
Renouard	25 décem.	14 fév. 1823	1,500	66 vol. in-8°	99,000
Touquet { édition de souscription }	21 sept.	30 déc. 1820	5,000	15 vol. in-12	75,000
Touquet { édition de ... propriété }	8 févr. 1821	non termin.	5,000	{ 67 vol. in-12 au lieu de 95 }	301,000
Enneaux	15 nov.	12 oct. 8 24	3,000	65 vol. in-8°	195,000
Dupont	24 jan. 1823	non termin.	2,600	70 vol. in-8°	182,000
Dalibon	20 juil. 1824	idem	1,000	75 vol. in-8°	75,000
TOTAL			51,600		1,598,000
J.-J. ROUSSEAU.					
Belin	28 mars 1817	2 déc. 1817	1,500	8 vol. in-8°	12,000
Lefèvre et Deterville	24 juillet	22 juin 1818	1,500	18 vol. in-8°	27,000
Ledoux et Tenré	15 oct. 1818	19 juin 1819	3,000	20 vol. in-18	60,000
Vᵉ Pérroneau et Guillaume	12 octobre	1ᵉʳ août 1820	2,000	22 vol. in-12	44,000
Lefèvre	15 juil. 1819	9 sept.	1,000	22 vol. in-8°	22,000
Lequien	5 oct. 1820	20 mars 1823	1,500	20 vol. in-8°	50,000
Touquet	22 décem.	12 déc. 1821	3,000	12 vol. in-12	36,000
Thomine et Fortic	6 avril 1824	4 mars 1824	2,000	25 vol. in-18	50,000
Desoër	30 août	21 nov.	3,000	21 vol. in-18	63,000
Lequien	1ᵉʳ juil. 1823	non termin.	1,500	21 vol. in-8°	51,500
Masset-Pathay	1ᵉʳ sept.	7 déc. 1824	2,000	22 vol. in-8°	44,000
Gamery	25 mars 1824	non termin.	1,500	24 vol. in-12	36,000
Dalibon	24 juillet	idem	1,000	25 vol. in-8°	25,000
Total			24,500		480,500

Figure 21. Table of the publication of the works of Voltaire and Rousseau between February 1817 and December 31, 1824. This table and numerous others were printed in *Des Abus de la liberté de la presse, depuis la restauration, ou Considération sur la propagation des mauvais livres* (Paris, 1826), a work distributed free to all subscribers to the Bibliothèque Catholique.

to overturn altars, and to topple thrones. By mere contact, they could consign a soul to a life of perdition or an eternity of hell. But these very facts also pointed the way to a third strategy in checking the influence of *mauvais livres*. One could ban them and one could burn them, but one could also fight their evil influence with the power of the good. Just as a soul might be lost through contact with evil, it could be transformed in the presence of righteousness. As *La France Chrétienne* affirmed, the best way to fight the "poison" of *mauvais livres* was with antitoxin, the "counter-poison" of *bons livres*.[76]

This was hardly a new proposition. Despite lingering Catholic uneasiness about placing Scripture and theology in unlearned hands, a significant devotional literature had grown up in the wake of the Reformation. First, when church authorities were forced to respond directly to the onslaught of Protestantism, and then in the eighteenth century, when they engaged with the *philosophes* in the literary public sphere, orthodox Catholics generated a significant body of "good books" that were aimed at protecting the faithful and reigning in the errant. The numbers, as we have seen, were significant, and the variety of genres impressive.[77]

There was, however, an original fervor of purpose in the way in which the Restoration book war was carried out and a willingness to experiment with new forms and methods. Fought in the context of the most committed effort to re-Catholicize France since the Counter-Reformation and in full appreciation of the contemporary efforts of international Protestant Bible societies to distribute Scripture throughout the world, this war marshaled the resources, both financial and spiritual, of men and women who had been told for years that the text was the chief weapon in the *philosophe* arsenal.[78] In their view, the stakes were enormous. The fate of France, as elsewhere, would be read in an open book.

This realization was a natural corollary to that other great Restoration effort to spread the word—the over 1500 Catholic missions carried out in France between 1815 and 1830.[79] Weeks-long gatherings of processions, lectures, sermons, fellowship, spiritual teaching, and masses, the missions were at once efforts to atone for the sins of the Revolution, to rebaptize a country that for over twenty years had been seriously deprived of religious instruction, and to help overcome the shortages in a priesthood depleted by death, destruction, and the ravages of time. By descending on a town or city for relatively brief but intensive periods, the missions could reach areas understaffed by regular clergy. They made the most of their opportunity, filling dawn to dusk with fervent spiritual activities and elaborately staged rallies, cross plantings, and mass expiations. In Marseilles in 1820, penitents erected a massive cross that required three thousand men to raise, and crowds that frequently numbered in the tens of thousands gathered to hear talented orators praise the faithful and condemn the wicked. It was in such environments that book burnings took place and during such occasions that the faithful sought to purge sites sullied during the Revolution, rebuilding churches, repairing statues, and reconsecrating the profaned. In late 1821, the former church of Sainte Geneviève (the Pantheon) was restored to religious worship, cleansed of the sacrilegious remains of Voltaire and Rousseau. And during the novena celebrating the church's patron saint in early January 1822, vast flocks of penitents, renouncing Satan, helped to complete the exorcism of what the abbé Maccarthy described in his presiding sermon as this "beautiful building" that had served until only recently "as a gallows."[80] Not surprisingly, missionaries regularly preached violent sermons against the *philosophes* at these gatherings, warning their flocks, whether or not they had ever heard of these men, to beware.[81]

In this environment, in which religious education played such a central role, it was only natural that missionaries would make efforts to distribute edifying literature. As early as 1812, the enterprising vicar of the parish of Saint-Paul, the abbé Barault, established a lending library of *bons livres* to serve his flock in the Bordeaux region.[82] Gradually expanded, this innovative project took on impetus in the wake of the Berry assassination, capturing the attention of Charles-François d'Aviau Dubois de Sanzai, the archbishop of Bordeaux, who recognized it as a useful means of inoculating the population against *mauvais livres*. Providing ecclesiastical and financial support, the archbishop charged Barault with broadening his network of lending libraries. As the 1821 prospectus of the *oeuvre* makes clear, the project was conceived in direct response to the proliferation of philosophic texts:

> For half a century, impiety has spared nothing to facilitate and expand the reading of *mauvais livres*. It was with this battering ram that it laid the groundwork for the Revolution. . . . The tactic has not changed. The most infamous books against religion, the throne, morals, and virtue are exhumed, reprinted, disseminated, flogged in the streets, and delivered up at low prices to serve as every day catechisms of depravity and license.[83]

Given this state of affairs, the *oeuvre des bons livres* would confront *philosophie* on its own terms. The archbishop envisioned the establishment of "depots" throughout the diocese for the purpose of "multiplying, disseminating, and facilitating the reading of good books." Each depot, through its agents, would serve as a dropping point at which to surrender *mauvais livres*, as well as a place to "present good books and to sell them at a large discount conducive to easy purchase."[84] In addition, private libraries would be established there to lend works to those who could not afford them. Overseen and carried out by both laity and ecclesiastics, the administration of the *oeuvre* was conferred on a central office of six (including a vice-president, a general librarian, treasurer, and secretary), as well as a directing council made up of the members of the central office, the superiors of the seminaries and missions, the chiefs of private libraries that took part in the work, and those who paid an annual subscription of at least thirty francs. Underwritten by the archbishopric and by contributions from private donors, the *oeuvre* would appeal to anyone it could, targeting above all young men and women in an effort to warn them "of the danger of bad books" at a formative stage in their development.[85]

Part of a much wider effort to reestablish and expand Catholic influence over the French educational process—a struggle that would continue through the nineteenth century—the Bordeaux *oeuvre* sought to take the battle against *mauvais livres* out of the classroom and into the countryside. Thus it opened up a new front against the secular forces of *philosophie*, holding out a prospect of extraordinary appeal to those concerned with the salvation of souls and the safekeeping of throne and altar. By 1822, the *oeuvre* had established twenty-nine depots in the Bordeaux diocese (106 by 1835), transforming itself into an almost exclusively charitable organization with a special vocation to the poor.[86] In recognition of its efforts, the Vatican granted the *oeuvre* numerous indulgences, conferring the status of a religious confraternity in 1824.[87] By this time, other regions were beginning to establish organizations based directly on the Bordeaux example, with *oeuvres des bons livres* initiated in Vendôme (1824); Lille, Tours, and Nantes (1825); and Autun, Bourg, and Lyon (1827) to complement those already underway in Amiens, Grenoble, and Nevers.[88] Many of these local *oeuvres* would thrive well into the twentieth century, making important contributions to the dissemination of the faith, as well as to the development of a national system of public libraries.[89]

Initiated by local efforts and staffed by local personnel, these various *oeuvres* attempted to adapt themselves to regional circumstances and particularities. The Parisian-based Société catholique des bons livres, by contrast, operated on a national scale. Founded in August 1824 by members of the devout secret society, the Chevaliers de la foi, the Société catholique also aimed to heal through the written word.[90] As its opening prospectus affirmed, "It is by books that society has been spoiled. It is by books that it must be cured." Vowing to establish "in Paris and the provinces, depots for these works in order to lend or give them away at the lowest prices possible," the Société catholique instituted to that end a directing office of five under the presidency of Mathieu de Montmorency, grandmaster of the Chevaliers de la foi, as well as a general council of twenty-four, made up of Parisian curates, ecclesiastics, deputies, peers, and sundry faithful, charged with convening at least four times a year to oversee the Société catholique's affairs. Enjoying government sanction and, in 1827, the official approval of the Holy See, the Société catholique des bons livres could count on secular and ecclesiastical support of the highest order.

Although in these respects this joint lay and ecclesiastical venture strongly resembled its Bordeaux counterpart, there were essential differences. Whereas the Bordeaux *oeuvre* was devoted above all to circulating *bons livres*—a task that it carried out almost entirely free of charge through its many depots and lending branches—the Société catholique emphasized the *sale* of its works, overseeing their editing and publication as well. Publishing between eight and eleven volumes each year, the society solicited annual subscriptions for the entire series at the rate of twenty francs (later twenty-five) per annum. Every subscriber then received three copies of each work, two of which they were expected to give away to whomever they saw fit. Though this method of diffusion necessarily depended on the generosity and means of local benefactors, the aggregate numbers were impressive. In its first three years, the society counted 7,500, 6,400, and 6,000 subscribers, respectively, distributing over 900,000 *bons livres* by the end of 1827.[91] As the *Ami de la religion* commented, these were figures that "would please friends of religion and order."[92]

Friends of religion had other causes for satisfaction. The same year that saw the establishment of the Société catholique des bons livres witnessed the foundation of another national subscription service, the Bibliothèque catholique. Undertaken to complement its friendly rival, the Bibliothèque catholique shared a common aim. As its opening prospectus explained,

> This collection is intended to spread our best works in theology, piety, history, and literature at low prices, and was begun in order to help pastors establish stores of useful and agreeable books in our cities and in the countryside. It also may serve as a stock from which to lend, free of charge, the most suitable works to all sorts of persons, depending on their age, their estate, their taste, and their level of education; a stock from which to provide children and people of scant means books which may instruct them in religion . . . in short, a stock from which to

substitute religious and orthodox works for those of corruption and impiety.[93]

Conceived under a somewhat different format than that of the Société catholique des bons livres, the Bibliothèque catholique relied on direct subscriptions to finance its low-cost religious books, dividing them into various "series" appropriate to different readers (ecclesiastical, apologetic, historical, and literary, as well as a series for children). Publishing twenty-four volumes each year for subscribers—one on the first calendar day of each month and another on the tenth—the undertaking was very much a weapon of war in the battle of the books, a "powerful rampart," the *Mémorial catholique* observed, "with which to contain the torrent of corrupting works that flooded France."[94]

But just what sort of *bons livres* were the Bibliothèque catholique and its kindred societies distributing, and to whom? Although these important questions cannot be answered with the precision they deserve until historians devote greater attention to the nineteenth-century Catholic *oeuvres*, it is possible to make several general observations with a reasonable degree of certainty. First, it seems clear that the overwhelming majority of so-called *bons livres* circulating during the Restoration had been written previously.[95] Constrained by time and circumstances to reproduce titles immediately at hand, the directors edited and pasted copiously from the great Christian classics: the works of the church fathers and medieval theologians, the lives of the saints, and inspirational histories of the pious.[96] They drew extensively on the towering figures of the seventeenth century: Bossuet, Massillon, Bourdaloue, and Fénelon. And they dipped time and again into the output of eighteenth-century religious writers, publishing the works of the abbé Proyart, Barthélemy Baudrand, F.-X. Feller, and Jacob Moreau, to name only a few. Indeed, it was in large part to remedy this problem that the Bibliothèque catholique proposed in late 1825 an annual essay contest with a prize of two thousand francs for "the best work that, in a simple but piquant way, responds to objections made by the people against religion, the sacred mysteries, the Bible, the clergy, the authority of the Church, and so forth." It was not enough, the editors admitted, simply to "reproduce old works composed for another time and other needs."[97] For similar reasons, the Société catholique des bons livres began to sponsor its own yearly contest in 1826.[98]

Part expediency and part failure of imagination, this reliance on previously composed works had important repercussions. Undoubtedly it sapped much of the vitality of the good-books offensive, giving the appeal to renew the faith a dated (if also a timeless) feel. But even when the organizers did try to incorporate more current writings into their arsenal, these often had such contemporary and stridently political agendas that it is questionable how effective they were as purely religious weapons. The Ultra organizers of the Société des bons livres, for example, did not hesitate to include the maudlin account of Louis XVI's last days, the *Journal de ce qui s'est passé à la tour du Temple pendant la captivité de Louis XVI*, at the top of their list for 1826.[99] Nor, in the same year, did the directors of the Bibliothèque catholique see any discrepancy in issuing, free to all subscribers, *De la liberté de la presse, depuis la restauration, ou Considération sur la propagation des mauvais livres*. A collection of pamphlets, articles, sermons, pastoral letters, and legal *arrêts* that condemned the proliferation of *mauvais livres*, the work was a sustained Ultra attack on the government's unwillingness to censor Liberal and philosophic publications.[100] At heart, the volume was designed to convert the mind, not the soul, to shape *political* convictions, not religious beliefs.

Coming from an organization devoted to combating *mauvais livres*, this position is not at all surprising. Nor is one shocked to find the *oeuvres*' lists dotted with titles that lauded the Vendée rebellion, excoriated the Terror, attacked Liberals, or vilified the Revolution.[101] To those directing the war against bad books, the conflation of the political and the religious was second nature—the defense of the throne tied intimately to the defense of the altar. However natural, this conflation almost certainly weakened the strictly religious impact of the good-books campaign by tying the faith inextricably to a counterrevolutionary political agenda. One wonders how many otherwise potentially sympathetic readers were alienated by the political posturing of the books and representatives of the *oeuvres*.

To enter into this line of inquiry is to pose, in turn, the question of audience. Who was reading these *bons livres* and just whom were they intended to persuade? The fact that the funding of the Société catholique des bons livres, the Bibliothèque catholique, and other subscription services of the kind was largely underwritten by paying subscribers significantly determined the nature of the product. Their books catered to the level, tastes, and education of readers able to afford them—a relative elite.[102] And though it is true that the Société catholique did maintain *cabinets des lectures* aimed at working-class readers in Paris and other cities and that both it and the Bibliothèque catholique issued titles for circulation among artisans and peasants, there is no real reason to believe that their success was great.[103] In this respect, the failure of an ambitious effort by the Société catholique in 1827 to appeal to "poor families" through the establishment of a national network of lending depots modeled on the Bordeaux *oeuvre* was symptomatic.[104] For the most part, neither of the two national societies nor its regional subscription counterparts were able to make significant inroads among popular milieux, and in 1830 the Société catholique was forced to close because of financial difficulties.

The Bordeaux *oeuvre*, by contrast, with its commitment to the free distribution of *bons livres*, had far greater success among the people, establishing a network of *dépôts* in working-class quarters and in the small villages of the countryside.[105] Repeated with similar results at the popular level around Nantes and Toulouse, the Bordeaux experiment helps to remind us of the considerable gains made by Catholic proselytes in this period and of the solid foundation they laid for the future. Over the course of the nineteenth century, the *oeuvre des bons livres* would become a standard feature of the French landscape, a principal means through which the church was able to project the word and so maintain a delicate balance between literacy and the faith. In the context of the 1820s, however, the limited gains of the Bordeaux *oeuvre* and its more successful imitators were relatively circumscribed, set off against twenty-five years of religious neglect and revolutionary experience. Encouraging for the long run, these organizations were now only fledglings, ill suited, on their own, to withstand the secular tide. Even when joined with the kindred forces of the missions, the pious organizations, and the national and regional societies that distributed hundreds of thousands of *bons livres* during the Restoration, none of these efforts could arrest the philosophically inspired current that flooded France with *mauvais livres*. It is telling that in 1829 the regional subscription library, the Bibliothèque de Lille, issued free to all subscribers the *Suites funestes de la lecture des mauvaises livres*, the tale of a young bourgeoise, her servants, and her friends whose lives are decimated by reading evil books. Although they are, in the end, rescued by repentance and the pity of Christ, it is unlikely that such literary conventions provided much consolation to men and women who read the wider book of France with alarm.[106] Notwithstanding the ascension in 1824 of a new king committed to the protection of religion, defenders of the altar continued to bewail the lack of assistance from the throne.

Eternal Return

It is more than a little ironic that the Restoration king so intent on strengthening the bond between throne and altar ultimately hastened its undoing. Deeply pious and far less compromising than his worldly predecessor, Charles X came to the throne in 1824 with visions of making France what his brother had not: a Christian monarchy in keeping with the Ultra ideal. The story of his failure in this regard—the bumbling, lachrymose coronation ceremony at Reims in 1825; the passage of the Sacrilege Law in the same year, making the defamation of religious property an offense punishable by mutilation and death; the inept effort to indemnify the émigrés for property seized during the Revolution; and ultimately, the halting attempts to regulate the press and electorate that precipitated his final downfall—is a tale familiar to those acquainted with the conventional history of the Restoration. What is less often appreciated is just how superficial, in the end, were these efforts to unify throne and altar, to make the Bourbon reign the reign of God.[107] However much Charles might personally have sympathized with the cause of his more devout clerical allies, his ability to aid them was limited. Consider, for example, the fact that despite the rigorous terms of the 1825 Sacrilege Law, it was never once enforced. Decrees passed in the same year that mandated a greater role for the church in public secondary education were quickly repealed in the face of public protests. Time and again, royal officials in the provinces worked to curtail or even circumvent what they felt were the disruptive and overly zealous activities of the missions, and despite Charles's stated support for the various *oeuvres des bons livres*, his regime did almost nothing to curb the extensive traffic in anticlerical publications and philosophic books.[108] Finally, despite the widespread public perception that Charles was aiding a nationwide Jesuit resurgence (and had even joined the order himself), government support for the controversial order was negligible. Leaving aside the received image of a reactionary throne and altar entente, Charles X's regime continued what was the dominant pattern of the Restoration and of the century as a whole—the ever greater secularization of political authority.

Despite the truth of these statements, it is also clear that they were largely irrelevant to a great many French observers in the 1820s. To these men and women, truth lay in appearance (image was everything), and the image of Charles X prostrate before the crucifix at his lavish coronation ceremony or walking barefoot in purple robes among the penitents at the Papal Jubilee of 1826 was enough to convince them that this king was in thrall to men in black. To protest that servitude and to forestall an even closer union between throne and altar than apparently already existed, French activists took up their pens and placards in a wave of anti-clerical defiance that historians agree rose dramatically in the wake of Charles's coronation. Reviving a discourse used to great effect during the Old Regime, journalists and pamphleteers spun tales of a horrible clerical plot, a vast conspiracy stretching from Rome to the inner sanctum of Charles's court, designed to usurp political power and place it in the hands of the church. Singling out the Jesuits for particular vilification, this myth gained truly astounding national currency, becoming the subject of a number of best-selling publications by otherwise "respectable" royalists and filling the columns of Liberal newspapers and the correspondence of royal administrators throughout the country.[109]

To bolster this effort, publishers continued their campaign of reprinting key Enlightenment texts in the form of pamphlets and cheap editions easily affordable to workers, artisans, and peasants. One enterprising publisher brought out a fireproof edition of Voltaire, boasting that "at a time when one so charitably burns so many of our most useful and philosophical works, the precaution is not without use."[110] The publisher expressed confidence, however, that the phoenix would rise from the flames. *Le Constitutionnel* concurred, exulting in 1825 that "the more of Voltaire the missionaries obtain for their *auto-da-fés*, the more [his] works . . . are sought after. The number of publications surpasses the number of burnings." "Never," the paper continued elsewhere, has Voltaire "enjoyed such widespread popularity in France"[111] (see Figure 22).

This popularity only increased as Voltaire, Rousseau, and their *philosophe* brethren were taken up as popular symbols of resistance to the clerical order, penetrating into the furthest reaches of society. The names of leading Enlightenment authors became "common currency" for ordinary men and women, employed, along with their slogans, as symbols of defiance to altar and throne.[112] While the names and words of the *philosophes* thus gained genuinely widespread recognition, so did their appearances, sustaining a buoyant trade in images, engravings, and prints. In the Breton town of Vannes in 1824, one could even purchase "razors bearing the likeness of the author of *Candide*, or of Montesquieu"—just two of the many items that ingenious marketers brought out to satisfy the popular yearning to demonstrate solidarity with the men and ideals of the century of lights.[113]

Others assumed more active roles, expressing their resistance to the clerical order by singing seditious songs, disrupting church services and processions, affixing scurrilous placards, and hanging priests in effigy. From 1825 to 1830, France witnessed a wave of sacrilegious crimes of the very kind the 1825 law was designed to curtail: attacks on mission crosses, robberies in churches, desecration of the host and sacred vessels, and profanation of the altar. In a particularly unsavory incident, young men urinated and defecated on a large calvary in the department

Figure 22. The Phoenix Reborn from Its Ashes (1817). A group of religious students at Bourges dances around a burning pile of *mauvais livres*, including works by Raynal, Diderot, Voltaire, and Mably. The phoenix of *philosophie*, however, rises from the flames.

of the Drôme. Elsewhere, protesters trampled the sacraments underfoot and defaced church property with grafitti, leaving behind pointed if unsubtle messages: "Down with Charles X, down with the Catholic clergy" or simply "Shit for the priests."[114]

Anathema of this kind and on this scale would doubtless disconcert even the inured faithful of the early twenty-first century. To Restoration Catholics, convinced that God had only just demonstrated the extent of his might by punishing France for the sins of the eighteenth century, the anticlerical campaign of the final years of the Bourbon monarchy was nearly incomprehensible in its perversity—appalling evidence of the will to defy and of the utter depravity of humanity. "Lift your heads, Christian brothers," urged the Bishop of Dijon in his Lenten *mandement* of 1826, "and look at what is happening around you. What a century and what morals! What a world in which we are condemned to live."[115] "Let us not fool ourselves about what has become of human society," concurred the Bishop of Chartres in his Jubilee *mandement* of the same year: "See for yourself—not a single doctrine of Christianity is respected, not a single scrap of truth is left. . . . Impiety rushes headlong . . . [toward] the frightful abyss of atheism."[116]

This frantic rush to the abyss was incomprehensible. Its cause was not.

The Catholic Right had no doubt that it was witnessing the continued development of an epic struggle between religion and philosophy—one that transcended the present moment and that surpassed the spatial limits of national frontiers. With the great boldness of Liberal and anticlerical activity in the final years of Charles X's reign, French observers tended increasingly to see their own battle as part of a much larger drama.[117] The horrible, pregnant system of *philosophie* had spawned international mutations, spreading in the form of Liberal uprisings to Spain, Portugal, and the Italian peninsula.[118] France's tremors were only reverberations of shock waves being felt throughout Metternichian Europe and, from there, the world.[119] "Let us cast an eye on the principal events that for several years have afflicted Europe," the counterrevolutionary polemicist Nicholas Rosset commented in his 1827 *Lettre au peuple français*, "and let us blush at our own credulity."[120] For too long French observers had remained blind to the international activity of the "impious sect" that was plotting "the destruction of all monarchies." Even in the New World one could see evidence of these machinations in the marauding activities of Simón Bolívar.[121] When, two years later, news of a bloody uprising in Mexico City reached France, *La Quotidienne* slotted the news neatly into this larger, world-historical narrative: "Thousands of citizens chased from their homes, five hundred opulent families reduced to poverty, eight hundred men butchered, women raped, children violated, an immense city turned over to pillage, and twenty-five million rendered the prey of brigands—here is the liberty of Liberalism . . . the application of the doctrine of *philosophes*."[122] Surely, what the *Conservateur de la Restauration* described as the Liberal-philosophical "representative fever" was sweeping the globe.[123]

This situation boded ill for the future precisely because it was so reminiscent of the past. Reviewing a newly abridged version of the abbé Barruel's *Memoires pour servir à l'histoire du Jacobinisme* in late 1829, the *Ami de la Religion et du roi* was forced to remark on the disturbing parallels between Europe on the eve of the Revolution of 1789 and the present: "We see exactly the same systems and the same principles reproducing themselves with striking resemblance." "The same methods are today put into effect," with the one difference that in this corrupt, contemporary age there was no longer "any hindrance to impede" the modern *philosophes incrédules*.[124]

The journal was by no means alone in drawing frightening parallels with 1789. Since the onset of the Restoration, observers had warned repeatedly that like causes produced like effects; that the proliferation of philosophically inspired literature would bring down Louis XVIII and Charles X, as it had their elder brother. "What state can hold out against this permanent assault . . . this frightening circulation of impious and corrupting books?" Boulogne had asked in 1819.[125] A decade later, the author of the *Tableau des trois époques,* or *The Philosophes Before, During, and After the Revolution,* compiled a table to more graphically illustrate the extent of the coming danger. In one column, he listed the characteristics of 1789–1792, and in the other those of 1829, concluding that all clear-eyed observers would see the obvious—"that danger is approaching, that the altar and throne are going to be overthrown again, and that France will once more be delivered up to the horror of anarchy."[126] Unfortunately, "men of state" could not readily be counted among the lucid, for they remained "without worry concerning the dangers threatening religion," undisturbed by the machinations of nineteenth-century philosophers, worthy successors to those of the eighteenth century."[127] The militant *Conservateur de la Restauration,* too, consistently adopted this outlook of incredulous, bitter comparison, warning repeatedly between 1828 and 1830 of the similarities between 1789 and the present: "What one saw then, one sees today," the journal lamented, adding in frustration that

> for ten years, wise men . . . have not ceased to warn those in power of the abyss to which a passionate sect is leading us. . . . But today, like [during the eighteenth century], these sage warnings are scorned; eyes and ears are closed so as not to see and hear. The revolution is knocking at the door, but unhappy France does not want to recognize the monster that is waiting to devour its children. What is one to do in the midst of a blindness that nothing can cure and which seems humanly impossible to explain?[128]

This question captured perfectly the sense of helplessness of those who considered themselves the regime's most resolute defenders. Attacked on one side by a seemingly insurmountable coalition of modern-day *philosophes,* and abandoned on the other by a monarchy unable or unwilling to uphold the altar that maintained the throne, the Catholic Right retreated in the Restoration's final hours into a role that it had played before: that of Cassandra.[129] Just as in the years preceding 1789 and on the eve of the Berry assassination, observers on the Right bemoaned again what they considered to be the utter folly of the present course, gave voice to a sense of recrimination that their warnings were brushed aside, and took solace in predicting the disasters that would most certainly follow from this negligence. In the face of efforts on the part of ministers of Charles X to backtrack, proposing compromises with the ascendant opposition forces of Liberals and moderate Royalists in the final years of the regime, men and women of the Right remained recalcitrant, decrying what they termed this perilous *modérantisme* that would only open the floodgates to greater disasters. As the *Conservateur de la Restauration* argued just months before the final fall, all those suggesting a "middle way" between the two "extremes" of Liberalism and Royalism were horribly misguided. In truth, there were only those, on the one hand, who sought to "abolish the Catholic religion" and "carry out in the State and Europe as a whole a general upheaval," and those, on the other hand, who worked to "maintain at all costs the Catholic religion in France, and defend until the last breath the legitimacy of the Bourbons."[130] In such a world, configured along eschatological lines, there could be no middle course, only light and darkness, truth and error. Far better to remain unsullied on high ground, as the dark waters rose, than to plunge in with the enemy.

CONCLUSION

*I*f one is to pose the perennial, and perhaps unanswerable, question "Do philosophical books make revolutions?" there is probably more cause to do so in connection with the French Revolution of 1830 than with that of 1789.[1] It would seem difficult to deny that the vast proliferation of works by Voltaire, Rousseau, and other leading *philosophes* played at least some role in preparing the way for the final undoing of the Bourbons. Whether this role was merely symbolic, the expression of deeper shifts in French culture, or an immediate cause in its own right is hard to say. In any case, that question lies beyond the purview of this book. To the men and women under consideration here at least, *philosophie* was as guilty in the second Bourbon downfall as in the first—a charge that they were making within days of the July Revolution and that many would repeat well into the nineteenth century.[2]

Such relatively undiscriminating assertions aside, however, there can be little doubt that the Right's own internal disintegration, as much or more than any external, philosophic threat, played a crucial role in hastening its downfall. Despite the insistence of right-wing commentators on construing their world in terms of starkly cast oppositions—*philosophie* and religion; the cause of the Revolution and the cause of royalty; or as Bonald opined more sharply, the "state of war between good and evil"—it is evident that such divisions were as unfit to comprehend the political environment of Restoration France as they were the France of the Revolution.[3] Between these poles lay—both within the narrow electorate of the Restoration and outside in the country at large—a considerable range of opinions about the relative merits of the Old Regime, the Revolution, and the compromises to be effected between the two. Even at the Ultra extreme, opinion was by no means unanimous.[4]

To be sure, men and women of the Right—which is to say, in the context of the Restoration, Ultra-Royalists—did share a good deal of common ground, general principles bequeathed by their anti-*philosophe* and counterrevolutionary forebears.[5] Almost all could agree, for example, on the need for a strong, strategic alliance of throne and altar to prevent the resurgence of revolutionary forces.[6] Yet when it came to configuring that alliance—establishing the terms of power between the church and the crown—fault lines that had plagued these two institutions for centuries quickly reemerged, undermining their unity in practical, institutional terms. Closely related was the question of where the ultimate basis of spiritual authority lay, in the traditional, Gallican church, with its locus in the collective power of the French bishops appointed by the crown, or "over the mountains" in the confines of the Vatican. If at the outset of the Restoration the better part of the clergy was Gallican, faithful to the French church's peculiar traditions and historic rights, by the end many were less sure, disillusioned by the vacillation and creeping secularism of the monarchy and seeing in Rome a far more steadfast ally. Friction between Gallicans and Ultramontanes, as a result, proved another inherent weakness that divided the Right from within.

Tensions also arose over the nature and extent of royal power. In principle, most Ultras espoused a belief in the unified, indivisible, and divinely consecrated status of royal authority. Yet Louis XVIII's role in dissolving the Incomparable Chamber and his frequent disagreements with the Ultra deputies in the first years of his reign highlighted the precariousness of admitting too much authority to the crown. Summoning the ghosts of hallowed antagonisms between the aristocracy and the monarchy, these squabbles highlighted the embarrassing question of what to do with an unreliable king, leading a number of Ultras to develop defenses of the sovereignty of the chamber that struck more doctrinaire absolutists like Bonald as smacking dangerously of liberalism.[7]

Similar tensions arose over the sweep and scope of central authority in relation to the privileges of corporate bodies—intermediate institutions such as the local collectivity, the provincial administration, and the courts. Here, once again, long-standing fissures reappeared, revealing that the foundations of history were not so solid as many proclaimed. Although Ultras unanimously regarded the past as the font of all knowledge of humankind and society, that past, the experience of the Restoration underscored, was capable of generating a variety of different lessons and interpretations, producing, in turn, conflicting privileges, prerogatives, and principles. On closer examination, even such an idyllic moment as the golden age of Louis XIV revealed trenchant conflicts among a centralizing monarchy, the church, and the aristocracy, sending some of those who would search for models of corporate symbiosis and organic social harmony further back in time—to a vague and poorly documented Middle Ages, in which imagination and myth could hold much freer sway.[8]

Finally, even the seemingly unbreakable Ultra consensus against freedom of expression and religious tolerance proved subject to dispute. Whereas the great majority of Ultras advocated careful control of the written and spoken word, some balked when Louis XVIII attempted to turn the censor against the Ultras themselves in the years before the Berry assassination, and they came to support, with varying degrees of sincerity, freedom of expression as a necessary means to guarantee the dissemination of their own views.[9]

Ultra-Royalism, then, was inherently unstable, and when forced to engage in the practical project of ruling, prone to the divisive thrusts of its political enemies to the Left, who proved tremendously adept at "splitting the Ultra coalition" of monarchists, aristocrats, and clergy in the waning years of the Restoration.[10] In certain respects this was the simple result of Ultra-Royalism's relatively narrow base of popular support. But, arguably, as important a cause of the failure of the Right in this period (and in later periods as well) was the fact that its intellectual capital was shaped fundamentally through opposition. Both the anti-*philosophe* discourse of the *ancien régime* and the more extreme of the successive counterrevolutionary doctrines were born out of radical defiance—dogged antagonism to threats both real and perceived. "Anti" the *philosophes*, "counter" the Revolution, "against" the Enlightenment, polemicists adopting these stances articulated animosities in great detail, painting powerful pictures of what they opposed.[11] But when it came to presenting a carefully delineated portrait of the social and political world that should replace the one sullied by *philosophes* and revolutionaries, anti-*philosophes*, counterrevolutionaries, and ultimately the Ultras spoke with a good deal less sharpness, precision, and consistency. They invoked the need for the unity of throne and altar to fight their collective enemies yet failed to specify the terms and limits of that alliance. They glorified power, hierarchy, and deference yet were quick to break ranks when their particular interests clashed. They spoke of the need to conserve yet advocated the undoing of much of what had been done. Ultimately, the French Right, in all its various early guises, was far more coherent in opposition than in power.

There is another, closely related reason for the practical failure of the Right in this period, a reason, strangely, that was also a cause of its enduring appeal—its idealism. This is not a word generally associated with the rightward end of the political spectrum, yet the early French

Right was undoubtedly idealist, both literally, in that it saw ideas as constitutive of social reality, and more broadly, in that it continually refused to accept the world as given. From its birth, the Right was never really conservative in a strict sense but, rather, sought radical change, the profound alteration of a world infected to the core by *philosophie*. During the Old Regime, this impulse took the form of a bitter criticism of existing social mores, of the cultural devastation wrought by an alien creed, and of the reluctance of the state to wage war against it. With the triumph of the Revolution, erstwhile anti-*philosophes* and newly consecrated counterrevolutionaries were then forced to advocate the reversal of concrete political and institutional changes to accompany the reversal they sought in spiritual matters. And during the Restoration, the attempt to carry out this project—most evident in the great Catholic cultural revolution of the missions—met not only with the "conservative" resistance of those shaped by the historical experience of 1789–1815 but also with that of men and women who, monarchist in theory, were nonetheless unwilling to participate fully in what seemed to be a utopian venture: the effort to cleanse France of all trace of the Enlightenment and of the Revolution and to invest its inhabitants with a spiritual piety more intense than the eighteenth century had ever known. On the surface, this was a journey to the mythic past. But in truth the world that the men and women of the far Right aimed to create was not that of the *ancien régime*, the former regime. The world to which they hoped to return existed only in their minds.

The practical experience of power, then, betrayed the visionary, even revolutionary tendency at the Catholic extreme, pointing out the fault lines, tensions, and divisions in the right-wing constellation. In these respects, the Restoration marked the culmination in failure of the early French Right, dealing a definitive setback to the Catholic Counter-Enlightenment. But although down, that movement was not out. Its legacy would prove lasting.

Most immediately, enemies of the Enlightenment left behind a construction of the Enlightenment itself that was destined to exert a persistent hold on subsequent interpretations. In their daily polemics, carried out for over half a century and filling thousands of pamphlets, books, articles, sermons, and orations, anti-*philosophes* had wound their accusations tightly about their foes, tying them into positions from which the *philosophes* would find it difficult to escape. The works of Baudrand, Feller, Barruel, Proyart, and Gérard, to name only a few, were reprinted with great consistency into the nineteenth century, passing on their defenses of religion and criticism of the Enlightenment wholly intact.[12] Ironically, an age generally thought to be one of spiritual and theological sterility nonetheless produced an apologetic literature and a vision of its defining movement that far outlived it.

This is to speak only of works written in the eighteenth century itself. In the nineteenth century, many continued to rail in very similar terms against the age seen as the germinating source of the major problems of modernity. In the genre of *bon livre*, for example, Catholics spread piety and anti-*philosophe* criticism of the Enlightenment in such volume and with such acerbity that one Catholic official, R. P. Delaporte, argued that they were doing the faith a disservice. "Superficial, flimsy, boring," the "bad good book" impeded true Catholic enlightenment, Delaporte charged before the General Assembly of the Catholic Committees of France in 1880, urging, in a strange twist, that they be thrown into the flames. "Burn them all!" he exhorted: "Throw them to the shredder. . . . The *mauvais bon livre* will serve the Catholic cause only in its death."[13] Few, if any, took him at his word. The *bon livre* continued to line bookstalls throughout France, reflecting the animosity toward the Enlightenment that they were first designed to instill. In churches, catechisms, and classrooms, many in the Catholic educational establishment perpetuated these biases, insinuating remnants of the anti-*philosophe* discourse into the cultural fabric of France. Such diffusion helped to ensure that hostility to the Enlightenment remained a staple of Catholic, conservative, and right-wing thought into the twentieth century.

Particular thinkers embellished and adapted the original anti-*philosophe* portrait in different ways, putting its charges to varied purposes, but on the whole they left the principal allegations intact. Thus, in the pages of authors as far afield as Tocqueville, Taine, Cochin, Maurras, and Gaxotte, one finds a dogged insistence on the *philosophes'* responsibility for the excesses of the Revolution.[14] They were accused of being abstract speculators, spreading atheism and unbelief among the highest and lowest orders and preparing the "mob" that would trample down altars, as well as the aristocrats who would betray their class and king. Intolerant and fanatical, they exercised a stranglehold on the Old Regime world of letters that was the direct precursor of the tyranny of the Jacobins. As Cochin observed in 1911 in a scathing critique of *philosophisme*, "Before the bloody terror of 1793, there was, from 1765 to 1780, a dry terror whose Committee of Public Safety was the *Encyclopédie* and whose Robespierre was d'Alembert."[15]

Writing at almost exactly the same time, Gustave Gautherot, professor of the history of the French Revolution at the Institut Catholique in Paris, devoted an entire book to chronicling the relationship between the *philosophes* and the radical phase of the Revolution, repeating the anti-*philosophe* discourse in full.[16] For Gautherot, however, *philosophisme* was not just the animating principle of the Revolution but also a motive force in the "gigantic drama that continues in the world between Christian civilization and the counter-civilization issued from *Encyclopédisme*."[17] Unfolding this drama in detail, he charged the *philosophes* with responsibility for everything from the ravages of capitalist individualism to the international pacifism of Gustave Hervé. He dwelled at length, too, on the original *philosophe* conspiracy and its relation to the ongoing machinations of Freemasonry.[18]

Gautherot's work highlights the way in which anti-*philosophe* plot language could be refitted to account for later developments. Providing a model of Manichean opposition and an archetype of conspiratorial design, theories of *philosophe* conspiracies were frequently employed by Catholics during the nineteenth and first half of the twentieth centuries, swept up into other narratives and applied to more immediate enemies.[19] As the German scholar Johannes Rogalla von Bieberstein has pointed out, it is possible to trace the charge of "conspirator against the social order" in a clear line of descent from the *philosophe* bugbear of the eighteenth century through the Freemason, Jewish, liberal, and socialist pariahs of the nineteenth and twentieth centuries.[20] If the *philosophes* occupied an increasingly less illustrious place in this pantheon of living demons, their influence continued to be felt in the notion of the plot itself, in the conception of the world as a battleground between good and evil. And when it came, specifically, to the historical phenomenon of the French Revolution, the theory of the *philosophe* conspiracy displayed incredible longevity. As the British historian William Doyle observes, the oldest theory of the origins of the French Revolution—"that it was some sort of intellectual conspiracy or plot"—continues to find adherents even today.[21] Right-wing book shops throughout Europe are well stocked with such texts, decrying the "noxiousness and perversity of the philosophy of the Enlightenment."[22]

Given this undeniable persistence, the long resonance of arguments crafted over two centuries ago, it is worth emphasizing one last time how seductive could be the most compelling rhetorical tropes at the disposal of enemies of the Enlightenment, that is, that they were right. They had predicted—had they not?—the terrible events of the French Revolution, the excesses wrought by men whose heads were full of *philosophie*. They had warned—had they not?—that the indulgence of the early Restoration would lead to horrific deeds, a prediction that took shape in the murder of the Duke of Berry. And they had foreseen—had they not?—that the failure of Charles X to arrest the tide of philosophic books and the *libéralisme* that was their child would bring down the

Bourbons in yet another revolution. To accept the premise, that *philosophie* was a protean cause, was to admit the clairvoyance of those who had cautioned that the century of light bore darkness at its heart. Seen from this perspective, the Right, unequivocally, was right.

Looking at the Western world through this lens in the nineteenth and twentieth centuries, more than a few intelligent observers were persuaded by this basic claim. The decline of the faith, the isolation of the individual, the breakup of the family, moral turpitude, the separation of the church and state, political upheaval, and unbridled tolerance—all this could be traced to an infectious source. Liberalism itself was regarded as *philosophie* in disguise. Should we really be surprised that Pius IX condemned it as one of the principal errors of the modern world in his infamous Syllabus of 1864? If considerable numbers of Catholics continued to resist basic liberal tenets into this century and continued to see the Enlightenment as a dark moment in European history, it was due in no small part to this long anti-*philosophe* heritage. It is far too easy to forget that what to many today seem perfectly innocuous values—tolerance, free speech, civil marriage and divorce, moral and economic laissez faire, democracy, and natural rights—were for many, for long, infected at their source.

Nor was this skepticism about the Enlightenment and its values simply confined to France. Around the Catholic world, one can follow the main outlines of the anti-*philosophe* portrait. Exported throughout Europe after the Terror, it was maintained in the nineteenth century in sermons, pamphlets, newspaper articles, and disquisitions in Italy, Germany, Spain, Portugal, Ireland, Québec, Poland, Hungary, Martinique, and many parts of Latin America. One finds its principal outlines into the 1970s in textbooks in Franco's Spain and in Salazar's Portugal, and there are more than a few who can still remember reading such accounts in the Argentina of Perón, the Brazil of Getulio Vargas, the France of Vichy, or the Chile of General Pinochet. Just as the Enlightenment was an international phenomenon, so was the Counter-Enlightenment. That story deserves to be told in much greater detail.

Bequeathing an image of its enemy that long outlived it, the French Counter-Enlightenment, too, passed on a structure of opposition and a set of recurrent themes that would resurface in right-wing thought even to the present day. The foundations for that endurance were religious, for as we have seen, the motive force shaping the early French Right was the Catholic conviction of militants whose views were hardened in response to the threats—both real and perceived—of the Enlightenment. Although one can point to the likes of the atheist Rivarol, question the depth of conviction of a La Harpe, or scoff at the orthodoxy of a Sabatier, on the whole these are exceptions that prove the rule—that the early French Right was founded on sincere belief in the sanctity and necessity of the Roman Catholic faith.[23]

Too many observers, however, continue to harbor the received notion that the European Right was, or must have been, exclusively self-serving in its origins, the justification of antiquated social privilege, political power, and economic interest. To take only one example, the eminent social scientist Albert O. Hirschman bases his important, recent study of "reactionary rhetoric" in the West on a model that sees the principal galvanizing movements in modern conservative thought as responses to three great progressive "thrusts": the struggle to secure the *civil* dimension of citizenship (civil rights and equality before the law); the *political* effort to extend the suffrage; and the push for *social* rights to education, health, and economic well-being.[24] Carried out in the West in successive waves since the eighteenth century, each of these thrusts, Hirschman affirms, generated powerful and inveterate "counter-thrusts" of such rhetorical consistency and argumentative force that they would seem to confirm Whitehead's famous remark that "The major advances in civilization are processes which all but wreck the societies in which they occur."[25]

Hirschman's primary concern was to lay bare the rhetorical strategies at work in these principal counterthrusts, a task he fulfills admirably. His model of "action and reaction," moreover, is compelling. Certainly it presents a much more sophisticated framework for understanding Western development than did the theories of earlier sociologists, such as T. H. Marshall, who were inclined to see the great movements of history as triumphant, linear advances, victories over barriers that impeded the course of progress. Yet in important ways, as Hirschman himself freely acknowledges, he is indebted to this earlier sociology, drawing from it the original schema of civil, political, and social advance to which reactionaries then responded.[26] As a consequence, he pays almost no attention to religion, leaving one with the impression that Western right-wing thought arose primarily in response to civil, political, and economic dynamics to safeguard threatened interests. Beginning his account only at the time of the French Revolution, Hirschman neglects the response to the Enlightenment altogether.

This is not to suggest that civil, political, and economic interests were unimportant factors in shaping the attitudes of adherents of the early Right. In their view, the Enlightenment, and more directly the Revolution, challenged their prerogatives in all these areas, a fact that only sharpened their hostility to both. Yet in considering the arguments of the men and women treated in this text, it is also clear that their sense of anxiety arose first and foremost from the secular thrust of the Enlightenment, from its alleged, unmitigated attack on religion. Other concerns—civil, political, and economic—flowed from this basic preoccupation. One is struck by how overwhelmingly moral was their criticism of the Enlightenment and by how overwhelmingly cultural were their arguments on behalf of the world for which they fought. Religion, to reiterate, was the primary concern, and Hirschman's failure to treat it causes him and many others to miss what was most compelling about this early, reactionary rhetoric.

For all their exaggeration, hatred, and hostility, enemies of the Enlightenment captured something essential about the modern world, intuited early on that the secularization of society and the desacralization of government would have profound and lasting consequences. In this, whatever their other shortcomings, they were right. It was their ability to play on this realization—to dramatize the cultural costs of disenchantment—that gave their vision sustenance and power.

This, in turn, highlights another important aspect of the early Right: its modernity. Admittedly, that term is vague, and as no shortage of postmodern theorists have reminded us, it is rarely value-free. In fact, when used in reference to a state or process of historical development, "modernity" generally reveals its Enlightenment origins. Although the self-conscious embrace of the modern had even earlier roots, in the seventeenth-century fight against the ancients, the idea of doing progressive battle against forces who refused to cede to the light of the times was quintessentially an Enlightenment construct.[27] The *philosophes* saw and presented themselves as modern and progressive, labeling their enemies as archaic and retrograde. These labels, the Enlightenment's labels, have proved difficult to shake.

Of course, the *philosophes* did not choose their terms entirely without justification, for in certain fundamental respects enemies of the Enlightenment *were* opposed to what they conceived as the noxious consequences of modern thought. Yet as even a cursory consideration of the writings of Rousseau will make clear, opposition to modernity is itself a modern phenomenon. In the same way, the men and women of the French Counter-Enlightenment, so heavily indebted to him, were very much the product of their time. Although prone to great exaggeration and tremendous oversimplification, they nonetheless understood, in ways that perhaps only Vico had before them, the implications for faith of the corrosive effects of reason and the social ramifications of secularism, individualism, and materialism.[28] Arguably, they were prescient, discerning early on that Enlightenment ideas would undermine the structure of the patriarchal family; encourage sexual liberation; dissolve established hierarchies; and provide an ethics of utility, self-interest, and pleasure to serve a new type of social order.

For the most part, it is true, French enemies of the Enlightenment were silent about the ramifications of industrial capitalism, which was in any case only in its nascent stages. But when they did speak of the social effects of machine production, wage labor, and urbanization, they were often farsighted in perceiving its deleterious consequences.[29] The criticism of *luxe*, sensual pleasure, and individualism provided a solid foundation for later, corporatist criticism of the atomizing effects of market mechanisms and consumer culture. And their argument that the progress of science and technology failed to ensure moral improvement prepared successors to cast critical eyes on the benefits of capitalism.

Enemies of the Enlightenment, however, did more than just anticipate the changes on the horizon of the modern world. They responded to them in novel ways, meeting their adversaries' innovative attacks with innovation of their own. In doing so, members of the nascent Right necessarily borrowed from the past, drawing particularly on the venerable arsenal of Catholic theology. But they marshaled their arguments originally, in new alignments and new formations, basing them on simple, stilted oppositions that were formed in direct response to the great progressive movement of the age. Reactive and not always stellar, they were nonetheless, in their ensemble, as new to the century as the Enlightenment itself.

Thus, whereas the *philosophes* undermined religion with ridicule and reason, tilling the soil of atheism, anti-*philosophes* responded by asserting reason's inherent weakness and the necessity of faith to individual happiness and social well-being. Religion was true because it was useful, useful because it was true, an affirmation that was confirmed by feeling and by the heart. Few would have defended the faith in these terms at the beginning of the eighteenth century. By the dawn of the nineteenth, they were commonplace.[30]

Similarly, whereas the *philosophes* urged the satisfaction of personal pleasures and the sanctity of individual rights, anti-*philosophes* stressed the incumbency of duty, the priority of the social whole. In a manner that was not radically different from the response of the emerging communitarian Left to the atomizing individualism of modern society, the Right created its own image of idealized, organic community. True, it located that ideal in the past, but then so did the early Jacobin Left, which sought to usher in the future by way of a return to the purity of classical antiquity. In both cases, the past was only an idealized response to the present, the reflex of men and women moved by a sense of loss and alienation from a fractured social whole. That response, too, was modern.

The Right's rhetoric of family was also a product of contemporary conditions. If patriarchy was as old as the patriarchs and the oppression of women the most venerable form of slavery, the self-conscious defense of fathers and families was a response to perceived attacks on both. In the same way that few would have thought to organize against same-sex marriages at the dawn of the twentieth century, few, in France at least, were arguing the prerogatives of fathers or the indissolubility of the marital tie at the dawn of the Enlightenment with anywhere near their later sense of urgency or conviction.

The same can be said for what would seem to be the most archaic of the early Right's argumentative tropes—the defensive alliance of throne and altar. Although the ideological foundations for the union of the two were laid long before the eighteenth century, it can be argued that their self-conscious defense arose only when that union was truly threatened.[31] How many in the previous century were urging partisans to rally in support of "God, king, and country" in the manner of such contemporary enemies of the Enlightenment as Élie Harel? The throne and altar entente was asserted most forcefully only when it was challenged, not just by the criticism of the *philosophes*, but far more decisively by the secular drift of the modern state. This was a desperate plea, ultimately futile, to shore up a threatened alliance, a plea to put religion *back* into politics from whence, the Right claimed, it had been banished. As every American living at the beginning of the twenty-first century can confirm, this, too, is a modern goal.

The same dynamic is apparent in the Right's defense of tradition. Whereas the *philosophes* allegedly spoke in ungrounded abstractions, opposing inherited customs and prejudices with the speculations of reason, anti-*philosophes* emphasized the rootedness of the past, the primacy of history over change and of human fallibility over utopian promise. These claims were new, and indeed could not have been otherwise. As Clifford Geertz has observed, "one constructs arguments for tradition only when its credentials have been questioned."[32] The Right began to value a world that was lost, only as it slipped away; appreciated the inertia of history, only when that force was challenged.

Finally, enemies of the Enlightenment argued all these points with means that were state of the art. Suspicious of reason, they brought reason to bear nonetheless in the new world of the republic of letters, producing a voluminous literature that competed for the attention of an evolving public sphere. Enemies of the Enlightenment distrusted that sphere—hated it, really—judging that indiscriminate tolerance of opinions and unrestrained freedom of the press were forces for cultural undoing. But that same conviction led them to a profoundly modern understanding of the power of language to shape and distort human reality. The *philosophes*, their enemies believed, had made a Revolution with words, molding society through abstract concepts, such as despotism, liberty, fanaticism, and superstition, that obscured what they claimed to represent. To counteract and expose that power, the early Right was thus forced to descend into the messy world of the public sphere. Doubtless they would have preferred an absolute monarchy to a republic of letters, but they participated in it all the same, showing a willingness to use, in the great cultural campaign of the Restoration battle of the books, mass mobilization, propaganda, and indoctrination to achieve their aims when the free play of ideas appeared to fail. Their means were as yet imperfect, their techniques unrefined. But they were up to date.[33]

It is therefore misleading, whether wittingly or not, to accept the Enlightenment's characterization of its enemies as relics of a bygone era and of their arguments as atavisms of the past. The weight of history, the primacy of the social whole, the centrality of the family, the necessity of religion, and the dangers of tolerance—these principles were both modern and timeless. Long after the reign of the Ultras had come to an end, their ideas endured, finding their way into the panoply of right-wing ideologies that would dot the French and European landscapes in the nineteenth and twentieth centuries.

Full appreciation of that fact challenges us to conceive of the process of modernity in new and surprising ways. Rather than think of opponents of the principal "advances" in modern civilization as somehow acting outside the flow of historical time—as atavisms, or prisoners of the past—we would do better to think of them as endemic to modernity itself. In this view, the men and women of the French Counter-Enlightenment, the men and women of the early French Right, were bound up in a common process with the very movement they sought to destroy. Whereas the Enlightenment summoned its enemies into existence through its unprecedented attack on revealed religion, the Counter-Enlightenment in turn "created" the Enlightenment as the specter and source of modernity's ills, reaffirming religion's place in the modern world and prescribing a program to heal it that was both idealistic and radical. This reaffirming process—generative of so much polarized opposition and hate—was then carried into the Revolution, radicalized, accelerated, and sustained.

It was this vicious dialectic of mutually exclusive and mutually reaffirming opposition that created the circumstances for the terrible violence of the Revolution. The Terror was not, as both contemporaries and subsequent critics have alleged, the product of forces inherent in either the Enlightenment or the Revolution alone but the tragic outcome of the interplay of these forces with their corresponding Counter-Enlightenment and counterrevolutionary extremes. Rather than see this great bloodletting in the revolutionaries' own terms as a battle of the new versus the old, we should think of the Terror as the result of the conflict of the new versus the new, the clash of two opposed and incompatible visions of the world, brought into being, in part, by each other. The great chasm opened up by this conflict was then replayed and reaffirmed on a lesser scale during the cultural battles of the Restoration, ensuring that such opposition would remain a central feature of the modern French landscape.

This dialectic of Enlightenment and Counter-Enlightenment was peculiar but not exclusive to France. As I have suggested, similar processes of mutual reification were replicated in settings throughout Europe and the New World, where religious activists created similar constructions of the force they took to be the bearer of modernity (*philosophie*) and which they then struggled to oppose. These were, it bears repeating, "constructions," which did great violence to the movements they portrayed, in the same way that Enlightenment constructions of religion were frequently marred by distortion. But the adoption and use by contemporaries of such reifications not only permits us to do the same—to think of Enlightenment and Counter-Enlightenment movements as coherent, reaffirming forces—but also suggests that we should see in their conflict and interaction the source of historical developments not attributable to either force alone. Just as it is insufficient to think of the Revolution as singularly responsible for the Terror, it is deeply misleading to the think of the Enlightenment as singularly responsible for modernity's ills.

This, of course, was precisely the charge of its contemporary opponents, repeated by critics on the Right to the present day. In more recent times, however, the charge has been taken up by the Left. Max Horkheimer and Theodor Adorno argued famously in 1944 that the Enlightenment contained within itself a dialectic that "self-destructed" over time. Defying its original project of liberation, the Enlightenment turned totalitarian, resulting in "disaster triumphant" whose ultimate expression was the Holocaust.[34] Widely influential, this line of inquiry has been adopted and embellished by later, postmodern critics, who have charged the Enlightenment with nurturing many of the ills of modernity: totalitarianism, environmental destruction, the hegemony of reason, racism, antisemitism, imperialism, misogyny, and moral tyranny. Gestating in the Enlightenment's own, dark underbelly, this insidious dialectical force emerged to ravage the world.

As a number of recent observers have pointed out, much of this criticism is woefully reductive, tending to conflate the Enlightenment as a historical movement with the general advance (or dissolution) of Western civilization.[35] Moreover, it has been conducted in total neglect or total ignorance of the fact that the Enlightenment generated militant hostility from the start. It may be that this neglect is not entirely unconscious, for ironically many of postmodernism's most sweeping condemnations of the Enlightenment (totalitarianism, the hegemony of reason, intolerance, and the will to power) sound suspiciously like those of more avowedly conservative critics.[36] Both, in turn, bear more than a passing resemblance to the charges of their Counter-Enlightenment predecessors. Philosophy, it would seem, like politics, makes strange bedfellows.

Surely, it is more sensible to see the dialectic of Enlightenment as consisting not in an internal undoing of the movement itself but in its charged, developmental struggle with the oppositional movements it brought into being. This dialectical process would then be seen, collectively, as constitutive of modernity. The process necessarily differed extensively from national context to context. But as I have suggested, there is scope for thinking of the French pattern as at least partly applicable to other Christian (especially Catholic) cultures. And it may be that a conception of modernity that makes room for the religious reactions it provokes could be applied to non-Western cultures as well. As the sociologist of religion Mark Juergensmeyer has argued, the explicit rejection of Western, secular ideology that is a standard feature of religious nationalist movements in many parts of the world today does not render them, ipso facto, unmodern.[37] However comforting the thought may be for some observers, it makes little sense to see the Iranian revolutionaries who overthrew the shah, the religious activists with important power bases in India's ruling BJP party, the Buddhist monks so prominent in post-Soviet Mongolia, or Algeria's Islamic Salvation Front as historical relics who will simply crumble with time. Indigenous responses to their own processes of modernity, these movements and numerous others are very much products of our age. We may have to learn to live with them. At the very least, Western observers must recognize that religion has played a similarly complicated role in shaping and informing our own modern paths.

In closing, it is worth noting that the hostility to the Enlightenment chronicled here had one other lasting consequence, which was also, ironically, profoundly modern. It reaffirmed a belief in the power of the individual mind to make human history. When Maistre declared that the Revolution was the fault of Voltaire and Rousseau; when Sabatier described *gens d'esprit* as the "first pontiffs, the first legislators, the first kings" of nations; when Bonald deemed men of letters "either the ornament or the plague of society," they conceded as much power to the individual intellect as did any high priest of the Pantheon.[38] By repeating such charges through the decades, the Enlightenment's most virulent opponents perpetuated, despite themselves, a myth of omnipotence that helped to render it true. In their quest to make men through God, enemies of the Enlightenment made gods of men.

NOTES

Introduction

1. For the following account of Voltaire's apotheosis, I have relied heavily on René Pomeau, ed., *Voltaire en son temps*, 5 vols. (Oxford, 1994), 5:205–333; Gustave Desnoiresterres, *Voltaire et la société au XVIIIe*, 8 vols. (Paris, 1876); and J. A. Leith, "Les Trois apothéoses de Voltaire," *Annales historiques de la Révolution française* 51 (1979):161–209.

2. *Correspondance littéraire, philosophique et critique par Grimm, Diderot, Raynal, Meister, etc.*, ed. Maurice Tourneux, 16 vols. (Paris, 1877–1882), 12:67 (March 1778).

3. Pomeau, *Voltaire en son temps*, 5:297.

4. On this episode, see chapter 1.

5. On Beauregard, see [Louis Petit de Bachaumont], *Mémoires secrets pour servir à l'histoire de la république des lettres en France*, 36 vols. (London, 1777–1789), 11:234 (April 20, 1778).

6. *Journal historique et littéraire*, i (April 1, 1778):537–540.

7. The term "anti-*philosophe*" appeared at roughly the same time that the Encyclopedists began to claim the mantle *philosophe* for themselves. See, for example, Abbé Allamand's *Pensées anti-philosophiques* (La Haye, 1751), a refutation of Diderot's *Pensées philosophiques* of 1747 or Louis Mayeul Chaudon's *Dictionnaire anti-philosophique* (Avignon, 1767), a "commentary on" and "corrective of" Voltaire's *Dictionnaire philosophique*.

8. For essential introductions to the subject of the rise of the writer, see Paul Bénichou, *Le Sacre de l'écrivain 1750–1830: Essai sur l'avènement d'un pouvoir spirituel laïque dans la France moderne* (Paris, 1973); Jean-Claude Bonnet, *Naissance du panthéon: Essai sur le culte des grands hommes* (Paris, 1998); John Lough, *Writer and Public in France: From the Middle Ages to the Present Day* (Oxford, 1978); and Alain Viala, *Naissance de l'écrivain. Sociologie de la littérature à l'âge classique* (Paris, 1985).

9. This is from Voltaire's article, "Gens de Lettres," included in the *Encyclopédie ou dictionnaire raisonné des sciences des arts et des métiers*, new ed., 35 vols. (Stuttgart, 1966–1967), 7:599–600. Voltaire was not always so sanguine about the status of writers in France.

10. Cited in Maurice Pellisson, *Les Hommes de lettres au XVIIIe siècle* (Paris, 1911), 60.

11. Cited in Éric Walter, "Les auteurs et le champ littéraire," in Roger Chartier

and Henri-Jean Martin, eds., *Histoire de l'édition française*, 4 vols. (Paris, 1982–1986), 2:391.

12. Cited in Lough, *Writer and Public*, 235.

13. Robert Darnton, "The High Enlightenment and the Low-Life of Literature," *The Literary Underground of the Old Regime* (Cambridge, Mass., 1982). For important reflections on the multivalence of the term *philosophe*, see the indispensable volume by Hans Ulrich Gumbrecht and Rolf Reichardt, *Philosophe, Philosophie*, Vol. 3 of Rolf Reichardt and Eberhard Schmitt, eds., *Handbuch politisch-sozialer Grundbegriffe in Frankreich 1680–1820*, 10 vols. (Munich, 1985–). For a more circumscribed discussion of who constituted the party of the *philosophes*, see John Lough, "Who Were the Philosophes?" in J. H. Fox, M. H. Waddicor and Derek A. Watts, eds., *Studies in Eighteenth-Century French Literature* (Exeter, 1975); and Robert Shackleton, "When did the French *Philosophes* Become a Party?" *Bulletin of the John Rylands University Library of Manchester*, 60 (1977):181–199.

14. Lucien Brunel, *Les Philosophes et l'Académie Française au dix-huitième siècle* (Paris, 1884), Appendix II: 367.

15. In addition to Darnton's classic account of this process in "High Enlightenment," 1–15, see Alan Charles Kors, *D'Holbach's Coterie: An Enlightenment in Paris* (Princeton, N.J., 1976), esp. 184–257.

16. Cited in Jean-Claude Bonnet, "Les morts illustres: Oraison funèbre, éloge académique, nécrologie," in Pierre Nora, ed., *Les Lieux de mémoire*, 3 vols. (Paris, 1984–1992), 2, Part 3:217–241.

17. Sébastien-Roch-Nicholas Chamfort, *Combien le génie des grands écrivains influe sur l'esprit de leur siècle*, in *Oeuvres complètes de Chamfort*, 5 vols. (Paris, 1824), 1:203–204, 212. The prize was awarded by the Académie of Marseilles in 1767.

18. On the inclusion of *hommes de lettres* in the pantheon of modern heroes, see Jean-Claude Bonnet's *Naissance du panthéon*, as well as his "Les morts illustres," in *Les Lieux de mémoire*, 2, Part 3:217–241; Mona Ozouf, "Le panthéon: L'école normale des morts," in *Les Lieux de mémoire*, 1:139–165. On pilgrimages to the great *philosophes*, see Olivier Nora, "La visite au grand écrivain," in *Les Lieux de mémoire*, 2, Part 3:563–587; and Anna Ridehalgh, "Preromantic Attitudes and the Birth of a legend: French Pilgrimages to Ermonville, 1778–1789," *Studies on Voltaire and the Eighteenth Century*, 215 (1982):231–252.

19. See Gumbrecht and Reichardt, *Philosophe, Philosophie*, 59–61. A reproduction of *philosophe* cards is provided in Roger Chartier and Henri-Jean Martin, eds., *Histoire de l'édition française*, 4 vols. (Paris, 1982–1986), 2:416. Pipes and other Voltaire paraphernalia are reproduced in the catalogue of the Voltaire exhibition held at the Hôtel de la monnaie in Paris during the fall of 1994, *Voltaire et l'Europe* (Bruxelles, 1994).

20. See, for example, Robert Darnton, *Mesmerism and the End of the Enlightenment in France* (Cambridge, Mass., 1968).

21. Robert R. Palmer, *Catholics and Unbelievers in Eighteenth-Century France* (Princeton, N.J., 1939), 4.

22. Ibid., 21.

23. The principal text here is Berlin's classic essay, "The Counter-Enlightenment," reproduced in Isaiah Berlin, *Against the Current: Essays in the History of Ideas*, ed. Henry Hardy (New York, 1980). Important reflections may also be found in *Vico and Herder: Two Studies in the History of Ideas* (London, 1976); *The Magus of the North: J. G. Hamann and the Origins of Modern Irrationalism*, ed. Henry Hardy (London, 1993); and "Joseph de Maistre and the Origins of Fascism,"

in Isaiah Berlin, *The Crooked Timber of Humanity*, ed. Henry Hardy (London, 1992).

24. Berlin, "Joseph de Maistre," 101, 110. On Maistre, see also Richard Lebrun, *Joseph de Maistre: An Intellectual Militant* (Montreal, 1988).

25. I take Quentin Skinner's "Meaning and Understanding in the History of Ideas," *History and Theory*, 8 (1969):3–53 to be the point of departure for any modern study of intellectual history and the programmatic statement of the shortcomings of the great thinker/great ideas approach. For a more detailed methodological and substantive critique of Berlin's understanding of the Counter-Enlightenment, see Graeme Garrard, "The Counter-Enlightenment Liberalism of Isaiah Berlin," *Journal of Political Ideologies*, 2/3 (1997):281–291, as well as my own article, "What is the Counter-Enlightenment? The Case of France," forthcoming in a volume of collected essays on the Counter-Enlightenment, to be edited by Robert Wokler.

26. The classic work of Jacques Godechot, *The Counter-Revolution Doctrine and Action, 1789–1804*, trans. Salvator Attanasio (Princeton, N.J., 1971), is characteristic of this tendency. I emphasize that I am referring here to the *thought* of the Counter-Revolution. Its social history has been studied in great depth.

27. Of the many scholars whose methods have influenced my own, I note above all the work of Keith Michael Baker and Robert Darnton. For Baker's theoretical vision, which draws on the writings of J. G. A. Pocock and Quentin Skinner, see the Introduction and the classic "On the Problem of the Ideological Origins of the French Revolution," in Baker, *Inventing the French Revolution: Essays on French Political Culture in the Eighteenth Century* (Cambridge, 1990). Darnton's methods are summarized in "The Social History of Ideas" and other articles in *The Kiss of Lamourette: Reflections in Cultural History* (New York, 1990). The phrase "the social history of ideas" was first coined by Peter Gay, who arguably practiced it with greater care than Darnton appreciated.

28. Roy Porter has recently challenged this conventional understanding, arguing compellingly that an Enlightenment in Britain preceded varietal movements on the continent. A characteristic feature of the British Enlightenment, however, seems to have been a much less antagonistic relationship with Christianity than was the case in France. See Roy Porter, *The Creation of the Modern World: The Untold Story of the British Enlightenment* (New York, 2000).

29. Berlin included the Italian Giovanni Battista Vico (1668–1744) as a rare non-German in the pantheon of the Counter-Enlightenment. Vico, however, was almost completely unknown outside his native Naples until the nineteenth century. See the fine study by Mark Lilla, *G. B. Vico: The Making of an Anti-Modern* (Cambridge, Mass., 1993).

30. Although he formulated his definition of the Enlightenment in different ways at different times, a neat summary is provided in Berlin, "Counter-Enlightenment," 1–2.

31. Graeme Garrard has recently emphasized this point. See the introduction to his forthcoming *Counter-Enlightenment: From Rousseau to Rorty* (New York, 2001).

32. For an important argument that French religious writing in the eighteenth century was richer and more innovative than previously acknowledged, see William Everdell, *Christian Apologetics in France, 1730–1790: The Roots of Romantic Religion* (Lewiston, N.Y., 1987); and also Nigel Aston, "The Golden Autumn of Gallicanism? Religious History and Its Place in Current Writing on Eighteenth Century France," *French Historical Studies*, 13 (1999):187–222.

33. In addition to chapter 3, see my article "Seeing the Century of Lights as

a Time of Darkness: The Catholic Counter-Enlightenment in Europe and the Americas," in Florence Lotterie and Darrin M. McMahon, eds., *Les Lumières européennes dans leur relation avec les autres grandes cultures et religions du XVIIIe siècle* (Paris, 2001).

34. There is need for a thorough history (a *Begriffsgeschichte*) of the term "Enlightenment," in the principal Western languages. In English, "the Enlightenment," employed as a substantive to refer to a movement and period in European history, did not gain common usage until after the Second World War II. Thus, like other critics, I use it anachronistically, fully aware, moreover, of the dangers of reification implicit in its use. For thoughts on these matters, see John Lough, "Reflections on *Enlightenment* and *Lumières*," *British Journal for Eighteenth-Century Studies*, 8 (1985):1–17, and James Schmidt, ed., *What Is Enlightenment? Eighteenth-Century Answers and Twentieth-Century Questions* (Los Angeles, 1996).

35. Roger Chartier, *The Cultural Origins of the French Revolution*, trans. Lydia G. Cochrane (Durham, N.C., and London, 1991), 5, 87–89.

36. Daniel Mornet, *Les Origines intellectuelles de la Révolution française* (Paris, 1933), 205.

37. Donald Sutherland, *France 1789–1815: Revolution and Counterrevolution* (Oxford, 1985); Jean-Clément Martin, *Contre-Révolution, Révolution et Nation en France 1789–1799* (Paris, 1998).

38. Most notably Peter Gay's now classic study *The Enlightenment: An Interpretation*, Norton Library ed., 2 vols. (New York, 1977), originally published in successive volumes in 1966 and 1969.

39. See, for example, J. L. Talmon, *The Origins of Totalitarian Democracy* (London, 1952); Eric Voegelin, *From Enlightenment to Revolution*, ed. J. H. Hallowell (Durham, N.C., 1975); and John Gray, *Enlightenment's Wake: Politics and Culture at the Close of the Modern Age* (London and New York, 1995).

40. The writing in this vein is extensive, but any short list must include the influential work of Max Horkheimer and Theodor W. Adorno, *Dialectic of Enlightenment*, trans. John Cumming (New York,1944; New York, 1972); Richard Rorty, *Philosophy and the Mirror of Nature* (Princeton, N.J., 1979); and the various works of Michel Foucault. Other examples may be found in Thomas Docherty, ed., *Postmodernism: A Reader* (New York, 1993), as well as in Sven-Eric Liedman, ed., *The Postmodernist Critique of the Project of Enlightenment* (Amsterdam, 1997).

41. Klaus Epstein, for example, explored this connection fruitfully in the German case in *The Genesis of German Conservatism* (Princeton, N.J., 1966). J. M. Roberts posited a link between anti-*philosophe* rhetoric and the origins of the Right in France in his seminal article "The French Origins of the 'Right,'" *Transactions of the Royal Historical Society*, 23 (1973):27–53.

42. See, for example, Marcel Gauchet, "La droite et la gauche," in *Les Lieux de mémoire*, 3, Part 1:395–467; René Rémond, *The Right Wing in France: From 1815 to de Gaulle*, trans. James M. Laux, 2d ed. (Philadelphia, 1969); Jean-François Sirinelli and Éric Vigne, eds., *L'Histoire des droites en France*, 3 vols. (Paris, 1992), 1:x–xv; and Michel Winock, ed., *L'Histoire de l'extrême droite en France* (Paris, 1993).

43. See, for example, François Furet, *Interpreting the French Revolution*, trans. Elborg Forster (Cambridge, 1981).

44. See, in this connection, the insightful opening sections of Berlin's "Joseph de Maistre," where he characterizes Maistre as an "ultra-modern," "born not after but before his time" (96). Berlin, however, took pains to distinguish Maistre from Bonald, whom he dismisses as an "orthodox political medievalist" (102). As will

become apparent, I do not accept this distinction. For a more recent treatment of the theme of Maistre's modernity (and even postmodernity), see Owen Bradley, *A Modern Maistre: The Social and Political Thought of Joseph de Maistre* (Lincoln, Neb., 2000). Bradley is rightly dismissive of Berlin's charge of Maistre's protofascism.

45. The literature on the eighteenth-century public sphere is vast. Though criticized extensively, the fundamental theoretical text remains Jürgen Habermas, *The Structural Transformation of the Public Sphere: An Inquiry Into a Category of Bourgeois Society*, trans. Thomas Burger and Frederick Lawrence (Cambridge, Mass., 1989). On the republic of letters, see Dena Goodman, *The Republic of Letters: A Cultural History of the French Enlightenment* (Ithaca, N.Y., and London, 1994).

46. Javier Herrero, *Los Origines del pensamiento reaccionario español* (Madrid, 1971), 24.

47. Ibid.

Chapter 1

1. Cited in René Pomeau, ed., *Voltaire en son temps*, 5 vols. (Oxford, 1994), 5:286.

2. [Louis Petit de Bachaumont], *Mémoires secrets pour servir à l'histoire de la république des lettres en France*, 36 vols. (London, 1777–1789), 11:123 (February 28, 1778).

3. J. P. Migne, *Colléction intégrale et universelle des orateurs sacrés*, 99 vols. (Paris, 1844–1846), vol. 65, *Oeuvres complètes de Cambacérès*, Sermon III, "Sur les incrédules," 1047–1048.

4. There is great need for a comprehensive study of early opposition to the *philosophes*. For essential works in addition to those by Palmer and Everdell cited in the preceding chapter, see Jean Balcou, *Fréron contre les philosophes* (Geneva, 1975); D. W. Smith, *Helvétius: A Study in Persecution* (Oxford, 1965); Kurt Wais, *Das Antiphilosophische Weltbild des Französischen Sturm und Drang 1760–1789* (Berlin, 1934); and Furio Diaz, *Filosofia e politica nel Settecento francese* (Torino, 1962), Chap. 3, 131–229.

5. "Mémoire au roi," in *Procès-verbal de l'assemblée générale du clergé de France, tenue à Paris, au couvent des grands-augustins, en l'année mil sept cent cinquante-cinq* (Paris, 1764), 327–329.

6. *Censure de la faculté de théologie de Paris, contre le livre qui a pour titre, de l'Esprit* (Paris, 1759), 7–8.

7. *Procès-verbal de l'assemblée-générale du clergé de France, tenue à Paris, au couvent des grands-augustins, en l'année mil sept cent soixante-dix* (Paris, 1776), 124.

8. *Procès-verbal de l'assemblée-générale extraordinaire du clergé de France, tenue à Paris, au couvent des grands-augustins, en l'année mil sept cent quatre-vingt-deux* (Paris, 1783), 86–87.

9. *Procès-verbal de l'assemblée-générale du clergé de France, tenue à Paris, au couvent des grands-augustins en l'année mil sept cent quatre-vingt-cinq, et continué en l'année mil sept cent quatre-vingt-six* (Paris, 1786), 148.

10. Fleury, a scion of a distinguished parliamentary family, served as *avocat général* at the Paris *parlement* beginning in 1746, *premier avocat général* in 1756, and *président à mortier* from 1774 to 1790. Seguier was also an *avocat général* (1755–1771 and 1774–1790) and a member of the Académie française (1757).

11. B. N. MS Nouv. acq (*Collection Joly de Fleury*), Vol. 352, 3807–3819, folio 6.

Arrests de la cour du Parlement, portant condamnation de plusieurs livres et autres ouvrages imprimés. Extrait des registres de parlement du 23 Janvier 1759 (Paris, 1759), 2–4.

12. *Arrest de la cour de Parlement, qui condamne un Imprimé, in-8, ayant pour titre: Histoire philosophique & politique des établissemens & du commerce des Européens dans les deux Indes, par Guillaume-Thomas Raynal* (Paris, 1781). An extract from the registers of the Paris *parlement*, the text, though not written by Seguier, was read aloud by him on May 21, 1781. Seguier did compose the *Réquisitoire sur lequel est intervenu l'arrêt du Parlement du 18 août 1770, qui condamne à être brûlés différents livres ou brochures* . . . (Paris, 1770), a classic statement of anti-*philosophe* polemic. This same text was republished in Paris in 1790 (Chez N.Y. Nyon) as evidence of Seguier's prescient "anticipation" of the Revolution.

13. John Hardman, *Louis XVI* (New Haven, Conn., 1993), 20—this despite Louis XVI's personal animosity toward the *philosophes*.

14. John Hardman, *French Politics 1774–1789: From the Accession of Louis XVI to the Fall of the Bastille* (London, 1995), 36; and Munro Price, *Preserving the Monarchy: The Comte de Vergennes, 1774–1787* (Cambridge, 1995), 19, 27, 240.

15. On opposition to the *philosophes* in the secular republic of letters, see Darrin M. McMahon, "The Counter-Enlightenment and the Low-Life of Literature in Pre-Revolutionary France," *Past and Present*, 159 (1998):77–112.

16. Cited in Robert R. Palmer, *Catholics and Unbelievers in Eighteenth-Century France* (Princeton, N.J., 1939), 7.

17. [Gabriel Gauchat], *Lettres Critiques, ou Analyse et réfutation de divers écrits modernes contre la religion*, 19 vols. (Paris, 1755–1763), 1:7. In a similar vein, see the several thousand pages of *La Religion vengée, ou Réfutation des auteurs impies* . . . *par une Société de Gens de Lettres*, 21 vols. (Paris, 1757–1763), a journal edited by Jean G. Soret and Jean-Nicolas-Hubert Hayer.

18. *Discours prononcé dans l'Académie Françoise, le lundi 10 Mars M. DCCLX à la réception de M. Le Franc de Pompignan* (Paris, 1760), 4. For the later views of Pompignan, see the introduction to his collected works, *Oeuvres de M. le Marquis de Pompignan*, 4 vols. (Paris, 1784).

19. [Jean-Marie-Bernard Clément], *Satires, par M. C*** (Amsterdam, 1786), 68.

20. On anti-*philosophe* salons, see Jolanta T. Pekacz, *Conservative Tradition in Pre-Revolutionary France: Parisian Salon Women* (New York, 1999); and Dena Gooman, "Filial Rebellion in the Salon: Madame Geoffrin and Her Daughter, *French Historical Studies* 16 (1989):28-47. On patronage and social geography, see William Everdell, *Christian Apologetics in France, 1730–1790: The Roots of Romantic Religion* (Lewiston, N.Y., 1987), 17–22, 168–172, as well as McMahon, "Counter-Enlightenment," 84–85, 93–94, 98.

21. Bernard Plongeron, "Recherches sur l'Aufklärung catholique en Europe occidentale, 1777–1830," *Revue d'histoire moderne et contemporaine*, 16 (1969):555–605. Detailed analysis of the French church is provided in John McManner's sweeping *Church and Society in Eighteenth-Century France*, 2 vols. (Oxford, 1998). On the French hierarchy, see Nigel Aston's excellent *The End of an Élite: The French Bishops and the Coming of the French Revolution, 1786–1790* (Oxford, 1992).

22. Cited in John McManners, *The French Revolution and the Church* (London, 1969), 16.

23. On this theme, see Cyril B. O'Keefe, *Contemporary Reactions to the Enlightenment (1728–1762)* (Geneva, 1974), 76; and Alan Charles Kors, *D'Holbach's Coterie: An Enlightenment in Paris* (Princeton, 1976), 230–240.

24. *Épitre aux calomniateurs de la philosophie* (London, 1776), 3.

25. See, for example, Hans Ulrich Gumbrecht and Rolf Reichardt, *Philosophe, Philosophie,* vol. 3 of Rolf Reichardt and Eberhard Schmitt, eds., *Handbuch politisch-sozialer Grundbegriffe in Frankreich 1680–1820,* 10 vols. (Munich, 1985–), 48–51.

26. "L'innoculation du bon sens," *Journal ecclésiastique, ou Bibliothèque raisonnée des sciences ecclésiastiques,* 83, Part 2 (May 1781):156–157. A moderately priced monthly, the *Journal ecclésiastique* was founded in 1760 with the aim of reaching rural and provincial clergy. It coupled practical instruction in Christian dogma and duty with more learned disquisitions, including pastoral letters, book reviews, essays, and correspondence. Signficantly, the abbé Barruel assumed its editorship in 1788.

27. [Maximilien-Marie Harel, called le P. Élie], *Les Causes du désordre public, par un vrai citoyen* (Avignon, 1784), 11.

28. Some more recent observers have also noted this shift. See A. Bernard, *Le Sermon au XVIIIe siècle. Étude historique et critique sur la prédication en France, de 1715 à 1789* (Paris, 1901), 22, 469; Albert Monod, *De Pascal à Chateaubriand: Les défenseurs français du Christianisme de 1670 à 1802* (Paris, 1916), 488–489; and Everdell, *Christian Apologetics,* 281–282.

29. *Correspondance littéraire,* 11 (April, 1776): 244–245.

30. *La Satyre des satyres* (n.p., 1778): 27, n. 7.

31. *Correspondance littéraire,* 12 (May, 1778): 105–106.

32. Just how common, however, is a question impossible to answer with precision at this stage. I have based this conclusion on a comprehensive survey of the books listed and reviewed in *Affiches, annonces et avis divers; Année littéraire; Journal ecclésiastique; Journal historique et littéraire; Journal de littérature, des sciences et des arts; Journal de monsieur;* and *Nouvelles ecclésiastiques* for their respective runs since 1775.

33. The distribution of fliers, in Paris and in the provinces, announcing a forthcoming edition of the collected works of Voltaire elicited a violent anti-*philosophe* response, prefiguring the battle of the books that would rage during the Restoration. See, for example, [Jean-Jacques Duval d'Eprémesnil], *Dénonciation au parlement de la souscription pour les oeuvres de Voltaire* (n.p., [1781]); the clergy's "Mémoire au Roi, sur le projet d'une édition complète des oeuvres de Voltaire" (November 16, 1782), in *Procès-verbal de l'assemblée-générale* (1782), 169–170; the bishop of Amien, Louis-Charles de Machault, *Mandement de Monseigneur l'evêque d'Amiens, Au sujet de l'annonce publiée dans son diocèse d'une collection entière des Oeuvres du Sieur de Voltaire* (n.p., [1781]); and [Jean-George Le Franc de Pompignan], *Mandement de Monseigneur l'archevêque & comte de Vienne, touchant l'édition annoncée des Oeuvres du Sieur de Voltaire, donné à Vienne le 31 Mai 1781* (Vienne, 1781).

34. Everdell, *Christian Apologetics,* 168–172.

35. Royou, Geoffroy, Grosier, Pey, Gérard, and the abbé Crillon (all discussed below) served on the society's committee of judges. In 1781 the society awarded a prize of 1200 *livres* to the young priest Étienne-Antoine de Boulogne. See Bachaumont, *Mémoires secrets,* 14 (October 1, 1779):221–222 and 17 (January 1, 1781):3–5.

36. Details on all these journals and journalists can be found in Jean Sgard, ed., *Dictionnaire des journaux, 1600–1789,* 2 vols. (Paris, 1791); Jean Sgard, ed., *Dictionnaire des journalistes (1600–1789)* (Grenoble, 1976); and McMahon, "Counter-Enlightenment," 100–105. Feller was the one slight exception to this tightly knit

group, editing the bimonthly *Journal historique et littéraire* from Luxembourg. He was intimately tied to France, however. See chapter 3.

37. On French religious apologetic literature and its variants in the eighteenth century, see, in addition to the works by Monod and Everdell cited above, Sylviane Coppola, "Recherches sur la littérature apologétique catholique en France de 1730 à 1770," unpublished *thèse de doctorat*, Paris-Sorbonne IV (1981).

38. Amos Hofman also uses the term "anti-*philosophe* discourse" in his seminal article "The Origins of the Theory of the *Philosophe* Conspiracy," *French History*, 2 (1988):152–172. Although richly suggestive, Hofman's work concentrates almost exclusively on a handful of writers associated with the *Année littéraire* (chiefly the abbé Barruel). He limits his conception of "anti-*philosophe* discourse," moreover, to the language of conspiracy. As will be apparent, I employ the term more broadly.

39. In the remainder of the paragraph, I offer a counterpart to Darnton's argument in *The Forbidden Best-Sellers of Pre-Revolutionary France* (New York, 1996), 246, drawing on his language and formulations to do so.

40. Richard was the author of numerous religious apologies and attacks on the *philosophes*, including several viciously anti-Protestant and anti-Semitic works. His refutation of Voltaire, *Voltaire parmi les ombres* (Paris, 1775), was republished seven times before 1821. A nonjuring priest and vocal opponent of the Revolution, Richard was apprehended in Belgium by invading Jacobin forces in 1794 and executed for his authorship of *Parallèle des Juifs qui ont crucifié Jésus-Christ avec les Français qui ont tué leur roi* (Mons, 1794).

41. Charles-Louis Richard, *Exposition de la doctrine des philosophes modernes* (Lille, 1785), vii.

42. Ibid., 30.

43. Ibid., 33–38.

44. Ibid., 48.

45. Antoine Sabatier, *Les Trois siècles de la littérature françoise, ou Tableau de l'esprit de nos écrivains, depuis François I, jusqu'en 1781, par M. L'Abbé S*** de Castre*, 5th ed., 3 vols. (La Haye, 1781), 1:57. The fifth edition of 1781 includes the same "preliminary discourse" added to the 1779 edition. On Sabatier, see McMahon, "Counter-Enlightenment," 88–94.

46. [Stéphanie-Félicité Ducrest de Saint-Aubin de Genlis], *La Religion considérée comme l'unique base du bonheur & de la véritable philosophie. Ouvrage fait pour servir à l'éducation des enfans de son A.S. Mgr. le duc d'Orléans, & dans lequel on expose & l'on réfute les principes des prétendus philosophes modernes* (Paris, 1787). On the life of this colorful opponent of the *philosophes*, see Violet Wyndham, *Madame de Genlis: A Biography* (London, 1958).

47. "Avertissement de l'éditeur," in *Correspondance littéraire, ou Lettres critiques et impartiales sur la littérature française du XVIIIe siècle et sur les Trois Siècles de Mr. L'Abbé Sabatier* (London, 1780), ix.

48. Augustin Barruel, *Les Helviennes, ou Lettres provinciales philosophiques*, 5 vols. (Paris, 1781–1789). See *Année littéraire*, iii (1781):332–347; *Journal de littérature, des sciences et des arts*, iv (1781):241–278; *Journal de Monsieur*, ii (1781): 323–348; *Journal historique et littéraire*, ii (June 15, 1784):237–240, iii (November 1, 1784):319–343, iii (November 1, 1789):323–347, 1789, iii (December 1, 1789): 487–507, iii (December 15, 1789):569–578; *Affiches, annonces et avis divers*, no. 17 (April 25, 1781):66; and *Journal ecclésiastique* 100, Part 2 (August 1785):187–190, (June 1787):51–71, (July 1787):79–96.

49. Grosier, "Idées préliminaires sur la Critique," *Journal de littérature, des sci-

ences et des arts, i (1779):8–9. Grosier began the *Journal de littérature, des sciences, et des arts* in an effort to revive the defunct *Journal de Trévoux*. It folded in 1783, following difficulties with the government. See Sgard, *Dictionnaire des journalistes*, 185.

50. Ibid., 8, 27

51. René Liger, *Triomphe de la religion chrétienne, sur toutes les sectes philosophiques* (Paris, 1785), viii; Harel, *Causes du désordre*, 134.

52. Grosier, "Idées préliminaires sur la Critique," 9; Clément, *Satires*, 104; Harel, *La Vraie philosophie* (Strasbourg and Paris, 1783), v, viii.

53. Some of these terms were also used by proponents of *philosophie*. See Gumbrecht and Reichardt, *Philosophe, Philosophie*, 59–61. Simon-Nicolas-Henri Linguet, an implacable if eccentric opponent of the *philosophes*, coined a great many anti-*philosophe* neologisms in the pages of his *Annales politiques, civiles et littéraires du dix-huitième siècle*. See Darline Gay Levy, *The Ideas and Careers of Simon-Nicolas-Henri Linguet: A Study in Eighteenth-Century French Politics* (Urbana, Ill., 1980), 179.

54. My argument here should be compared with that of Roger Chartier, *The Cultural Origins, of the French Revolution*, trans. Lydia G. Cochrane (Durham and London, 1991), 5, 87–89.

55. Antoine-Adrien Lamourette, *Pensées sur la philosophie de l'incrédulité, ou Réflexions sur l'esprit et le dessein des philosophes irréligieux de ce siècle* (Paris, 1785), 26.

56. *Determinatio sacrae facultatis parisiensis in librum cui titulus: Histoire philosophique des établissements des Européens dans les deux Indes, par Guillaume Thomas Raynal* (Paris: 1781), 3–4.

57. On the anti-*philosophe* conspiracy theory, see Hofman, "Origins," 152–172, and chapter 2.

58. Genlis, *Religion*, 222.

59. *Instruction pastorale de Monseigneur l'évêque duc de Langres, sur l'excellence de la religion* (Paris, 1786). See also Jean Soret, *Essai sur les moeurs, nouvelle édition considérablement augmentée*, 2 vols. (Paris, 1784), 2:144.

60. *Année littéraire*, vi (1783):5.

61. Liger, *Triomphe de la religion*, viii; Harel, *Vraie philosophie*, 13.

62. On the revival of Pyrrhonism, see Richard H. Popkin, *The History of Scepticism from Erasmus to Spinoza* (Berkeley and Los Angeles, 1979).

63. Alan Charles Kors, *Atheism in France, 1650–1729* (Princeton, N.J., 1990), esp. Chap. 1, "Atheists Without Atheism," 17–44.

64. [Abbé Philippe-Louis Gérard], *Le Comte de Valmont, ou les Égarements de la raison*, 6 vols. (Paris, 1826), 2:20–32. The work's subtitle states its central theme. First published in 1774, *Comte de Valmont* was augmented and republished in at least seven editions by 1784. The work and its author were heavily indebted to Rousseau.

65. Most notably, Pascal's stress on human depravity, the shortcomings of reason, and our yearning for certain truth was seen as his strength. See, for example, [Louis Athanase des Balbes de Berton de Crillon], *Mémoires philosophiques du Baron De ***, 2d ed., 2 vols. (1779), 2:91; and Genlis, *Religion*, 79–86. Numerous apologists were inclined to borrow Pascal's arguments and even quote his words, without naming him directly.

66. In commenting on this influence, William Everdell goes so far as to call Rousseau "the founder of the Counter-Enlightenment in France" (89). He was, in any event, an extremely important voice. For the ways in which Catholics expropri-

ated Rousseau for their own purposes, see Everdell, *Christian Apologetics*, 86–109; Monod, *De Pascal à Chateaubriand*, 402–424, 475–489; Lionello Sozzi, "Interprétations de Rousseau pendant la Révolution," *Studies on Voltaire and the Eighteenth Century*, 64 (1968):190–194, esp.; and Pierre Maurice Masson's classic, *La Religion de Jean-Jacques Rousseau*, 3 vols. (Paris, 1916).

67. *Journal historique littéraire*, iii (September 15, 1780):90. It is revealing that an ardent Catholic opponent of the *philosophes*, the former Jesuit and archbishop of Bordeaux François-Antoine-Étienne de Gourcy chose to write a work "avenging" Rousseau from the attacks of his philosophic detractors. See his *Rousseau vengé* (Paris, 1772).

68. [Jean-George Le Franc de Pompignan], *Avertissement de l'assemblée-générale du clergé de France aux fidèles de ce royaume sur les avantages de la religion chrétienne et les effets pernicieux de l'incrédulité* (Paris, 1775), 5.

69. *Affiches, annonces et avis divers*, no. 11 (March 13, 1782):41.

70. *Oeuvres de M. le marquis de Pompignan*, 4 vols. (Paris, 1784), 1:xvii.

71. [Le P. Barthélémi Baudrand], *L'Âme affermie dans la foi, et prémunie contre la séduction de l'erreur; ou Preuves abrégées de la religion à la portée de tous les esprits & de tous les états*, rev. ed. (Lyon, 1781), 95–96. Written in response to the "flood" of *mauvais livres* of the century and in a style "at the disposal of everyone," Baudrand's concise, antiphilosophic work was reprinted twenty-eight times between 1781 and 1870.

72. Barruel, *Helviennes*, 4:457.

73. On the theme of crime, see Genlis, *Religion*, 209; Harel, *Causes du désordre*, 135; and Marquis de Fulvy's "L'Apprenti *philosophe* moderne," *Année littéraire*, ii (1789):237–238.

74. Gérard, *Valmont*, 1:212.

75. Crillon, *Mémoires philosophiques*, 1:135.

76. Liger, *Triomphe de la religion*, ix. See also pp.187ff.

77. Barruel, *Helviennes*, 4:298–301. The charge of the *philosophes'* promotion of egotism and self-interest was an extremely common anti-*philosophe* complaint. See, typically, Clément, *Satires*, 165; Genlis, *Religion*, 181–182; or *Journal de Monsieur*, i (1781):182–204.

78. [Abbé Étienne Bremont], *Représentations adressées a M. N*** [Necker]*, à *l'occasion de son ouvrage: De l'importance des opinions religieuses; suivies d'un supplément, contenant l'exposition sommaire & la réfutation succincte de la doctrine des philosophes-économistes* (Geneva and Paris, 1788), 272. In this vein, see also [Abbé Charles-François Le Gros], *Analyse et examen du système des philosophes économistes, par un solitaire* (Geneva and Paris, 1787).

79. *Journal ecclésiastique*, May 1787, 4; Gérard, *Valmont*, 2:272.

80. *Journal ecclésiatique*, 97, Part 2 (November, 1784):189.

81. Harel, *Causes du désordre*, 133.

82. Barruel, *Helviennes*, 5:81, 101, 106, 118.

83. Genlis, *Religion*, 182.

84. See, for example, Peter Gay, *The Enlightenment: An Interpretation*, 2 vols. (New York, 1977), 2:459–461; Norman Hampson, *The Enlightenment* (Middlesex, 1968), 98–99.

85. On the complexities of the *philosophes'* notions of happiness, see the classic study by Robert Mauzi, *L'Idée du bonheur dans la littérature et la pensée française au XVIIIe siècle* (Paris, 1979).

86. Gay, *Enlightenment*, 2:171–174, 191–201.

87. See Darnton, *Forbidden Best-Sellers*, 85–115; Jean-Marie Goulemot, *Forbid-*

den Texts: Erotic Literature and Its Readers in Eighteenth-Century France, trans. James Simpson (Cambridge, 1994).

88. Barruel, *Helviennes*, 4:174. This bestial language was not simply metaphorical. As the anti-*philosophes* emphasized, numerous *philosophes* suggested that the principal difference between human beings and animals was one of degree—a question of the size of the brain, the faculty of speech, or the superiority of the hand over hoof.

89. Harel, *Causes du désordre*, 6.

90. Defending the youth of France was the explicit goal of the abbé Guinot's *Leçons philosophiques ou le germe des connoissances humaines dans ses premiers développemens* (Paris, 1779). The threat of *philosophie* to women, frequently stressed by anti-*philosophe* writers, forms the sole subject of the pamphlet *L'Influence de la philosophie sur l'esprit et le coeur des femmes, ou Peinture des femmes philosophes de notre siècle* (Paris, 1784).

91. *Journal ecclésiastique*, 98, Part 2 (February 1785):163.

92. Liger, *Triomphe de la religion*, 437–438.

93. See Jeffrey Merrick, "Fathers and Kings: Patriarchalism and Absolutism in Eighteenth-century French Politics," *Studies on Voltaire and the Eighteenth Century*, 308 (1993):281–303; Merrick, "The Body Politics of French Absolutism," in Sara E. Melzer and Kathryn Norberg, eds., *From the Royal Will to the Republican Body* (Berkeley and Los Angeles, 1998), 11–31; and Sarah Hanley, "Engendering the State: Family Formation and State Building in Early Modern France: The Marriage Pact," *French Historical Studies*, 16 (1989):4–27.

94. On the *philosophes'* views of the family, see James F. Traer, *Marriage and the Family in Eighteenth-Century France* (Ithaca, N.Y., and London, 1980), 48–78; and William F. Edmiston, *Diderot and the Family: A Conflict of Nature and Law* (Saratoga, Cal., 1985).

95. [Antoine de Malvin de Montazet], "Instruction pastorale de Monseigneur l'archevêque de Lyon sur les sources de l'incrédulité, & les fondemens de la religion," *Journal ecclésiastique*, 100, Part 2 (August 1785):127–159.

96. Abbé Claude Yvon, *Histoire de la religion, où l'on accorde la philosophie avec le christianisme*, 2 vols. (Paris, 1785), 1:205. This was a common comparison. See, for example, *Année littéraire*, iv (1783):176–177.

97. *Année littéraire*, vi (1783):4–5. See also Harel, *Causes du désordre*, 3–4.

98. Jean-Antoine Rigoley de Juvigny, *De la décadence des lettres et des moeurs, depuis les Grecs et les Romains jusqu'à nos jours* (Paris, 1787), 452–453. Rigoley was a *conseiller honoraire* at the *parlement* of Metz and a member of the Académie des Sciences, Arts & Belles-Lettres de Dijon. For similarly sweeping summaries, see *Journal de Monsieur*, i (1779):69; and "Reflexions critiques sur la philosophie du siécle présent," *Journal ecclésiastique*, 84, Part 2 (August 1781):176.

99. Lamourette, *Pensées sur la philosophie*, 9, 74; Harel, *Vraie philosophie*, v; Liger, *Triomphe de la religion*, 33; "Tableau des révolutions de la littérature françoise," *Journal de Monsieur*, i (1781):28.

100. See, typically, Genlis, *Religion*, 209, 222, 231; Sabatier, *Trois siècles*, 1:58–61; Barruel, *Helviennes*, 5:378–388; Crillon, *Mémoires philosophiques*, 174; Liger, *Triomphe de la religion*, 431–436.

101. Gérard, *Valmont*, 3:189, n. 7. The charge of the *philosophes'* "Anglomania" was well established by this point. On the *philosophes'* praise for England and the anti-*philosophes'* condemnations, see Frances Acomb, *Anglophobia in France 1763–1789: An Essay in the History of Constitutionalism and Nationalism* (Durham,

N.C., 1950), and Josephine Grieder, *Anglomania in France: 1740–1789* (Geneva, 1985).

102. See, for example, Barruel, *Helviennes*, 5:388; Liger, *Triomphe de la religion*, 436.

103. [Abbé Liéven-Bonaventure Proyart], *Vie du Dauphin, père de Louis XVI*, 4th ed.. (Lyon, 1781), introductory "Éloge du Dauphin," 37. A prolific anti-*philosophe* who would later write a popular *philosophe* conspiracy interpretation of the Revolution, Proyart was a teacher at the prestigious Collège Louis-le-Grand and a member of the academies of Angers, Montauban, Offenbourg, and Rome. *Vie du Dauphin*, first published in 1777, achieved five editions by the outbreak of the Revolution and would be republished fourteen more times between 1788 and 1863.

104. [Abbé Jean Pey], *La Tolérance chrétienne opposée au tolérantisme philosophique, ou Lettre d'un patriote au soi-disant curé sur son dialogue au sujet des Protestants* (Fribourg, 1784), iii.

105. Barruel, *Helviennes*, 5:384–385, 387. See also *Année littéraire*, ii (1782):15; Rigoley de Juvigny, *De la décadence*, 491.

106. Soret, *Essai sur les moeurs*, 2:120–121.

107. *Discours sur la naissance de Monseigneur le Dauphin, le 22 d'Octobre 1781, prononcé en présence de l'Université de Paris, pendant l'office divin, le 12 du mois de décembre suivant, dans l'Eglise du College Mazarin*. Printed in *Supplement au Journal ecclésiastique*, 10, Part 3 (December 1786):231–255.

108. Richard, *Exposition de la doctrine des philosophes modernes*, 52–53.

109. See, for example, the virtually identical passage in Gérard, *Valmont*, 3:174; the bloody references in the Sorbonne's *Determinatio sacrae facultatis*, 112; and Barruel's extensive references to toppled thrones, "kings on the scaffold," and "revolt, blood, and carnage" in *Helviennes*, 5:400–403.

110. Marc-Antoine de Noé, *Discours sur l'état futur de l'Église* (Paris, 1785), in Migne, *Orateurs sacrés*, 71:1021. Although printed in Paris in 1785 and 1788 at the behest of the General Assembly of the Clergy (and also reprinted in Peau in 1789), the sermon was for some reason not actually delivered by Noé before the assembled clergy. See Everdell, *Christian Apologetics*, 175.

111. Hofman, "Origins," 168. See also Dale Van Kley's observations on the memory of the wars of religion in *The Religious Origins of the French Revolution: From Calvin to the Civil Constitution, 1560–1791* (New Haven, Conn., 1996), 160–164.

112. See Hofman's analysis in "Origins," 163–169, as well as the insightful reflections of J. M. Roberts in "The Origins of a Mythology: Freemasons, Protestants and the French Revolution," *Bulletin of the Institute of Historical Research*, 44 (1971).

113. Genlis, *Religion*, 230. The "fanaticism" of the *philosophes* was one of the most consistent and ubiquitous anti-*philosophe* criticisms. See Linguet's classic pamphlet *Le Fanatisme des philosophes* (London, 1764) or the long article "Réflexions préliminaires sur le fanatisme philosophique," *Année littéraire*, i (1786):3–30.

114. *Journal ecclésiastique*, 98 (January 1785):274. For typical examples in this vein, see [F.-X. Feller], *Catéchisme philosophique, ou Recueil d'observations propres à défendre la religion chrétienne contre ses ennemis* (Liege, 1773), Book 3, Chap. 4, "La Tolérance," 230–235, or Abbé Pey's *La Tolérance chrétienne*.

115. *Journal historique et littéraire*, iii (October 15, 1780):255.

116. For examples of the coupling of Protestantism and *philosophie* and allega-

tions of a joint conspiracy to overthrow the realm, see the *Mémoire au Roi, sur les entreprises des Protestans, tirée de procès-verbal de l'Assemblée* (Paris, 1780); *Remonstrances du clergé de France, assemblé en 1788, au roi, sur l'édit du mois de Novembre 1787, concernant les non-Catholiques* (Paris, 1788); [Abbé Lenfant], *Discours à lire au conseil, en présence du Roi, par un ministre patriote, sur le projet d'accorder l'état civil aux Protestants* (1787); and the [abbé Proyart], *Lettre à un magistrat du Parlement de Paris, au sujet de l'édit sur l'état civil des protestants* (n.p., n.d.).

117. Isaiah Berlin, "Joseph de Maistre and the Origins of Fascism," in *The Crooked Timber of Humanity*, ed. Henry Hardy (London, 1992), 112.

118. See, for example, Jean-Baptiste-Charles-Marie de Beauvais, *Oraison funèbre du très grand, très haut, très puissant et très excellent prince, Louis XV le bien-aimé . . . prononcée dans l'Église de l'Abbaye Royale de Saint-Denis le 27 Juillet 1774* (Paris, 1774), 33.

119. Lamourette, *Pensées sur la philosophie*, 49–50.

120. Liger, *Triomphe de la religion*, ix.

121. "Fanatisme philosophique," *Journal historique et littéraire*, i (February 1, 1786):230.

122. *Journal historique et littéraire*, iii (December 15, 1786):573–575.

123. For typical examples in addition to those provided above, see Harel, *Causes du désordre*, 3; Harel, *Vraie philosophie*, 168; *Journal ecclésiatique*, 99, Part 1 (April 1785):94; *Journal de Monsieur*, i (1779):69; and Lamourette, *Pensées sur la philosophie*, 89.

124. On the use of the term "revolution" in eighteenth-century political discourse, see Keith Michael Baker, "Revolution," in Keith Michael Baker, Colin Lucas, and François Furet, eds., *The French Revolution and the Creation of Modern Political Culture*, 4 vols. (Oxford, 1987–1994), 2:41–63.

125. Harel, *Vraie philosophie*, vii–viii.

126. Grosier, "Idées préliminaires sur la critique," *Journal de littérature, des sciences et des arts*, i (1779):27.

127. I am drawing here on Clifford Geertz's well-known essay, "Ideology as a Cultural System," in *The Interpretation of Cultures: Selected Essays* (New York, 1973), 217–218.

128. In this respect, anti-*philosophe* discourse was very much in keeping with the mode of Catholic apology that William Everdell terms "social-utilitarian apologetic." See Everdell, *Christian Apologetics*, Chap. 5, esp. 126–136.

129. See, characteristically, [François-Antoine-Étienne de Gourcy], *Essai sur le bonheur* (Vienne, 1778); or [Joseph-Aignan Sigaud de la Fond], *L'École du bonheur, par M**** (Paris, 1782).

130. "Mémoire au roi, concernant les mauvais livres" (July 20, 1780), in *Procès-verbal de l'assemblée-générale* (1780), 335–336. The *mémoire* proceeded directly to warn that "several more years of silence" and French society would be reduced to "debris and ruins."

131. See, for example, Jeffrey W. Merrick, *The Desacralization of the French Monarchy in the Eighteenth Century* (Baton Rouge, La., 1990).

132. Dale Van Kley, *The Jansenists and the Expulsion of the Jesuits from France, 1757–1765* (New Haven, Conn., 1975).

133. See Van Kley, *Religious Origins of the French Revolution*, 221–222. The alienation of fervent Catholics from the French throne had many precedents, including the militant rhetoric of the Catholic League during the wars of religion. See Frederic J. Baumgartner, *Radical Reactionaries: The Political Thought of the*

French Catholic League (Geneva, 1975); and Denis Crouzet, *Les Guerriers de Dieu: La violence au temps des troubles de religion vers 1525–1610*, 2 vols. (Seysell, 1990).

134. Harel, *Vraie philosophie*, 153.

135. Rigoley de Juvigny, *De la décadence*, 130.

136. Lamourette, *Pensées sur la philosophie*, 78.

137. *Année littéraire*, i (1783):3–4.

138. These are all classic citations from Burke's *Reflections on the Revolution in France*, ed. L. G. Mitchell (Oxford and New York, 1993), 95.

139. Rigoley de Juvigny, *De la décadence*, 331–349.

140. Gérard, *Valmont*, 3:174–180.

141. I follow closely here, as elsewhere, the definition of "Right" elaborated by J. M. Roberts in "The French Origins of the 'Right,'" *Transactions of the Royal Historical Society*, 23 (1973), esp. 27–35.

Chapter 2

1. [Yves-Alexandre de Marbeuf], *Les Malheurs actuels préedits par le prophète Isaïe et le célèbre Fénelon, ou Extrait du mandement de M. l'archevêque de Lyon, du 28 Janvier 1789, sur l'exemplaire imprimé à Lyon* (n.p., 1789), 4.

2. Among other passages, Marbeuf quotes Isaiah 24:1: "Behold, the Lord will lay waste the earth and make it desolate, and he will twist its surface and scatter its inhabitants. . . ."

3. Marbeuf, *Malheurs actuels*, 3.

4. Ibid., 6–7

5. F. Amable Coquet de la Minaudière, *Mandement de Monseigneur l'abbé de Val-Joyeux, sur l'abjection de l'état religieux* (n.p., [1789]), 2–4. The *mandement* is signed February 1, 1789.

6. Ibid., 2–4, 19.

7. *Journal ecclésiastique*, March 1789, 301–302. See also *Mandement de monseigneur l'archevêque de Paris, pour le saint temps du carême* (Paris, 1789).

8. Cited and translated in William Everdell, *Christian Apologetics in France, 1730–1790: The Roots of Romantic Religion* (Lewiston, N.Y., 1987), 225.

9. See, for example, Clarke Garrett, *Respectable Folly: Millenarians and the French Revolution in France and England* (Baltimore, 1975); or Antoine de Baecque, "L'Homme nouveau est arrivé: La 'régénération du français en 1789," *Dix-huitième siècle*, 20 (1988):193–208. On such an interpretation of the French Revolution in America, see Ruth Bloch's *Millennial Themes in American Thought, 1756–1800* (Cambridge, 1985), esp. 150–186.

10. See, for example, Michel Winock, "L'Héritage contre-révolutionnaire," in Michel Winock, ed., *Histoire de l'extrême droite en France*, (Paris, 1993), 32; or Massimo Boffa, "La Contre-Révolution, Joseph de Maistre," in Keith Michael Baker, Colin Lucas, and François Furet, eds., *The French Revolution and the Creation of Modern Political Culture*, 4 vols. (Oxford, 1987–94), 4:290–308. One notable exception is Jochen Schlobach. See his "Fortschritt oder Erlösung. Zu aufklärerischen und millenaristischen Begründungen der Revolution," *Archiv für Kulturgeschichte*, 72 (1990):201–222.

11. Marbeuf, *Malheurs actuels*, 6–7.

12. "L'Influence des moeurs et du philosophisme sur les événemens actuels," *Journal ecclésiastique*, January 1789, 1–34. This article, along with two others in the April edition of the *Journal ecclésiastique*, was published by Barruel in pamphlet

form as *Le Patriote véridique, ou Discours sur les vraies causes de la révolution actuelle* (Paris, 1789). Subsequent pagination refers to this edition.

13. *Patriote véridique*, 10–11.

14. Ibid., 20–21.

15. In addition to Amos Hofman's pioneering article "The Origins of the Theory of the *Philosophe* Conspiracy," *French History*, 2 (1988):152–172, see his "Anatomy of Conspiracy: The Origins of the Theory of the Philosophe Conspiracy 1750–1789," Ph.D. dissertation, University of Chicago, 1986.

16. See Hofman's analysis of the explicitly conspiratorial elements of Barruel's language in *Les Helviennes* (ibid. 26–39), as well as Chap. 3 of Michel Riquet's *Augustin de Barruel: Un jésuite face aux Jacobins francs-maçons 1741–1820* (Paris, 1989), 23–37. Hofman provides numerous examples of plot language from *Année littéraire*, noting that the "theory of *philosophe* conspiracy was first crystallized" there in the 1770s ("Origins," 154). One can, however, can find examples of the theory much earlier in the writings of Sorbonne censors and *parlementaires* in the 1750s. See, for example, *Arrests de la cour de parlement, portant condamnation de plusieurs livres et autres ouvrages imprimés. . . . Extrait des registres de parlement du 23 Janvier 1759* (Paris, 1759), 4; and *Censure de la faculté de théologie de Paris, contre le livre qui a pour titre, de l'Esprit* (Paris, 1759), 8.

17. [Abbé Philippe-Louis Gérard], *Le Comte de Valmont ou les Égarements de la raison*, 6 vols. (Paris, 1826), 3:354–355. The conspiracy is developed in detail in 3:308–359.

18. [Louis Athanase des Balbes de Berton de Crillon], *Mémoires philosophiques du Baron De****, 2d ed., 2 vols. (1779), 1:75–175.

19. Bertrand Capmartin de Chaupy, *Philosophie des lettres qui auroit pu tout sauver. Misophie Voltairienne qui n'a pu que tout perdre. Ouvrage inutile à la présente tenue des États, pour laquelle il avoit été entrepris, mais qui pourra servir à celle qui pourra lui succéder, si la mode s'en continue*, 2 vols. (Paris, 1789–1790), 1:viii. For a discussion of Capmartin de Chaupy's numerous anti-Jansenist and anti-*parlement* screeds of the 1750s, see Dale Van Kley, *The Religious Origins of the French Revolution: From Calvin to the Civil Constitution* (New Haven, Conn., 1996), 226–229.

20. Capmartin de Chaupy, *Philosophie des lettres*, 121.

21. Ibid., xxiii.

22. Ibid., 124.

23. Ibid., 122–123.

24. See Arlette Farge and Jacques Revel, *The Vanishing Children of Paris: Rumor and Politics Before the French Revolution*, trans. Claudia Mieville (Cambridge, Mass., 1991); and Steven L. Kaplan, "The Famine Plot Persuasion in Eighteenth Century France," *Transactions of the American Philosophical Society*, 72 (1982). David Bien also notes the prevalence of popular belief in Protestant conspiracies among Catholics in the Midi. See *The Calas Affair: Persecution, Toleration, and Heresy in Eighteenth-Century Toulouse* (Princeton, N.J., 1960), 188–200, 124, 146.

25. Joachim Duport du Tertre, *Histoire des conjurations, conspirations et révolutions célèbres, tant anciennes que modernes*, 10 vols. (Paris, 1754–1760), 1:1. Duport, however, makes no mention of *philosophe* conspiracies.

26. The Jesuits, in particular, were frequently singled out by *philosophes* and others for allegedly conspiring against France. See Dale Van Kley, *The Jansenists and the Expulsion of the Jesuits from France, 1757–1765* (New Haven, Conn., 1975), 62–89.

27. Jean-Jacques Rousseau, *Rousseau Juge de Jean-Jacques*, in *Oeuvres complètes*,

eds. Bernard Gagnebin and Marcel Raymond, 5 vols. (Paris, 1959–1995), 1:890–891, 967–968. Rousseau discusses the plot in detail in both the second dialogue (esp. 888–892) and the third (964–974).

28. All citations ibid., 965–969.

29. [Alfonse Muzzarelli], *Jean Jacques Rousseau accusateur des prétendus philosophes de son siècle, et prophète de leur destruction, traduit de l'Italien, d'après la dernière édition* (Rome, 1807). Muzzarelli was a censor at the Academy of the Catholic Religion in Rome. His pamphlet was published in France and elsewhere in numerous editions.

30. On this theme, see Roger Barny, "Les Aristocrates et Jean-Jacques Rousseau dans la Révolution," *Annales historiques de la Révolution française*, 50 (1978):534–568; Gordon H. McNeil, "The Anti-Revolutionary Rousseau," *The American Historical Review*, 58 (1953):808–823; and Joan McDonald, *Rousseau and the French Revolution* (London, 1965), Chap. 9, "The Counter-Revolutionary Appeal to Rousseau."

31. On this theme, see Gordon S. Wood, "Conspiracy and the Paranoid Style: Causality and Deceit in the Eighteenth Century," *William and Mary Quarterly*, 3d series, 39 (1982):401–404.

32. François Furet, *Interpreting the French Revolution*, trans. Elborg Forster (Cambridge, 1981), 54–55. Lynn Hunt also ascribes to conspiracy an important place in the rhetoric of the Revolution, although she views its role as less of a philosophically necessary product of revolutionary discourse than as a contingent result of the revolutionaries' confrontation with mass politics. See her influential *Politics, Culture, and Class in the French Revolution* (Berkeley and Los Angeles, 1984), 38–43.

33. Furet does not mention right-wing conspiracy theories at all except for one passing reference to Barruel's much later *Mémoires pour servir à l'histoire du jacobinisme*, a work, Furet implies, that was adapted from Thermidorian plot theories (Furet, *Interpreting the French Revolution*, 58). Hunt, by contrast, recognizes that "conspiracy rhetoric invaded all varieties of political discourse in France," but she sees the conservative variety as being largely derivative of the radical example, only taking on any real importance after the fall of Robespierre (*Politics, Culture, and Class*, 41).

34. Furet, *Interpreting the French Revolution*, 28–29, 43–45, 54. Similarly, see Patrice Gueniffey, *La Politique de la Terreur: Essai sur la violence révolutionnaire, 1789–1794* (Paris, 2000); Clarke Garrett, "The Myth of the Counterrevolution in 1789," *French Historical Studies*, 18 (1994):784–800; and Paul Beik, *The French Revolution Seen from the Right: Social Theories in Motion, 1789–1799* (Philadelphia, 1956), 341. It is revealing, in this connection, that Keith Baker's influential *Inventing the French Revolution: Essays on French Political Culture in the Eighteenth Century* (Cambridge, 1990) provides not a single index reference to the Counter-Revolution, leaving one to surmise that the Revolution was "invented" in the absence of opposition.

35. Furet, *Interpreting the French Revolution*, 54.

36. See Timothy Tackett, "Conspiracy Obsession in a Time of Revolution: French Elites and the Origins of the Terror, 1789–1792," *American Historical Review*, 105 (2000):698–699.

37. Jacques Linsolas, *L'Église clandestine de Lyon pendant la Révolution, 1789–1799*, 2 vols. (Lyon, 1987), 1:23. Linsolas was a priest at the collegial church of

Saint-Nizier in Lyon. He began his clandestine diary at the time of the Estates General. The passage is dated simply 1789.

38. *Journal politique-national,* no. 5, 3. Founded by Sabatier with Antoine Rivarol, the paper was quickly taken over by the latter after Sabatier's emigration in late July. See William J. Murray, *The Right-Wing Press in the French Revolution: 1789–1792* (Woodbridge, Suffolk, 1986), 12–17.

39. *Journal historique et littéraire,* iii (September 15, 1789):116. See also the analysis in the following issue, iii (October 1, 1789):220.

40. Hardy, "Mes loisirs," BN: MS. Fr. 6687 (June 24, 1789), 364, cited in Van Kley, *Religious Origins,* 363. Hardy claims that the archbishop singled out the newly appointed president of the National Assembly, the astronomer Jean-Sylvain Bailly, as the *philosophe,* and Necker as the Protestant.

41. [Augustin Jean François Chaillon de Joinville], *La Vérité dévoilée* (Cosmopolis, 1784). This work is attributed to Joinville, who had served as both a counselor and a *maître des requêtes* at the Paris *parlement.* Given the glaring contrast between this and Joinville's later works, it is possible that the attribution is mistaken. Such rapid reversals upon confrontation with the Revolution, however, were not uncommon.

42. [Augustin Jean François Chaillon de Joinville], *La Vraie philosophie* (Paris, 1789), iii.

43. *Discours à prononcer par un des membres des états-généraux* (Paris, 1789), 8. The pamphlet contains numerous references to the *philosophe* conspiracy.

44. Timothy Tackett, *Becoming a Revolutionary: The Deputies of the French National Assembly and the Emergence of a Revolutionary Culture (1789–1790)* (Princeton, N.J., 1996), 50–53. I am grateful to Professor Tackett for showing me additional, unpublished material from this important study.

45. Ibid., 68.

46. See, for example, Jack Richard Censer, *Prelude to Power: The Parisian Radical Press, 1789–1791* (Baltimore and London, 1976), 98–99.

47. On this point, see Roger Chartier, *The Cultural Origins of the French Revolution,* trans. Lydia G. Cochrane (Durham and London, 1991), 5; and Hans Ulrich Gumbrecht and Rolf Reichardt, *Philosophe, Philosophie,* vol. 3 of Rolf Reichardt and Eberhard Schmitt, ed., *Handbuch politish-sozialer Grundbegriffe in Frankreich 1680–1820,* 10 vols. (Munich, 1985–), 61–64.

48. *Année littéraire,* viii (1789):306–307.

49. M. J. Mavidal and M. E. Laurent, eds., *Archives parlementaires de 1787 à 1860, recueil complet des débats législatifs & politiques des chambres françaises,* Série 1 (1787–1799), 88 vols. (Paris, 1867–1913), 18:250. La Harpe delivered his discourse, accompanied by André Chénier, Louis-Sébastien Mercier, Nicolas Sébastien Roche Chamfort, and others on August 24, 1790.

50. *L'Ami du Roi, des François, de l'ordre, et surtout de la vérité, par les continuateurs de Fréron,* no. 87 (August 26, 1790). Felix-Christophe-Louis Ventre de la Touloubre, better known as Galart de Montjoye, was the son of a professor of law at the University of Aix-en-Provence. In the summer of 1790 he began to edit the daily *Ami du roi* with the veteran anti-*philosophe* Thomas-Marie Royou. The two fell out in August 1790, however, and Royou proceeded to found his own daily journal of the same name. See Murray, *Right-Wing Press,* 35.

51. *Journal politique-national,* no. 13, 3–5.

52. Cited in Tackett, *Becoming a Revolutionary,* 73.

53. *Journal politique-national*, no. 19, 5; Tackett, *Becoming a Revolutionary*, 182–184,

54. Edmund Burke, *Reflections on the Revolution in France*, ed. L. G. Mitchell (Oxford and New York, 1993), 21, 124.

55. Franciszek Draus, "Burke et les Français," in *French Revolution and Political Culture*, 3:79.

56. See Colin Lucas, "Edmund Burke and the Emigrés," in *French Revolution and Political Culture*, 3:101–114. It is also true that the portrayal of scientists and men of letters as abstruse systematizers, divorced from concrete reality, enjoyed a long tradition in England, figuring centrally, for example, in Swift's *Gulliver's Travels*, a work that Burke greatly admired.

57. See Burke's letter to Barruel, quoted in chapter 3.

58. Burke, *Reflections*, 111–112.

59. [Thomas-Marie Royou], *L'Ami du Roi, des Français, de l'ordre et surtout de la vérité, par les continuateurs de Fréron*, no. 1 (September 1, 1790):3.

60. *Journal historique et littéraire*, iii (December 1, 1789):542.

61. Ibid., 543.

62. *Apocalypse*, no. 10 (September 1790):8–9. André-Boniface-Louis, vicomte de Mirabeau, younger brother of the more famous count, earned the nickname *tonneau* ("barrel") because of his prodigious size.

63. See, for example, Sabatier, *Le Tocsin des politiques*, new ed. (n.p. [1791]), 102; and the *Journal historique et littéraire*, iii (September 1, 1789):59.

64. *Réflexions intéressantes sur les principes de la nouvelle constitution de la France, et sur quelques décréts de l'Assemblée Nationale, par un François* (Nivelles, 1790), 15–16, 47. The work is a point-by-point refutation of the Declaration of the Rights of Man and the Citizen.

65. [Étienne Bremont], *Apologie de mémoire présenté au roi, par Monseigneur comte d'Artois, M. le prince de Condé, M. le duc de Bourbon, M. le duc d'Enghien, & M. le prince de Conti. . . . Ouvrage dédié à l'Assemblée des Etats-Généraux, tenue à Versailles en 1789* (Amsterdam and Paris, 1789), 38. Bremont presented his work as a defense of the infamous *Mémoire des princes*, submitted by the Comte d'Artois and other peers of the realm to Louis XVI in the wake of the Assembly of Notables in 1788.

66. Chaillon de Joinville, *Vraie philosophie*, 3.

67. Capmartin de Chaupy, *Misophie Voltairienne*, 1:101. See also *Réflexions intéressantes*, 7–8.

68. *Réflexions intéressantes*, 47.

69. *Du Tolérantisme, et des peines auxquelles il peut donner lieu, suivant les lois de l'Église & de l'État* (Brussels, 1789), x. The text has been attributed both to F.-X. Feller and to Barthélemy Baudrand. See the enthusiastic reviews of the work and further attacks on the National Assembly's "tolerance strategy" in the *Journal ecclésiastique*, August and September 1789, 415–416 and 87ff., respectively.

70. *Journal historique et littéraire*, iii (November 1, 1789):381.

71. "Discours préliminaire sur l'état de France," *Ami du Roi*, no. 1 (June 1, 1790):1.

72. *Journal ecclésiastique*, January 1790, 6.

73. Ibid., 18.

74. Ibid., 21.

75. Jean-Jacques Duval d'Eprémesnil, *Observations de M. d'Eprémesnil, sur un sujet très important* (Paris, [1790]), 5–7, 11. The pamphlet is signed February 24,

1790. Eprémesnil had broken cleanly with the Committee of Thirty by late December 1788, establishing in response the conservative Committee of One Hundred, a group of nobles and clergy opposed to extending equal voting privileges to the Third Estate. See Tackett, *Becoming a Revolutionary*, 93–94.

76. Cited in Tackett, *Becoming a Revolutionary*, 289.

77. Ibid., 291.

78. [Léon de Castellane-Mazaugues], "Lettre Pastorale de Monsieur l'évêque de Toulon, aux fidèles de son diocèse," July 1, 1790, in Augustin Barruel, ed., *Collection ecclésiastique, ou Recueil complet des ouvrages faits depuis l'ouverture des états généraux, relativement au clergé*, 14 vols. (Paris, 1791–1793), 1:448–449. The bishop had particular reason to resent the Revolution. On March 23, 1789, crowds angered by bread shortages had ransacked his palace.

79. Ibid., 456.

80. *De la décadence de l'empire françois, fruit de la philosophie moderne adoptée par nos législateurs* (n.p. [1790]), 5. The author was a self-described "citizen of the order of the third estate."

81. Ibid., 22. Ironically, this quote was taken, although without attribution, from Pierre Bayle's article on "Uriel Acosta" in his *Dictionnaire historique et critique*.

82. Ibid.

83. See Robert Darnton, *The Kiss of Lamourette: Reflections in Cultural History*, (New York, 1990), xii–xiv

84. On the varieties of right-wing experience during this period, see Beik, *French Revolution Seen from the Right*; Jacques Godechot, *The Counter-Revolution Doctrine and Action, 1789–1804*, trans. Salvator Attanasio (Princeton, 1971), 3–50; and Murray, *Right-Wing Press*, 3–4, 158–173.

85. [François-Dominique de Reynaud de Montlosier], *Observations sur l'adresse à l'ordre de la noblesse française, de M. le comte d'Entraigues [sic], par M. de Montlosier* (n.p., [1792]), 6–8. On Montlosier and his politics, see Godechot, *Counter-Revolution*, 22–27.

86. "Discours préliminaire sur l'état de France," *L'Ami du Roi*, no. 1 (June 1, 1790); emphasis added.

87. On the need to purge and reform the clergy, see, for example, Barruel, "Discours sur l'influence du sacerdoce sur les progrès de la corruption des moeurs et philosophisme, sur la nécessité, et les moyens de réformer en France les abus du clergé," in *Journal ecclésiastique*, April 1789, 337–389.

88. On the principle of "no compromise" in the extreme right-wing press and criticism of the king, see Murray, *Right-Wing Press*, 158–159.

89. The question of armed resistance or foreign intervention was a divisive issue, even for the most extreme. The long-time anti-*philosophe* and virulent opponent of the Revolution the abbé Royou, for example, consistently opposed either of these options. By contrast, Louis-Abel Fontenai's *Journal général* and P. B. F. Rozoi's *Gazette de Paris* advocated armed foreign intervention from well before the king's flight to Varennes. See Murray, *Right-Wing Press*, 140–157.

90. Censer, *Prelude to Power*, 124–129.

91. Furet, *Interpreting the French Revolution*, 54–55.

92. The root of the French word for "conspiracy" (*conjuration*) is to "conjure," evoking association with the artifice of black magicians, sorcerers, and illusionists.

93. Louis Marie Stanislas Fréron (1754-1802) edited the violent revolutionary newspaper the *Orateur du peuple* and acted as an efficient "representative on mis-

sion" during the Terror. One of Fréron's colleagues at *Orateur du peuple*, Jean-Joseph Dussault, went on to become a prolific anti-*philosophe* during the reign of Napoleon and the Restoration.

94. See *Journal historique et littéraire*, ii (July 15, 1792):465, and ii (August 1, 1792):534–535. For other, similar characterizations of the *monarchiens*, see *Journal pie*, no. 2 (January 18, 1792); and Fontenai's *Journal général*, no. 197 (July 15, 1792).

95. See Hofman, "Anatomy of Conspiracy," Chap. 5, "The Theory of Conspiracy as a Defense of Absolutism," 239–279.

96. *Causes et agens des révolutions de France* (n.p., [1791]), 3. To emphasize the point, the author provided over fifteen pages of names of deputies to the National Assembly, classed according to their degree of criminality. For a discussion of this pamphlet and further reflections on the notion of a Protestant conspiracy, see J.M. Roberts, "The Origins of a Mythology: Freemasons, Protestants and The French Revolution," *Bulletin of the Institute of Historical Research* 44 (1971), 80–93.

97. Tackett identifies at least twenty-four Protestant deputies to the Estates General, the great majority of whom emerged as strong patriots (*Becoming a Revolutionary*, 65–66).

98. See the *Journal historique et littéraire*, ii (July 15, 1790):450. On charges of Protestant subversion leveled in the National Assembly, see Tackett, *Becoming a Revolutionary*, 268.

99. "Jansénisme, union de cette secte avec le philosophisme," *Journal historique et littéraire*, iii (October 15, 1790):290. See also ii (June 1, 1791):175, an appreciative review of Burke's *Reflections*, in which Feller faults the British author only for having overlooked the close ties between Jansenism and *philosophie*.

100. Van Kley, *Religious Origins*, 283.

101. See ibid., 343, for assertions of the Jansenist-Protestant-*philosophe* axis during the prerevolutionary period, as well as Jansenist rebuttals.

102. I draw heavily here on J. M. Roberts's indispensable *The Mythology of the Secret Societies* (New York, 1972), 146–154. See also Jacques Lemaire, *Les Origines françaises de l'antimaçonnisme (1744–1797)* (Brussels, 1985).

103. Roberts, *Mythology of the Secret Societies*, 129ff.

104. Ibid., 154.

105. Margaret Jacob, *Living the Enlightenment: Freemasonry and Politics in Eighteenth-Century Europe* (New York and Oxford, 1991).

106. *L'Esprit de la franc-maçonnerie dévoilé, relativement au danger qu'elle renferme, pour servir à MM. les ecclésiastiques et à tous les amis de la religion et du roi*, 2d ed. (Rome, 1790; reprint Montpellier, 1816), 40–41, 60. See also the abbé Le Franc's *Le voile levé pour les curieux, ou le secret de la révolution levé à l'aide de la franc-maçonnerie* (Paris, 1791), enthusiastically reviewed by Montjoye's *Ami du Roi*, no. 149 (September 6, 1791):995–996; and Lefranc's *Conjuration contre la religion catholique, et les souverains dont le projet conçu en France doit s'exécuter dans l'univers entier* (Paris, 1792). Roberts discusses both of Lefranc's works in "Origins of a Mythology," 82–85.

107. "Compte rendu a ses commettants par M. le comte de Pannetier," *Archives parlementaires*, Série 1, 32:494. The letter is dated July 15, 1791. Pannetier also cites in full a letter from First Estate colleagues, "Protestations contre tous les décrets de l'Assemblée nationale," drafted in June of 1790, which denounces a "general conspiracy" and vows to restore "the lustre and rights of our saintly religion, which *philosophes* and a handful of heretics have taken away" (ibid., 494–496).

108. See Godechot, *Counter-Revolution*, 29.

109. See, most notably, [Count Emmanuel-Louis-Henri-Alexandre de Launai d'Antraigues], *Dénonciation aux François catholiques, des moyens employés par l'Assemblée nationale, pour détruire en France, la religion catholique* (London and Paris, 1791); and *Adresse à l'ordre de la noblesse de France* (Paris, 1792). The work is dated November 25, 1791. On the life of this quizzical figure, see Colin Duckworth, *The D'Antraigues Phenomenon: The Making and Breaking of a Revolutionary Royalist Espionage Agent* (Newcastle, 1986); and Jacques Godechot, *Le Comte d'Antraigues, un espion dans l'Europe des émigrés* (Paris, 1986).

110. Murray, *Right-Wing Press*, 254. Murray refers to the first five journals. For Montjoye's *Ami de Roi*, see, for example, no. 149 (September 6, 1791):995–996. For Royou's *Ami de Roi*, see the unnumbered issue of September 13, 1791, 3. As editor of the *Année littéraire* through the spring of 1790, Royou had also voiced accusations of the conspiracy there. See *Année littéraire*, iv (1790):14–18. By 1792, charges of conspiracy were even more widespread. See, for example, *Journal pie*, no. 8 (January 30, 1792):7–8; and *L'Historien de France et de l'Europe*, no. 1 (April 12, 1792):1–2.

111. "Lettre de Pie VI" (April 13, 1791), printed in *Journal ecclésiastique*, May 1791, 92, 129.

112. [Abbé Balthazard], *L'Isle des philosophes et plusieurs autres, nouvellement découvertes, & remarquables var [sic] leurs rapports avec la France actuelle* (n.p., [1790]). On this text, see my "Narratives of Dystopia in the French Revolution: Enlightenment, Counter-Enlightenment, and the *Isle des philosophes* of the Abbé Balthazard," in Caroline Weber and Howard G. Lay, *Fictions of Revolution*, a special issue of *Yale French Studies*, 100 (2001).

113. See Timothy Tackett, *Religion, Revolution, and Regional Culture in Eighteenth-Century France: The Ecclesiastical Oath of 1791* (Princeton, N.J., 1986), esp. 2, 34–56.

114. See Tackett, "Conspiracy Obsession," 711–713.

115. On Voltaire's second apotheosis, see Raymond O. Rockwood, *The Cult of Voltaire to 1791: A Revolutionary Deity, 1789-May 30, 1791* (Chicago, 1937); J. A. Leith, "Les Trois apothéoses de Voltaire," *Annales historiques de la Révolution française* 51 (1979):161–209; and Simon Schama, *Citizens: A Chronicle of the French Revolution* (New York, 1989), 561–566.

116. Mona Ozouf, *Festivals and the French Revolution*, trans. Alan Sheridan (Cambridge and London, 1988), 265–282.

117. The French term *translation* (the movement of a body or relic of a saint from one place of internment to another) was habitually used in discussing the transfer of Voltaire's remains, further emphasizing the religious connection.

118. *Pétition à l'Assemblée Nationale, relative au transport de Voltaire*, new ed. (n.p., n.d.), A2 (first page of text). The first edition is essentially the same but contains fewer petitioning signatures.

119. Ibid., 5–6.

120. *Journal historique et littéraire*, ii (July 1, 1791):395. See also ii (May 1, 1791):52–53.

121. *Journal de la cour et de la ville*, no. 31 (May 31, 1791):241–242; no. 11 (July 11, 1791):81. For circulation figures, see Murray, *Right-Wing Press*, 86.

122. *Journal de la noblesse, de la magistature, du sacerdoce et du militaire*, no. 31, 53.

123. See Montjoye's *Ami du Roi*, no. 95 (April 5, 1791):378; no. 129 (May 9,

1791):514; and no. 194 (July 13, 1791):775–776. For publication figures, see Murray, *Right-Wing Press*, 87.

124. See Murray's tables in *Right-Wing Press*, 296, 302.

125. *Journal général*, no. 120 (May 31, 1791):483; *Journal général de France*, no. 151 (May 31, 1791):601. As late as 1792, Fontenai's *Journal général* was claiming daily sales of seven thousand copies, a figure that William Murray deems credible. The *Journal général de France*'s circulation rate probably approached three thousand copies per day. See Murray, *Right-Wing Press*, 86–87.

126. Émile Durkheim, *The Elementary Forms of Religious Life*, trans. Karen E. Fields (New York, 1995), 215.

127. See, for example, *Le Martirologe, ou L'Histoire des martyrs de la Révolution* (Coblentz and Paris, 1792), 12, 24.

128. [Augustin Jean François Chaillon de Joinville], *La Révolution de France prophétisée, ainsi que ses causes infernales, ses effets sinistres & ses suites heureuses, qui seront une restauration générale & une reforme complette de tous les abus en 1792*, 2 vols. (Paris, 1791), 1:20.

129. Ibid., 2:266–267.

130. Sabatier, *Tocsin*, 6.

131. Antraigues, *Adresse*, 100–101. The connection between the Santo Domingo rising and *philosophie* was made frequently. See, for example, *Journal pie*, no. 2 (January 18, 1792):4; *Journal historique et littéraire*, iii (December 1, 1791):557; and *Petit Gautier*, no. 4 (January 4, 1792):29.

132. *Journal pie*, no. 2 (January 18, 1792):4.

133. *Journal du peuple*, no. 31 (March 2, 1792):124.

134. "Discours préliminaire," *L'Historien de France et de l'Europe*, April 12, 1792. This short-lived publication, issued thrice weekly, examined in its opening number how "*philosophisme*" and "Cromwellism" had infected France, inciting the fever of the Revolution, which now threatened all of Europe.

135. "Discours préliminaire. Caractères de la Révolution," *Journal général*, January 1, 1792, 1.

136. Ibid. See also the long, four-part essay in the *Gazette de Paris* "Origine des maux présens soit de l'Eglise, soit de l'Etat," May 19, 21–23, 1792.

Chapter 3

1. William Doyle, *The Oxford History of the French Revolution* (Oxford, 1989), 253, 258–259.

2. Robert Darnton, *The Kiss of Lamourette: Reflections in Cultural History* (New York, 1990), 6–7.

3. Mona Ozouf, *Festivals and the French Revolution*, trans. Alan Sheridan (Cambridge and London, 1998), chap. X, "The Revolutionary Festival: A Transfer of Sacrality," 262–282.

4. On the emigration, see Donald Greer's seminal *The Incidence of the Emigration during the French Revolution* (Cambridge, Mass., 1951). Recent scholarship is summarized in Kirsty Carpenter and Philip Mansel, eds., *The French Émigrés in Europe and the Struggle against the Revolution, 1789–1814* (London and New York, 1999). See also Kirsty Carpenter, *Refugees of the French Revolution: Émigrés in London, 1789–1802* (London, 1999). I have drawn my figures from these sources.

5. Fernand Baldensperger, *Le Mouvement des idées dans l'émigration française 1789–1815*, 2 vols. (New York, 1968), 2:15–16. In general, see Vol. 2, Chap. 1, "La

Dénonciation de la 'secte' organisée," and Chap. 2, "Le Désaveu des 'lumières,'" as well as Jean Vidalenc, *Les Émigrés français 1789–1825* (Caen, 1963), 383.

6. André Morellet, "Apologie de la philosophie contre ceux qui l'accusent des maux de la Révolution" (1796), *Mélanges de littérature et de philosophie du 18e siècle*, 4 vols. (Paris, 1818), 4:308–332.

7. Honoré Riouffe, *Discours lu au Cercle Constitutionnel*, Le neuf messidor, an V (Paris, 1797), 10–12. Imprisoned by the Jacobins, Riouffe later served as a prefect under Napoleon, for which the title of baron and membership in the legion of honor were bestowed.

8. Augustin Barruel, *Le Patriote véridique, ou Discours sur les vraies causes de la révolution actuelle* (Paris, 1789), 11.

9. The citation is taken from an undated, introductory prospectus that announces the forthcoming journal *L'Ami du Roi, des français, de l'ordre et surtout de la vérité, par les continuateurs de Fréron*, published most likely in May 1790, with the epigraph *Pro Deo, Rege et Patria*.

10. Ibid. The claim to have foretold the Revolution was neither exclusively French nor Catholic. The anonymous English pamphlet *Prophetic Conjectures on the French Revolution, and Other Recent and Shortly Expected Events* (London, [1793]) stacked up quotations by British religious commentators, dating back to the sixteenth century, as proof of both God's revelation and the divination of prescient observers.

11. *Instructions aux Catholiques, sur les causes de la Révolution et les moyens d'en arrêter les progrès*, 2d ed. (Paris, 1792), 5.

12. [Abbé Duvoisin], *Examen des principes de la Révolution française* (Wolfenbuttel, 1795), 98. On Duvoisin's life and writings, see Jacques Godechot, *The Counter-Revolution Doctrine and Action, 1789–1804*, trans. Salvator Attanasio (Princeton, 1971), 41, 48–49.

13. Augustin Barruel, *Mémoires pour servir à l'histoire du jacobinisme*, 3d ed., 4 vols. (Ausbourg, 1797), 1:226.

14. For typical examples of what was a common practice, see Blanchandin-le-Chêne, *Hommage à l'immuable vérité, ou Discours à sa gloire, et dont l'objet encore est de la défendre des erreurs et des excès d'impiété des dernières années du dix-huitième siècle* (Bruxelles, 1802); and [Edme-Hilaire Garnier-Deschenses], *Chansons et prédictions, très-curieuses et relatives à la Révolution française où l'on voit la grande utilité du Christianisme, et les funestes effets de la soi-disant philosophie, qui l'attaque* (Paris, [1801]).

15. Chaillon de Joinville's *Révolution de France prophétisée, ainsi que ses causes infernales, ses effets sinistres & ses suites heureuses, qui seront une restauration générale & une reforme complette de tous les abus en 1792*, 2 vols. (Paris, 1791) purported to be an ancient prophecy found in the tombs of the French kings at St-Denis. See also *Prédiction de Cazotte, faite en 1788, et rapportée par La Harpe* (Paris, 1817), allegedly an unambiguous prediction of the Revolution made in 1788 by the anti-*philosophe hommes de lettres* Jacques Cazotte.

16. For a concise, early statement of this position, see Pierre Louis Roederer's *De la Philosophie moderne, et de la part qu'elle a eue à la révolution française, ou Examen de la brochure publiée par Rivarol sur la Philosophie moderne* (Paris, an VIII), a refutation of the work of Antoine Rivarol, discussed below.

17. *L'Accusateur public*, 1, no. 2 (n.d.):22–24.

18. *Journal littéraire*, no. 29 (March 23, 1797):165.

19. Antoine Rivarol, *De la Philosophie moderne* (n.p., [1797]). 66–68 (emphasis

in original). On Rivarol's life, see Bernard Fay, *Rivarol and the Revolution* (Paris, 1978), and Jean Lessay, *Rivarol* (Paris, 1989).

20. *Considérations sur l'intérêt des puissances de l'Europe dans la Révolution françoise*, 2d ed. (Londres, 1793), 9–10. See also *Considérations historiques sur la Révolution françoise, par un ami de l'ordre, de la liberté et du bonheur des peuples* (London, 1793), 11.

21. Rivarol, *Philosophie moderne*, 14; *Annales religieuses, politiques, et littéraires* (*Annales catholiques*) 3, no. 26 (1797):6; *La Véritable politique à l'usage des émigrés françois, ou Lettres du Marquis de *** au Chevalier **** (London, 1795), 43; [Auguste Danican], *Le Fléau des tyrans et des septembriseurs, ou Réflexion française, Ouvrage dans lequel on traite de la souveraineté du peuple, de l'esclavage, de la liberté, de la royauté, de la république, des économistes, des chevaliers du temple, illuminés & franc-maçons* (Lausanne and Paris, 1797), 132; Duvoisin, *Examen des principes*, 103, 148. See also the typically sweeping condemnation by Richer-Sérizy, *Accusateur public*, 1, nos. 9–11 (one issue, n.d.):22–23.

22. *Actes des Apôtres*, 2, no. 3 (1797):58.

23. J.-E.-M. Portalis, *De l'Usage et de l'abus de l'esprit philosophique durant le XVIIIe siècle*, 3d ed., 2 vols. (Paris, 1834), 1:113. Although written in 1798, the work was not published until 1820.

24. Rivarol, *Philosophie moderne*, 11.

25. Joseph de Maistre, *Considérations sur la France*, in Jean-Louis Darcel, ed., *Écrits sur la révolution* (Paris, 1989), 100, n. b. This passage, found in Maistre's draft manuscript of the *Considérations*, was excised from the first published version of 1797. It is nonetheless perfectly in keeping with Maistre's convictions. See, for example, his outbursts in Jean-Louis Darcel, ed., *Étude sur la souveraineté du peuple: Un Anti-contrat social* (Paris, 1992), 170–172.

26. The episode occurred on December 5, 1792, at a meeting of the Jacobin club in Paris. See Dr. Robinet, *Le Mouvement religieux à Paris pendant la Révolution* (1789–1801), 2 vols. (Paris, 1896–1898), 2:329–330.

27. *Accusateur publique*, 1, no. 2, 24. On perceptions of Rousseau, see Roger Barny, *Rousseau dans la Révolution: Le personnage de Jean-Jacques et les débuts du culte révolutionnaire* (*1787–1791*) (Oxford, 1986); and Jean Roussel, *Jean-Jacques Rousseau en France après la Révolution* (*1795–1830*) (Paris, 1972).

28. [François-Marie Bigex], *Le Missionaire Catholique, ou Instructions familières, sur la religion, en refutation des préjugés, des erreurs et des calomnies . . .* , 3d ed. (Paris, 1797), 4–5; Barruel, *Mémoires*, 1:5.

29. For discussions of the text, see Amos Hofman, "Opinion, Illusion, and the Illusion of Opinion: Barruel's Theory of Conspiracy, *Eighteenth-Century Studies*, 27 (Fall 1993): 27–61; and Michel Riquet's *Augustin de Barruel: Un jésuite face aux Jacobins francs-maçons 1741–1820* (Paris, 1989), 83–91.

30. Louis-Jacques Briel, *Les Principes fondamentaux de toute société, constitués avec l'homme, précédés d'un précis historique et critique des causes éloignées et prochaines de la Révolution en France*, 3 vols. (Paris, 1797), 1:29, 66, 3:8; *Journal littéraire*, no. 15 (5 Frimaire, an V):75–76; *Annales religieuses*, 1, no. 1 (1796):6–7.

31. *Actes des Apôtres*, 1, no. 6 (November 6, 1796):13.

32. Maistre, *Considérations sur la France*, 137.

33. Duvoisin, *Examen des principes*, 99.

34. Briel, *Principes fondamentaux*, 3:8, 69–70. On this theme of the passions, see also Barruel-Beauvert, *Lettres à un rentier, habitant une solitude au bord de la mer et ne*

vivant que de sa pêche (Paris, 1796), 63; *Accusateur public*, 2, no. 28, 15; and Maistre, "Trois fragments sur la France," in Darcel *Écrits sur la révolution*, 78.

35. Rivarol, *Philosophie moderne*, 37, 59–62, 66.

36. *Année littéraire*, ii (1772):305.

37. Duvoisin, *Examen des principes*, 98.

38. Ibid., 101.

39. *L'Invariable, Journal de politique et de littérature M. Royou*, no. 40 (July 24, 1797):2. The editor, Jacques-Corentin Royou, was the brother of the celebrated anti-*philosophe* Thomas-Marie Royou, who died in 1792.

40. *Le Déjeuner*, no. 135 (May 15, 1797):539.

41. *Journal littéraire* 1, no. 14 (25 Brumaire, an V):34. On the same theme, see *Accusateur public*, 1, no. 4, 21–22.

42. Bigex, *Missionaire Catholique*, 20.

43. *Thé*, no. 135 (August 28, 1797):538.

44. Rivarol, *Philosophie moderne*, 7.

45. *Politique chrétienne*, no. 24 (August 1, 1797):185. So did polemicists in this period continue to levy charges of the Protestant character of the Revolution and *philosophie*. See the classic conspiracy account by [F.-N. Sourdat de Troyes], *Les Véritables auteurs de la Révolution de France de 1789* (Neufchatel, 1797), as well as Joseph de Maistre's brief essay of 1798, "Réflexions sur le protestantisme dans ses rapports avec la souveraineté," in Darcel *Écrits*, 219–239.

46. *Considérations sur l'intérêt*, 10. On the larger theme of the man of letters as secular priest, see Rivarol, *Philosophie moderne*, 47–48; and Paul Bénichou, *Le Sacre de l'écrivain 1750–1830: Essai sur l'avènement d'un pouvoir spirituel laïque dans la France moderne* (Paris, 1973).

47. *Accusateur public*, 1, no. 4 (n.d.):18.

48. Ibid., 2, no. 28 (n.d.):7–8.

49. *Politique chrétienne*, no. 5 (May 17, 1797):39. See also *Déjeuner*, no. 99 (April 9, 1797):394–395, and *Journal général de France*, no. 127 (January 26, 1797):509–511, for further commentary linking Babeuf to the *philosophes*.

50. *Discours préliminaire au projet de constitution pour la république prononcé par Boissy-D'Anglas, au nom de la commision des onze* (Paris, an III), 3.

51. See Jeremy Popkin's indispensable *The Right Wing Press in France, 1792–1800* (Chapel Hill, N.C., 1980), 116–122. Popkin observes of this period that "blanket condemnations of eighteenth-century philosophy were less common in the right wing press than were attempts to discriminate between good and bad philosophes" (120). As a general characterization, this is probably true, although it should be noted that Popkin's definition of "right wing" is very broad, including not only constitutional monarchists but also anti-Jacobin republicans (8). Of those journals he describes as "royalist extremist" and "Catholic," the critique of *philosophie* presented here was the norm.

52. Biographical information is drawn from "Notice sur l'abbé Feller," in the posthumous edition of F-X. Feller's *Catéchisme philosophique, ou Recueil d'observations propres à défendre la religion chrétienne contre ses ennemis*, new ed. (Tournai, 1846), v–x.

53. See, for example, *Journal historique et littéraire*, i (February 1, 1780):178–187; ii (June 15, 1784):237–240; iii (November 1, 1784):319–343; iii (December 15, 1786):571–575; iii (October 1, 1787):159–171; iii (November 1, 1789):323–347, 1789; iii (December 1, 1789):487–507, and iii (December 15, 1789):569–578.

54. Dale K. Van Kley, "Piety and Politics in the Century of Lights," forthcoming in Robert Wokler, ed. *Cambridge History of Eighteenth-Century Political Thought*. I am grateful to Professor Van Kley for showing me this rich essay in unpublished form.

55. "Jansénisme, union de cette secte avec le philosophisme," *Journal historique et littéraire*, iii (October 15, 1790):290. Feller was speaking here in reference to the French National Assembly, but he drew the connection repeatedly about the Low Countries as well.

56. R. Bocca, *La lega della teologia moderna colla filosofia a danno della Chiesa di G.C.* (Rome, 1789). This text, republished in Foligno in 1792 and Milan in 1834, was also translated into Spanish at the behest of the Marqués de Mérito as *La liga de la teología moderna con la filosofía en daño de la iglesia de Jesucristo* (Madrid, 1798).

57. Van Kley, "Piety and Politics in the Century of Lights," section 2. For a more detailed treatment of Jansenism's role in galvanizing a Catholic Counter-Enlightenment response, see my "Seeing the Century of Lights as a Time of Darkness: The Catholic Counter-Enlightenment in Europe and the Americas," in Florence Lotterie and Darrin M. McMahon, eds., *Les Lumières européennes dans leur relation avec les autres grandes cultures et religions du XVIIIe siècle* (Paris, 2001).

58. Richard Herr, *The Eighteenth-Century Revolution in Spain* (Princeton, N.J., 1958), 213–214, 366–367; Javier Herrero, *Los Origines del pensamiento reaccionario español* (Madrid, 1971), 19, 35–45.

59. See Alfonso Prandi's classic *Religiosità e cultura nel '700 italiano* (Bologna, 1966); and more generally, Furio Diaz, *Filosofia e politica nel Settecento francese* (Torino, 1962), esp. 131–229.

60. Of the long list of Italian anti-*philosophe* authors, L. A. Muratori, Francesco Zanotti, D. Concina, T. Vincenzo Moniglia, G. S. Gerdil, A. Valsecchi, Ignazaio Danisi, G. B. Noghera, B. Scardua, T. M. Mamachi, Appiano Buonafede, A. M. Gardini, Luigi Mozzi, and Alfonso Muzzarelli are notable for their prolific production and familiarity with French sources. Gasparo Gozzi's various journals, *La Gazzeta Veneta*, *L'Osservatore*, and the *Sognatore italiano*, as well as the *Giornale ecclesiastico di Roma*, edited by Tommaso Maria Mamachi and Luigi Cuccagni, were also important sources of anti-*philosophe* invective.

61. See César Rouben, "Propagande antiphilosophique dans les gazettes de Montréal et de Québec après la fin du régime français," in *Littérature antiphilosophique et contre-révolutionnaire au XVIIIe siècle*, a special issue of *Revue de l'Université d'Ottawa*, 54 (1984):79–98.

62. Prandi, *Religiosità è cultura*, 81–164, 256–99; Herrero, *Origines del pensamiento reaccionario*, 27–110; Klaus Epstein, *The Genesis of German Conservatism*, (Princeton, N.J., 1966) Part 1, Chap. 1.

63. On Austria, see Elisabeth Kovacs, ed., *Katolishe Aufklärung und Josephinisumus* (Wien, 1979); and Derek Beales, "Christians and *philosophes*: The case of the Austrian Enlightenment," in Derek Beales and Geoffrey Best, eds., *History, Society and the Churches: Essays in Honour of Owen Chadwick* (Cambridge, 1985), 169–195. On Poland, see Henrik Hinz, "The Philosophy of the Polish Enlightenment and Its Opponents: The Origin of the Modern Polish Mind," *Slavic Review*, 30 (1971):340–349; and Andrzej Walicki, *Philosophy and Romantic Nationalism: The Case of Poland* (Oxford, 1982). Catholic opposition to the *philosophes* in Hungary was also vehement and significant, led by such important religious apologists as Lajos Csapodi, János Molnar, Ferenc Szuhányi, and Abrahám Szathmári Paksi. I

am grateful to Judit Fejes of the Central European University at Budapest for imparting her knowledge of the Hungarian case.

64. [Fernando de Zebollas], *La falsa filosofía, o el ateísmo, deísmo, materialismo y demás nuevas sectas convencidas de crimen de estado contra los soberanos y sus regalías, contra los magisrados y potestades legítimas. Se combaten las máximas sediciosas y subversiones de toda sociedad y aun de la humanidad*, 6 vols. (Madrid, 1775–1776). See the detailed analysis of this and related texts in Herrero, *Origines del pensamiento reaccionario*, 91–117.

65. Cited in Vincenzo Ferrone and Daniel Roche, "Historia e historiografía de la ilustración," in Vincenzo Ferrone and Daniel Roche, eds., *Diccionario histórico de la Ilustración* (Madrid, 1997), 422.

66. See the discussion in Epstein, *Genesis of German Conservatism*, Chap. 10, "The Conspiracy Theory of the Revolution."

67. Cited in Herr, *Eighteenth-Century Revolution*, 308.

68. See Herrero, *Origines del pensamiento reaccionario*, 117–159; Jean Sarrailh, *L'Espagne éclairée de la second moitié du XVIIIe siècle* (Paris, 1964), 207–221; and Herr, *Eighteenth-Century Revolution*, 305–311, 421ff.

69. On Italy, see Godechot, *Counter-Revolution*, 296.

70. Baldensperger, *Le Mouvement des idées*, 2:25

71. David Higgs, "The Impact of Counter-Revolutionary Literature in Late Eighteenth-Century Portugal," in *Littérature antiphilosophique et contre-révolutionnaire au XVIIIe siècle*, 59.

72. Ibid., 64.

73. On this conspiracy, see Kenneth R. Maxwell, *Conflicts and Conspiracies: Brazil and Portugal, 1750–1808* (Cambridge, 1973), esp. Chaps. 5–8.

74. Ibid., 126, 132.

75. Ibid., 202. On the 1794 investigation of the Rio Literary Society, and general fears of French ideas, see also David Higgs, "Unbelief and Politics in Rio de Janeiro During the 1790s," *Luso-Brazilian Review*, 21 (Summer 1984), 13–31.

76. See, for example, the alarmed comments of the royal censor, Mariano José Pereira da Fonseca, in 1819. National Archives of Brazil, Rio de Janeiro, Caixa 171, Doc. 25. I am grateful to Dr. Kirsten Schultz for providing this and other materials relevant to Portugal and Brazil.

77. On the Latin American Enlightenment, see Diana Soto Arango, Miguel Angel Puig Samper, and Luis Carlos Arboleda eds., *La Ilustración en América colonial: bibliografica crítica* (Madrid, 1995); Arthur Whitaker, ed., *Latin America and the Enlightenment* (Ithaca, N.Y., 1961); and the comprehensive account in D. A. Brading, *The First America: The Spanish Monarchy, Creole Patriots, and the Liberal State 1492–1867* (Cambridge, 1991).

78. Cited in N. M. Farriss, *Crown and Clergy in Colonial Mexico, 1759–1821: The Crisis of Ecclesiastical Privilege* (London, 1968), 192–193. The accused were all delegates to the liberal Cadiz *cortes*. On the Spanish mainland, too, orthodox Catholics viewed the Cadiz liberals as a product of modern philosophy. See Lluis Roura I Aulinas, "La Pensée antiphilosophique et contre-révolutionnaire de la hiérarchie ecclésiastique espagnole," in *Littérature antiphilosophique et contre-révolutionnaire au XVIIIe siècle*, 99–112.

79. BM (Madrid), Mss 12 463, *Copia literal de los informes pedidos a various sujetos con fecha de 21 de mayo de 1814*, Madrid, July 6, 1814, cited in Brian R. Hamnett, *Revolución y contrarrevolución en México y el Perú: Liberalismo, Realeza y Separatismo, 1800–1824* (Mexico City, 1978), 205.

80. Cited in Hamnett, *Revolución y contrarrevolución*, 234.

81. See, for example, ibid., 226–227, 237, 244.

82. On the English reception of Barruel, see Bernard N. Schilling, *Conservative England and the Case Against Voltaire* (New York, 1950), 248–277, and Seamus Deane, *French Revolution and Enlightenment in England, 1789–1832* (Cambridge, Mass., 1988), 11. James J. Sack, however, warns against overestimating the impact of Barruel in England. See his comments in *From Jacobite to Conservative: Reaction and Orthodoxy in Britain, c. 1760–1832* (Cambridge, 1993), 32–33.

83. Edmund Burke to Abbé Barruel, May 1, 1797, in Thomas W. Copeland, ed., *The Correspondence of Edmund Burke*, 10 vols. (Chicago and Cambridge, 1958–1978), 9:319–320.

84. Ibid., 320. Burke visited France in 1773, where he met Mirabeau, André Morellet, and Thomas Paine, all of whom he implicated in the plot. He may also have known Diderot, Necker, Turgot, and the duc d'Orléans, on whom he casts aspersions as well. For some of Burke's many post-*Reflections* tirades against *philosophes*, see, in particular, "A Letter to a Noble Lord," in Daniel E. Ritchie, ed., *Further Reflections on the Revolution in France* (Indianapolis, Ind., 1992), 314–316.

85. Cited in *Lettres d'un voyageur à l'Abbé Barruel* (n.p., 1800), 161–167.

86. Joseph de Maistre, himself a former Mason, denounced the Masonic element of Barruel's thesis, despite sharing many of his other views. Ironically, Barruel, too, had been a member of a Masonic lodge. See Riquet, *Augustin de Barruel*, 113–120.

87. Epstein, *Genesis of German Conservatism*, 504. No publishing history of the *Mémoires pour servir à l'histoire du jacobinisme* exists. I have compiled this list, which is doubtless incomplete (limited moreover to editions published before the Restoration), from the National Union Catalogue of the Library of Congress and from those of the British Library, the New York Public Library, and the Bibliothèque Nationale.

88. Cited ibid., 506.

89. Publishing information is provided by Vernon Stauffer, *New England and the Bavarian Illuminati* (New York, 1918), 200, n. 1; Robison is cited on 203.

90. Cited ibid., 228.

91. See Schilling, *Conservative England*, 248–277.

92. On the general importance of conspiracy rhetoric in eighteenth-century American political thought, see Bernard Bailyn, *The Ideological Origins of the American Revolution* (Cambridge, Mass., 1992), 86–90, 105–110, 145–149; Richard Hofstadter, *The Paranoid Style in American Politics and Other Essays* (New York, 1965), 10–15; and Gordon S. Wood, "Conspiracy and the Paranoid Style: Causality and Deceit in the Eighteenth Century," *William and Mary Quarterly*, 3d Series, 39 (1982):401–404. On the reception of Barruel and Robison in particular, see Stauffer, *New England and the Bavarian Illuminati*, 229ff.

93. Cited in Stauffer, *New England and the Bavarian Illuminati*, 85, 246–251.

94. Ibid., 250–251.

95. Ibid., 103–160. Stauffer cites a long passage from Hamilton that outlines the organized "plan" to subvert and destroy the Christian religion during the *ancien régime*, as well as the "alarmingly visible" "symptoms" of this revolutionary "system" in the United States (139–141).

96. Wood, "Conspiracy and the Paranoid Style," 433.

97. On this theme, see David A. Bell, *The National and the Sacred: Religion and the Origins of Nationalism in Eighteenth-Century France* (Cambridge, Mass., 2001).

98. I wish to thank Professor Paul Robinson of Stanford University for suggesting this parallel.

99. This figure is taken from Gumbrecht and Reichardt, who do not give specific dates of publication but comment simply, "Ausgelöst aber wurde sie vor allem durch La Harpes in kürzester Zeit mindestens 19mal aufgelegtes Pamphlet Du Fanatisme . . . " Hans Ulrich Gumbrecht and Rolf Reichardt, *Philosophe, Philosophie*, vol. 3 of Rolf Reichardt and Eberhard Schmitt, eds., *Handbuch politisch-sozialer Grundbegriffe in Frankreich 1680–1820*, 10 vols. (Munich, 1985–), 75.

100. Christopher Todd, *Voltaire's Disciple: Jean-François de la Harpe* (London, 1972). On the life of La Harpe, see also Alexandre Jovicevich, *Jean-François de la Harpe, adepte et renégat des Lumières* (South Orange, N.J., 1972).

101. Todd, *Voltaire's Disciple*, 52–54.

102. Ibid., 55–56.

103. Jean-François de la Harpe, *Du Fanatisme dans la langue révolutionnaire, ou de la Persécution suscitée par les barbares du dix-huitième siècle, contre la religion et ses ministres*, 2d ed. (Paris, 1797), 5.

104. Ibid.

105. Ibid., 3–4, n. 2. La Harpe makes scattered mention of Diderot, Helvétius, and Voltaire (see, e.g., 80, n. 1) but in general abstains from specific recriminations in this work. He employed a similar strategy in his Lycée lecture of December 1796, published as *De l'état des lettres en Europe, depuis la fin du siècle qui a suivi celui d'Auguste, jusqu'au règne de Louis XIV* (Paris, 1797), a polemic replete with condemnation of the *philosophes*. More direct attacks, however, are leveled in *Réfutation du livre de l'Esprit* (Paris, 1797) and the posthumously published *Philosophie du XVIIIe siècle*, 2 vols (Paris, 1818).

106. La Harpe, *Du Fanatisme*, 4, n.1.

107. Ibid., 1–2.

108. Ibid., 7.

109. Ibid., 43.

110. Ibid., 44–45.

111. Ibid., 72.

112. Ibid.

113. Ibid., 27.

114. Ibid., 72–73.

115. Ibid., 74–75.

116. Ibid., 72.

117. Lynn Hunt, *Politics, Culture, and Class in the French Revolution* (Berkeley and Los Angeles, 1984), 19.

118. For examples from the Republican press, see Todd, *Voltaire's Disciple*, 64ff. The most vicious anti-La Harpe pamphlet was written by the self-described "French republican" Guy Chaumontquitry, *De la Persécution suscitée par Jean-François La Harpe, contre La Philosophie et ses partisans* (Paris, an VIII), a point-by-point refutation of *Du Fanatisme*.

119. *Annales religieuses*, 3, no. 32, 390.

120. *Journal général de France*, no. 193 (April 2, 1797):52.

121. *Actes des Apôtres*, 2, no. 11 (March 12, 1797):283; no. 12 (March 19, 1797):315–327; and no. 13 (March 26, 1797):351–355.

122. *Déjeuner*, no. 60 (March 1, 1797):237.

123. *Le Véridique, ou Courrier universel*, 1 (March 18, 1797):2–3.

124. *L'Historien*, no. 486 (March 21, 1797): 3–4. See also J. M. B. Clément's

delight in La Harpe's conversion in *Journal littéraire*, no. 29 (March 23, 1797): 162.

125. *Annales réligieuses*, 3, no. 27, 90.

126. Maistre, *Considérations*, 95.

127. Barruel, *Mémoires*, 1:x.

128. Todd, *Voltaire's Disciple*, 61, 66–67.

Chapter 4

1. *L'Antidote, ou L'Année philosophique et littéraire, par J. C. H. Méhée*, Cahier 1 (n.d.), 3, 7, 24, 38. A fervent revolutionary, Méhée had played a key role in the September massacres. His journal was quickly shut down by Napoleon.

2. *La Décade philosophique, littéraire et politique*, 20 Fructidor, an IX (September 7, 1801), 453. On *La Décade*, see Joanna Kitchin, *Un Journal "Philosophique": La Décade (1794–1807)* (Paris, 1965); and Marc Regaldo, *Un Milieu intellectuel: la Décade philosophique (1794–1807)*, 5 vols. (Lille and Paris, 1976).

3. [Marie-Joseph-Blaise Chénier], *Les Nouveaux saints*, 3d ed. (Paris, an IX), 1, 4. For another, considerably longer satire of the "new saints," see [J. L. Piestre], *Les Crimes de la philosophie, ou Tableau succinct des effets qu'elle a opérés dans la plupart des sciences et des arts, et dans le régime des associations politiques* (Paris, an XII). The work is written as a parody of the anti-*philosophe* voice.

4. *Journal des débats*, 28 Fructidor, an X (September 15, 1802), 3. On this abrupt shift, see the observations of Kitchen, *Journal "Philosophique,"* 72; Paul Bénichou, *Le Sacre de l'écrivain, 1750–1830: Essai sur l'avènement d'un pouvoir spirituel laïque dans la France moderne*, (Paris, 1973), 112; and Regaldo, *Milieu intellectuel*, 2:530.

5. Chateaubriand, "Sur les *Annales littéraires, ou De la Littérature avant et après la restauration*, ouvrage de M. Dussault" (1819), *Mélanges littéraires*, in *Oeuvres complètes de Chateaubriand*, new ed., 12 vols. (Paris, 1861), 6:527.

6. Cited in Eugène Hatin, *Histoire politique et littéraire de la presse en France*, 8 vols. (Paris, 1859–1861), 7:471–473.

7. Donald Sutherland, *France 1789–1815: Revolution and Counterrevolution*, (Oxford, 1985), 342; Jean Tulard, *Napoleon: The Myth of the Saviour*, trans. Teresa Waugh (London, 1977), 73.

8. On Napoleon's lopsided dealings with the Right, see Louis Bergeron, *France Under Napoleon*, trans. R. R. Palmer (Princeton, N.J., 1981), 14–15.

9. There is not to my knowledge any detailed study of France's religious revival during this period. For general commentary, see ibid., 191–194; Sergio Moravia, *Il Tramonto dell'illuminismo: Filosofia e politica nella società francese (1770–1810)* (Bari, 1968), "La reazione spiritualistica e religiosa," 509ff.; and Sutherland, *Revolution and Counterrevolution*, 282.

10. Bergeron, *France Under Napoleon*, 18; Robert Gildea, *The Past in French History* (New Haven, Conn., 1994), 66.

11. Cited in Jacques Godechot, *The Counter-Revolution Doctrine and Action, 1789–1804*, trans. Salvator Attanasio (Princeton, 1971), 362.

12. Strongly ultramontane, Barruel resolutely supported the legitimacy of the Concordat, defending the arrangement in his *Du Pape et de ses droits religieux, à l'occasion du Concordat*, 2 vols. (Paris, 1803). With the exception of this work, however, Barruel published little, passing his time during Napoleon's rule in relative seclusion in Paris. See Michel Riquet's *Augustine de Barruel: un jésuite face aux Jacobins francs-maçons 1741–1820* (Paris, 1989), 121–136.

13. Cited in Kitchen, *Journal "Philosophique,"* 72.

14. "Aux apologistes de la philosophie," *Journal des débats*, 26 Frimaire, an XII (December 18, 1803), 3.

15. *Année littéraire*, 3 (an IX [1801]):284.

16. R. Fargher, "The Retreat from Voltairianism, 1800–1815," in Will Moore, Rhoda Sutherland and Enid Starkie, eds., *The French Mind: Studies in Honour of Gustave Rudler* (Oxford, 1952), 220–221. *Journal des débats* boasted such contributors as Geoffroy, Boissonade, Dussault, Feletz, Fiévée, Delalot, Saint-Victor, and the abbé de Boulogne. Its close ally, *Mercure*, garnered the talents of La Harpe, the abbé de Vauxcelles, Fiévée, François Michaud, Guéneau de Mussy, Fontanes, Bonald, and Chateaubriand. For general information on these journals, see André Cabanis, *La Presse sous le consulat et l'Empire, 1799–1814* (Paris, 1975), and Alfred Nettement, *Histoire politique, anecdotique et littéraire du Journal des débats*, 2 vols. (Paris, 1938).

17. Joseph Fiévée, *Lettres sur l'Angleterre, et réflexions sur la philosophie du XVIIIe siècle* (Paris, 1802), 10.

18. *Mercure*, 11 (Nivôse, an XI [1802–1803]): 160–163. Charges of the *philosophes'* formal conspiracy to destroy the *ancien régime* remained a staple of anti-*philosophe* rhetoric during this period. For noteworthy examples, see the *Année littéraire*, 2 (an X [1800]):145–168; *Annales philosophiques, morales et littéraire*, 3 (1801):347–360; and *Journal des débats*, 26 Frimaire, an XI (December 17, 1802), 3–4; 7 Prairial, an X (May 27, 1802), 3–4; and 17 Germinal, an XI (April 7, 1803), 3–4.

19. *Journal des débats*, 18 Frimaire, an XII (December 10, 1803), 3–4. The article singled out Diderot, Voltaire, and Raynal for particular opprobrium. For a similarly "precise" definition of *philosophie*, see "Ce qu'on doit entendre par philosophie du XVIIIe," *Journal des débats*, January 4, 1806, 3–4.

20. *Le Citoyen français*, nos. 526, 528, cited in *Année littéraire*, 4 (an IX [1810]):99

21. Bénichou, *Sacre de l'écrivain*, 114.

22. *Annales de la religion, ou Mémoires pour servir à l'histoire des 18e et 19e siècle*, 12 (an IX [1800]):22.

23. *Annales philosophiques, morales et littéraires*, 1 (1800):3.

24. *Journal des débats*, 6 Ventôse, an X (February 25, 1802), 3–4. See, similarly, *Mercure*, 13 (20 Messidor, an XI [July 9, 1803]):107.

25. René-Auguste de Chateaubriand, *Génie du christianisme*, ed. Pierre Reboul, 2 vols. (Paris, 1966), 2:252–253.

26. Ibid, 1:203; emphasis added.

27. "Réflexions sur la prétension des philosophes, que la religion n'est bonne que pour le peuple," *Annales morales, philosophiques et littéraires*, 4 (1801):73. See also "Du retour à la Religion," *Journal des débats*, 6 Ventôse, an X (February 25, 1802), 3; and "De l'accord de l'utile et du vrai," *Journal des débats*, 22 Vendémiaire, an XIII (October 14, 1804), 3–4.

28. "Réflexions sur la prétension des philosophes," 67.

29. See, for example, *Journal des débats*, 11 Germinal, an XII (April 1, 1804), 3–4; and "Des grands et des philosophes du siècle dernier," *Journal des débats*, 22 Fructidor, an XIII (September 10, 1804).

30. *Annales de la religion*, 14 (an X [1801]):193.

31. *Hommage à l'immuable vérité, ou Discours à sa gloire, et dont l'objet encore est de la défendre des erreurs et des excès d'impiété des dernières années du dix-huitième*

siècle, par M. Blanchandin-le-Chêne, prêtre, ancien Supr. Rx., etc. etc. (Bruxelles, 1802), Preface.

32. See, for example, *Mercure*, 17 (9 Thermidor, an XII [July 28, 1804]): 258–266; and *Annales philosophiques, morales et littéraires*, 1 (1800):21.

33. *Journal des débats*, 19 Floréal, an VIII (May 9, 1800), 4. See also *Mercure*, 1 (Messidor, an VIII [1800]):18.

34. *Journal des débats*, 19 Floréal, an VIII (May 9, 1800), 4.

35. Ibid. On the contrast between the happiness of faith and the despair of the *philosophe*, see also Fiévée's portrait in "L'esprit littéraire de XVIIIe siècle," *Mercure* 15 (21 Pluviôse, an XII [February 11, 1804]), and Philippe-Louis Gérard's *La Théorie du bonheur, ou L'art de se rendre heureux, mis à la portée de tous les hommes, faisant suite au Comte de Valmont* (Paris, an IX [1801]).

36. Bénichou also notes the general reclamation of Pascal during this period, a trend that had begun prior to the Revolution (*Sacre de l'écrivain*, 147).

37. *Journal des débats*, February 4, 1807, 4.

38. Chateaubriand, *Génie*, 1:197–198.

39. *Mercure* 9 (28 Messidor, an IX [July 17, 1801]):185–186.

40. *Ibid.*, 6 (Brumaire, an X [1801]):272. See further examples below.

41. Louis de Bonald, "Réflexions philosophiques sur la tolérance des opinions," *Mélanges littéraires, politiques et philosophiques* (Paris, 1852), 124. The article was originally published in *Mercure*, 24 (June 21, 1806):533–554, and was also excerpted in *Journal des débats*, June 29, 1806, 3–4.

42. *Journal des débats*, February 4, 1807, 3.

43. Bonald, "Réflexions," 124.

44. *Journal des débats*, 18 Ventôse, an XIII (March 9, 1805), 3–4. The article, significantly, was a favorable review of M. J. B. Duvoisin's *Démonstration évangélique, suivi d'un Essai sur la tolérance*, 4th ed. (Paris, 1804). Duvoisin returned to France in 1802 and was subsequently appointed bishop of Nantes during the Empire.

45. Bonald, "Réflexions," 125.

46. [Stéphanie Félicité Ducrest de St. Aubin de Genlis], *Suite des souvenirs* (Paris, 1807), 364. See also, Bonald, "Réflexions," 135–136, where he argues that faith cannot be coerced.

47. Bonald, "Reflexions," 133.

48. Antoine Sabatier, *Considérations politiques sur les gens d'esprit et de talent tirées d'un ouvrage inédit de M. l'abbé Sabatier de Castres*, ed., L. Bonumville (Paris, 1804), 36, 40–41, 89–90.

49. *Journal des débats*, 22 Fructidor, an XIII (September 10, 1805), 4. The author of *Le Danger des mauvais livres, ou Sermon sur l'apocalypse* (Valence, n.d.), attributed to J.-Isaac. Sam. Cellerier, exhorted his readers to "imitate the generous Christians of Ephesius who, touched by grace, burned the pernicious books they had seized at the feet of the apostles" (39). Zealous *dévots* would translate such exhortations into action during the book burnings of the Restoration.

50. Genlis, *Suite des Souvenirs*, 358–362.

51. *Mercure*, 5 (Brumaire, an X [1801]):248.

52. Historians have generated a significant literature about the family and the French Revolution in recent years. For an essential introduction, see Marcel Garaud, *La Révolution française et la famille* (Paris, 1978); Lynn Hunt, *The Family Romance of the French Revolution* (Berkeley and Los Angeles, 1992); Marie-Françoise Lévy, ed., *L'Enfant, la famille et la Révolution française* (Paris, 1990); Suzanne Desan, "Reconstituting the Social After the Terror," *Past and Present*, 164 (1999);

and James F. Traer, *Marriage and Family in Eighteenth-Century France*, (Ithaca, N.Y. and London, 1980) 79–192.

53. *Année littéraire*, 6 (an IX, [1801]):370.

54. André Burguière, "Demande d'état et aspirations individualistes. Les attentats contradictoires des familles à la veille de la Révolution," in Levy, *L'Enfant*, 25.

55. See, typically, J. M. B. Clément, *Tableau annuel de la littérature*, 3 vols. (Paris, 1801), 2:338; and *Année littéraire*, 1 (an X [1800]):219.

56. *Mercure*, 5 (Thermidor, an IX [1801]):278.

57. *Journal des débats*, 4 Germinal, an VIII (March 25, 1800), 2.

58. Hunt, *Family Romance*, 65. See her summary of revolutionary legislation against paternal authority on 40–42.

59. Louis Gabriel Ambroise de Bonald, *On Divorce*, trans. Nicholas Davidson (New Brunswick, N.J., and London, 1992), 55.

60. *Journal des débats*, 4 Germinal, an VIII (March 25, 1800), 3.

61. Ibid., 10 Pluviôse, an XII (January 31, 1804), 2–3.

62. *Mercure*, 19 (13 Pluviôse, an XIII [February 2, 1805]):319.

63. *Année littéraire*, 1 (an X [1800]):243–244.

64. *Mercure*, 19 (1 Nivôse, an XIII [December 22, 1804]):319.

65. On this theme, see Olwen H. Hufton, "In Search of Counter-Revolutionary Women," *Women and the Limits of Citizenship in the French Revolution. The Donald G. Creighton Lectures, 1989* (Toronto, 1992), 96–97, 102–130; Sutherland, *Revolution and Counterrevolution*, 282.

66. See, for example, *Des Services que les femmes peuvent rendre à la religion: Ouvrage suivi de la Vie des Dames françaises les plus illustres en ce genre, dans le dix-septième siècle* (Paris, an X).

67. Chateaubriand, *Génie*, 1:97. See also his contrasting portrait of the incredulous wife seduced by *fausse philosophie* (211–212).

68. See, for example, Joan B. Landes, *Women and the Public Sphere in the Age of the French Revolution* (London and Ithaca, N.Y., 1988), and Hunt's superbly nuanced account in *Family Romance*.

69. Most notable, Carole Pateman, *The Sexual Contract* (Stanford, Cal., 1988); and Joan Wallach Scott, *Only Paradoxes to Offer: French Feminists and the Rights of Man* (Cambridge, Mass., 1996). Joan Landes focuses her criticism on Rousseau and the Revolution, yet she tends to see the author of *Émile* as representative of the Enlightenment. (See *Women and the Public Sphere*, esp. 88–89).

70. See, for example, Karen Offen, "Reclaiming the European Enlightenment for Feminism: Or Prologemena to Any Future History of Eighteenth-Century Europe," in Tjitske Akkerman and Siep Stuurman, eds., *Perspectives on Feminist Political Thought in European History: From the Middles Ages to the Present* (London, 1998); and Daniel Gordon, "Philosophy, Sociology, and Gender in the Enlightenment Conception of Public Opinion," *French Historical Studies*, 17 (1992). Dena Goodman's *The Republic of Letters: A Cultural History of the French Enlightenment* (Ithaca, N.Y. and London, 1994) also provides a more positive assessment of the role and agency of women in the Enlightenment.

71. *Mercure*, 14 (18 Frimaire, an XII [December 10, 1803]):554.

72. On background to the Catholic critique carried out under Napoleon, see Suzanne Desan, "Marriage, Religion, and Moral Order: The Catholic Critique of Divorce During the Directory," in Renée Waldinger, Philip Dawson, and Isser Woloch, eds., *The French Revolution and the Meaning of Citizenship* (Westport, Conn., 1993).

73. *Journal des débats*, 4 Brumaire, an X (October 26, 1801), 3. For the reviews and extracts of *On Divorce*, see also ibid., 16 Brumaire, an X (November 7, 1801), 3–4; *Mercure*, 6 (Brumaire, an 10 [1801]):248–270; *Annales philosophiques, morales et littéraires* 4 (1801):127–139; and *Année littéraire*, 6 (an IX [1801]):361–387.

74. I draw here largely on Bonald's *On Divorce*, one of a number of longer conservative treatises written against the practice in the first years of the century. See the many texts mentioned in Traer, *Marriage and Family*, 167–170.

75. *Annales philosophiques, morales et littéraires*, 4 (1801):130–131.

76. On the drafting of the family and divorce legislation of the Civil Code, see Garaud, *Révolution française*, 177–181; and Traer, *Marriage and Family*, 166–191.

77. Outside of France, especially on the Italian peninsula, the code's "provision for divorce and insistence on civil marriage" was greeted by many Europeans as "anathema." See Michael Broers, *Europe Under Napoleon, 1799–1815* (London, 1996), 53.

78. *Journal des débats*, 26 Floréal, an IX (May 16, 1801), 3.

79. *Mercure*, 10 (22 Brumaire, an XI [November 13, 1802]):362.

80. *Ibid.*, 13 (6 Messidor, an XI [June 25, 1803]):106.

81. *Journal de débats*, 7 Prairial, an X (May 27, 1802), 3.

82. *Ibid.*, March 14, 1806, 3.

83. [Joseph-Elzéar-Dominique Bernardi], *De l'Influence de la philosophie, sur les forfaits de la Révolution, par un Officier de Cavalerie* (Paris, [1800]), Chap. 2, "D'une erreur fondamentale de la philosophie," 19. This text was an abrupt departure from Bernardi's earlier work, a fact that perhaps influenced his decision to publish under a false identity.

84. Ibid., Chap. 5, "De la véritable nature de l'homme," 44–45.

85. Bonald, "Réflexions sur l'esprit et le génie," in *Mélanges littéraires, politiques et philosophiques* (Paris, 1852), 102. See also *Annales philosophiques, morales et littéraires* 1 (1800):3; *Journal des débats*, 26 Floréal, an IX (May 16, 1801), 3.

86. *Année littéraire*, 1 (an IX [1800]):300–301.

87. "Sur la perfectibilité," *Journal des débats*, 19 Fructidor, an XI (September 6, 1803), 4.

88. *Mercure*, 1 (1 Messidor, an VIII [June 20, 1800]):23.

89. Ibid., 24.

90. "Philosophie moderne," *Journal des débats*, 3 Ventôse, an X (February 22, 1802), 3–4.

91. *Mercure*, 1 (1 Messidor, an VIII [June 20, 1800]):27.

92. *Année littéraire*, 1 (an IX [1800]):302.

93. "Lettre à un philosophe, sur les préjugés," *Mercure*, 11 (28 Ventôse, an XI [March 19, 1803]):595.

94. Ibid., 594–595, 599.

95. Ibid., 602. Michaud cites numerous phrases from the famous passage of the *Reflections*, beginning "You see, Sir, that in this enlightened age I am bold enough to confess, that we are generally men of untaught feelings. . . ." Rather than retranslate from Michaud's French, I have cited Burke here in the original from *Reflections on the Revolution in France*, ed. L. G. Mitchell (Oxford and New York, 1993), 97.

96. Ibid.

97. Claude-François Beaulieu, *Essais historiques sur les causes et les effets de la Révolution de France, avec des notes sur quelques événements et quelques institutions*, 3 vols. (Paris, 1801–1803), x.

98. It was perhaps this conviction that led certain anti-*philosophes* during this period to qualify their appraisals of Montesquieu, disassociating him from other *philosophes*. See, for example, La Harpe's article in *Mercure*, 11 (4 Nivôse, an XI [December 25, 1802]):55–70; and that of "P," ibid., 18 (21 Vendémiaire, an XIII [October 13, 1804]):182–183. For differing judgments on Montesquieu's views on England, see "Des Opinions de Montesquieu sur les Anglais," *Journal des débats*, 10 Ventôse, an XII (March 1, 1804), 3–4; and 26 Pluviôse, an XII (February 16, 1804), 2–3; and *Mercure*, 17 (21 Fructidor, an XII [September 8, 1804]):587.

99. *Journal des débats*, 26 Pluviôse, an XIII (February 16, 1804), 2.

100. Fiévée, *Lettres sur l'Angleterre*, 113. Many of these letters were originally published separately in *Mercure*, relayed by Fiévée from England, where he spent the better part of 1801 as an emissary of Napoleon, charged with reporting on English affairs and public opinion. On Fiévée, see Jean Tulard, *Joseph Fiévée: Conseiller secret de Napoléon* (Paris, 1985).

101. Ibid., 233.

102. Genlis, *Suite des souvenirs*, 51–59.

103. The characterization of English political institutions as "stormy and bizarre" was a commonplace of eighteenth-century French political discourse— one shared by observers of varying outlooks. See Keith Michael Baker, "Public Opinion as Political Invention," in *Inventing the French Revolution: Essays on French Political Culture in the Eighteenth Century*, (Cambridge, 1990), esp. 178–185; and Frances Acomb, *Anglophobia in France 1763–1789: An Essay in the History of Constitutionalism and Nationalism* (Durham, 1950), 30–50.

104. *Journal des débats*, January 4, 1807, 3–4.

105. Ibid., 26 Pluviôse, an XII (February 16, 1804), 2.

106. "De l'Anglomanie," *Année littéraire*, 2 (an IX [1800]):365–366. An abbreviated version of the same article was also printed in *Journal des débats*, 10 Germinal, an IX (March 31, 1801), 3–4.

107. *Mercure*, 10 (15 Brumaire, an XI [November 6, 1801]):306–307.

108. Bonald, "Considérations sur la France et sur l'Angleterre," *Mercure* 24 (April 12, 1806):57–70 (Part I), and 24 (April 19, 1802):103–113 (Part II). See also Count Louis-Mathieu Molé, *Essai de morale et de politique* (Paris, 1805), for a similar comparison of the "natural" perfection of absolute monarchy and the corresponding perversion of the English constitution.

109. See Donald Cohen, "The Vicomte de Bonald's Critique of Industrialism," *Journal of Modern History*, 41 (December 1969): 475–484.

110. *Journal des débats*, 10 Pluviôse, an X (January 30, 1802), 3.

111. "Sur la position respective de la France et de l'Angleterre," *Mercure*, 8 (25 Prairial, an X [June 14, 1802]):468.

112. "Sur l'usure," *Journal des débats*, September 24, 1806, 2.

113. Fiévée, *Lettres sur l'Angleterre*, 34, 233–234.

114. J. M. B. Clément, *Tableau annuel de la littérature*, 3 vols. (Paris, 1801), 1:i.

115. *Journal des débats*, 2 Ventôse, an X (February 21, 1802), 2.

116. "Sur la perfectibilité," *Journal des débats*, 19 Fructidor, an XI (September 6, 1803). 3.

117. Chateaubriand, *Génie*, 2:29.

118. *Mercure*, 16 (3 Germinal, an XII [March 24, 1804]):22. On this theme, see also Joseph Fiévée, "L'Esprit littéraire de 18e siècle," *Mercure*, 15 (21 Pluviôse, an XII [February 11, 1804]):396–397.

119. *Mercure*, 16 (3 Germinal, an XII [March 24, 1804]):11.

120. "De l'Anglomanie," *Année littéraire*, 2 (an IX [1800]):362.

121. *Journal des débats*, 8 Fructidor, an XI (August 26, 1803), 3.

122. *Mercure*, 15 (21 Pluviôse, an XII [February 11, 1804]):395–396.

123. Ibid., 13 (6 Messidor, an XI [June 25, 1803]):30.

124. *Journal des débats*, 3 Messidor, an XI (June 22, 1803), 4.

125. *Mercure*, 10 (3 Vendémiaire, an XI [September 25, 1802]):11. On charges of the *philosophes*' destruction of the poetic spirit, see Bénichou, *Sacre de l'écrivain*, 128–134; on the praise for classical drama, see Charles-Marc Des Granges, *Geoffroy et la critique dramatique sous le consulat et l'empire, 1800–1814* (Paris, 1897); and on the elevation of seventeenth-century aesthetics in general, see Pierre Moreau, *Le Classicisme des romantiques* (Paris, 1932), esp. Chap. 3, "La Géneration du *Génie du christianisme*," 57–129.

126. Roland Mortier, "L'idée de décadence littéraire au XVIIIe siècle," *Studies on Voltaire and the Eighteenth Century* 57 (1967):1013–1029. Mortier confines his discussion of the idea of decadence in the eighteenth century to the *philosophes* and their supporters.

127. Bénichou, *Sacre de l'écrivain*, 122. Bonald stressed this theme and cited the phrase repeatedly. See, specifically, "Du Tableau littéraire de la France au dix-huitième siècle," in *Mélanges littéraires politiques et philosophiques*, (Paris, 1852), 321–338.

128. Bonald, "Du Style et de la littérature," in *Mélanges littéraires politiques et philosophique*, (Paris, 1852), 190–191. This article was first published in August 1806.

129. Genlis, *Suite des Souvenirs*, 49–50.

130. *Année littéraire*, 2 (an X [1800]):146. The author mentions Corneille, Boileau, Bourdaloue, Bossuet, Fénélon, Massillon, Pascal, and other *grands hommes*.

131. F.-G. de la Rochefoucauld, *Esprit des écrivains du 18e siècle; extraits de l'histoire de la langue et de la littérature française* (Paris, 1809), 9–10. See also Chateaubriand, *Génie*, 2:26–27. Rochefoucauld, of great aristocratic lineage, served Napoleon as subprefect of Clermont-Oise.

132. Cited in Hatin, *Histoire politique*, 7:480.

133. [Pierre-Louis Roederer], *Observations morales et politiques sur les journaux détracteurs du 18e siècle, de la philosophie & de la Révolution* (n.p. [1805]), 33. The pamphlet assembled articles from the *Journal de Paris* and other publications sympathetic to the *philosophes* that attacked the anti-*philosophe* and counterrevolutionary pronouncements of *Mercure* and *Journal des débats*.

134. This is also the opinion of Hatin, *Histoire politique*, 7:491; and Abel-François Villemain, *Souvenirs contemporains d'histoire et de littérature*, 2 vols., 3d ed. (Paris, 1854), 1:439.

135. Cited in Hatin, *Histoire politique*, 7:503.

136. Cited in Louis de Villefosse et Janine Bouissonouse, *L'Opposition à Napoléon* (Paris, 1969), epigraph and 202; and Fargher, "Retreat from Voltairianism," 224.

137. Fréderic Bluche, *Le Bonapartisme: aux origines de la droite autoritaire, 1800–1850* (Paris, 1980), 46. See also the comments of Moravia, *Il Tramonto*, 551.

138. Cited in Cabanis, *La Presse*, 208, n.12.

139. "Note à Fiévée," cited in Hatin, *Histoire politique*, 7:503–504.

140. Cited in Cabanis, *La Presse*, 208–209. Earlier, in October 1804, Napoleon had similarly complained to Fouché, citing the *Mercure* in particular, "that several journals are obsessed with denouncing the *philosophes* and attacking them *en masse*" (cited in Tulard, *Fiévée*, 122).

141. On Napoleon's moves against *Journal des débats* and *Mercure*, see Hatin, *Histoire politique*, 7:92–529; and Claude Bellanger, Jacques Godechot, Pierre Guiral, and Fernand Terrou, eds., *Histoire générale de la presse française*, 5 vols. (Paris, 1969), 1:560–561.

142. Cited in Moravia, *Il Tramonto*, 560.

143. The contest was organized with the specific intent of counteracting the anti-*philosophe* onslaught. The responses were so disappointing, however, that the institute solicited essays in four successive contests, not issuing a prize (to Antoine Jay and Victorin Fabre jointly) until 1810. On the competition, see Roland Mortier, *Le "Tableau littéraire de la France au XVIIIe siècle." Un épisode de la "guerre philosophique" à l'Académie française sous l'Empire (1804–1810)* (Bruxelles, 1972).

144. Archives de l'Institut, 2D3 (Premier concours, an XIII–XIV), Manuscript #2, attributed to Gallon de Bastide, 1.

145. Ibid., Manuscript #6, attributed to Amaury Duval, 98.

146. Ibid., 2D4 (Concours de 1807), Manuscript #3, signed "Le Clerc, ancien professeur de littérature," 9, 14.

147. Alexis de Tocqueville, *The Old Régime and the French Revolution*, trans. Stuart Gilbert (New York, 1955), 139.

Chapter 5

1. M. J. Mavidal and M. E. Laurent, eds., *Archives parlementaires de 1787 à 1860, recueil complet des débats législatifs & politiques des chambres françaises*, Série 2 (1800–1860), 127 vols. (Paris, 1867–1913), 26:193.

2. Ibid., 195.

3. *Le Drapeau blanc*, February 14, 1820, 1.

4. François Furet, *Revolutionary France 1770–1880*, trans. Antonia Nevill (Oxford, 1992), 282.

5. Excerpted in *L'Ami de la religion et du roi. Journal ecclésiastique, politique et littéraire*, 7, no. 160 (February 21, 1816):43.

6. Ibid., 10, no. 252 (January 8, 1817):269.

7. Ibid., 9, no. 210 (August 16, 1816):1–2.

8. The blanket term "Liberal" was used to refer not only to the Independents and their supporters outside the Chamber but also to the so-called Doctrinaires, the left-center grouping around Royer-Collard, Guizot, Barante, and Broglie. On Restoration liberalism in general, see L. Girard, *Les Libéraux français (1814–1875)* (Auber, 1985), and Pierre Manent, *Les Libéraux*, 2 vols. (Paris, 1986).

9. Éphraïm Harpaz, *L'École libérale sous la Restauration: Le "Mercure" et la "Minerve" (1817–1820)* (Geneva, 1968).

10. On the term "Ultra," see René Rémond, *The Right Wing in France: From 1815 to de Gaulle*, trans. James M. Laux, 2d ed. (Philadelphia, 1969), 37. On the Ultras in general, see Michel Denis, "Que faire de la Révolution française?" in Jean-François Sirinelli and Éric Vigne, eds., *L'Histoire des droites en France*, 3 vols. (Paris, 1992), 1:13–89; Jean El Gammal, "L'apprentissage de la pluralité," in *Histoire des droites*, 1:491–517; Brian Fitzpatrick, *Catholic Royalism in the Department of the Gard, 1814–1852* (Cambridge, 1983); David Higgs, *Ultraroyalism in Toulouse from Its Origins to 1830* (Baltimore, 1973); Nora E. Hudson, *Ultra-Royalism and the French Restoration* (Cambridge, 1936); J. J. Oechslin, *Le Mouvement ultra-royaliste sous la restauration: son idéologie et son action politique 1814–1830* (Paris, 1960).

11. Martyn Lyons, "Fires of Expiation: Book-Burnings and Catholic Missions

in Restoration France," *French History,* 10 (1996), 253–256, 263–266. See also Martyn Lyons, *Le Triomphe du livre: Une histoire sociologique de la lecture dans la France du XIXe siècle* (Paris, 1987), Chap. 5.

12. See Sheryl Kroen, *Politics and Theater: The Crisis of Legitimacy in Restoration France, 1815–1830* (Berkeley and Los Angeles, 2000), 185–187. I am grateful to Professor Kroen for allowing me to consult this important study while still in manuscript form.

13. *Les Fidèles catholiques aux évêques, et à tous les pasteurs de l'Église de France, au sujet des nouvelles éditions des oeuvres de Voltaire et de Rousseau* (Paris, 1821), 4, 9–10. This pamphlet was first published in early 1817 and then reissued in 1821 with a new *avertissement.* I have cited here only material included in the 1817 text. The authors of the pamphlet may have been linked to the secret Ultra-Royalist brotherhood, the Chevaliers de la foi.

14. *Mandement de Messieurs les vicaires généraux du chapitre métropolitain de Paris, le siége vacant, pour le saint temps du carême* (Paris, 1817), 9.

15. As an indication of the importance attributed to the republication of the works of Voltaire and Rousseau, see the many articles devoted to the subject in *Ami de la religion* during the first months of 1817, especially "Nouvelles réflexions sur les éditions de Voltaire et de Rousseau," 11, no. 264 (February 19, 1817):33–41; "Sur quelques écrits publiés à l'occasion de la nouvelle édition des *Oeuvres de Voltaire,*" 11, no. 270 (March 12, 1817):129–137; and "Questions importantes sur les nouvelles éditions des *Oeuvres complètes* de Voltaire et de J. J. Rousseau," 11, no. 274 (March 26, 1817):193–205.

16. *Fidèles catholiques,* 5.

17. [Claude-Hippolyte Clausel de Montals], *Questions importantes sur les nouvelles éditions des Oeuvres complètes de Voltaire et de J.-J Rousseau* (Paris, 1817), 33.

18. [Maximilien-Marie Harel, called le P. Élie], *Voltaire: Particularités curieuses de a vie et de sa mort, avec des Réflexions sur le Mandement de MM. les vicaires généraux, administrateurs du diocèse de Paris, contre la nouvelle édition de ses Oeuvres et de celle de J. J. Rousseau, par M. Élie Harel* (Paris, 1817), xii, 133. This scurrilous attack on Voltaire was first published in 1781 and subsequently republished and translated into numerous languages. "Réflexions sur le Mandement de MM. les Vicaires-généraux," from which I quote, was added in 1817.

19. See, typically, Clausel de Montals's *Questions importantes,* for which the phrase served as an epigraph. Louis XVI did, in fact, make this statement. See John Hardman, *Louis XVI,* (New Haven, Conn. 1993), 220.

20. *Mandement de Messieurs les vicaires généraux,* 8.

21. Clausel de Montals, *Questions importantes,* 47 (emphasis added).

22. *Fidèles catholiques,* 13.

23. "Sur quelques écrits publiés à l'occasion de la nouvelle édition des Oeuvres de Voltaire," *Ami de la religion,* 11, no. 270 (March 12, 1817):135.

24. *De la Monarchie avec les philosophes, les révolutionnaires et les Jacobins, par J.A.P. de Lyon* (Lyon, 1817), 12.

25. See Kroen, *Politics and Theater,* chapters 1–3; and Sheryl Kroen, "Revolutionizing Religious Politics During the Restoration," *French Historical Studies,* 21 (1998).

26. *Quotidienne,* February 27, 1817, 1.

27. *Ami de la religion,* 12, no. 296 (June 11, 1817):140.

28. Ibid.

29. *Coup d'oeil sur l'Église de France, ou Observations adressées aux Catholiques, sur l'état présent de la religion dans ce royaume, par M. l'abbé Clausel de Montals* (Paris, 1818).

30. Ibid., 44, 14.

31. Harel, *Réflexions sur le mandement de MM*, 177–178.

32. "Sur quelques nouvelles productions philosophiques," *Ami de la religion*, 15, no. 370 (February 25, 1818):48.

33. Félicité de Lamennais, "L'Influence des doctrines philosophiques sur la société" (1815), *Réflexions sur l'etat de l'église en France pendant le dix-huitième siècle, et sur sa situation actuelle; suivies de Mélanges religieux et philosophiques* (Paris, 1819).

34. Ibid., 165.

35. Ibid.

36. Stanley Mellon, *The Political Uses of History: A Study of Historians in the French Restoration* (Stanford, Cal., 1958), 74–75, 77.

37. *Ami de la religion*, 21, no. 538 (October 6, 1819), 256. On this theme, see also Viscount Suleau's "De la lutte des opinions monarchiques et religieuses, avec les intérêts révolutionnaires," *Le Conservateur*, 5 (1819):345–354.

38. Ironically, Grégoire's election during the Restoration was made possible in part by the votes of 88 (of 220) Ultras in the department of the Isère, who voted for him in a *politique du pire* rather than support the ministerial candidate. See Guillaume Bertier de Sauvigny, *The Bourbon Restoration*, trans. Lynn M. Case (Philadelphia, 1966), 163.

39. *Quotidienne*, January 18, 1820, 3.

40. [Antoine-Eugène de] Genoude, "Qu'il faut être Royaliste ou Révolutionnaire," *Conservateur*, 4 (1819):607. See also [Charles-Joseph-Fortuné d'] Herbouville, "L'Harmonie sociale considérée relativement à notre situation," *Conservateur*, 2 (1819):397. On the *Conservateur*, see Guillaume de Bertier de Sauvigny, "L'image de la Révolution française dans *Le Conservateur*," in Roger Dufraise and Elisabeth Müller-Luckner, eds., *Revolution und Gegenrevolution 1789–1830: Zur geistigen Auseinandersetzung in Frankreich und Deutschland* (Munich, 1991); and Pierre Reboul, *Chateaubriand et le Conservateur* (Lille and Paris, 1973).

41. See Bonald, "Sur les partis," and "Sur les circonstances présentes," *Conservateur*, 5 (1819):599 and 171, respectively.

42. Although the Restoration was in fact rife with plots and conspiracies of both liberal and conservative design, Louvel undoubtedly acted alone. On Liberal conspiracies, see Rafael Sánchez Mantero, *Las Conspiraciónes liberales en Francia (1815–1823)* (Sevilla, 1972); for the conservative side, see Guillaume Bertier de Sauvigny, *Le Comte Ferdinand de Bertier et l'énigme de la congrégation* (Paris, 1948).

43. *Archives parlementaires*, Série 2, 26:195.

44. Cited in Bertier de Sauvigny, *Bourbon Restoration*, 165. In the same vein, see *Quotidienne*, March 1, 1820, 3.

45. *Quotidienne*, January 9, 1822, 4.

46. L.-F. de Robiano de Borsbeek, *Essai sur l'action du philosophisme et sur celle du Christianisme* (Paris, 1820). Although Borsbeek was from the Pays-Bas, his book was well received in France. See the glowing review in *Ami de la religion*, 20, no. 661 (December 9, 1820):113–117.

47. *Drapeau blanc*, June 7, 1826, 2. On the conflation of nineteenth-century liberalism and eighteenth-century *philosophie*, see also Antoine Madrolle, *Défense de*

l'ordre social attaqué dans ses fondemens, au nom du libéralisme du XIX siècle (Paris, 1826); and the anonymous *Tableau des trois époques, ou Les Philosophes avant, pendant et après la Révolution* (Paris, 1829).

48. "Des Variations du système libéral," *Le Mémorial catholique*, 1 (March 1824):197–205. The article, the first of several installments, was signed "Haller."

49. M. Beauchamp, *Du Libéralisme, ou La Véritée vengée* (Paris, 1822).

50. Ibid., 31, 36–37.

51. *Le Libéralisme dévoilé, chant anti-philosophique* (Paris, 1822).

52. Haller, "Variations du système libéral," 133–140.

53. "Libéralisme, son origine et ses effets," *Mémorial catholique*, 2 (August 1824):81–85.

54. See, for example, *Drapeau blanc*, July 4, 1821, 1.

55. Beauchamp, *Libéralisme*, 32. Slightly later, see *Conservateur de la Restauration*, 9, no. 103 (1830):102.

56. "Sur la politique de l'Europe dans les circonstances actuelles," *Drapeau blanc*, January 12, 1826, 1–2. On the same theme in the thought of Bonald, see Donald Cohen, "The Vicomte de Bonald's Critique of Industrialism," *Journal of Modern History*, 41 (December 1969):475–484.

57. *Quotidienne*, June 15, 1825, 2.

58. "Plan des Libéraux pour recommencer la révolution," *La France Chrétienne: Journal religieux, politique, et littéraire*, 2 (1821):49–58. The article, the second of two parts, was signed "Z".

59. *Ami de la religion*, 33, no. 859 (November 2, 1822):383–384.

60. Lyon, "Fires of Expiation," 252. Lyons's fine article concentrates almost exclusively on efforts to destroy *mauvais livres*, not on those to disseminate the good.

61. Cited in Roland Mortier, *Le "Tableau littéraire de la France au XVIIIe siècle." Un épisode de la "guerre philosophique" à l'Académie française sous l'Empire (1804–1810)* (Bruxelles, 1972), 8. Thierry's comments were originally published in *Le Censeur européen* in 1820.

62. *Ami de la religion*, 22, no. 569 (January 22, 1820):329.

63. Ibid., 25, no. 649 (October 28, 1820):359.

64. Ibid., 360.

65. Étienne-Antoine de Boulogne, *Instruction pastorale sur l'impression des mauvais livres, et notamment sur les nouvelles oeuvres complètes de Voltaire et Rousseau*, du 28 août 1821, in *Oeuvres de M. de Boulogne, évêque de Troyes*, 6 vols. (Paris, 1827), 5:241.

66. Ibid., 242–243, 245, 267.

67. Ibid., 281.

68. *La France Chrétienne*, 4 (1821):17; *Quotidienne*, January 9, 1822, 4.

69. Denis de Frayssinous, "Conférence sur les mauvais livres," excerpted in *Ami de la religion*, 1, no. 803 (April 20, 1822):310–313. Frayssinous's important conference was attended by, among others, the Duchess of Berry.

70. See, for example, the two-part article "Réclamations du clergé contre la circulation des mauvais livres," *Ami de la religion*, 46, nos. 1189 and 1191 (December 31, 1825, and January 7, 1826):225–230 and 257–262.

71. Lyons, "Fires of Expiation," 253.

72. Ibid., 242–243.

73. Ibid., 248, 258.

74. Lyons maintains that the renewed "publishing initiatives were not in them-

selves responsible for the outbreaks of book burnings," as the latter were "under way early in 1817, well before the new editions of Voltaire had been put into circulation" (ibid., 251). This is to ignore, however, the violent reaction to efforts to publicize the new editions in late 1816 and early 1817, as well as the long anti-*philosophe* background that made such reactions more comprehensible.

75. *Mandement du carême*, cited in *Ami de la religion*, 59, no. 1522 (March 11, 1829):113. On book burning, see also Étienne-Antoine de Boulogne's *Instruction pastorale sur l'éducation chrétienne, à l'occasion du carême du 19 février 1822*, in *Oeuvres de M. de Boulogne, Évêque de Troyes* 6 vols. (Paris, 1827), 5:286–287.

76. *La France Chrétienne*, 4 (1821):44.

77. In addition to the material in chapter 1, see Robert Mandrou's discussion of the religious *bibliothèque bleu* in Chap. 4 of his *De la culture populaire aux XVIIe et XVIIIe siècles: La Bibliothèque bleu de Troyes* (Paris, 1964).

78. On Protestant Bible societies, see, for example, *Ami de la religion*, 12, no. 306 (July 16, 1817):291.

79. The standard account of the missions is Ernest Sevrin, *Les Missions religieuses en France sous la Restauration*, 2 vols. (Paris, 1959). English-speaking readers will benefit from Kroen's account in *Politics and Theater*, 76–109. I am grateful to Maria Riasanovsky for generously relating some of her extensive knowledge of the missions and of Restoration history in general.

80. See Louis XVIII's ordinance of December 12, 1821, excerpted in *L'Ami de la religion*, 30, no. 770 (December 26, 1821):196–199; and the account of Maccarthy's sermon and the other lavish events of the novena, ibid., 33, no. 776 (January 16, 1822):293–295.

81. Kroen, *Politics and Theater*, 90, 100–102.

82. I am grateful to M. Noë Richter for sending me his pamphlet about the establishment of the Bordeaux *oeuvre*, *L'Oeuvre des bons livres de Bordeaux: Les Années de formation, 1812–1840* (Bernay, 1997). On the Bordeaux *oeuvre* in general, see also the brief account in Claude Savart's indispensable *Les Catholiques en France au XIXe siècle: Le Témoignage du livre religieux* (Paris, 1985), 396–402.

83. "Prospectus," *Oeuvre des bons livres*, printed in *La France chrétienne*, 4 (1821):43.

84. Ibid., 44–45.

85. On the Bordeaux *oeuvre*'s administrative structure, goals, and policy, see *Oeuvre des bons livres, fondée par Monseigneur d'Aviau, archevêque de Bordeaux. . . . Manuel de l'Oeuvre* (Bordeaux and Nantes, 1827).

86. Richter, *L'Oeuvre des bons livres de Bordeaux*, 13; Savart, *Catholiques en France*, 397.

87. Richter, *L'Oeuvre des bons livres de Bordeaux*, 10; Savart, *Catholiques en France*, 400.

88. Noë Richter, *La Lecture et ses institutions, 1700–1918* (Le Mans, 1987), 81–82; Claude Savart, "Les Bibliothèques paroissiales," in Dominique Carry, ed., *Les bibliothèques de la Révolution et du XIXe siècle, 1789–1914* (Paris, 1991), 537–538, Vol. 3 of Claude Jolly and André Vernet, eds., *Histoire des bibliothèques française*, 4 vols. (Paris, 1988-1991).

89. Richter, *L'Oeuvre des bons livres de Bordeaux*, 10–11.

90. On the connection with the Chevaliers, see Geoffroy de Grandmaison, *La Congrégation, 1801–1830* (Paris, 1890); and Jean-Baptiste Duroselle, "Les filiales de la Congrégation," *Revue d'histoire ecclésiastique*, 50 (1955): 867–891.

91. *Ami de la religion*, 57, no. 1479 (October 11, 1828): 279–281. These figures are corroborated by Savart, *Catholiques en France*, 394.

92. *Ami de la religion*, 45, no. 1158 (September 14, 1825):150–151. In its first year, the Société published eight works in eleven volumes at press runs of 25,000–27,000 each for a total of 285,000.

93. Prospectus to the Bibliothèque catholique, cited in *Mémorial catholique*, 2 (September, 1824):143–144. On the mutual aims of and cordial relations between the Société catholique des bons livres and the Bibliothèque catholique, see *Ami de la religion*, 43, no. 1825 (May 11, 1825):401–405.

94. *Mémorial catholique*, 2 (September 1824):144.

95. See the comments in *Ami de la religion*, 57, no. 1479 (October 11, 1828):279.

96. In its first year, for example, the Société catholique des bons livres published eight works in eleven volumes, all of which were either classics or long-established books of piety. See ibid., 45, no. 1158 (September 14, 1825):150–151.

97. "Program du concours pour le meilleur ouvrage en réponse aux objections populaires contre la religion," ibid., no. 1170 (October 26, 1825):350–351.

98. See the account in *Rapport présenté au conseil général de la société catholique des bons livres, par M. Laurentie, secrétaire de la direction de la société* (Paris, 1827), 13–24; the commentary of *Ami de la religion*, 47, no. 1209 (March 11, 1826):116–117; and *Quotidienne*, February 19, 1829, 3

99. *Ami de la religion*, 45, no. 1158 (September 14, 1825):150–151.

100. *Des Abus de la liberté de la presse, depuis la restauration, ou Considération sur la propagation des mauvais livres* (Paris, 1826).

101. *Quotidienne*, January 11, 1829, 4.

102. This is a point noted by Claude Savart in reference to the Société catholique des bons livres (*Catholiques en France*, 394).

103. Richter, *Lecture et ses institutions*, 83. Titles included *La Bonne journée ou la manière de sanctifier la journée, pour les artisans et les gens de la campagne*, as well as the Prince de Beaumont's *Trésor des artisans domestiques et gens de la campagne*. Cited in *Ami de la religion*, 45, no. 1173 (November 5, 1825):389–391, and 43, no. 1122 (May 11, 1825):401–405. Other regional *bibliothèques* made similar efforts to include works deemed suitable for artisans, peasants, and laborers. See *Ami de la religion*, 60, no. 1558 (July 15, 1829), 304.

104. The prospectus of this proposed venture is printed in *Ami de la religion*, 51, no. 1307 (February 17, 1827):22–23. It never appears to have gotten off the ground, because of in part squabbles between Gallicans and Ultramontanes in the society's organizing committee and lack of funds.

105. Richter, *L'Oeuvre des bons livres de Bordeaux*, 18–19; Savart, *Catholiques en France*, 402.

106. *Suites funestes de la lecture des mauvais livres, par l'auteur de la Famille heureuse*, 2 vols. (Lille, 1829).

107. In what follows, I draw heavily on the excellent analysis of Kroen, *Politics and Theater*, chapters 1–3.

108. Sevrin, *Missions religieuses en France*, 2:18.

109. See Geoffey Cubitt, *The Jesuit Myth: Conspiracy Theory and Politics in Nineteenth-Century France* (Oxford, 1993), and Kroen, *Politics and Theater*, 216–228.

110. Cited in Kroen, *Politics and Theater*, 188.

111. Cited ibid., 187.

112. See Kroen's fascinating description, ibid., 185–189.

113. Ibid., 191.

114. In a sign of the times, the *Ami de la religion* began running a column in 1828 entitled *vols sacrilèges*, which reported regularly on sacrilegious crimes.

115. *Mandement pour la carême de M. de Boisville, évêque de Dijon*, cited ibid., 47, no. 1204 (February 22, 1826):43–44.

116. *Mandement de Monseigneur l'évêque de Chartres sur le Jubilé*, cited in *Ami de la religion*, 47, no. 1212 (March 22, 1826):161.

117. See, for example, "Sur la disposition actuelle des esprits en Europe, par rapport à la religion," *Mémorial catholique*, 4 (August, 1825):118.

118. "Plan des Libéraux pour recommencer la révolution," *La France Chrétienne*, 1 (1821):401–402. See also "Des sociétés secrètes," *Mémorial catholique*, 1 (January, 1824):37–41, the first of at least five articles that chronicle the history and present activity of secret societies in Europe; "Des sociétés secrètes en Espagne," *Mémorial catholique*, 2 (October 1824):198–210; and "Chronique de la Révolution du Portugal, de 1820 a 1826," *Mémorial catholique*, 7 (June 1827):445–461.

119. Metternich himself shared these sentiments, ascribing European unrest to a network of closely allied secret societies. See J. M. Roberts, *The Mythology of the Secret Societies* (New York, 1972), 301.

120. [Natalis Rosset], *Lettres au peuple français, sur la véritable conspiration du moment* (Paris, 1827), 41. (Rosset, a former *avocat*, also wrote for the virulently Ultra *Conservateur de la Restauration* between 1828 and 1830.)

121. Ibid., 39, 50.

122. *Quotidienne*, February 27, 1829, 2. The *Conservateur de la Restauration* gave a similarly graphic account of the bloodshed in Mexico, charging French liberals with complicity. "Révolution arrivée au mexique," *Conservateur de la Restauration*, 4, no. 43 (1829):225–227. On the alleged role of *philosophes* and liberals in Robert Owen's experiments in England, see *Ami de la religion*, 59, no. 1528 (April 1, 1829):215–216.

123. "De la nature, des obstacles, des chances et de la destinée probables du gouvernement représentatif en France," *Conservateur de la Restauration*, 2, no. 19 (1828):174–186.

124. *Ami de la religion*, 61, no. 1576 (September 16, 1829):162.

125. *Mandement pour la carême*, ibid., 19, no. 482 (March 24, 1819):183–184.

126. *Tableau des trois époques*, 409. See also the graphic predictions in Rosset, *Lettres au peuple français*, 82, 99.

127. Ibid., 315, 290–293.

128. "Des dangers qui nous menaçent," *Conservateur de la Restauration*, 3, no. 34 (1828):297. See also in the same journal "De la vraie source de nos maux," 2, no. 15 (1828):34–41; "De l'Entraînement des conséquences en 1789 et par conséquent en 1829," 3, no. 28 (1828):97–100; "De l'Hypocrisie des libéraux," 3, no. 29 (1828):131–134; "Coup d'oeil sur le libéralisme du moment," 4, no. 43 (1829):204–208.

129. See, for example, M. l'évêque de Bayeux, *Mandement pour annoncer le jubilé à son diocèse de 16 septembre 1829*, in *Ami de la religion*, 61, no. 1585 (October 17, 1829):311; *Instruction pastorale de M. l'évêque de Chartres, à l'occasion du jubilé*, in *Ami de la religion*, 61, no. 1587 (October 24, 1829):337–339; and M. l'évêque de Saint-Claude, *Mandement de 29 novembre 1829*, in *Ami de la religion*, 62, no. 1599 (December 5, 1829):104–105.

130. "Il faut éviter les deux extrêmes," *Conservateur de la Restauration*, 8, no. 94 (1830):217–224. The article was devoted to combating the dictum of its title.

Conclusion

1. This is the suggestion of Martyn Lyons in "Fires of Expiation: Book-Burnings and Catholic Missions in Restoration France," *French History*, 10 (1996), 256. The question of whether books make revolutions is treated in depth in Roger Chartier, *The Cultural Origins of the French Revolution*, trans. Lydia G. Cochrane (Durham and London, 1991), 67–92, and Robert Darnton, *The Forbidden Best-Sellers of Pre-Revolutionary France*, (New York, 1996), 167–246.

2. See, for example, *Ami de la religion et du roi*, 64, no. 1661 (July 10, 1830):273–281, or 65, no. 1688 (September 23, 1830):363–364, which analyzes the Revolution of 1830 in terms of a Carbonari-*philosophe* conspiracy.

3. See, for example, [Louis-Ange-Antoine-Elysée de] Suleau, "De la Lutte des Opinions monarchiques et religieuses, avec les Intérêts révolutionnaires," *Conservateur*, 5 (1819):346; [Louis-Gabriel-Ambroise de] Bonald, "Sur les partis," *Conservateur*, 5 (1819):596, and E. G., "Qu'il faut être Royaliste ou Révolutionnaire," *Conservateur*, 4 (1819):606–610.

4. See, for example, René Rémond, *The Right Wing in France: From 1815 to de Gaulle*, trans. James M. Laux, 2d ed. (Philadelphia, 1969), 63; Jean El Gammal, "L'apprentissage de la pluralité," in Jean-François Sirinelli and Éric Vigne, eds., *L'Histoire des droites en France*, 3 vols. (Paris, 1992), 1:493; and James Roberts, *The Counter-Revolution in France, 1787–1830* (New York, 1990), 79–85.

5. El Gammal, "L'apprentissage," 493.

6. J. J. Oechslin, *Le Mouvement ultra-royaliste sous la Restauration: son idéologie et son action politique 1814–1830*, (Paris, 1960), 143.

7. Nora E. Hudson, *Ultra-Royalism and the French Restoration* (Cambridge, 1936), 71.

8. Rémond, *Right Wing*, 49. On Ultra defenses of and attacks on Louis XIV, see Michel Denis, "Que faire de la Révolution française?," in *Histoire des droites*, 1:36, and Stanley Mellon, *Political Uses of History: A Study of Historians in the French Restoration* (Stanford, 1958), 65–66.

9. El Gammal, "L'apprentissage," 502.

10. On this subject, see Mellon, *Political Uses of History*, Chap. 7, "The Splitting of the Coalition," 150–193.

11. James Sack has observed about England, "What is perhaps less emphasized in modern discussions of the meaning of early modern conservatism is the role which unalloyed hatred played in defining ideology." This comment applies equally to France. See James J. Sack, *From Jacobite to Conservative: Reaction and Orthodoxy in Britain, c. 1760–1832*, (Cambridge, 1993), 38.

12. See the countless reeditions of these authors' works listed in the printed catalogue of the Bibliothèque nationale.

13. Cited in Claude Savart, "Les Bibliothèques paroissiales," in Dominique Carry, ed., *Les Bibliothèques de la Révolution et du XIX siécle, 1789–1914* (Paris, 1991), 544, vol. 3 of Claude Jolly and André Vernet, eds., *Histoire des bibliothèques française*, 4 vols. (Paris, 1988–1991).

14. See, for example, the famous Chapter 1 Part 3 of Alexis de Tocqueville, *The Old Régime and the French Revolution*, trans. Stuart Gilbert (New York, 1955), first published in 1856; Hippolyte Taine, *Les Origines de la France contemporaine*, 2 vols. (Paris, 1876–1896), esp. Vol. 1, *L'Ancien Régime*, Chap. 3, "L'Esprit et la doctrine," and Chap. 4, "La Propagation de la doctrine"; Augustin Cochin, "Les Philosophes," in *Les Sociétés de pensée et la démocratie moderne* (Paris, 1978), origi-

nally delivered as a lecture at the Conférences Chateaubriand, held in Paris on May 15, 1912; and Pierre Gaxotte, *La Révolution française*, 2 vols. (Paris, 1930), esp. Chap. 3, "La doctrine révolutionnaire," and Chap. 4, "La crise de l'autorité." On Maurras, see Maurice Weyenbergh, *Charles Maurras et la Révolution de 1789* (Paris, 1992), 29–38.

15. Cochin, "Les Philosophes," 13, 23.

16. Gustave Gautherot, *L'Assemblée Constituante: Le philosophisme révolutionnaire en action* (Paris, 1911).

17. Ibid., xv.

18. Gautherot's readiness to implicate the Masons in revolutionary and postrevolutionary conspiracies—a trait shared by Cochin as well—was characteristic of this period. See, for example, Gustave Bord's *La Conspiration révolutionnaire de 1789, Les complices, les victimes* (Paris, 1909), as well as the comments in J. M. Roberts, *The Mythology of the Secret Societies*, (New York, 1972), 8–11.

19. On the persistence of Catholic plot theories of the Revolution and the readiness to see the Third Republic as the plaything of conspiratorial sects (Jacobin, Freemason, Protestant, or Jewish), see Robert Gildea, *The Past in French History*, (New Haven, Conn., 1994) 225–233, 248.

20. Johannes Rogalla von Bieberstein, *Die These von der Verschwörung 1776–1945: Philosophen, Freimaurer, Juden, Liberalen und Sozialisten als Verschwörer gegen di Sozialordnung* (Berne, 1976).

21. William Doyle, *Origins of the French Revolution* (Oxford, 1988), 24–25.

22. This is the description of Louis Pozzo di Borgo's *Après nous le déluge* in the right-wing, Catholic book catalogue *Pour une Croisade du livre Contre-révolutionnaire*, 256 (February 1999), 3. The catalogue advertises a disturbingly long list of such titles, many frankly antisemitic and anti-Masonic. They are directly for sale at the association's Parisian bookstore, Duquesne Diffusion.

23. In alleging this close connection, I am far from implying that French Catholicism was somehow inherently conservative or inherently counterrevolutionary. Dale Van Kley makes a powerful case for linking certain strains of French Catholic thought directly to support for the Revolution in *The Religious Origins of the French Revolution: From Calvin to the Civil Constitution, 1560–1791*, (New Haven, 1996) and during the Restoration one sees the beginnings of a current of "social Catholicism"—progressive, reform-minded, and directly concerned with effecting social change. See, notably, Jean-Baptiste Duroselle, *Les Débuts du catholicisme social en France (1822–1870)* (Paris, 1951).

24. Albert O. Hirschman, *The Rhetoric of Reaction: Perversity, Futility, Jeopardy* (Cambridge, Mass., 1991), 1–6.

25. Cited ibid., 4.

26. Hirschman's point of departure was T. H. Marshall's series of lectures "Citizenship and Social Class," delivered at Cambridge University in 1949. See ibid., 1–3.

27. On the ancient-modern debate, see Joseph M. Levine, *The Battle of the Books: History and Literature in the Augustan Age* (Ithaca, N.Y., and London, 1991). On the Enlightenment embrace of the modern, see, for example, Jean-François Lyotard, *The Postmodern Condition: A Report on Knowledge,* trans. Geoff Bennington and Brian Massumi (Minneapolis, Minn., 1989), xxiii–xxiv.

28. See Mark Lilla, *G. B. Vico: The Making of an Anti-Modern*, (Cambridge, Mass., 1993), 232–233.

29. See, for example, Donald Cohen, "The Vicomte de Bonald's Critique of Industrialism," *Journal of Modern History*, 41 (December, 1969), 481–482.

30. On the innovation, change, and modernity of French Catholic apologetic writing in the eighteenth century, see William Everdell, *Christian Apologetics in France, 1730–1790: The Roots of Romantic Religion* (Lewiston, N.Y., 1987). esp. 284–286.

31. On this point, see the always perceptive comments of Van Kley, *Religious Origins of the French Revolution*, 221–222.

32. Clifford Geertz, "Ideology as a Cultural System," *The Interpretation of Cultures: Selected Essays* (New York, 1973), 218–219, n. 42. Geertz makes this observation in the context of a discussion of "reactionary ideologies," the formation of which, however, he believes did not occur until the onset of the French Revolution.

33. On the compatibility of reaction and modern technology in the very different context of Germany in the 1930s, see Jeffrey Herf, *Reactionary Modernism: Technology, Culture, and Politics in Weimar and the Third Reich* (Cambridge, 1984).

34. Max Horkheimer and Theodor W. Adorno, *Dialectic of Enlightenment*, trans. John Cumming (1944; New York, 1972), xiii, 3, 6.

35. For a spirited and damning analysis of postmodern understandings of the Enlightenment, see Robert Darnton, "George Washington's False Teeth," *New York Review of Books*, 44 (March 27, 1997):34–38; Robert Wokler, "The Enlightenment Project and Its Critics," in Sven-Eric Liedman, ed., *Postmodernist Critique of the Project of Enlightenment*, (Amsterdam, 1997), 13–30; and the many trenchant articles in Daniel Gordon, ed., *Postmodernism and the French Enlightenment*, a special edition of *Historical Reflections-Réflexions Historiques*, 25 (Summer 1999).

36. In ways different from my own and each other, Jürgen Habermas and Chantal Mouffe have also leveled this charge. See Habermas, "Modernity vs. Postmodernity," *New German Critique*, 22 (1981):3–14; his *The Philosophical Discourse of Modernity: Twelve Lectures*, trans. Frederick Lawrence (Cambridge, 1987); and Mouffe, "Radical Democracy: Modern or Postmodern?" in Andrew Ross, ed., *Universal Abandon: The Politics of Postmodernism* (Minneapolis, Minn., 1998), 31–45.

37. Mark Juergensmeyer, *The New Cold War? Religious Nationalism Confronts the Secular State* (Berkeley and Los Angeles, 1993), esp. 5–6, 190–192, and his *Terror in the Mind of God: The Global Rise of Religious Violence* (New York and Los Angeles, 2000). For useful speculation on the need to revise the standard assumption, evident from Max Weber to Peter Berger, that modernity and religion are fundamentally incompatible, see the special issue of *Daedalus* 129 (Winter 2000), "Multiple Modernities."

38. Joseph de Maistre, *Étude sur la souveraineté du peuple: Un Anti-contrat social*, ed. Jean-Louis Darcel (Paris, 1992), 171–172; Antoine Sabatier, *Considérations politiques sur les gens d'esprit et de talent tirées d'un ouvrage inédit de M. l'abbé Sabatier de Castres*, ed., L. Bonumville (Paris, 1804), 88; Louis de Bonald, "Réflexions sur les questions de l'indépendance des gens de lettres" (1805) in *Mélanges littéraires, politiques et philosophiques* (Paris, 1852), 33.

INDEX

as engine of the Revolution, 67
and ethics of pleasure and pain, 29,
  37–38
Herder, J. G., 8
Herr, Richard, 109
Herrero, Javier, 15
Hervé, Gustave, 194
Higgs, David, 111
Hirschman, Albert O., 196–197
Historien, 119
Hofman, Amos, 44, 212 n. 38
Holbach, Paul Henri Dietrich, baron
  d', 29, 30, 157
Horkheimer, Max, 201
Human nature, 139–140. *See also* Sin
Hundred Days, 156
Hunt, Lynn, 118, 220 nn. 32–33,

Ideologues, 122, 123, 144, 149, 151
Illuminati, 77, 80, 113, 114
Independent party. *See* Liberal party
Invariable, 103
Isaiah, book of, 56

Jacob, Margaret, 80
Jacobi, Friedrich, 8
Jacobins, 98, 105, 106, 117, 125, 193
  compared to far Right, 75–77
  early formation of, 75
  as participants in conspiracy, 78
  as *philosophes*, 76
  power of, 75
  Rousseau and, 63
Jansenism, 35, 78–80
  and age of Louis XIV, 147
  and alliance with *philosophes*, 49
  and conspiracy, 78–80, 111
  as crypto-Protestantism, 78
  and Enlightenment, 108–109
  and expulsion of Jesuits, 49
J. A. P., 153, 161
Jefferson, Thomas, 114
Jesuits
  as anti-*philosophe* journalists, 27
  and Charles X, 183
  compared to *philosophes*, 63
  and conspiracy, 62, 184
  expulsion of, 22, 49–50, 101, 112

Jews
  antisemitic references to, 212 n. 40,
    249 n. 22
  included in conspiracy accounts, 194,
    249 n. 19
  granted civil rights, 149
Joly de Fleury, Jean Omer, 21, 109, 209
  n. 10
Joseph II, 50
*Journal de la cour et de la ville. See Petit
  Gautier*
Journal des débats, 122, 123, 126, 148
  on Adam Smith, 144
  advocates book burning, 133
  criticized by Napoleon, 150–151
  defines *philosophie*, 127
  on divorce, 137
  on history, 138
  name changed to *Journal de l'Empire*,
    150
  on paternal authority, 134, 135
  on perfectibility, 140
  on *philosophie*'s destruction of hap-
    piness, 130
  on Protestantism, 143–144
  on religion and law, 129
  on weakness of reason, 131
  on women, 135
  writers of, 235 n. 16
Journal ecclésiatique, 26, 27, 30, 57, 58,
  72, 81
*Journal de l'Empire. See Journal des
  débats*
Journal général, 86, 88, 226 n. 125
Journal général de France, 81, 119, 226
  n. 125,
Journal historique et littéraire, 27, 30,
  46–47, 81, 107
Journal littéraire, 1797
*Journal de littérature, des sciences et des
  arts*, 27, 30
Journal de Monsieur, 27, 30
Journal de la noblesse, 86
Journal de Paris, 123, 148
Journal du peuple, 81
Journal pie, 87
Journal politique national, 97, 221 n. 38
Juergensmeyer, Mark, 202

Kant, Immanuel, 32
Kroen, Sheryl, 162

La Beaumelle, Laurent Angliviel de, 30
Labourdonnaye, comte de, 154
Lafayette, Marie-Josèphe Paul Yves
Roche Gilbert du Motier, marquis
de, 157
Lafitte, Jacques, 158
La Harpe, Jean-François, 3, 7, 122, 126,
195
as anti-*philosophe* hero, 118–119
conversion of, 116
and *Du fanatisme dans la langue révo-
lutionnaire*, 115–120
praises men of letters as source of
Revolution, 67
and Richer-Sérizy, 120
Lamennais, Félicité Robert de, 166, 167
critique of liberalism, 164–165
La Mettrie, Julien Offroy de, 29, 67,
157
Lamourette, Antoine-Adrien, abbé, 46,
73
Langres, bishop of, 33
Le Clerc de Juigné, Antoine-Elénore-
Léon, 66
Le Clerc de Lassigny, Louis-Jean-
Baptiste, 68
Le Franc de Pompignan, Jean-Georges
(archbishop of Vienne), 214 n. 68
Le Franc de Pompignan, Jean-Jacques,
marquis, 24, 36
Leopold, Peter, grand duke of Tuscany,
50
Lettres critiques (anti-*philosophe* journal), 24
Liberal interpretation of Revolution,
96, 165
Liberalism
charged with Berry assassination,
154, 166
criticism of, 164–170, 195
international spread of, 186
as new form of *philosophie*, 155,
164–170, 186, 195
and Protestantism, 168
and women, 136–137

Liberal party, 157–158, 164–165, 241
n. 8
and conspiracy, 165, 170
defends Enlightenment, 165
publishes works by *philosophes*, 158
Liberal press, 162
Liger, René, abbé, 33, 37, 40, 46, 108
Linsolas, Jacques, 65
Locke, John, 37, 44
Loménie de Brienne, Étienne Charles,
25
Louis XIV
golden age of, 52, 190, 145–147, 152
Louis XV, 21, 22, 49, 84
Louis XVI, 21, 49, 90, 125, 181
accuses Voltaire and Rousseau of
ruining France, 161
on appointment of archbishop of
Paris, 25
faith of, 22
far Right criticism of, 75
Louis XVIII, 154, 157, 158, 167, 191
dissolves chambre introuvable,
190
Louvel, Louis-Pierre, 154, 166
Luther, Martin, 168

Mably, Gabriel Bonnot de, 30, 111
Maccarthy, abbé, 177
Mackintosh, James, 113
Maistre, Joseph de, 9, 119, 202
on guilt of Voltaire, 99
and Isaiah Berlin, 9, 46
and providence, 58
violence and modernity of, 46
on war of Christianity and
philosophisme, 101–102
Malesherbes, Chrétien-Guillaume
Lamoignon de, 7, 22
Malvin de Montazet, Antoine de (arch-
bishop of Lyon), 40
Manuel, Jacques, 157
Marat, Jean-Paul, 98, 99, 117
Marbeuf, Yves-Alexandre de (arch-
bishop of Lyon), 56–57, 58
Marmontel, Jean-François, 7
Marshall, T. H., 196
Massillon, Jean-Baptiste, 180

Masonry. *See* Freemasonry
Maurepas, Jean Frédéric Phélypeaux, comte de, 22
Maurras, Charles, 193
Maury, Jean-Siffrein, abbé, 81
Méhée, J. C. H., 234 n. 1
Mémoires secrets, 18
Mémorial catholique, 168, 180
Men of letters, 6–8, 203. *See also philosophes*
Mercure de France littéraire et politique, 122, 126, 144
  on age of Louis XIV, 145–146
  confiscated by Napoleon, 151
  on family and state, 133
  on history, 139
  on paternal power, 134
  on perfectibility, 140
  on prejudice, 142
  on religious tolerance, 131
  on women, 135
  writers for, 235 n. 16
Mérito, marqués del, 108
Michaud, Joseph, 142, 145
Mirabeau, André-Boniface-Louis, vicomte de ("Mirabeau-Tonneau"), 70
Mirabeau, Victor de Riqueti, marquis de, 29
Missions, Catholic, 173, 176–177
Modernity, process of, 200–202
Montesquieu, Charles de Secondat, baron de, 69, 184, 239 n. 98
Montjoye, Galart de, 67, 74, 86, 221 n. 50
Montlosier, François-Dominique de Reynaud, comte de, 74
Montmorency, Mathieu de, 179
Moreau, Jacob, 180
Morellet, André, 93, 151
Mornet, Daniel, 12
Möser, Justus, 8
Muzzarelli, Alfonse, 220 n. 29

Naigeon, Jacques-André, 30
Napoleon I, 112
  and anti-*philosophes*, 123, 148–151
  authoritarian ideology of, 149

criticism of *philosophes*, 149, 150, 240 n. 140
politics of, 123–125, 147–148
and Revolution, 124–125
National Assembly, 67, 116
  attacks church, 70–73
  honors Voltaire, 83–84, 86
  as sect of *philosophes*, 55, 66, 76, 81
National Convention, 90, 91, 106, 116, 117
National Institute, 122, 123, 150, 151
Necker, Jacques, 81
Newton, Isaac, 44
Nodier, Charles, 166
Noé, Marc Antoine de (bishop of Lescar), 43, 216 n. 110
Nonnotte, Claude-François, abbé, 109

Oeuvres des bons livres, 177–179, 182
Orléans, Louis Philippe Joseph, duc d', 80
Ostolaza, Blas, 112
Ozouf, Mona, 83

Palmer, Robert R., 8
Pannetier, comte de, 81
Pantheon, 83–84, *illus.* 85, 99, *illus.* 100, 177, 203
Paquot, J. N., 107
Pascal, Blaise, influence of, 34–35, 131, 213 n. 65
Passions, critique of, 36–37, 102
Patriarchal family. *See* Family values
Petit Gautier, 84
Pey, Jean, abbé, 42, 108, 211 n. 35
Philosophes
  alleged cohesion of, 31–32
  alleged intolerance of, 45, 63, 69, 102–103, 110, 117
  Anglomania of, 41, 142–143, 169
  as conspirators, 58–62, 76
  and history, 139
  as new cultural heroes, 7–8
  as revolutionary forefathers, 67
  and revolutionary violence, 96–99
  rise of, 6–8
  self-conception of, 7
  view of human nature, 38

Throne and Altar
  competing attitudes toward past, 162
  unity of, 49–50, 199
  tensions between, 49–50, 162, 190
Tindal, Matthew, 44
Tocqueville, Alexis de, 152, 193
Tolerance, critique of, 44–45, 71, 78,
    102–103, 131–133, 168
Tradition, defense of, 50–51, 141–145,
    199
Tuileries, 90
Turgot, Anne Robert Jacques, baron
    de, 3

Ultramontanism, 190
Ultra-Royalism
  and criticism of crown, 158, 161
  ideological origins of, 152
  internal tensions in, 189–191
  revolutionary aspirations of, 155–156
  use of term, 241 n. 10
  See also Right
Ultras. *See* Ultra-Royalism

Van Kley, Dale, 108
Ventre de la Touloubre, Felix-Louis-
    Christophe. *See* Montjoye, Galart
    de
Vergennes, Charles Gravier, comte de,
    22
Véridique, 119
Vicars General of Paris, 159
Vico, Giovanni Battista, 9, 197, 207
    n. 29

Voltaire, 29, 30, 66, 81, 109, 111, 119
  attacks Fréron, 24
  books burned, 184
  corrupts students at Yale, 114
  first apotheosis of, 3–5, 18
  in flagrant delight, *illus.* 39
  guilt of, 99, 100
  images of, 7, 184
  Jean-Baptiste Pigalle statue of, *illus.*
    60
  publication of works by, 27, 158–159,
    162, 211 n. 33, 170–172, *illus.* 175
  second apotheosis of, 83–86
  on treatment of men of letters, 6
  writings as cause in 1830 revolution,
    189

Wagnière, 18
Waterloo, 155, 156
Weishaupt, Adam, 80
Well, Bernard, abbé, 109
Whitehead, Alfred North, 196
White Terror, 156
Wiener Zeitschrift, 111
Women
  anti-*philosophe* conceptions of,
    135–137
  and religion, 135–136
Wood, Gordon, 114

Yvon, Claude, abbé (canon of
    Coutances), 40

Zeballos, Fernando de, 110

Printed in the United Kingdom
by Lightning Source UK Ltd.
136147UK00002B/64/A